# BETWEEN

# CULTURE

# AND

# FANTASY

# BETWEEN

# CULTURE

# AND

# FANTASY

## A New Guinea Highlands Mythology

## GILLIAN GILLISON

THE UNIVERSITY OF CHICAGO PRESS
CHICAGO AND LONDON

Gillian Gillison is associate professor of anthropology at the University of Toronto.

The University of Chicago Press, Chicago 60637
The University of Chicago Press, Ltd., London
© 1993 by The University of Chicago
All rights reserved. Published 1993
Printed in the United States of America

02 01 00 99 98 97 96 95 94 93    5 4 3 2 1

Library of Congress Cataloging-in-Publication Data

Gillison, Gillian.
      Between culture and fantasy : a New Guinea highlands mythology /
      Gillian Gillison.
            p.      cm.
      Includes bibliographical references and index.
            1. Gimi (Papua New Guinea people)—Folklore.   2. Women, Gimi—
      Social conditions.   3. Women, Gimi—Psychology.   4. Gimi (Papua New
      Guinea people)—Attitudes.   5. Gimi (Papua New Guinea people)—
      Social life and customs.   6. Ceremonial exchange—Papua New Guinea.
      I. Title.
      GR385.P36G55   1993
      398'.0899912—dc20                                                              92-11319
                                                                                          CIP

ISBN (cloth): 0-226-29380-7
ISBN (paper): 0-226-29381-5

Photographs are by David Gillison

♾ The paper used in this publication meets the minimum requirements of the American National Standard for Information Sciences—Permanence of Paper for Printed Library Materials, ANSI Z39.48-1984.

75958

For
Samantha
and
Douglas

# CONTENTS

Contents

# PHOTOGRAPHS

# FIGURES

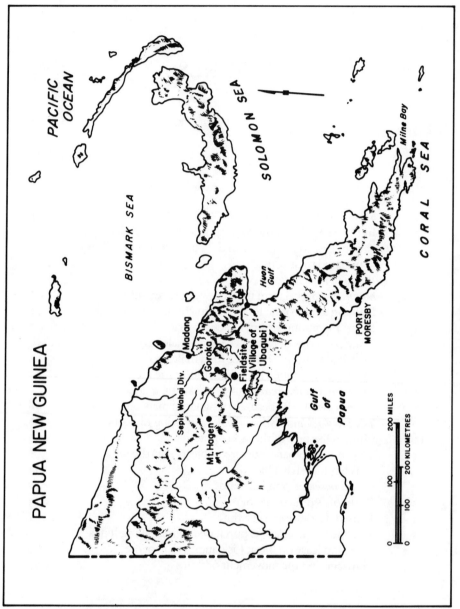

Figure 1. Map of Papua New Guinea.

# PREFACE

The fieldwork upon which this book is based was carried out mainly in Ubagubi, a village of Gimi-speaking people in the Eastern Highlands Province of Papua New Guinea, and covers a span of a dozen years. My work began in 1973–74 with twenty months in the field, followed in 1975 by a further six-month stay, and then continued, in the form of intermittent summer visits of three to four months, until 1985. In the early 1970s, most Highlands ethnographies were written by men from a male point of view. Even when the events of women's lives were well described, and even when the ethnographers were women, Highlands women themselves seemed to have no voice. Like women in most ethnographies, they were mute at the level of interpretation, reflecting the inclination of ethnographers to rely overwhelmingly upon men to decipher and translate the cultures they studied and thus to collude in presenting men's theories of the origin and nature of social life. This tendency was accentuated in the New Guinea Highlands by extreme forms of sexual segregation and antagonism, according to which men lived communally, were accustomed to traveling abroad, and were thus far more accessible and practiced as informants than their wives. Besides being forbidden to enter men's houses and to participate in men's sacred rites and lore, Highlands women had little time or liberty to converse with curious outsiders and, in any case, rarely spoke (or admitted to speaking) Melanesian Pidgin, the lingua franca of colonial contact. While men remained inside the settlement for much of the day, women went off to work in distant gardens or to chase pigs that foraged at the edges of the forest.

The impetus for my original research among the Gimi was to describe the society from a female point of view, to use women's own accounts, life histories, attitudes to men, etc., to portray the lives of both sexes.

During the period of fieldwork I was married to David Gillison, an Australian artist and lithographer who, as a result of his experience among the Gimi, became a photographer and rainforest conservationist. As a man, and an Australian with the stature of a *kiap* or patrol officer, he was naturally the one whom the men of Ubagubi approached to negotiate the terms of our presence in the village. David arranged the use of land for a house and garden, the purchase of trees, thatch, bamboo, and other materials, and the labor to build the house. He also organized the supply of firewood and water. Without a husband, my stay among the Gimi would have been infinitely more difficult from both material and psychological standpoints. David's existence immediately identified me to the Gimi as a wife, as one who usually, or publicly at least, remained aloof from men's affairs. He was my route to discrete, restricted relationships with the men who came to our house in the evening to plan the next day's outing into the bush to photograph Birds of Paradise. During a fertility festival that took place early in 1974, in a village about a day's walk from Ubagubi, David tape-recorded songs and initiation rites that were taking place inside the men's houses while I was inside the women's houses participating in marriage ceremonies. After a period of nine or ten months during which my only extended conversations were with women, I transcribed and translated David's recordings with the help of several of his guides and, eventually, used their contents as the basis for interviews and discussions with a wide range of men.

After Douglas Gillison was born in 1978, David returned to the Highlands several times without me, receiving grants from *National Geographic Magazine* to photograph Birds of Paradise and from the New York Zoological Society to help establish a wildlife refuge and national park in the vicinity of Ubagubi. These summer visits provided continuity in our relations in the village and allowed me, although I was in New York with Douglas, to keep alive connections with women and men that had become vitally important to the coherence and evolution of my work.

Beginning in 1983, Douglas accompanied us to the field where he was an exciting addition to our ménage and a constant source of the unexpected. Ten years earlier, when we had first arrived in Ubagubi, Samantha Gillison was already six years old. Her presence and personality gave me an immediate rapport with the women, and helped me establish an intimacy with the mothers and grandmothers of her closest friends that, in time, extended into relationships with other women. Samantha began to converse freely in Gimi after about six weeks, and soon afterward understood another dialect of the language spoken only by married women who were born in a distant region. My daughter initiated me into the complexities of the language and the subtleties of Gimi etiquette, explaining the effect of my smiling too much or of "pulling my nose" (frowning). Her young friends, some of whom are now mothers with children the age they were when I met them nearly twenty years ago, also became charming and valued informants.

Despite the early familiarity with women that I gained as a mother, it took me nearly two years, until my first follow-up study in 1975, to realize that the bedtime songs and stories women told inside their own houses, and that Samantha often overheard, had a significance far beyond preparing children for sleep. Gimi women possess myths of their own that, looked at in combination with men's myths, seem to be part of a conversation with men, as if the myths themselves were engaged in discourse, as if the sexes were able to carry on a clandestine debate while avoiding or ignoring each other in much of their daily lives. Through the process of collecting the myths of women and men, and by returning to the field repeatedly, studying the myths on my own in New York and then going back to informants to test and explore my interpretations, I gained an understanding of the sexes' mythic argument and the premises that underlie it, realizing that there were unspoken terms upon which the *myths* agreed to differ. Over the years, I became convinced that this unspoken agreement between the sexes, the shared set of assumptions upon which rests the logic of their mythic debate, also constitutes the deepest structure of Gimi social life.

Throughout the book I try to show how the conflictual, mythological basis of Gimi society is rooted in the overriding idea that exchange has a profoundly sexual origin and meaning; and, conversely, that the sexual relation is a *transaction* of which one party—and which one is at the heart of the debate—is symbolically unaware, or "still a child," and, therefore, innocent of the disastrous outcome. For the Gimi, the gift or object of exchange not only signifies a person, or part of a person, as Marcel Mauss observed long ago (1967 [1925]:10), but also stands for a child conceived and lost without awareness, one created and killed during the first sexual abandon so it never emerged into the world fully formed or alive. The one who had been asleep awoke from the dream of sex, realized what the other had done, and retaliated, "killing the child"—or producing the menstrual flow—in revenge for the first penetration. In conflicting versions, but often from the vantage point of the unborn child, the myths of women and men describe the primordial union that gave rise simultaneously to life and death, producing a "firstborn child the same as menstrual blood." The mythic child observes the first copulation from the unique perspective of the womb, bearing witness to its own demise, and thus condemns the other sex, accusing it of harboring too much desire, initiating the first encounter, and thus causing the death that ensues.

The myths of men and women argue over who instigated the first sex but agree that, whoever is to blame, the outcome is the same: the first gift, the firstborn child, arrives as "dead womb blood." The project of ritual, in these terms, is to bring each person to life by replacing him or her inside a different kind of transaction, one that will counteract the original exchange that occurred with such ill effect in the mythic or prenatal past. If the encounter between the first man and woman had a grievous outcome, then other exchanges, conducted in the ritual present, are designed to undo it and achieve a better result. Life is made possible, to adopt the male view, because men confiscate the child from women and circulate it entirely among themselves. In the various secret and public phases of life-cycle rituals, the subject of the ritual—the newborn, initiate, bride, groom, deceased, etc.—is reproduced in secret artifacts, like sacred flutes or tokens of menstrual blood, and in publicly offered payments like cooked pork, marsupial furs, Bird of Paradise plumages, and other valuables called "the head of the child." Through the various transactions of these items, men reclaim the child women stole from them in the mythic past and launch it in exchanges with other men, thus resurrecting the one women delivered stillborn.

By presenting "the head of the child" to women, men accuse them of appropriating men's gift, of stealing the life-producing substance while men were asleep or transported in copulation, and of refusing afterward to give back a *living* person. Men who receive head payments are likewise accused in this complex mythic sense, in terms that thus express the female "side" in the debate with men. But men can give back the "head"—and the blame—by initiating exchanges on their own, a right women never acquire. Before marriage, a woman functions, like her brother, as an object of exchange, as one in whose name and on whose behalf her father presents head payments to her mother's brother. But once a woman marries, she drops out of circulation among men: her daughter and son replace her and her brother as the impetus for payments from her husband to her brother. A woman is "killed" at marriage, punished for her mythic desires, in the sense that she is no longer an object of exchange between her father and mother's brother, no longer a child the two men continually transact to life, and that, unlike her brother, she does not inherit the father's role as a donor of head payments. Unlike a man, she cannot divest herself of the guilt that being a recipient always conveys, guilt for initiating the first coitus, causing the first menstrual loss, murdering the firstborn, etc.

My interpretation of Gimi exchanges relates to one Marilyn Strathern has recently offered for Melanesia in general. "Often gifts subsume persons themselves, especially under patrilineal regimes where women move in marriage from one set of men to another. . . . However, one cannot read . . . gender ascriptions off in advance, not even when women appear to be the very items which are gifted" (1988:xi). My argument for the Gimi is that, as a gift or object of exchange, a woman carries a neutral or *male* identity: as a child and, later on, as a bride, she has the phallic status of her father's mythic wife, of one who "stole his head" during the first copulation and keeps it hidden inside her, giving her whole body a phallic significance and dimension. But after marriage, when a woman ceases to serve as exchange object, she loses her father-derived masculinity: with her father's connivance, her brother, who is still a "small boy" according to men's myth, steals from her the thing she took from their father while the old man was asleep or off guard. In men's view, a woman ceases to be fully alive after she marries because she is no longer her father's mythic wife: she no longer possesses his child to give away and, instead, receives one from a new husband, a man to whom her father gives the "same name" as her brother. Upon marriage, only the brother/husband graduates from the childlike status of exchange object, or head payment, into a role as *both* donor *and* recipient of head payments. A married woman only receives these payments, an activity Gimi describe as "eating the head of the child." "The basis for [gender] classification does not inhere in the objects themselves," Strathern says, "but in how they are transacted and to what ends. The action is the gendered activity" (ibid.). Drawing upon both Freud and Lévi-Strauss, Gayle Rubin expresses the idea that women's role as eternal recipients, their exclusion as initiators of exchange, symbolizes both female sexual identity and secondary status: "The girl . . . can 'get' the phallus—in intercourse, or as a child—but only as a gift from a man. *She never gets to give it away*" (Rubin 1975:195; my emphasis).

The idea that the things Gimi exchange, head payments and, secretly, men's sacred bamboo flutes, embody the mythic firstborn, the child that the first woman—or man—would rather keep by turning to blood than give back alive, etc., means that the gift has the significance of both an accusation and a rescue operation: as a replacement for the "head of the child," it is also an inducement to stop devouring the real head and thus an indictment of the recipient for having already committed the mythic crime. On an implicit or covert level of culture, the gift is designed to create enduring social ties by severing others that preexist in fantasy or in the mythic past. In this vein, I argue that Gimi exchanges are contrived to undo deadly mythic entanglements mainly by blaming women for their invention; and I suggest that women, despite their emphatic mythic protest, generally confirm men's conclusion for reasons of their own.

As the prelude to life-cycle transactions, women are draped and festooned with men's "murdered gift": at marriage, the mothers of the bride transport the wedding pigs by wearing charred sections of the animals on their heads and hips; and at death, the women mourners put on various relics of the deceased which they continue to wear until they are paid to take them off, removing their mourning raiments in exchange for head payments in one rite after another. In the chapters on mortuary and marriage ritual, I suggest that women's elaborate decorations give to the transference of goods between men the literal or symbolic meaning of a *divestiture* of women, as if the only way for men to come to terms with each other were to deprive and diminish women, to treat "the child" as something women stole from men, dismantled, and then connived to make seem an integral part of themselves. Seen in these terms, acts of exchange repeatedly demonstrate women's guilt and illegitimacy as donors.

If Gimi ritual and exchange are indeed organized around such fantastic mythic themes, around the notion that death can be overcome or delayed if only it could be decided which sex invented it, then these themes and debates tend to pervade the whole culture. The very nature of fantasy, its impossibility and often unutterability, makes it greatly in need of demonstration and repetition. Myths are unattainable, or, if achieved momentarily in a ritual context, unsustainable, so that their premises have to be played out again and again, reasserted at every crisis, celebrated every time there is a birth, marriage, death, initiation, suspicion of sorcery, etc. It is this ritual repetition, a continual striving after what is paradoxical or futile, that constitutes myth's great organizational force, making the illogic of myth a reliable, if highly elliptic, guide for understanding the construction of social life. My reiteration of certain mythic themes, arguments, and ideas throughout the text is thus the result not only of my own struggle to elucidate what I consider to be extremely complex and difficult material but also of the character of fantasy itself.

# ACKNOWLEDGMENTS

Every ethnographer knows that the quality of one's work depends upon the friendship and help received in the field. My debt to my Gimi friends and informants and to my family is beyond measure. Thirteen women and twelve men in Ubagubi were regular informants whom I consulted more or less systematically to provide background information about events I witnessed in the village, dispute settlements or *kot,* sorcery trials, and other public rituals. Generally speaking, these people were not among the five or six men and women with whom I gossiped on a daily basis, who provided me with their life histories, detailed insights into rituals, myths, and current events. Over the years, as my interests became increasingly centered on myth and ritual theater, I sometimes gave my tape recorder to those with whom I was working closely and encouraged them to conduct interviews, gather new material, and instruct me in its interpretation. On one occasion, I arrived in the field with color xeroxes of David's photographs of ritual theater and gave these out to my assistants, asking them to elicit anecdotes from the performers. Having identified the village of Ubagubi, I feel I cannot name my intimate associates and use pseudonyms throughout the text for individuals and clans. However, Ms. Otanumo Kuabe, a woman of great sophistication and knowledge about myth and ritual, and Mr. Babogu Kuipaba deserve special mention and my deepest gratitude, as do two field assistants, Mr. Fobora Autiaba and Mr. Farau Idoru. Many other women and men of Ubagubi, whom I do not name, have been extraordinarily generous to me both in friendship and as consistent sources of insight.

In the fall of 1973, Sam and Nancy McBride of the Summer Institute of Linguistics gave generously of their time and knowledge, and provided me with their Gimi Grammar Essentials, a description of a dialect spoken in Okapa Subdistrict, which helped me to instruct myself in the dialects of Unavi. Mr. Tony Thatcher, the assistant district commissioner at Lufa Station in 1973–74, invited us to join his patrol into Labogai and Unavi Census

Divisions and suggested Ubagubi as a field site. Both he and his successor, Mr. Craig McConaghy and Ms. Jennifer McConaghy, furnished us with logistical support and excellent companionship. During visits to Goroka we received hospitality, help, encouragement, and penetrating discussions of fieldwork problems from Mr. George Malynicz of the Tropical Pig Breeding Establishment, Department of Agriculture, Stock and Fisheries, and his wife, Anna; from Dr. Gregor Lawrence of the Institute of Medical Research and his wife, Lynn; and from the Institute's director, Dr. R. W. Hornabrook.

In Port Moresby, Professor Marilyn Strathern proved to be an unswerving friend and guide through the intricacies of New Guinea life, indigenous and expatriate. Later, in England, she was a tireless and inspiring reader of my Ph.D. dissertation, and in the years since has remained a steady source of encouragement and new ideas. Also in Port Moresby, Ulli and Georgina Beier of the Institute of Papua New Guinea Studies offered warm support and comfort on my infrequent sojourns in that city.

The National Science Foundation and the Canada Council gave initial financial support to my undertaking. In later years, David Gillison and I received funds from the New York Zoological Society and from *National Geographic Magazine,* where we were fortunate to come under the tutelage of Mary Griswold Smith. I want to express my thanks to Professor Maurice Godelier who, in 1985, at a time when I had no university affiliation, invited me to work in Paris, beginning a fruitful relationship with the Laboratoire d'Anthropologie Sociale founded by Professor Claude Lévi-Strauss and now headed by Professor Françoise Héritier-Augé. Over the years, the officers and members of the Laboratoire, in particular Marie-Élisabeth Handman, have generously provided me with the opportunity to continue my work and engage in stimulating discussion. Among the members of the Laboratoire, Patrice Bidou has consistently challenged my interpretations and pushed me to clarify my ideas and my writing.

Douglas Newton, Gananath Obeyesekere, Robert Paul, and Marilyn Strathern also have read portions or all of the present manuscript and offered encouragement and invaluable criticism. To each of them I express my deepest appreciation.

# NOTE ON ORTHOGRAPHY

All words in Gimi, except personal names, are written in italics. The spelling of Gimi words is not phonological because this dialect of the language is not yet described by a specialist. The approximate phonetic values of the symbols are:

## Consonants

*b, f, h, m, n, p, s, t* are close to the sounds of English
*b* is sometimes pronounced as the English *w*
*h* is often added to a word that begins with *a* when the word is uttered alone or at the start of a phrase
*r* is a flap similar to the *r* in the Spanish "caro"
*ϑ* is pronounced as the voiced *th* in "that" or as the *d* in "dare" or as the *y* in "yellow"
*k* and *g* are hard and soft glottal stops
An apostrophe (') indicates that *k* or *g* is usually glottalized (see the Morphophonemic Note in the front of the Glossary)

## Vowels

*a* is like the *a* in "mama"
*e* is like the *a* in "late"
*i* is like the *ee* in "feet"
*o* is like the *oa* in "boat"
*u* is like the *oo* in "root"
*3* is like the *e* in "ebb"
*E* is like *i*, above, but follows a dropped or silent glottal
*I* is like the *igh* in "high"

# BETWEEN

# CULTURE

# AND

# FANTASY

# INTRODUCTION

A group of women in Ubagubi. The woman with her back to the camera is netting a string bag.

# ONE

# The Argument among Myths

Gimi myths seem not only to "think among themselves," as Lévi-Strauss says, but also to speak to one another, to protest, alter, and enlarge upon myths of the other sex. The myths of Gimi women and men "read" like entries in a covert dispute, fantasies produced in response to other fantasies, as if the sexes—while openly avoiding each other—were communicating through separate "secret" myths and rites, arguing over who is to blame for life's impermanence and human misfortune. "The ideas elaborated by myth and spun out into narrative are especially painful," Malinowski noted (1954 [1926]:137). "They all refer to what might be called the . . . unpleasant or negative truths; the loss of rejuvenation, the onset of disease, the loss of life by sorcery" (ibid., 136). Gimi myths describe human mortality as if it were the fault of one sex or the other, as if the first woman or man had invented death and misery in the course of satisfying incestuous wishes. Each sex portrays itself as culture hero, as the one who took the initiative in curbing the other's inordinate desires.

Gimi men and women cast blame in the esoteric imagery of myth but then dramatize their accusations in public ritual. In celebrations of death, birth, marriage, and male initiation, men and women cooperate in shows of conflict and resolution that demonstrate women's guilt and leave men in control of the main transactions. At the start of the rites, men indict women for a mythic crime that, according to men's lore, was committed by the first woman, thus creating the pretext to exclude women as initiators of exchange. When the myths of men and women are factored into the analysis of ritual, the logic of ritual, and indeed the whole organizational basis of Gimi society, seem to lie in the unspoken terms upon which the myths agree to differ. Life-cycle rites play out a mythic debate between the sexes and then override women's side, translating the "secret" premises of their defeat into the ordinary conventions of kinship, marriage, and exchange.

When I set out to do fieldwork in the New Guinea Highlands, I was looking for some kind of female protest or counterculture, hoping to find among women ideas and opinions that would revise the classic descriptions of male dominance, sexual segregation, and antagonism. In the era that ended with the *pax australiana*, established in the aftermath of World War II, warfare in the Highlands was chronic and determined most of the material conditions of life. Settlements were perched on steep ridges and often surrounded by palisades. Men and boys over the age of about fifteen ate and slept in communal "men's houses" and spent much of their time preparing for war while women did the main daily work of subsistence, tending sweet potato gardens and small herds of pigs. Women, children, and pigs lived in outlying houses which sometimes served as early warning: an alarm from a woman's house at the start of a raid woke the men and gave them precious moments to rally.

Men believed the intimate company of wives and children dulled their alertness and agility and thus jeopardized the whole community in time of attack. Having sex with a woman, accepting food from her hands, or fondling an unweaned child on the eve of battle could leave a man utterly debilitated, unable to string a bow or shoot an arrow or lift an ax without cutting himself. The source of a woman's danger was her menstrual blood, and during her periods she was banished to a tiny shelter on the outskirts of the settlement. But even when a woman was no longer menstruating and emerged from seclusion, vestiges of blood remained beneath her fingernails and in the crevices of her vagina so that she was always polluted to some degree, infecting whatever she handled or stepped over and so "passed between her thighs." In the days of war, men regarded their wives as the enemy within, capable not only of ruining their husbands' prowess by mere proximity but also of transmitting war plans to their fathers and brothers in other villages. Fighting men performed regular rites of purification, letting blood from their noses or penes or swallowing cane to induce vomiting that would rid their bodies of the inevitable accumulations of female influence. Highlands men fought each other in constant wars, yet seemed more afraid of the women and children in their midst, believing their own health and vigor to be threatened more by menstrual blood, which was hidden and pervasive, than by their enemies' spears and arrows. Men treated menstruation and childbirth as hostile and contagious acts. A woman with her period, or holding a newborn child, was dangerous and had to be confined and avoided in the same way as a warrior who had just slain one of the enemy.

In the Eastern Highlands, men expressed their fears in elaborate flute cults (Read 1952; R. Berndt 1962; Salisbury 1965; Langness 1967, 1974; Herdt 1981; Godelier 1986; etc.). They believed that the ability to wage war and dominate women, and thus to uphold the social order, rested with those who possessed sacred bamboo flutes called "birds." Men kept the flutes in the rafters of their communal houses and forbade women to look at them on pain of death, refusing even to let women walk on the paths that led to men's houses. Yet, according to men's own myth, the flute was invented by a woman who was supremely independent and lived without a husband. One night her haunting music woke a small boy asleep in the men's house. The boy crawled in the darkness to her house, waited until morning, and then crept inside and stole her flute. Robbed of her "bird," the woman began to menstruate and lost her independence. But she said nothing and died without telling other women what she had once had and lost. If men fail to keep this secret, their myths warns, if they allow even one woman to lay eyes on the flutes—and live to speak of it—women will "take back" the flutes and regain their ancient autonomy. Men's enemies will defeat them in battle; gardens and pig herds will fail; seasons will falter; birds and marsupials will disappear from clan forests; life will lose any semblance of meaning or order.

Do Highlands women know the flute myth? Do they consider menstrual blood poisonous to men or to themselves? Do they have secret myths and rites centered on men's sexuality? In the early 1960s a missionary embarked on a walking tour through Unavi Census Division, demanding in each village that the flutes be shown to the women and children. In some villages, the missionary entered the men's houses, carried out the sacred instruments, and told the men to play them publicly. When the display was over, he placed the flutes in a pile, burned them, threw the ashes into a river, and then baptized the whole village. When this happened in Ubagubi, men report, there was a prolonged period of mourning, anger at the mission, and resistance to Christian teaching. The mission also forbade the construction of men's houses, because they prevented nuclear family life, and it ordered the burning of menstrual huts, perhaps because they were called *kami ðama*, literally, "flute houses" (*kamiba*/flute + *nama*/house). By 1973, when we first arrived in Unavi, there was a revival of traditional practices, and men in many Unavi villages were rebuilding men's houses and holding initiations for adolescent boys. But menstrual huts, the other flute houses, were not rebuilt.[1]

1. The first missionary in Ubagubi, and in most of Unavi Census Division, was the Reverend Ben Wertz who established the Faith Mission at Gono, southwest of Lufa Station, in 1954. Having entered a controlled area against the wishes of the Australian administration, he confined his activities to the outskirts of Unavi until about 1962. The New Tribes mission moved into the area of Yani River Gimi, within the jurisdiction of Okapa Station, in 1957; and in 1959, the Lutheran mission arrived at Agotu.

In the opinion of some researchers, "the Gimi have been slower to change their traditional ways than their closely related neighbors, the Fore and Keiagana. They accepted the new ideas of the administration . . . but did not immediately discard their old modes of dress or housing, or the practice of cannibalism" (Gajdusek and Alpers 1972:18). Since 1985, roughly half the 1000 adults in Ubagubi have become nominal adherents of either the Faith Mission or Seventh Day Adventists.

Our family lived under one roof, conforming to the missionized pattern of about half the families in Ubagubi, but David had a life separate from Samantha and me, spending much of his time with other men in the forest trying to photograph the elusive Birds of Paradise. Samantha and I followed the women to their gardens and sat with them inside the compounds. But the more time I spent in women's company in the early months of fieldwork, the more I felt left out of the real business of village life. Women waited for food to cook inside earth ovens, nursed infants, twisted shredded bark into string, netted the string into carrying bags, deloused one another and their children, carried on intermittant conversations about a recent betrothal or troublesome pig while often, at the other end of a compound, men were in the midst of a sorcery trial making dramatic speeches and accusations. When I strained to listen, or coaxed other women to move within earshot, they reminded me that only men are sorcerers and "only men understand sorcery." When I changed the subject to women's affairs, repeating to one woman that I had seen another do in her garden or heard her say, groping for an explanation, the usual response was, "Who told you that?! . . . Well, then, ask *her!*"

After about nine months, I asked one of David's bird guides to help me translate a tape recording I had made of one of men's public meetings and to collect genealogies. Seeing me work closely with men, several women asked to put their garden magic into my book. "She puts talk into books and takes food out of tins," they remarked. "No other woman will give you the spells I do," one woman boasted. "But I won't come to your house if it is always crowded!" "When you talk to us older women," her companion advised, "keep away the men and other women and children. Shut your door and let no one else inside."

Inadvertently, I had lured women out of their gardens and into my house. They came alone or in pairs to recite private repertoires of garden songs and spells. "We name many, many things in our songs so that the *auna,* the spirit of the song, will go inside the food." A woman flatters her nurtured objects to make them grow, addressing her "darling" sweet potato as a beautiful bird, her precious pig as a giant echidna. In rhythmic phrases, she names the muddy pools where her pig likes to wallow, the grubs and nuts it finds delectable, punctuating references to its pleasures with the mellifluous nonsense sounds and sweet nothings she whispers to her child. Some women reminisced about their initiations and marriages, occasions when they were taught garden magic, and some went on to describe their first loves. Because I was still struggling with the language, I taped these early conversations; and as I listened to a passage again and again, straining to hear the distinctive sounds, I often heard a line of reasoning I had missed during the live interview, a tacit theme linking the topics of conversation. But as I tried to follow this other theme, I usually found I had cut it off by interrupting with a prearranged question. The more I listened to women, the more I came to regard my questions as fatal distractions from the more revealing other stories beneath their words.

Yet in twenty-two months of conversations and interviews I did not find women to be subversive nor opposed to prevalent cultural norms (see M. Strathern 1972:150; Kelly 1976:45). When asked outright, women said their mothers and grandmothers never saw the flutes and that they themselves had no notion why menstrual huts were called "flute houses." Menstrual blood could indeed be fatal to their husbands, and even to themselves, so that they had still to take elaborate precautions, to stay in seclusion, to wash their hands repeatedly with soap, etc. Older women, especially, promoted men's rules and values by imposing them on younger women during the initial secret phases of marriage and initiation, blaming brides in advance for adultery and making them responsible for protecting their husbands' welfare, as if the threat to men indeed stemmed from woman's own lethal nature. Women seemed to accept, and even embrace, men's characterization of their sex as part of an ancestral order that was beyond question or doubt. "If that be mystification, the outcome of male ideological hegemony," as Keesing says of Kwaio women, "they are fully taken in by it; if that simply be 'Kwaio culture' they fully subscribe to it" (Keesing 1987:38).

Out of the field, rereading my notes on women's conversations, I came across a description of the first Gimi man, a single reference to a bizarre creature with an enormously long penis that he wound in coils, like a rope of liana vine, and carried about inside a net bag. The bag hung from his neck and protruded in a lump over his belly. Returning to the Gimi some six months later, I described this fabulous man to one of David's guides. "That is a *nene* man," he told me. "You are speaking *nenekaina*. Ask my wife. *nenekaina* is women's talk." *nenekaina* are stories told after dark inside women's houses. The *nene* is the "gist" or "allegory." *nenekaina* is "talk" (*kaina*) charged with meaning. Learning this word, ironically from a man, changed my relationship with women by allowing me to name the thing I had been looking for.

When I asked a few women to tell me *nenekaina,* they told others of my request, and women from every part of the village, and from other villages, appeared at my door to tell stories in the versions and dialects of their birthplaces. Among the first to offer her stories was Rubake, a woman of about thirty-five who lived in a neighboring compound and whom many regarded as odd or disturbed. Her tales were longer than the others and seemed to be a chaotic mixture of the characters and episodes of many *nene*. But as I worked on her voluminous texts, I realized that Rubake had systematically raided various *nenekaina* to "cut and paste" accounts of her own life. By selecting and rearranging pieces of several myths, she had created personal histories that vividly presented her own version of her marriage, the deaths of her children, her husband's infidelities, the arrival of a co-wife, etc. Like entries on a Rosetta stone, Rubake's stories made it possible to lay out with dramatic clarity connections among personal symbols and collective representations, showing how "myth can be regarded as constituting the furthest background of a continuous perspective which ranges from an individual's personal concerns, fears, and sorrows . . . right back into the epoch where a similar fact is imagined to have occurred for the first time" (Malinowski 1954 [1926]:136).

During the next ten years of intermittant fieldwork, *nenekaina* became the key to my understanding of Gimi women's protests—and acquiescence—in the "male ideological hegemony" of Gimi culture. Women may never have laid eyes on flutes, or never have done so publicly before the arrival of missionaries, but their myths indicate they have always known the secret. The association of *nenekaina* with women's houses suggests that women may even participate in, or influence, the creation of men's myths—a priority that men's myth seems to recognize in the premise that the first woman invented the flute by herself. Children of both sexes sleep with their mothers, giving males an intimate knowledge of women and women's bedtime stories. But women have no counterpart knowledge of men, as some men point out, because they have no parallel experience in childhood of living for years alone with their fathers: on the contrary, they are traditionally kept apart. *biϑokaina,* or tales of the men's house, may be considered in this light not simply as the male equivalent of *nenekaina* but also as a response or appropriation of the *nene,* incorporating, elaborating, translating into the terms of a male ethic stories men heard in infancy. Whatever the direction—or mutuality—of influence, the tales told "in secret" inside men's and women's separate houses seem to speak to one another across the night.

### The Mythic Argument

An interpretation of culture based upon the content of belief is inherently unwieldy. In speaking of two sides of a hidden dispute between the sexes, I have used certain key myths to express the gist of hundreds. To summarize the mythic argument in a preliminary way, I present just two of these key myths, treating them to a kind of diagrammatic reduction in lieu of fuller versions that will appear later on. Aside from deleting narrative complexity, sometimes to the point of parody, such treatment gives the impression that I constructed an argument between the sexes simply by comparing their myths. In fact, I was able to see connections among the myths only through the "detour" of ritual enactment. The myths' relations with each other became apparent from associations informants made, not among the narratives themselves but between certain mythic events and ritual performances. When I examined the spoken content of a myth, and even accompanying exegeses, in the context of their often multiple ritual correlates, I saw that the myth could hide, distort, or even reverse the meanings it acquired in relation to ritual; and that these hidden meanings were sometimes *explicit premises* of other myths, especially those of the opposite sex. Associations with ritual revealed correspondences among myths and even suggested levels of meaning within a myth. While I follow Lévi-Strauss in "reading myths as a whole," I do not treat them as a closed system of meaning, as if "myth itself provides its own context" (Lévi-Strauss 1967:211).

My interpretations of myths are tied to the rites of death, birth, marriage, initiation, and sorcery. Like a rite of passage or curing, a Gimi myth always has a central character, one who represents the deceased, newborn, bride, groom, initiate, patient, etc., the one on whose behalf the ritual is performed, though in myth the subject is often "out of sight," behind the scenes, circulating in concealment, as it were, among the objects and episodes of the narrative. In the sense that a myth, like a ritual, always has a hero or heroine, one whose life is at stake or in the process of transformation, it is like a dream or personal narrative: everything in the myth masks—and in that sense depicts—a singular point of view or experience. I present the argument between men's and women's myths in these terms, as if they were concocted by an archtypical boy and girl, or man and women, and addressed to each other. But the analysis is actually routed through ritual performance: it is ritual that grounds my interpretations of the myths and allows me to speak of a male or female view, of the mutual containment of views, of women's unspoken protest, agreement, or collusion with men, etc.

Let me stress at the outset that the relentless sexuality and violence of most Gimi myths do not translate in any direct or obvious way into behavior. When I propose that complex collaborations among women's and men's fantasies provide the structural basis of kinship and exchange, I do not imply that Gimi are more sexual, incestuous, or death-obsessed in their personal relations than other people. Cunnilingus is alluded to in the flute myth, and in women's myth of the giant penis, although both sexes expressly forbid mouth-to-genital contact. While oral sex is sometimes performed, as far as I know it is hardly the general practice. Symbolic male homosexuality is a more prominent, though covert, theme, in my view, in the myths of both sexes. Indeed, I suggest that symbolic male homosexual incest, an encounter between father and son in the prenatal and primordial past, is the organizing principle of marriage and exchange and a focus of life-crisis rites (see Chaps. 7, 8, and 9). Yet, unlike men in some New Guinea societies (e.g., Williams 1969 [1936]; Kelly 1976; Schiefflin 1976; Herdt 1981), Gimi men do not practice ritual homosexuality, and they deny they engage in homosexual acts. To plead with another man, or express extreme deference or gratitude, a Gimi man says, "Let me eat your penis." But men insist the expression has only metaphoric meaning. Gajdusek (diary entry) reports no overt homosexuality among Gimi men; and over a period of nearly twenty years, during trips into the forest to photograph Birds of Paradise, D. Gillison observed "no sign or hint" of homosexual conduct among his companions. When, prodded by me, he put the question directly, men replied that they were not dogs, and did not "act like dogs—nor like men in the Sepik!" Although one man alluded to the time when "a Big Man is sweet on a young boy," he refused to elaborate. Whatever the facts of Gimi men's sexual conduct, in a sense they are peripheral to the connection I propose between culture and fantasy. The reality to which I tie mythic elements, including a symbolic homosexuality between father and son, is not the incidence of apparently equivalent events in real life, parallels to mythic incidents in the lives or behavior of individuals, but rather the intrinsic logic of social rules and arrangements.

According to men's flute myth, the first couple was composed of a woman and a boy who were sister and brother. One night, the cries of the woman's flute awoke the "small boy" asleep in the men's house and he crawled to her house, hiding himself in the tall grass outside her door. In the morning, after his sister had gone to her garden, the boy crept into her house and stole her flute from the head of her bed or, as told in other versions, he took it from the grass where she had left it. When he put the instrument to his mouth to play, he found that she had closed the blowing hole with a plug of her pubic hair. The boy's lips touched the plug and his sister's hair began to grow around his mouth, which is why men nowadays have beards. By stealing the flute, the boy not only acquired a beard; he also caused his sister to menstruate for the first time. But when she saw that her flute was gone and heard it "crying" inside the men's house, she was not angry, men's myth insists, and did not try to take it back. "She forgot everything that happened and died," their myth says. "But, in truth, the flute was once something that belonged *only* to women. It wasn't ours! We men stole it!"

According to the *nenekaina*, the primordial couple were not the woman with the flute and her brother but the *nene* man with the giant penis and a virgin girl who, in some versions, is identified as his daughter. What caused the "first appearance" of menstrual blood was not the boy stealing his sister's flute and removing the plug of her pubic hair but the girl cutting her father down to size. During the night, while the *nene* man lay fast asleep inside his house, his penis awoke "out of hunger" and went out alone to search for the vagina. The penis was blind and followed his nose into the woman's house. But she was fast asleep, and her vagina was closed. "The man slept. The woman slept. The penis came alone." He searched in vain for the opening and finally "ate a part of the hole to open it. Then he entered and ejaculated." The woman awoke with a start and took the penis in her hand. She walked to the man's house and, while he still lay sleeping, cut his penis to the length of a section and a half of sugarcane, throwing the huge severed portion into a river. The blood of the maimed giant was the blood of first menses.

Women's myth has a kind of public currency in the sense that it corresponds to the meaning of the Gimi term "to menstruate," *hibo fa,* which may be translated as either "to kill" or "be killed by the Moon" (*hik*/moon + *mo*/the + *fa*/hit, strike, [im]plant or kill). The Moon is "every woman's first husband," men and women say. When there is a full Moon, some men add, women run off. The Moon "throws his giant penis out of the sky" and copulates with them all, making their blood flow. Both sexes refer to menstrual blood as "dead womb blood" and as "the same as a firstborn child," suggesting that it signifies not only penetration by the Moon but also a stillbirth, the lifeless residue of a child. Among the neighboring Siane, according to Salisbury, "a girl's first menses are treated as a form of pregnancy, heralded similarly by her swelling breasts, but giving birth to paternal blood alone" (Salisbury 1965:72; see Newman 1965:76). The Mountain Arapesh also see "menstruation . . . as the act of not having children, of expelling the blood which might have been cherished to make a child" (Mead 1970:248).

In the use of idioms like "menstruate" and in other ways, Gimi men and women treat menstruation as if it were simultaneously a birth and a death, the issue of a mythic first marriage to the Moon. But if they agree on one level that the blood embodies a "killed child" and tells of a marriage, in their separate myths they seem to argue over which sex instigated the marriage, provoking the other sex to commit the theft that caused the first loss of blood. Who is to blame for the first desire? the myths seem to ask. Who is responsible for its fatal consequences? According to the flute myth, woman woke her brother and lured him into her house with the siren calls of her flute, tempting him to steal it and put his lips on her pubic hair. In women's tale, the woman is asleep and a virgin. The penis seeks her out by himself, roused in the night by his own hunger, and "eats" his way inside her, moving her to cut him down to size. The myths present dramatically different accounts of the first coitus and first menstruation, each claiming the innocence and heroism of a child of the opposite sex, but they are alike in one feature: each deletes or deactivates the Moon or primordial father. In women's myth, the Moon, or first *nene* man, lies fast asleep while his penis "does the walking" to woman's house. But in the flute myth he is entirely absent. There were no men in the primordial era, men's myth says: only "small boys" slept in men's houses. Woman invented the flute by herself and stuffed the blowing hole with only her pubic hair.

Some men hint at the Moon's presence, however, when they add in an epilogue that woman was inspired to make the flute and to use her hair as a plug after she "looked down" at her sex, recalling that she was inside the *kami ðama* or "flute house" because she was menstruating, being "killed by the Moon." In exegeses of other myths, men also say that the small boy who visited his sister in her menstrual hut was "the same as the Moon," implying that his deeds recapitulate the Moon's first copulation. Outside the main narrative, before the myth begins, as it were, before the boy awakes to the cries of his sister's flute, men's remarks suggest that the Moon or his giant penis finds her and plugs her hole. To express an unarticulated male view, one that is consistent with the explicit content of the *nene*, we might say that if the boy is the culture hero, then the one he defeats is not simply an omnipotent or flute-owning woman but also a distant or invisible man, a man as unnoticed as the plug of pubic hair, as inert yet domineering as the Moon (Gillison 1989).

The flute myth is more radical than women's *nenekaina* in the way it symbolizes the Moon's absence or nonparticipation in the first copulation. But once men admit the Moon into their narrative in parenthetical or exegetical remarks, once the flute appears as something that may have originated with a man as well as a woman, the myth takes on a decided resemblance to women's tale. Considered in the terms of the *nene*, the theft of the flute seems to be also a countertheft, part of a cycle in which one sex "steals the flute" or "cuts off the penis" of the other. Analyzed together, men's and women's myths reciprocally imply that, in the very first instance, before time began, during the silent sleep of the first night, etc., only the other sex "had the penis," only the other was grown-up and possessed sexual appetite. The other sex was the first one to awake so that it alone is responsible for the fatal outcome of first desire (see Kelly 1976:49).

The heroism of the small boy or virgin girl lies in curtailing this inordinate desire and suffering the inevitable consequences, acquiring the same "gigantic" first wishes he or she inhibits in the other. The only way to get rid of appetite is to satisfy it. But feeding someone else unavoidably transfers the appetite to oneself, as the boy acquires his sister's pubic hair around his mouth after he steals her flute, and as the girl's vagina fills with the blood of her father's penis after she cuts it off in a fury. The heroic child-thief is afflicted with the same voracity he or she takes away from the sibling or parent. The contagion of desire, the terrible hunger that infects whoever overthrows the first woman or man, makes the question of blame—and of who was first—irresolvable at the level of myth. But accusations cast in the veiled imagery of myth are also enacted in the various secret and public rites of both sexes. The work of life-cycle rituals, as I try to show in later chapters, is to convert the automatic or involuntary transfers of incest wishes described in myth into deliberate exchanges of flutes and head payments so that the mythic question of blame can be decided, at least temporarily, in men's favor.

On an implicit level of culture, I argue, ritual payments have the meaning of accusations, and the items themselves, which are called "the head of the child," stand for the corpus delecti, symbol of the Moon's firstborn. The transfer of the gift or head payment shifts primordial blame onto the recipient by making him or her the original site of the crime, the place where the firstborn, and first blood, appears. The act of receiving, which Gimi call "eating the head of the child," testifies to the recipient's inordinate hunger, indicating that he or she initiated the first copulation, invented death, etc., and has to be induced to cease and desist, offered something to replace the real and preferred "head." The gift indicts the recipient in the sense that it is designed to satisfy an original *mythic* hunger, to stop another kind of eating and end the carnage.

The only way to expunge the guilt of receiving is to shift it back onto the donor with a countergift. The compulsive character of exchange derives, in this sense, not only from the notion that the gift represents a part of the donor (see Mauss 1967 [1925]) but also from the idea that, implicit in the act of giving, is the element of exoneration, of divesting oneself of blame as if it were a stillborn child, a dead but detachable aspect of the person, a thing that can be objectified and cast off, leaving the person intact and renewed like a snake that has just shed its skin. But the rules of Gimi society bar women from initiating exchanges so that only men can achieve this expiation and renewal. Women can never give back the gift of blame, nor achieve a lasting immortality, because, as recipients in public transactions and as objects of exchange in marriage, they cannot launch the transactions that would enable them to shed their mortal aspect.

Before the public celebrations, during separate rites in which each sex enacts its own myths "out of sight" of the other, each concedes the presence of the Moon or mythic father and thus implicates him in woman's primordial crime. The study of men's and women's "secrets" suggests that they are designed not to hide information nor limit the other sex's understanding but rather to keep unacknowledged, and out of the public domain, mutual awareness of the father's mythic role, so that the conflict that arises from it, and that the rites of exchange publicly resolve by blaming women, can continue inside men's and women's separate houses and undermine the public conclusion, making woman's defeat eternally tentative, transitory, and in need of repetition.

## The Relation between Ritual and Myth

By the time I was inundated with *nenekaina*, I had some knowledge of the Gimi language but could hardly translate the myths alone. The woman who recounted a tale was rarely interested in reviewing it with me afterward, so I relied upon other women, mainly ritual experts, to extend my understanding of a myth, often by revealing its association with other myths in the same category or cycle. When I ventured an interpretation of a myth or mythic element, women sometimes recited another *nene* with the same theme or element, implying a comparison that confirmed the connection I had made without discussing or analyzing it directly. When I was off the mark, I got little response; if I persisted, the women changed the subject. To protect my relationships with women, I at first limited discussions with men, depending upon them only as translators. But after several months, I let the work of translation expand into interpretation, and it was then that men pointed out connections between the narratives and certain rituals. During a translation of women's myth of the giant penis, one man compared it to the concluding rite of female initiation (an event staged by both sexes) though the myth itself contains no mention of initiation (Gillison 1987). Men also told me that women "invented" ritual theater and that some of the playlets I had seen performed as nighttime entertainments during marriages and male initiations were enactments of *nenekaina* (Gillison 1983a, 1983b; see Chaps. 3 and 6).

When I first realized that myth and rite were connected, I thought they were "one and the same," as Leach suggests, the myth saying in words what the rite says in action (Leach 1954:13). Associated with the characters and objects of myth, ritual actors and artifacts seemed to acquire an explanatory text, to take on meaning within an expanded frame. I saw myth as the full scenario and ritual as the performance of key episodes, a reduction or condensation of the myth's narrative complexity. "No ritual copies the consecutive acts described in a myth," Newton observes, "Kwoma ritual re-enacts [some] procedures but not others" (Newton, n.d.:13). Malinowski describes the ellipsis of Trobriand myth in song. The song "is very condensed and impressionistic. A word or two indicates rather than describes whole [mythic] scenes and incidents, and the traditional commentary . . . is necessary for full understanding. . . . one might even say [the song is] futuristic, since several scenes are crowded simultaneously into the picture" (Malinowski 1922:295). But as I studied the relation between ritual performance and mythic episode, I saw that the myth, too, was highly condensed, that its events and characters concealed corresponding ritual elements and combined events and relations that were distinct in ritual. Compared with its ritual performance or counterpart(s), an episode in myth often appeared to be a blend of elements, just as the ritual seemed to deconstruct the myth, breaking apart its static, superimposed images into separate, transactable items. The more precisely I was able to associate a particular cycle of myths with a sequence of rites, the more the movement of ritual objects, the exchange of flutes, brides, head payments and other valuables seemed to undo the myth and to "open" its densely compacted images.

### The Work of Ritual: The Exchange of Women and Flutes and the Deconstruction of Myth

During the public celebration of marriage, men stage a "secret" performance of the flute myth that provides a dramatic example of the ritual process of deconstructing myth.

Several months before the marriage, the father of the bride has a "beard" tattooed on her face. He also makes a pair of flutes for the groom, incising the areas around the blowing holes or "mouths" of the flutes with the same designs used in his daughter's tattoos. The bride's beard is a kind of latter-day revenge, men say, a "return" for the beard the first woman planted around her brother's mouth after he stole her flute and put his lips on the plug of her pubic hair. In the matching designs around the mouths of the bride and the flutes, the father of the bride reproduces the mythic plug the first woman used to close her instrument. He recreates the plug yet again by stuffing his new flutes with chunks of cooked pig or marsupial, animals men describe in this context as "covered with hair." The father makes a new set of instruments, "plugs" them, and then hides them inside the bride's net bag, supposedly without her knowledge, so that, when he sends her to the groom, she unwittingly brings him her father's flutes. A man gives away his daughter and flutes together, as a secret icon of the first flute-holding woman, but he does it in a way that contradicts men's myth, revealing through his ritual deeds that she did not invent the flutes nor fill them by herself.

A Gimi marriage is ideally an exchange of sisters so that the father of a bride is also the father of a groom. The "sameness" of the fathers is accentuated in the way names are exchanged when the couples are betrothed. Each intended spouse receives the "same name" as the other's sibling of opposite sex: a bride is given the name of her groom's sister and a groom is given the name of his bride's brother. Every Gimi marriage unites a brother and sister in this sense regardless of the degree to which it conforms to other rules. The flute the groom acquires "in secret" with the bride thus belongs not only to his "sister," as it did in the myth, but also to his "father," whose ritual acts say to him, in effect: "Look! Your sister is not alone nor without a man as she appears. Her flute is not empty as it first seemed to the small boy in the myth. I plugged her hole. I put my meat inside her."

When the groom receives the flute, he, or his father acting in his stead, "unplugs" it by pulling out the chunks of "hairy" meat. But unlike the boy in the myth who put the plug to his lips and grew a beard, the groom (or his father acting on his behalf) places the flute food directly into the bride's newly bearded mouth, "giving her back her father's meat," as men point out. Men's secret exchange of flutes contradicts the overt premise of their myth by exposing the true content of the plug. The exchange deconstructs the myth, as it were, to reveal the presence of the Moon or primordial father at the marriage of brother and sister, showing that he was hiding inside the mouth of the flute and that he used his position and invisibility to mastermind the theft (see Bidou 1989).

In enacting the unspoken content of their own myth, acknowledging that the flutes the groom takes from the bride, and the things he removes from the mouths of the flutes, are phallic or father-derived objects, men play out a fantasy that closely resembles the explicit counterpremise of women's myth, in which the heroine removes the head of a giant penis. Through the transfer of flutes, men set up a connection with women's myth that they undo as soon as the exchange is made. The whole elaborate transaction between the father of the bride and the groom will fail, men say, unless it is kept utterly secret from the bride. If she "finds out her father's tricks" and *sees his flute*, if she realizes that the bamboo container stuffed with meat is not a container of salt, as her father tells her, she will smash it, opening the bamboo as if it were an ordinary cooking vessel, and remove the meat herself. She will eat the delicious morsels with no help from the groom. In terms of the episode in women's myth to which this part of men's rite corresponds, she will "kill the Moon" in a fury of revenge in the way the first woman cut off the giant penis after it "ate open" her vagina. If the bride finds out what men do in secret, smashes her father's flute and eats his meat herself—placing it into her mouth "with her own hands"—as men explain, she will "menstruate forever." She will produce no surviving child to continue the groom's lineage, and the marriage will fail.

Men's secret transfer of flutes links the objects of men's and women's myths, implying a correspondence between the flute plug—the "hairy" meat the bride's father stuffs into the flutes—and the head of the giant penis the woman cuts off and discards in anger. But the moment men acknowledge a kind of agreement with women, the moment they invoke women's premise, as it were, they override it. As soon as the groom receives the flutes, he empties them and feeds the bride, placing her father's meat directly into her mouth so her hands never touch it. The ritual that immediately follows the transfer of flutes is both a repetition and a denial or undoing of a combined mythic scenario: when the groom feeds the bride, he feeds *her instead* of himself. By not eating the contents of the flute, the groom disidentifies himself both with the boy who pressed his lips on the plug of pubic hair and with the giant who ate open the vagina. In the marriage ritual, it is the bride who eats the hairy plug—and gets a beard—not the groom. It is she who receives the first gift and "eats the head of the child" and is thus blamed for initiating the first copulation. In the sense that men's secret ritual enacts an explicit premise of women's *nene*, it also reverses women's meaning, replacing one fantasy of the first marriage with another. In the ritual, the bride's mouth is closed or "filled with blame" because she eats her father's gift without awareness and so cannot even think of making a return.

## The Gift as Accusation

The "hair-covered" food inside the flute is not only the secret ritual version of the mythic plug of pubic hair. It is also the original head payment (see Bowden 1988). When a child is born or has a new experience or becomes vulnerable, when it is named several months after birth, has its first haircut, falls ill or is injured, when it is initiated at adolescence, the father and other men of his patrilineage present the wife's father and brothers with payments called "the head of the child." Head payments consist of the same items as bridewealth, mainly live pigs, cooked pork, whole marsupials, marsupial furs, Bird of Paradise plumages, and lately manufactured goods and money, and are presented in amounts that vary with the importance of the transition the child undergoes. When the mother's brother and other matrikin receive these payments, Gimi say, they "eat the head of the child." A mother's brother is required to give regular gifts of food, clothing, and items of body decoration to his sister's children while they are young. The children's father pays the mother's brother and he reciprocates—but does not pay—with new gifts. When a girl is betrothed or initiated, her father makes a final head payment to her mother's brother that transfers his rights in her to her brother, so that when she marries her brother is the one who receives her bridewealth and, later, the head payments her husband will make on behalf of her children. But when a man marries, his mother's brother's investment in him does not end. A man takes over his father's obligations so that an asymmetrical exchange relationship, like the one between the brothers-in-law, continues between him and his mother's brother (or mother's brother's son) for the duration of his life. When a man or unmarried girl dies, the "head" or death payment goes to the mother's brother or his son; but when a married woman dies, her brother (or his lineal heir) "eats her head" (see Wagner 1967).[2]

When a bride eats the contents of her father's flute, "eats the head of his child," she initiates the flow of head payments to her brother and other pa-

2. Among the peoples of Mount Hagen, the most important type of prestation likely to be expanded into *moka* exchange is that of war compensations, either "man head" payments to an enemy, or "dead man" payments to an ally for the loss of a man fighting on one's own behalf. Both payments are elicited by the victim offering an initiatory "man bone" gift. "It is said that the killers (or allies) have 'eaten' the victim, and are now willing to hand over his bones in return for a payment. . . . 'You killed our man, but you did not really eat him . . . so now we have brought you this cooked pork, so that you may eat it, feel good, and pay "man head" to us'" (A. Strathern 1971:94).

ternal kinsmen. Her ritual meal inaugurates the exchange in the sense that, symbolically at least, she eats unknowingly. If she were to "see" her father's flute, she would smash it so there could be no exchange. In the terms of the fantasy the ritual recreates, she would finish her father's meat by herself and leave nothing to send back. Like the heroine of women's myth, she would act alone and "cut off the giant's head," leaving only blood in its place. Men keep the flute a secret from the bride, in this sense, in order to salvage her brother and her child.

Marriage and every other rite of exchange commence with a presentation of head payments to women. In the following chapters, I suggest that these initial rites are each a symbolic instance of men giving women the "head" or child in good faith and of women refusing to offer a suitable return. This nonreturn symbolizes the consequence and proof of a mythic crime, as if women had collectively devoured the firstborn child, or turned the small boy to menstrual blood, so they could not send him back to the men alive. By forbidding women to participate as donors in ritual exchanges, men dramatize their guilt and incapacity, showing that woman's only response to being offered the head of the child is to eat it. No matter how many times men present women the "head" in preliminary rites, the women fail to reciprocate, refuse to transact the child to life, leaving men no choice, as it were, but to "steal the flute" and circulate it entirely among themselves.

According to my analysis, every Gimi life-crisis rite centers around a set of exchanges that enacts the myth of the flute in a way that blames, or treats as possessed of demonic rage, a ritual counterpart of the first woman—bride, mother of the deceased, mother of the newborn, mother of the initiate, etc. In the actuality of ritual, it is the mother or grown-up sister, not the "small boy," who puts her mouth on the hair and eats the head of the child. The unborn, deceased, newborn, initiate, etc., not only undergoes a symbolic death in the classic sense of Van Gennep, he or she is also killed by the mother—surreptitiously devoured in the form of a head payment. The ritual subject is afterward reborn because the subsequent exchanges absolve the mythic father. Whenever the myth of the father's guilt threatens to come true, as it were, whenever there is a crisis in the life of an individual, men exchange the "head" in order to confiscate it from the mother, a move that acquits the father by publicly denying his original presence. But the father is really there in hiding, as we have seen, concealed like the plug in a flute, and

---

Like a "man bone" gift in Hagen, Gimi "head" payments have an accusatory meaning, although the crime to which they allude is entirely mythic. Like a man bone gift, the Gimi offer of a head payment is a demand for a bigger and better return. In the sense that women cannot initiate head payments, offering them the head is a demonstration of their incapacity (see Chap. 9).

he directs the theft or expropriation from behind the scenes, sending his sons to the rescue: men remove the flute and its contents from the mother and then send them *back* to her father, rescuing the child by making it the object of their own secret alliance.

Each life-crisis rite sets forth a version of the first marriage in which the woman is left alone and kills—or has to be stopped from killing—the child, stopped from smashing the flute and feeding herself the contents. Each rite promotes men's side in the mythic debate by revealing and then overturning women's account of the first union. Men celebrate primordial woman's rage, in these terms, as the pretext and justification for their own domination (see Bamberger 1974). Men's myth says that the first woman gave up her flute without a fight, without speaking of her loss, as if she, too, recognized her unworthiness. Even in secret rites of dissent, women seem to collude with men in the idea of their guilt by treating menstrual blood as a deadly substance (see Chap. 6). Though men subject women to ritual threats of violence and may, for that reason, be said to coerce them into cooperating in the public rituals of their defeat, women also seem to arrive at men's conclusion—though not without protest—for reasons of their own. Women join men "in the festivals that celebrate the successes and victories of the males, . . . [finding] in their heart of hearts confirmation of the masculine pretensions" (de Beauvoir cited in Ortner 1974:76).

If woman's primordial vexation and bleeding "head" justifies her subjugation—and if women themselves are inclined to accept this idea— why do men dramatize it as a secret? In order to make sense of woman's anger men have to reveal the presence of the mythic father: they have to contradict their own myth which says men are absent, as distant as the Moon, as blameless as a small boy, as inconsequential as a plug of pubic hair, etc. Men affirm the logic of women's view, in this sense, but *only as a secret among men*. A society's symbolic forms may thus "enact that female model of the world which has been lacking" (Ardener 1975:5). Their "surface may express the male view of the world, obscuring the existence at deeper levels of an autonomous female view" (ibid.). In the Gimi case, and in the New Guinea Highlands generally, the absence of a female model hardly reflects women's "inarticulateness" or "lack of a metalanguage for the discussion of social life," as Ardener presumes. Women's low profile seems rather to indicate men's systematic suppression of women's views in public ritual, a project in which they may indeed have help from women themselves as well as from ethnographers.

Gimi myth and ritual are not the perfect match Leach supposed. The ritual performance parallels the myths of both sexes at many points, linking this marriage, birth, initiation, death, etc., to the very first, imbuing these participants with the vigor and heroic dimension unique to their mythic counterparts (see Lincoln 1981:24). But the rite also departs from the myth, demonstrating meanings that contradict the myth's spoken content and the direct exegeses of informants. Ritual implicates newborn, initiate, groom, sick person, deceased, etc., in the myth of the first marriage but arranges that he or she escape the fate of the firstborn by transacting the "head" and undoing the myth, unplugging the flute in a way that avoids the flow of blood. Exchanges are a rescue, in this sense, a method for averting the disasters that originate in myth but often threaten to come true in the life of an individual. Each life-crisis rite follows a mythic scenario of "inevitable and ruthless fatality" (Malinowski 1954 [1926]:137). But by *reasserting the distinctions* that myths suppress, breaking the mythic fusion of family relationships, the rite alters the mythic outcome and forestalls the death of the firstborn.

The myths of Gimi men and women revolve around a primordial pair—the meandering penis and sleeping virgin, the flute-owning sister and sleeping boy. The Moon in men's myths and the *nene* man in women's tales are either external to the narrative or outside its main action. Unlike myth, however, the performance of ritual depends upon three dramatis personnae because it is always founded upon the exchange of brides and flutes or head payments between male affines. The exchange splits the male's mythic role: it makes the father appear in the guise of wife giver, highlighting the father-son boundary that the myths of both sexes ignore or underplay.

### The Social Status of Unconscious Thought

There was a time in anthropology when myths and procreation beliefs were treated as a kind of cultural theory. In the opening pages of *The Sexual Life of Savages,* Malinowski describes the Trobriand notion of virgin birth as the basis for "the rule governing descent, inheritance, succession in rank, chieftainship, hereditary offices, and magic—[for] every regulation, in fact, concerning transmission by kinship" (1929:4).

> The idea that it is solely and exclusively the mother who builds up the child's body, the man in no way contributing to its formation, is the most important factor in the legal system of the Trobriands. (Ibid., 3)

To a Trobriand child, the father is a "stranger," an "outsider," one whom the child addresses as *tama* or "husband of my mother." Malinowski regarded what he believed to be Trobrianders' ignorance "of the man's share in the begetting of children" as the basis of kin terms and marriage rules. "Love-making, marriage, and kinship are three aspects of the same subject," he said (ibid., 8).

Ashley Montagu arrived at a similar conclusion about Australian Aborigines:

> It is clear that the procreative beliefs of the Aborigines constitute the foundation stones of their cosmogony, kinship system, religion, and social organization and possess a significance the ramifications of which far exceed in importance any question of whether or not the Aborigines are in some cases ignorant of the fact of procreation. (1974 [1937]:230)

The problem with Malinowski's and Montagu's point of view, according to most of their contemporaries, was that it provided little basis for systematic comparison. The aim of fieldwork was to produce descriptions of societies that would make them comparable. Notions of virgin birth, myths of insemination by ancestral spirits, etc., were themselves irrational ideas that could hardly be used to generate reliable categories. To move the study of social structure onto what they held to be a higher, more theoretical plane, British functionalists discounted indigenous misconceptions about where babies come from and created classifications based instead upon residence rules, kin terms, and the linearity of descent. In keeping with Durkheim, functionalists rejected the idea that "religion [and culture] originated in a mere mistake, an illusion, a kind of hallucination . . . [that] a vain fantasy . . . produced law, science, and morals" (Evans-Pritchard 1965:53).

But procreation beliefs are not merely fantastic and irrational. They are also graphically sexual. Considered as "foundation stones" of the social order, they create the unacceptable impression that other people devise rules governing "descent, inheritance, succession in rank," etc., on the basis of sexual fantasies; and hence that they actually believe their fantasies and are deficient natural historians, ignorant of the facts of life—a conclusion that to some sounds supercilious and racist (e.g., Leach 1961, 1966). But there is another kind of explanation that gives myth a central place in the analysis of social forms yet does not insinuate an insulting lack of "scientific" understanding. Commenting in 1925 upon Malinowski's assertion of Trobrianders' ignorance "of the man's share in the begetting of children," Jones suggested, consistent with a psychoanalytic theory of unconscious thought and repression, that the father's role is disguised and denied rather than unknown; that "the father disappears from the scene only to reappear . . . [as] an ancestral spirit, who in a supernatural manner impregnates the mother" (Jones 1925:122; see Róheim 1933; and Spiro 1968).

Dismissing the relevance of psychoanalysis, anthropologists continued for years to debate the sexual ignorance of savages, arguing over whether Trobriand Islanders or Australian Aborigines indeed failed to grasp the "fertilizing agency of the male seed" (Spiro 1968:248); whether they actually believed, as Austin reported of Trobrianders, that the "man's contribution towards the new life in the mother's body was nil" (cited in ibid). Anthropologists refused to consider the fact that, at the same time as Trobriand informants emphatically denied the father's role, their myths and procreation beliefs gave ample evidence of a precise, although disguised, understanding of the male function (Malinowski 1929). What Trobrianders were "ignoring," it seems to me in extrapolating from Gimi data, was not the biological contribution of the male but the symbolic presence of the father.

In terms of their articulated views, Gimi appear in striking contrast to the classic aboriginal. Gimi men and women assert that a husband's semen forms the whole child and that a woman's body is merely the receptacle (see Chap. 7). But in denying the mother's active role, Gimi also seem to deny the hidden presence of her father and thereby hide the alliance of husband's semen and father's blood, obscuring the symbolically homosexual connection between men that Gimi of both sexes seem to consider the final cause of life. From this point of view, Trobrianders' insistence upon the primacy of ancestral spirit in causing conception achieves the same end by an opposite tactic: whereas Gimi absent the spirit-father or Moon or mythic giant, Trobrianders and Australians sacrifice the living penetrator in favor of a disembodied ancestor. Each gets rid of *one* of the men, mythic or real, who penetrates woman's body and thereby conceals their "homosexual" relation. If Gimi rules of kinship and marriage indeed enact such tacit beliefs, they suggest that a symbolic male homosexuality is at the basis of Gimi social organization (see Devereux 1965). Looked at in this light, exchanges of wives and head payments are a means to subvert men's sexual aims by carrying them out in disguised form, a means for men to counteract yet achieve unspeakable secrets implied in the argument between men's and women's myths.

From the perspective of myth and procreation belief, the essence of society's work is to recruit new members *one at a time,* to transform each new crop of children into men and women with the skill and strength to replace those who die, avenge their deaths, fight other wars, hunt new game, raise new crops, etc. The radicalism of this unremarkable view is that it treats society as a collection of individuals rather than of "social facts" or institutions and ties social organization, and the mechanics of group reproduction, to the growth and maturation of individuals, to the rituals that celebrate birth, marriage, initiation, and the achievement of an afterlife. But if the individual is to ascend to social status in this sense so, by inevitable corollary, must the fantasied dilemmas that threaten his or her development.[3] The private

3. Individual enterprise and initiative and the concept of the person are traditional themes in Melanesian ethnography (e.g., Read 1955; Barnes 1962; Sahlins 1963). My focus upon the individual as *the* constituent element of society is both an interpretation of Gimi concepts and a theoretical point of view (see M. Strathern 1988:3 ff.).

world of fantasy can no longer be "shut off, closeted as it were, from public culture" (Obeyesekere 1990:xix). Oedipal conflict ceases to be some private psychic process, internal to the individual and inaccessible except through "atrocious techniques of hit or miss intuition" (Leach 1967 [1958]:80), and becomes instead the centerpiece of collective life, the theme of lengthy, repetitive, directly observable performances of myths and rites. Motherhood is sexualized, and violence is transposed from the social periphery into the heart of the family. The unspoken meaning of public symbols, the invisible thing that really exists and "arouse[s] the sensation of the divine . . . [giving] the feeling of perpetual dependence" is not simply the idea of society, as Durkheim proposed (Evans-Pritchard 1965:57), but also unconscious wishes of the kind Freud described (e.g., 1960 [1913]). In the Freudian unconscious, similarities are treated as identities, negatives are equated with positives, the whole is represented by a part or by its opposite or by other distortions, expressing all at once, in one object or image, utterly incompatible impulses, aims, and ideas. When Gimi myths are analyzed in these terms, preexisting categories of relations disappear, and there is, instead, the fantasy of universal incest, a primordial era or realm in which self-evident distinctions of time, space, and relationship are lost or blatantly ignored.

If myth and unconscious fantasy, analyzed in terms that are consistent with basic psychoanalytic principles, are to be granted a role in determining the social design, then they have to be accompanied by a theory of negation or denial, some account of the complex social processes by which a people regularly create unambiguous categories and oppositions. In early functionalist studies, kinship and descent were treated quite apart from beliefs or practices that dealt explicitly with sex and copulation. The rules and actual incidence of marriages, sometimes called "ideal" and "statistical norms," encapsulated the system by which a society reproduced itself. Social reproduction was to be understood in abstract, even quasi-mathematical terms, as closed sets of logical relations that could be collected and catalogued "like butterflies" in Leach's phrase. Underlying these theories was the assumption that the work of society lay in forging bonds among already-distinct entities. The separations-in-existence which social symbols replicate were treated as manifest and unproblematic, generated automatically by participation in social life or, according to a structuralist view, by a distinction-making template in the brain. Lévi-Strauss avoided the circularity of locating in social experience the categories upon which social order rests by postulating the innate capacity for language, or a congruent "structure in the brain," as the source of logical oppositions. Traditional anthropology took for granted "the innateness of kin differentiation—the notion that the genealogical breakdown into 'father,' 'mother,' and so forth, is a natural fact, and that it is

a human responsibility to integrate them into particular kinship 'systems'"
(Wagner 1977:623).[4]

"Consider [instead] a situation in which all kin relations and all kinds of
relatives are basically alike, and it is a human responsibility to differentiate
them" (ibid). From this starting point, which closely resembles the mythic
beginning, the work of society is to sever the fantasied connections that
make human relations too entangled to fit into a kinship system. From the
perspective of myth, the first problem of order is not to combine but to *eliminate:* to create a "sister" who is not also a "mother," a "mother's brother"
who is not also a "father," etc.; to establish rules that arrest the promiscuous
flow of sameness among individuals (see Kelly 1976). According to my analysis of the Gimi, the deepest structure of kinship and marriage resides in the
dissociation of their terms through exchanges that undo the mythic first
marriage. The critical negations that underlie Gimi collective categories are
not given in any automatic or invisible way, it seems to me, but are achieved
with great effort through exchanges of flutes and head payments that "pull
out the plug" or "cut off the giant's head," breaking static images of the
myths into visibly distinct and negotiable items.

4. If much of traditional anthropology rests upon the assumption that some kind of "genealogical breakdown . . . is a natural fact," that assumption seems to stem, in particular, from
the way anthropologists have followed conventional wisdom and used the mother-child relation as the foundation of kinship (e.g., Schneider 1961; Fox 1967; Barnes 1973:68). "Maternity is
a question of fact, paternity a question of opinion" (Schouten cited in Jones 1925:114), or, in the
terms of an older Latin dictum, *pater semper incertus est, mater certissima.* Women are the known
parents, the ones whose bonds to children are demonstrated and undeniable. "The mother-
child tie is inevitable and given," says Fox. "The 'conjugal' tie is variable" (Fox 1967:39–40).
Because motherhood is manifest at birth and continues for years in the symbiotic tie of mother
and child, the argument runs, it is not dependent upon any kind of symbolic ratification. Fatherhood, on the contrary, is a wholly symbolic status that can be asserted only through a system of kinship, only by exchanging women in marriage and exploiting their conspicuous ties to
the next generation. For men, parenthood is just an idea: it is always a symbolic co-optation of
women's role as natural mothers (see Mitchell 1974a:393–95 summarizing views of Lévi-
Strauss, Freud, and Lacan).

According to at least one current line of feminist thinking, the notion that women are more
in nature than men, or less part of a symbolic cultural system, is an idea whose time has come:

> There are no "facts," biological or material, that have social consequences and cul-
> tural meanings in and of themselves. Sexual intercourse, pregnancy, and parturition
> are cultural facts, whose form, consequences, and meanings are socially constructed
> in any society, as are mothering, fathering, . . . and talking with the gods.
> (Yanagisako and Collier 1987:39; see Rosaldo and Lamphere 1974:4–6)

While I disagree with Yanagisako and Collier's further assertion that "there are no material
'facts' that can be treated as precultural givens," I concur that social or cultural categories are
never automatic or self evident but always in the process of being constructed and revised.
Chapters 3, 4, and 5, devoted to myths of cannibalism and rites of death, demonstrate how
elaborate and ongoing is the Gimi invention of motherhood.

# TWO

# The Gimi of Highland New Guinea

Gimi is the name of a language spoken by some 16,000–20,000 people who live in the southwestern corner of the Eastern Highlands Province just north of the Papuan border.[1] Gimi have probably always been a peripheral people, isolated by the terrain from centers of population in the Asaro and Wahgi River valleys. The first Australian patrols did not cross Gimi territory until 1948 or 1949, but residents of Ubagubi recall that a party of Japanese soldiers, coming from the direction of Papua, arrived some six or seven years earlier and conscripted men into their service, paying them with teaspoonsful of salt, an item Gimi traditionally manufactured by a laborious process of extraction from cultivated swamps or from the ashes of certain tree ferns.

Australian Patrol Posts were established at Lufa and Okapa in 1954 and 1955, but the area was not officially pacified or "decontrolled" until the late 1950s and early 1960s. Gimi are spread out rather sparsely, about twenty per square mile, in three Census Divisions: Labogai and Unavi in Lufa Sub-Province and Gimi in Okapa Sub-Province. Their neighbors on the east are South Fore, and on the north lie groups of Nomane, Elimbari, Siane, Yagaria, and Keiagana. To the west, across ranges that extend into the Karimui Plateau, are the seminomadic Pawaian people with whom Gimi trade and exchange wives.

The village of Ubagubi lies in the northeastern section of Unavi Census Division.[2] Unavi is bordered on the north by the wide Tua River, an eastern tributary of the Purari that runs through dramatic fold valleys clothed in oak

1. The Gimi language is part of the Fore-Gimi subfamily of the East-Central (Gende-Siane-Gahuku-Kamano-Fore) family of the East New Guinea Highlands stock (Wurm 1961, 1962).

2. Ubagubi can be reached by flying seventy air kilometers on a bearing of 229 degrees from Goroka, the provincial capital. Our usual means of entering the village between 1973 and 1983 was on foot, at the conclusion of a six-hour walk from the end of a road that meandered precariously in a southwesterly direction some thirty miles beyond Lufa Station. By 1985, the road extended into Ubagubi but was often impassable in the wet season.

and conifers. The Tua separates some 4000 Gimi from Siane and outlying Chimbu groups to the north. In a southwesterly direction Unavi is met by a no-man's-land; and on the east it is bounded by mountain ranges that extend from the southern spurs of Mount Michael and by the Tsoma River, which feeds into the Pio, a southern tributary of the Purari.

From the air one can see that most of Unavi is composed of steep, uncultivated slopes, deeply scored by white-water streams and waterfalls overhung with palms and giant ferns. Dense stands of Klinkii Pine (*Araucaria hunsteinii*) and groves of oak and beech are interspersed with rhododendrons, schefflera, and endless varieties of aroids, orchids, and other flowering epiphytes. The wilderness is a source of pride to men of Unavi and of envy to those of the grassland whose forests have been destroyed by repeated firings in warfare and hunting and who have traditionally traveled here to trade stone axes for marsupial furs and Bird of Paradise and parrot plumages. The derisive comments of outsiders who call the Gimi *bus kanaka,* the Melanesian equivalent of hillbillies, are reciprocated with equal feeling by the Gimi who refer to men of the treeless valleys around Goroka and Chimbu as *kunai* or "swordgrass" and liken them to scavenging kites and buzzards. "What do they know of hunting in the high forests?" Gimi say. "Birds of Paradise have vanished from their lands and the cassowaries we keep as pets are but fond memories of old men."

The people of Unavi have no name for themselves nor for their Labogai neighbors whom they recognize simply as *ikika kaina* or "one talk" (lit: *ikika*/one + *kaina*/speech or talk). They call *kimi,* literally, "they," those who live on the Yani River watershed in Gimi Census Division and speak another dialect of their language (McBride and McBride 1973).

## The Village of Ubagubi

Ubagubi is a collection of some twenty-one compounds spaced along a wide mountain shelf that lies within an altitudinal range of 5300–6000 feet. Each compound houses about four to twenty-five adults, organized around a patrilineal core, and is surrounded by a low wooden-stake fence to keep out pigs. A few outlying compounds are built in the traditional manner with one or more centrally located men's houses and two to six smaller women's houses scattered near the periphery or outside the fence. Each woman's house lodges a married woman, her mother-in-law or co-wife, young children, unmarried daughters, and several pigs. If two adult women share a house, each has her own entry, straddled by pig stalls, and her own hearth on one side of a central partition. Most compounds reflect the changes demanded by missionaries and patrol officers and are laid out along a broad, bare-earth thoroughfare bordered irregularly on one or both sides by a

The edge of a traditional compound in Ubagubi.

dozen or more houses occupied by nuclear families. At the far end of the compound is also usually one or two low, oval "men's houses" where adolescent boys sleep and married men stay while their wives are menstruating or confined after childbirth or when they are about to embark on a journey or important venture. Surrounding or adjacent to the men's house is a fenced plot of taro and bananas cultivated and used only by the men.

Family dwellings are built in the traditional mode—round, slightly below ground level, with walls made of bark and vines—or missionary style—rectangular, raised off the ground on three-foot posts, with walls of woven wild sugarcane. Roofs are made of heavy thatch blackened by smoke with pale green weeds, sprouted from seeds dropped by birds or fruit bats, often growing incongruously amid the fibers. Each family dwelling has a large central fireplace, a square mound of ash surrounded by logs. Across the back wall, about two feet from the packed-earth floor, there is a platform where the husband sleeps and stores his possessions, including a blanket, a suitcase containing a mirror and body decorations, and some folded coffee sacks. Displayed on nails above the platform are tightly netted carrying bags of the kind only men wear around their necks, a headdress of black cassowary feathers, and gourds containing salt and *ϑarĪ*, a mixture of pig fat and red pandanus oil used to coat the body on ritual occasions. Wives and children sleep on mats against the side walls. Women who live in the same houses as their husbands usually also have "pig houses" some distance from the compounds where they often sleep and keep their pigs at night in stalls built on either side of the entry.

Men plant coffee trees beside the compounds. Australian officers brought coffee plants on early patrols, introducing a cash crop so they could collect a head tax. Women pick, husk, and dry the beans. Five or six times a year, before the construction of a road in 1983, women helped their husbands haul heavy sacks to the roadhead where coffee buyers brought their trucks, a trek of some five or six hours. At a mission store near Lufa Station and at Chinese trade stores in Goroka, men exchange coffee revenues for steel ax heads, bush knives, metal pots and bowls, blankets, leather belts, safety pins, razor blades, matches, mirrors, shirts, shorts, soaps and perfumes, face paints, colored beads, lengths of cloth for women to wear as rear aprons, sacks of rice, tinned mackerel, bags of salt, sticks of molasses-dipped twist tobacco, and sheets of old Australian newspapers to make cigarettes. Until about 1979, cash and tinned food were used only as ritual gifts and as compensation for property damage or theft.

Before the *pax australiana,* Gimi settlements were smaller, more compact, and situated at higher altitudes. On crests of ridges some 2000 feet above Ubagubi, in what is now well-established forest, one can see large shallow oval depressions that were the floors of men's houses and pole holes from former palisades (see R. Berndt 1964). Judging by the rings of felled trees, these sites were abandoned no longer ago than the early 1950s. A few are so steep that Gimi say some residents had to tie themselves to the mountainside in order to work in their gardens. With pacification, settlements fell from their strategic perches and expanded in the flatter terrain.[3]

Men of every clan claim that, in the remembered past, all the members still lived together in the home of their eponymous founder, the "Father of the Flutes," *nimi kamibamosu aba* (*nimi*/bird + *kamiba*/flute + *mo*/the + *su*/poss. + *aba*/father), a man with many wives whose sons gave rise to all the men of the clan. But the upheaval of war makes it hard to imagine a time

3. In late 1973, Ubagubi had a population of 599. There were 292 females of which 157 were over the approximate age of fifteen years. Of the 307 males, 178 were over age fifteen. (See Chap. 8 for a comment on the high proportion of males.) According to a census made in 1991, Ubagubi now has some 1000 adult residents.

when a single patrilineal descent group could have remained undivided and alone in one locality. It was always likely that part of a residence group would be routed in combat with a neighbor, or accused of sorcery and forced to flee, while refugees from distant disputes arrived to take their place. The original father clan usually divided long ago into *oraratubana* (*oraratu*/senior + *bana*/man) and *aratubana* (lit: *aratu*/junior + *bana*), brother clans who reside in villages far from their ancestral home. Today a father clan shares little but a prohibition on marriage. A Gimi clan in my usage is an exogamous group of men who claim descent from the eponymous founder, trace four generations of patrilineal ties (without precise knowledge after the third ascending generation), and reside, together with their wives, children, and unmarried daughters, in one village, usually in neighboring compounds.[4]

A clan is emphatically a group of men, literally *ababana* (*aba*/father + *bana*/man). A woman may be called *ðufasu baðaha*, "woman of *ðufa* clan," because she is married to a *ðufa* man, or identified as the wife of her husband, but she is not a member of his group and is often referred to, even in old age, as "a foreign girl" or "a girl from Gotuha," her natal village. Throughout her marriage, her father and other men of her natal clan retain magical control over her fertility and still count her a daughter of their clan, collecting her head payments when she dies (see M. Strathern 1972:124).

Lineages are three generations in depth, and sometimes are subject to marriage prohibitions from which the other patrilines of the clan are exempt (see below, this chap.). Men of a lineage make gardens together, select wives for their sons, and rear or assemble pigs for the brideprice, but they often act in concert with men of one or more other lineages of their clan, especially if a Big Man is a member of another group. In general, lineages have few corporate responsibilities, reflecting the fact that Gimi "accord them strictly secondary significance" (Glick 1963:23). Throughout my account, I refer to both clans and lineages as *ababana* since they usually act together in the rituals and exchanges I describe. Some lineages, or lineage members, may reside in compounds with lineages of other clans, reflecting the traditional pattern, discouraged by Australian census takers, in which allied lineages of different clans shared a single men's house.

## Before the *pax australiana*

In the past, each ridgetop hamlet had formal enemy relations with two or three of its neighbors. The impetus to fight arose in disputes over land or women, theft, poaching of wildlife, and other problems of proximity and

4. I never encountered an informant with genealogical knowledge or interest beyond the fourth ascending generation.

regular contact. Enemies had to be near enough to allow swift retreat so that men who set out on raids before dawn could arrive behind their own palisades by nightfall. Two or three other neighbors were designated as allies and occasionally sent men to fight on one's side. Allies supplied wives although enemies sometimes exchanged women to make peace or create enclaves of alliance. "My father and Kuamoiaba were enemies, but they exchanged their daughters in marriage and stopped fighting," one man past fifty remarked. But allies—new or old—sometimes gave shelter to one's enemies by taking in refugees from other struggles and incorporating them into their territory. The designation of a village as friend, *regesubana,* literally, "our own men" (*rege*/we + *su*/poss. + *bana*/man), or foe, *ragamebana* (lit: *r*/our + *agame*/enemy + *bana*), thus signified not whether one might raid it, or try to ambush the inhabitants, but the degree to which such an attack would be abetted or undermined by the presence of enemies among allies and vice versa (see Gluckman 1963:1–26).

When a settlement faced attack, the residents united to defend it. But in offensive war or in hunting, trapping, and gathering forest products, the rights and allegiances of coresident clans or clan fragments, of older residents and newly arrived refugees, were often divided. Internecine wars sparked by accusations of sorcery were not uncommon and seem to have been deadlier than wars between settlements. Sorcery was, and is, practiced mainly through the theft and destruction of a man's *autaisana* or leavings (lit: *au*/body + *tai*/dir. + *sa*/poss. + *na*/thing). In the old days, men kept large bamboo tubes inside the men's house next to their weapons and deposited dried blood from the ends of their arrows and other *autaisana* "stolen" from their enemies, adding poisons to speed decomposition. The "sorcery bamboo" stood as a symbol of the trust and solidarity among comrades-in-arms by showing that they constantly resisted the temptations intimacy offered. Living in one men's house offered unparalleled opportunities for the theft of leavings, giving men constant access to each other's hair or feces, tattered bits of sweat-saturated clothing, tufts of fur or feathers that fell from a man's headdress while he danced, crumbs of tobacco that fell from his pipe, maize husks or sweet potato skins he discarded after a meal, etc.— prime sorcery material that might be passed to his "true enemies" in other houses or hamlets. In the past, men say, people die not die as often of sorcery because they killed the enemy face-to-face before he could act in secret and steal the capacity to retaliate. But pacification has "opened the roads" between settlements, men complain, giving safe passage to sorcerers and intensifying the traffic in men's leavings.

Men say that their best allies were "brothers," clans or lineages in their own or other villages linked to their clan or lineage as *ara'e a'au'e* (lit: *ara*/younger brother + *a'au*/elder brother), men with whom, generally speaking, they did not exchange wives. Brothers are "our own men." But conflicts between coresident *ara'e a'au'e* clans were often massacres, according to men's accounts of their history, because one brother clan could disarm the other with familiarity (see Chap. 10). Men also say that "a true affine is a true enemy!" Yet many of a clan's allies were distant affines or *abogofa* (lit: *abogo*/marriageable cousin + *fa*/pl.) acquired as part of a deliberate policy of dispersing sisters in marriage to villages where one might some day seek refuge.

Just prior to the first Australian patrols, men of Ubagubi recall, all the members of two clans were killed or routed from the village. Of the nine clans or clan fragments that remained in 1973, only one, Clan *A*, has an undisputed claim to be original settlers. Clan *B* is the "younger brother" of Clan *A* and shares some of its status in the sense that the circumstances of their arrival have been officially forgotten. Soon after the coming of Clan *B*, some of Clan *A* were killed or routed. Big Men of Clan *A* who remained in Ubagubi gave land and women to a neighboring hamlet to establish peace and, to augment their own ranks, took in men of Clan *C* who were refugees from another conflict. Clan *C* soon attracted men of Clan *D*, pursued by a common enemy. About the same time, Clan *B* sponsored a large group of Clan *E* with whom they and Clan *A* are now heavily intermarried. Clans *A*, *B*, and *E* are today the most numerous residents of Ubagubi, together occupying twelve of the twenty-one compounds. Indeed, the latest arrival of the big three, Clan *E*, is the largest clan. Since Clan *E* settled in Ubagubi, it has annihilated an "elder brother" clan and hosted four groups of refugees.[5]

Refugees were sponsored by individual clan leaders, called "Big Men."[6] A Big Man offered to take in his own or his father's *abogofa*, or their allies, and converted them to subordinate "younger brothers." The exchange of women in marriage, which had been the basis of long-distance alliance, was prohibited once the refugees took up residence in the same men's house and became comrades-in-arms, men say, because marriage would have undermined the trust upon which men relied in war. Though the new arrivals were designated "younger brothers," they referred to their patrons not as "elder brothers" but as *regesu rano*, literally "our mothers," a term that marked the change in status by emphasizing the maternal-avuncular aspect of the original affinal tie. Whereas the husband of a man's sister is his "taboo" and "true enemy," his sister's child is his *anu* or "spirit child" just as he is the child's *he-ano* or "spirit mother" (lit: *he*/spirit + *ano*/mother) and *kisa aba* or "true father" (lit: *kisa*/true + *aba*/father). To illustrate this relationship,

5. Throughout the text, I use letters or pseudonyms for the names of individuals, clans, and other villages.

6. Big Men are described throughout the New Guinea Highlands. See, e.g., Sahlins 1963; Salisbury 1964; Watson 1967; and Godelier and Strathern 1991.

Uarafu described his tie to Noromi. "My father's [classificatory] sister bore Noromi," he said. "Noromi is my *nabogo*. My fathers call him 'my child.'" Added Noromi: "Uarafu's father is *nanati* [lit: *n*/my + *anati*/mother's brother] . . . [but] I call him *naba* or 'father' [lit: *n*/my + *aba*/father]. Uarafu and I both are his children." In the past, if a man's comrades tried to shoot his real or close classificatory *anati* during a raid on another village, he stood or lay beside him and declared, "I am his child," or "He is my mother. If you kill him you must kill me!" His cohorts did not shoot because "they saw his child beside him and took pity." A man also avoided his own brother-in-law (*atu*) during fights and might even secretly inform him of impending raids.

The designation of refugees as the children or *anumona* of their sponsors also implied (in the most ambiguous way possible, as we see in Part 4) that the new arrivals would not steal their "mothers'" leavings and, reciprocally, that the mothers would refuse to provide their children's leavings to enemies who, having just put them to rout, were likely still in pursuit. A sponsoring Big Man was like a mother, men say, also because he supplied food to men whose women had mostly been killed or captured and so "had no mothers to feed them." He provided the refugees with access to garden land, pandanus orchards, clan forests, rivers, and stands of bamboo and wild sugarcane.

> . . . when we [men of Reko clan] arrived, men of Manoke gave us pigs to care for and many kinds of food. They said to our fathers, "Watch these red pandanus and these white pandanus. When they bear fruit it is yours to eat. . . . You have just arrived so we will show you our land and give you food like a mother."
>
> Basika [the sponsoring Manoke Big Man] looked after us as his own true children . . . and his sons are now my brothers.

When the sons of refugees reached the age of ten or fifteen, the sponsoring Big Man initiated them by showing them his flutes and feeding them "flute food," cooked blood drawn from his arm and from the arms of other Big Men (see Chap. 9). Much of *apina*, or first-stage male initiation, was devoted to replacing "mother's food," sweet potato and the produce of women's gardens, with male crops like taro, sugarcane, and bananas. For years after *apina*, initiates were forbidden to eat anything with female associations: possums with fur like pubic hair, mushrooms that smelled "like vaginas," red pandanus fruit that had the color and texture of blood, insects that burrowed in the ground or "hid" under rocks, going into seclusion like menstruating women. Men also tabooed hard white pandanus nuts, snakes, birds with long noses, and other foods with phallic qualities that might overwhelm and stunt the young male's emerging manhood. To counteract and replace the influence of mothers, men plied the initiates with concoctions of feral pigs and fruits taken from the clan forests and with other "wild foods" imbued with ancestral *kore* or spirit. "Food [that grows] on the land is impregnated with ancestral spirit. Locality and descent are in this set of ideas exactly fused" (A. Strathern, referring to Salisbury's account of Siane, 1975a:31).

By ingesting the foods of male "mothers" and ancestors, foods reaped from men's gardens and clan forests, initiates were "reborn" into a new territory, one they had to know intimately and defend with their lives. *apina* produced groups of men with territorial—not female—roots: the children of co-initiates, men who had seen the flutes at the same time, were related to each as "true" siblings, in the same terms as children of men born of the same woman. The system of initiation typically divided brothers so that the older ones, initiated in a prior cycle of rites, were themselves and their children subject to a different set of incest taboos and marriage prohibitions from the younger ones and their offspring (fig. 2). As brothers might be separated in

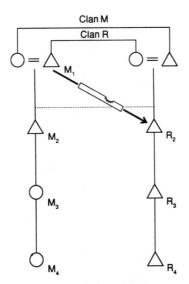

Figure 2. In war, refugees fled to their affines who were Big Men. The Big Men sponsored them, converted them to "younger brothers," and initiated their sons at adolescence. Clan *M* and Clan *R* were *abogofa* until $M_1$ gave refuge to a part of Clan *R*. As coresidents, Clans *M* and *R* became *ara'e a'au'e*. After seeing $M_1$'s flutes together, during the same rites of initiation, $M_2$ and $R_2$ became "true brothers" and their children "true brothers and sisters." $M_3$ and $R_3$ refer to each other as *kisa nasi* and may not marry each other. $M_4$ and $R_4$ refer to each other as *kisa nabogo* and also may not marry. But after each marries someone else, they become *amene asi* or classificatory brother and sister whose children may and, indeed, should intermarry.

this way, so might distantly related affines be united as brothers. In a situation where warfare and residential dislocation were the norm, Gimi men remade kinship by symbolically altering the sex of the mother: Big Men begat the initiates by feeding them arm blood and other male foods, deposing the female mother by replacing the blood of her womb and the food of her hands.

"The man who shows me his flute buys my wife," Gimi men say, enunciating a general rule of marriage. When a Big Man gave shelter to his affines and initiated their sons, converting the refugees to "younger brothers" and their sons to the "true" siblings of his own children, he instated a taboo on marriage in his own house. He found wives for his new "sons" not among his own daughters but among collateral lineages, offering his brothers' daughters or granddaughters in the male line:

> We [men of] Manoke warned [the men of] Reko while they were still living at Nema, "Men of Nema are trying to kill you!" So Reko ran here and Basika gave them refuge and looked after them like a mother. . . . He showed his flutes to their sons, and his son showed flutes to their sons' sons. . . . When Reko were at Nema they were our true affines, but we took them inside our house and made them our brothers. . . .
>
> The Manoke sons of Basika are his *arak* [lit: infant or child]. His Reko sons are his *anu* [lit: fetus or spirit-child]. Men of Reko say, "We have seen Basika's flute and cannot marry his daughters. His children are our own true brothers and sisters. . . . But Bigeke, who was Basika's brother, did not show us his flute nor buy us wives so we still call his sons *nabogofa* and marry his daughters. (Fig. 2*a*)

In the days of war, a sister's husband or son was often the first refuge. When a Big Man took in his *anatiraha* after a rout, he turned their sons into his "children" and set up a prohibition on marriage within his own lineage. But the prohibition was also a prescription for marriage with a brother lineage, thus maintaining the refugees' affinal relation to collateral lineages of his clan.[7] The patron's own sons and grandsons in the male line renewed the taboo he established and continued to supply their clients with wives from other patrilines of their clan and to exact the contingent payments. But after three generations or more, refugees who had managed to remain in their host's village often became a preferred source of wives. After three genera-

---

7. Discussing Sepik River social systems, Bowden makes the important point that "marriage prohibitions in these societies (contrary to the Lévi-Strauss model of Crow/Omaha systems) do not apply to clans as wholes, but only to specific descent lines" (Bowden 1991:230–31).

34

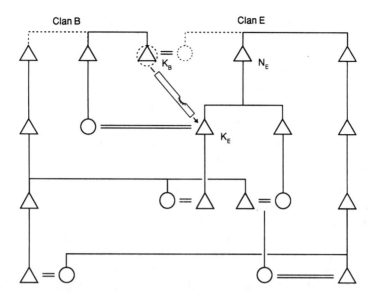

Figure 2a. Clan B and Clan E were *abogofa* until a Big Man of Clan B named K took in men of Clan E after a rout and turned them into his "younger brothers." Lineages established by $K_B$ and $N_E$ became *ara'e a'au'e* and could no longer exchange wives. Men of Clan B referred to the new arrivals as *anumona* or "spirit children," and men of Clan E referred to their hosts as *nanoha* (our mothers). As a "mother" and source of refuge, the Big Man K showed $K_E$ his flute during *apina*, gave him his name, and later provided him with a wife from a collateral line, maintaining the tradition of marriage between Clans B and E while excepting his own lineage.

tions they had increased in number and acquired more land, mainly through affinal grants. Their original sponsors, once rich in land but short of men to cultivate or defend it, often found themselves in the opposite predicament, wanting to regain rights to garden land from their former clients. With the passage of time, hosts and clients might decide to intermarry and redistribute their holdings, though the men continued to reside in a single men's house and refer to each other as "brothers." A Manoke man commented upon three "incestuous" unions between his clan and Patupo, the clan that gave them refuge in Ubagubi. A true FZD marriage and an exchange of sisters between male cross-cousins seem to have been contracted as a deliberate strategy to realign the two groups:

> The men of Patupo are our *a'au'e*, our elder brothers, but the women are our *abogofa* [marriageable cousins]. We marry our brothers' sisters and they marry ours. If we let our women marry into other clans, their sons will swell other ranks. . . . Patupo

have the same fear. They worry about the numbers of their sisters' sons. So we keep our daughters and sisters and give them to Patupo . . . and the sons they bear increase our own ranks.

If we give our sisters to our true *abogo,* they will work sorcery against us and we will die.

The term *ara'e a'au'e* thus described sharply differing kinds of relations between clans or lineages. Some "brothers" lived under one roof and observed an incest taboo because they considered themselves to be actual patrilineal relations. Others were fictive patrikin, former refugees and patrons, who had begun to intermarry after observing a taboo on marriage for at least three generations. Other *ara'e a'au'e* were worst enemies who lived in different villages because one had tried to annihilate the other. But they still shared a patrilineal ancestor and did not intermarry. The designation *abogofa* similarly described a broad range of affinal alliance. Some *abogofa* were indistinguishable from *ara'e a'au'e* who had been refugees and patrons but decided to intermarry, though they were still close allies and slept in the same men's house. Other *abogofa* lived in other villages and had various wartime statuses as enemies, noncombatants, potential sources of refuge, or allies in combat.

Though men define *abogofa* and *ara'e a'au'e* as opposite kinds of relations, each term seems to have applied to many gradations of enmity and alliance, some of which overlapped, obscuring phases in the oscillation between affinity and consanguinity. Genealogies reflect this state of flux in the sense that they lack generational depth but specify ties to living kin and affines, connections that were vital in finding refuge or in recruiting new allies to a depleted fighting unit. The vagaries of illness and war, fission among real or ritually created *ara'e a'au'e,* suspicions of sorcery that ended in massacre or dispersal, wars with other settlements that forced a part of the residence group to flee, etc., continually altered de facto relations among lineages, clans, and villages, outpacing and thus often contradicting formalized ties.

## Subsistence

Gimi consider the onset of drier weather in April or May to be critical for undertaking communal activities, especially the clearing of new gardens from secondary or tertiary forest and the celebration of major rituals like marriage and male initiation. Each year, Big Men of a village together gauge a combination of subtle environmental changes that signal the coming of the dry season, which is called *esara fo,* literally "cicada-sun," because of the arrival of screeching cicadas within the settlement.[8] Big Men are considered

---

8. According to estimates by outsiders, Ubagubi has no dry season. Records of rainfall kept at Lufa station over a sixteen-year period from 1957 to 1973 indicate that the four driest consecu-

especially astute in calculating the position of the sun as it rises, which is the main indicator of seasonal shift, and in observing the arrival of strong north-westerly winds funneled from the higher valleys or the appearance of honey eaters and Superb Birds of Paradise feeding upon the newly ripened fruits and blossoms of trees specially transplanted to coffee gardens. Big Men are not only perspicacious in noticing these signals; they also have the authority to be mistaken when they make the pronouncement that starts the round of garden clearings while it is still too wet.

### The Alternation of Seasons and Sexual Division of Labor

The alternation of seasons, slight though it is at these latitudes, combines with variations in altitude to produce a subtle temporal and spatial pattern of subsistence activities that corresponds in some respects with the sexual division of labor.

Compounds and gardens cut from forest appear around 5000 feet and pe-ter out over 6500 feet. This is also the range within which pigs forage, dig-ging up small tubers left unharvested in abandoned gardens or rooting for grubs and vegetable residue in once-cultivated secondary forest. Deeper in Unavi, in villages situated between 4000 and 5000 feet, women leave pigs over a certain age to fend for themselves, and men go out to hunt them years later when they are needed for ritual or exchange. But in Ubagubi, toward the end of the dry season, in September or October, women escort pigs des-tined to be slaughtered into groves of *ugami* to fatten them on the nuts that litter the ground.[9] *ugami* groves lie below the settlement, between 4500 and 5000 feet, and women who accompany their pigs may arrange assignations in the surrounding forest or in nearby orchards of red pandanus that are tended only by men.

Red pandanus, a large oily fruit used in ceremonial exchange, ripens over a long period but is abundant toward the end of the wet season, around March, due no doubt to men's efforts to improve yields by planting trees in the naturally occurring groves. Men also tend stands of white pandanus that grow above the settlement, just below 6000 feet, and that fruit in November and December. Young pigs that have survived the rituals of the dry season are fed a small part of the crop of delicious white nuts. White pandanus leaves are sewn together to make rain capes and sleeping or burial mats, and leaves of both pandanus types are used for roofing garden or bush shelters and hunting hides.

---

tive months together have an average of fifty-five rainy days. For Unavi, the number would be considerably more and, certainly, exceeds the forty-day limit set by Van Steenis to define an "everwet" climate (Clark 1971:44–45).

9. I have been unable to identify *ugami*. None of the "Fruits Used as Nuts" listed in the *Encyclopaedia of Papua New Guinea* seems to resemble this small hazel-nut-like fruit (1972:230).

Men point out that they tend the tall trees of white and red pandanus that grow "wild" at the upper and lower limits of settled terrain while women plant sweet potato, a fully domesticated subterranean tuber, by building mounds and keeping their heads "close to the ground." Whereas all men of a clan have access to the unfenced groves of pandanus, women toil alone much of the day in gardens men have subdivided and fenced. Men contain women within the settlement and within individual plots, keeping them apart both from the forest and each other. Comparing the sexes' differing roles in subsistence, men contrast the hard white pandanus (*huik*) that grows high at the river's mouth, and ripens at the end of the busy dry season, with the soft red pandanus (*kabai*) that grows at the river's lower reaches and ripens at the end of the dormant wet season. *huik* and *kabai* are like bone and blood, men say, and symbolize the "upper" and "lower" realms of men's and women's work.

Clan hunting grounds extend mainly south of the village to altitudes of 10,000 or 11,000 feet. In the late wet season and in the dry, men climb to a pass at about 9000 feet and fan out to their respective clan territories. Dogs range behind and ahead of a party of hunters, giving out excited yowls when they tree a possum or merely catch the scent. A dozen men may capture or kill thirty to forty tree kangaroos, wallabies, marsupial cats, and possums in three days of hunting; two men may take ten to twelve animals in five or six days. The highly prized meat is eaten mainly during rites of birth, death, and male and female initiations. In parts of Unavi closer to Papua, marsupials are still the only meat consumed on these occasions, a practice that was everywhere the rule, Gimi say, until several generations ago when men began to acquire pigs in numbers. Birds of Paradise are killed mainly for plumages, and their capture is an added feature to a hunting expedition. Cassowaries are tracked but seldom taken except as chicks to be reared in cages. Rarely, pythons are killed in the high forest and brought back to the village to eat.

Inside the forest, men gather vines to tie fences and house walls, timbers for weapons and utensils, delicacies like mushrooms and hearts of palm, yellow bamboos and other plants for body decoration, and medicinal barks and leaves. In the past, men combined hunting with travel to other villages for trade.[10] In place of such lofty pursuits, women collect ferns, parsley,

---

10. "Prior to Australian control, the Gimi seldom ventured into the territory of neighboring peoples . . . but . . . carried on a regular trade. Stone axes and feather headdresses from the Western Gimi and the nearby Chimbu traveled through Gimi territory, village by village, and eventually reached the Yagaria and Fore; in return, pigs moved westward from the Yagaria. . . . The southeastern region, poor in other resources, traded esoteric medicinal materials northwestward. The Gimi of the extreme southwestern pocket reportedly made three- or four-day trips to the Papuan lowlands, where they traded for shells and European goods" (Glick 1963: 3–4).

watercress, and other uncultivated greens and scavenge for rats, mice, lizards, snakes, beetles, frogs, grubs, grasshoppers, cicadas, spiders, and other tiny earthbound creatures that inhabit the edges of their gardens. Larger animals found within the settlement, such as eels, wild ducks, and birds are trapped or shot by the men. Men construct all the dwellings, but women fetch the tall grasses used as thatch. Men repair damages to other men's gardens attributed to their pigs. But when a pig is lost, women may join in the search.

### Sweet Potatoes and Pigs

Women do the daily, repetitive work of tending gardens and pig herds and caring for young children while men undertake more varied, adventurous, and seasonal tasks like hunting, clearing the forest, building houses and fences, and planning rituals (see Clark 1971:174). Men construct the physical and administrative boundaries within which women work, determining the size and composition of pig herds and deciding when to plant, what land to clear, and how to divide gardens among crops and gardeners.

Rules of patrilineal inheritance and of affinal or refugee grants ensure that all men resident in a village have rights to garden land. Boys may be told during *apina* which plots they will cultivate as married men. Former fight leaders, orators, and Big Men generally retain the best sites and often determine the allocation of other land according to the state of relations with neighboring clans or villages. One way to discern a man's status in the village is to calculate the position, number, incline, and accessibility of his gardens.[11] Some sweet potato gardens are located on gentle slopes outside the village. Others are cut into steep slopes as far as two hours' walk from the owners' houses.

Gardens also vary in size, crop content, and restrictions placed on access and use. There are two basic types: large supermarket gardens, some as much as twenty acres in extent, planted mainly with sweet potatoes and cultivated by women; and kitchen gardens of well under an acre, located near dwellings and filled with the luxury crops of taro and bananas and with small amounts of beans, maize, cucumbers, *pitpit* (a cultivated form of wild sugarcane), greens, yams and tobacco. Many of these small gardens are cultivated exclusively by men, by two brothers or a father and son, and females are forbidden to enter. Women who have their own gardens of taros and yams

---

11. By this guide, a few men and their families are considered to be of very low status, to "eat excreta" in the Gimi idiom or to be *rabis* in Melanesian Pidgin, "a poor person, a beggar . . . a worthless individual" (Mihalic 1971:162). In Ubagubi, a *rabisman* often has no garden because he has no wife and has become the dependent of a Big Man, helping the Big Man's wives in their gardens, carrying firewood, etc.

pause at the gate to purify themselves, reciting spells that expel the "dirt" of sex and menstruation (see Chap. 6). Women also may plant taro at the edges of large gardens that border streams, since taro needs wetter soil than sweet potato. Within the bounds of a large garden, men of a clan or lineage establish communal stands of sugarcane, interspersing the tall stems with sweet potatoes to be harvested at times when they cannot take food from women. Like bamboo and bananas, sugarcane is considered a male crop.

Once Big Men have agreed upon the imminence of the dry season, teams of men begin to cut a series of new supermarket gardens from the forest. After the men do the initial cutting of a site, a party of some fifty men and women finish the clearing. A work party can clear an acre or more in a strenuous day's work. The men climb the trees still standing and lop off the top branches, felling some and leaving the rest to dry out for firewood. They split the fallen trunks into planks and begin the fence, ramming the sharpened planks into the moist ground and binding crosspieces with heavy vines or bark rope. The men plant *Cordyline fructiosa* amid the posts and incorporate, here and there, a stand of wild sugarcane as a natural barrier to pigs. Fence construction takes several weeks but is hereafter the task of the garden owner alone. The women work far ahead, out of sight of the men, moving up the slope ten or so abreast, cutting the dense undergrowth with their husbands' bush knives, uprooting saplings and hacking off lower branches of trees. The women work in twenty-minute shifts, pausing briefly to nurse infants in the shade. Mid-afternoon rains bring the cutting and clearing to a halt and the workers gather in the compound of the garden proprietor to receive a meal of sweet potato, taro, and banana to repay the day's effort.

The male holder of a sweet potato garden takes one or more female partners: his wife or wives, mother, or married sisters. If he is a man of prominence, he may also allot a part of his garden to an age-mate or male affine who in turn subdivides it among his wives and daughters-in-law, one of whom is likely the proprietor's own daughter. A complex set of taboos called *aꝺaoina* prevent a man, his wife, and his own parents from eating the first fruits of his own and his wife's combined labors, especially the first crop his wife produces on land he cleared and fenced. Until a woman has produced five living children, according to the rules of *aꝺaoina,* she avoids her husband and serves as a wife to his patrilineage, making good their investment in her brideprice by turning over her pigs and the first crops of her gardens.

By taking a married sister or daughter as a garden partner, a man produces foods that can circulate in the complex system of exchanges within the extended family. When a man's sister gardens his land, she can supply him and their parents with food untouched by his wife; and she can produce food for her husband's parents untouched by her husband (fig. 3). In figure 3, *S* and *U* have adjacent plots in *T*'s garden. Until *S* bears five surviving children, *T* will

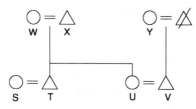

Figure 3. Rules of *a ϑaoina*.

avoid eating the food she grows and will take food instead from the plots of
$U$ and $W$. $W$ and $X$ also avoid the products of $S$'s new gardens because they
represent the "firstborn" labor of $S$ and $T$. But $W$ and $X$ do take food grown
by $S$ apart from their son on land fenced and cleared by another man. The
same applies to $Y$, who is a widow:

> What is $U$'s, $T$ eats. That is why she comes inside his garden to
> plant. $Y$ eats the food $U$ plants in $T$'s garden. Because $U$ is inside
> her brother's garden, her husband's mother can eat. . . . When
> $V$ makes a new garden with $U$, $Y$ cannot have that food! When
> the garden gets old, when a second crop has ripened, it is alright.

Once a man's garden is established, no one besides he and his female partners, parents, and full brothers enter without an invitation. Men who were
initiated together and sleep in the same men's house may make lengthy de-
tours to avoid trespassing each other's gardens.

After the initial clearing, the proprietor and his partners work sporad-
ically for about six weeks to ready the land for planting. The man creates
internal partitions that separate the women's sections, and each gardener
completes the clearing of her own plots, using a bush knife, a long sharp
digging stick, and her hands to hack, root out, and pull at the remaining
vegetation and shake it free of earth. The debris is left to dry out for about
two weeks and then collected into piles for burning. While the last debris
fires smolder, women begin the work of mound building, filtering loose
roots and stringy matter between their fingers and shaping the earth into
low piles some two-and-a-half feet apart. The mound builder makes a tunnel
toward the center of each heap, inserts several sweet potato vines with a
twisting movement, and pulls the other ends out the top of the mound,
propping them up with handfuls of earth and singing or reciting spells as
she works (see Chap. 6). Later, she will plant decorative coleus alongside the
markers of her plots and her husband may add banana plants or sugarcane to
emphasize the internal division of his garden. During the weeks or months a
garden is being established, the men keep watch at night to ward off ma-

rauding rats, sitting around a small fire and hooting or shaking a rattle made of pebbles inside a tin can.

Some three months after the final clearing, cucumbers begin to ripen and, for twenty months or more, the harvest continues without interruption, crops yielding like waves that rise and subside in time and position on the slope. After cucumbers have borne for about a month, leafy greens are ready, followed by maize, beans, pumpkins, squash, and other gourds. After five or six months, when the first sweet potatoes mature, the cucumbers at the top of the garden are nearly finished. In the next few months, *pipit* becomes abundant while beans, maize, and pumpkins decline. At nine or ten months, sugarcane and bananas are the last crops to bear. In large, well-situated gardens, a second crop of sweet potatoes, called *fiꝺa,* is planted on top of the first, some twelve to eighteen months after the initial planting. After *fiꝺa,* a garden lies fallow for ten to thirty years and becomes covered in scrubby growth and wild sugarcane or reverts to forest.

If men did not carefully divide the land, one Big Man told me, women would work haphazardly so that no one knew who planted what. Plants could not identify their "mothers." The garden holder would not know whose crops he took. He would be unable to avoid his wife's produce and to calculate her output in relation to other gardeners. He could not estimate the total amount of food at his disposal, not only to sustain his family and herds but also to stage feasts and meet obligations to trading partners. In the same way a man oversees his gardens, he manages his herd, which consists of some two to six pigs. He kills a part of every litter and assigns daily care of the rest to one or more women. He decides when to destroy sick animals and when, and from whom, to acquire new ones.

Unlike land, the care of pigs is carried out within the patrilineage: a man disperses his herd only among his wife, mother, other wives of his father, and wives of his brothers. One benefit in taking his sister as a garden partner is that, although most of her produce accrues to another lineage, the area she cultivates extends the range in which his pigs will forage for unharvested tubers. One man estimated that an adult pig eats about twenty tubers a day. Women save the skins of cooked potatoes and hand other scraps to piglets who graze around the edges of earth ovens. Men also feed their pigs, giving them husks of *pitpit* or the uncooked fruit itself and, as a special inducement to grow, smoked white pandanus nuts or cooked sweet potatoes.

When a sow produces a litter, the owner calculates the number of women he can call upon to care for it, taking into account how many other pigs each is already rearing. Both sexes believe that shoats and new crops, no less than human infants, depend for survival upon intense and prolonged involvement with women (see Chap. 6). Describing the role of attachment behavior and "positive affect" between woman and pig in creating tractable herds among the Maring, Rappaport quotes animal studies which suggest that the "tactile communication" crucial to "the psychic development and socialization of human infants" may also be indispensible "for the infants of other species as well" (Rappaport 1968:59). Gimi women carry shoats like babies inside net bags to their gardens and go to sleep in rain shelters, or inside their houses at night, embracing and sometimes nursing both their young. As her animals mature, a woman lets them forage in wild oak and chestnut groves and in abandoned sweet potato gardens. But in late afternoon she summons them with high-pitched ululating calls and ushers them into the stalls inside her house. When one of her pigs is killed and set out for distribution at a feast, she sits weeping beside the pile of charred slabs, swatting away flies, wearing the pig's tail around her neck and chanting its name.

Men are keenly aware of women's differing capacities for productive attachments, and they take them fully into account in assigning their herds and in acquiring garden partners. At regular intervals during an eighteen-month period between 1973 and 1975, I recorded the weights of every infant and shoat in Ubagubi and the numbers and approximate sizes of gardens cultivated by their caretakers. Based on weight gains and other data, I found that women who excel in one kind of nurturance tend to excel in all and vice versa. Of forty-six lactating women, nine or about one-fifth had no pigs. The same number had between four and eight pigs in their care, and the remaining three-fifths had charge of one to three pigs each. To cite an extreme example of the variation among women, a lactating mother of several children caring for six pigs and raising much of the sweet potato to feed them had a co-wife with no children, no pigs, and one small garden. After menapause, women tend to increase their output (see below, this chap.).

## Relations among Women

### Co-Wives

Of 115 marriages in Ubagubi in 1974, only fourteen were polygynous. Yet many women report having ousted a co-wife and complain that their husbands pressure them to accept others. If a man has more than one wife, he builds each a house or partitions the woman's house so that each has her own hearth, pig stalls, and entrance. Co-wives compete for their husband's favor and may come to blows if he allocates one wife more pigs or garden sections or a larger portion of meat at a feast. On the rare occasions when a woman openly blames her husband for conflict with a co-wife, or retaliates by refusing to bring firewood or prepare his evening meal, he usually beats her. If she persists, she risks giving her rival the advantage. In an effort to dominate a co-wife, a woman may encourage her husband to take a third wife and rear the pigs he needs for the brideprice, using her industry to demand a voice in the selection. In two or three cases where such an arrangement seems to have been made, the enterprising co-wife makes the new wife her ally, takes her part in disputes with their husband, and speaks out on her behalf in public if she is slighted in a distribution of food. But such alliances are temporary and virtually never extend into wider ties with other women.

In a polygynous household, when one wife falls ill, the other may bring her sweet potatoes or care for her child. And when a child gets sick or dies, the co-wife may remain secluded with the mother. A co-wife may yell abuse at a man she catches stealing sweet potatoes from the other woman's garden. But co-wives have no obligation to help each other in these ways and are often enemies. If a man's affair seems to anticipate marriage, his wife may make strenuous objection, blaming the other woman even when her husband admits to being the seducer. One man publicly justified taking sexual favors from his clansman's wife in lieu of the pigs he was owed in return for his contribution to her brideprice. "I paid a lot for Rati but she doesn't raise pigs. The man she married does no 'business' with her so I'll take her as my wife!" When his own wife objected, he berated her as an adulteress, a poor gardener and pig herder. When the wife persisted, he beat her, and she attacked Rati in retaliation: "He broke my arm and my back!" she cried. "I hit Rati to get back for that!"

Sometimes a group of women, headed by the angry wife, launch an assault upon an adulteress. When that happens, the woman's lover, husband, lineage brothers, immediate brothers of the aggrieved wife, and other men may join in the attack on her or stand idly by. If a woman is badly beaten, hit with stones, humiliated by her assailants thrusting their pudenda into her mouth, her "mothers," women of her father's patriclan, may afterward come to her defense. The morning after Peruta was beaten, women of her natal Ketope clan arrived in a delegation at her house, surrounded her, and shouted abuse at the women who had led the assault:

> Peruta is not the child of a dog! or a pig! or a tree! She is the child of a *man!* She had many fathers but they have died. And you think her mothers are dead, too, . . . but we are still here to fight you.

From a position outside the compound fence, Peruta's assailants and their allies took up the challenge:

> You want to make Peruta the wife of someone else and we'd like to discuss that! . . . All you Ketope women are adulteresses, purveyors of semen, man-killers! You are all *kore baðaha,* "wild women," hungry for men! . . . Your cunts are stinking black holes oozing with sores and infested with vermin!

During these salvos, one woman accused the adulterer of starting the trouble and suggested that he and the cuckold fight it out between them. But others insisted, "This is women's fight! We don't need men to help us!" Typically, a clan brother of the beaten woman stepped into the women's midst and examined her wounds, swollen face, and blood-matted skirts. Recalling the amount of her brideprice, he said that the injuries and the children she had borne had "eaten her pay" so that her kinsmen could now take her to live in their compound without debt to her affines. But his speech turned out to be a grandstand rather than a serious threat. After he left, the women exchanged more invectives and threatened to take up the fight with sticks.

The standoff continued for hours until senior women on each side approached one another. The mother of Peruta's lover made the first move, walking alone into the enemy's midst. "I am not angry," she said as she sat down to rub the leg of one of the senior women who had led the fight on Peruta's behalf. "I told my son not to have sex with her. 'She'll steal your semen and give it to a sorcerer and you'll die!' I told him." The older women negotiated a sum of money to compensate the adulteress for her injuries, including in their calculations sums she owed to men she had inadvertently struck with mud or a stone in attempting to defend herself, or who were harmed as bystanders in the fray she had caused. Even the women who defend a battered woman view her as a guilty party, calculating the men *she has injured* and, therefore, has the responsibility to compensate.

After the women's meeting, men hold their own *kot* to decide if the sum women have reckoned, or any sum, shall be paid.[12] While the men discuss her case, the woman sits alone at the bare center of the compound, slumped under a blanket to hide her wounds. Her female defenders remain on the sidelines now, a subdued audience who groom one another, twist string, suckle infants, or sleep under trees. If the adulterer insists repeatedly that she seduced him, and if she does not vigorously deny it, her case may be lost, and the wife who led the attack against her may be awarded the damages instead.

### *namau, namau:* My Husband's Sister, My Brother's Wife

When a married woman is in need or distress, when she menstruates or goes into labor or is confined with a newborn, when she shames herself by bearing a child while she has another still at the breast, when she is in mourning and cannot enter her gardens, she receives help from her *amau,* her husband's sister or brother's wife, who is the same woman when men exchange

---

12. *kot* is the Pidgin term for the system of "courts" or dispute settlement procedures introduced by the Australian administration to hear noncriminal cases. *kot* are held at the clan or village level and are presided over by the *komiti* men elected in each clan.

sisters (fig. 4). Because a woman's husband is the reason for his sisters' support, she does not get it when either she or her husband is discovered in
adultery. When a man is caught, his wife may get vocal encouragement from
her brothers' wives, especially if they are themselves polygynously married
and the affair seems bound for marriage.

A woman's two or three principal *amau* are selected by her husband from
among his immediate sisters. If the husband is a firstborn child, the wife was
given at betrothal the "same name" as the sister closest to him in age or adjacent in order of birth. When bride or groom is a firstborn or eldest surviving
child, the parents give to the intended the name of a child of opposite sex
next in order of birth so that spouse and cross-sex sibling are *ahamoina,*
those with the same name (lit: *aha*/same + *mo*/the + *na*/thing). An eldest
sibling pair is thus replicated in name in each of their marriages (fig. 4*a*). But
even if neither of the married pairs contains an eldest child, the two
hus-bands (*aturaha;* lit: *atu*/taboo + *raha*/pl.) and two wives (*amauraha*)
are still *ahamoina* and address each other as "*nahamo*" on ritual occasions. In name at least, every Gimi marriage unites a "brother" and a "sister."
Ideally, a woman's *amau* is the husband's sister whose "same name" she
shares.

If none of a man's "true" sisters are alive or married within the village, the
*amau* may be one of his patrilateral parallel cousins or classificatory sisters.
Because descent is patrilineal and marriage normally virilocal, two *amau*
rarely reside in the same compound. But they are likely to live in the same
village, especially since pacification and the attendant increase in settlement
size and endogamy. The pool of a man's sisters (lit: *asi*/sibling of opposite
sex) is composed of his immediate siblings, his "true" MBD and FZD, and
all the women who are his MBD and FZD in the classificatory or "not true"
sense and thus fall into the category of preferred spouse—yet whose bridal
pork he is entitled to eat. "Asked why a girl in another sib is called *nasi* (my
sister), a Gimi does not explain that she is his own cousin. He says, 'She is
*nasi* because when she marries I will eat her pork'" (Glick 1963:58n.). As we
have seen, a man may recruit "true sisters" among the daughters of refugees
sponsored by his father or paternal grandfather, women who are likely to

Figure 4. *amau:* reciprocal term used between sisters-in-law (BW/HZ).

Figure 4a. Naming at betrothal for firstborn children. M is a firstborn child. When she was betrothed, her parents gave the groom-to-be the name of her brother, R. Years later when R was betrothed, M bestowed her own name upon her much younger *amau*.

have married into collateral lineages of his clan. The potential of the same woman to serve as wife or sister, depending upon the vagaries of war and men's alliances, means, from a woman's standpoint, that her *amau* may be a coresident.

Actual marriage patterns affect the range and choice of a woman's *amau* because they determine the ways brother-sister pairs are traced. Ideally, a woman's HZ and BW are one person and the relation is perfectly reciprocal. In most cases, however, a woman receives services from her HZ which she tends not to reciprocate but to deliver instead to her BW (fig. 5). In figure 5, B, C, or D will serve as midwife when A bears a child; when D has a child, E will be on hand; when E has a child, F will assist her; etc.

*Case 1.* A was born in a distant village. Her husband's own three sisters, all married in Ubagubi, are her *amauraha*. A is also regarded as the "sister" of one of her husband's clan brothers whose mother is a member of A's natal clan: the same link that made her husband's brother a potential spouse was converted to a sibling tie after her marriage to another man. This "brother's" wife is also her *amau*.

*Case 2.* After her marriage, B continued to reside in the compound of her father, a Big Man. One of her husband's clan sisters married a coresident brother and became her *amau*. Her husband's immediate sister, who resides in another compound, is also her *amau*.

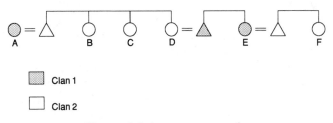

Clan 1

Clan 2

Figure 5. Relations among *amauraha*.

*Case 3. R* was born in a distant village. Her husband's own sister died soon after she arrived in Ubagubi. His "true" FBD and "true" MBD (a member of a refugee group from *R*'s home village) became her *amauraha*.

The help a woman receives from her *amau* is rooted in her husband's well-being: the *amau* acts as his surrogate and protector, safeguarding his interests while isolating him from the danger the wife emits, especially during childbirth (see Chap. 8). Giving birth is the same as being "killed by the Moon," men and women say. The child's body is "the same as [what] the Moon kills," and anyone who touches the newborn or the mother, or the mother's food, cannot handle the father's food, nor touch his hearth, nor blow into the embers of his fire lest he fall ill and die. The *amau* attends the birth to make sure the afterbirth is properly emptied of blood so that no traces are left on nearby rocks or leaves of overhanging trees whence they might fall into sorcerer's hands. At the start of fieldwork, the death of a young married man was attributed directly to the carelessness of his wife's midwives. During the recent birth of his son, the deceased's mother and sisters charged, other women had left pieces of the placenta at the water's edge and let drops of blood become absorbed into their string skirts whence they were retrieved by the sorcerer. An ordinary man stays far away from his wife when she menstruates or gives birth to a child "because he is afraid of dying! The heat of the child would enter his nose and have no way to get out! The heat would fill his whole body and kill him." But a sorcerer watches birth with immunity. In the past, sorcerers followed women to menstrual huts, hoping to get hold of discarded tampons and use the dried blood in spells against the husbands.

After the birth, mother and child remain in seclusion in her "pig house" which is often used, nowadays, as a menstrual hut. During the month or more of confinement, the *amau* keeps the new mother supplied with firewood and cooks the evening meal in her hearth, grooming her, serving as wet-nurse if she has not enough milk, and netting a new net bag as the baby's cradle. The food and firewood the *amau* brings usually come from the woman's own garden, which the *amau*—who is likely a garden partner—weeds and tends while she is indisposed. The *amau* cares for mother and child, and sometimes attends to the mother's other young children, while most of the women who live in the compound avoid them so they can continue to provide food to the husband.

The continuing role of the *amau* after confinement is illustrated in the following case of a woman whose husband was embarrassed by the recent birth of a second child before the first was weaned. During preparations for a feast, the man stood in the doorway of his wife's house and shouted angrily at her, "Get some water, lazy!"

The *amau* sat outside holding her own baby but did not converse with other women at the gathering, concentrating instead
upon her brother's domestic scene inside the house. There were
his wife, two infants, and mother. The old woman peeled wild
sugarcane to feed her pig while the elder child slept in her lap.
When the new baby began to cry, she yelled, "Look at that! Her
child cries and she just lies there!"

Hearing the mother's contemptuous remarks, the *amau*
rushed into the house and gave the crying child her breast. With
her own child slung across her back inside a net bag, she carried
the baby outside, saying nothing to the beleaguered wife.
Throughout that day, the *amau* helped care for her brother's two
children while her husband assisted her brother in preparing
red-fruited pandanus for distribution.

The conspicuous support given by the *amau* on such occasions belies underlying tension. The competition inherent in the *amau* relation becomes evident in later years, especially when the two women take up what seem to be
petty disputes between their children, investing them with incongruous importance (see Chap. 8).

### *nanatu, nanatu*: Woman My Pigs Made a Wife, Woman Whose Pigs Made Me a Wife

A man's mother and wife often live in the same house and share in the daily
upkeep of his household. But the mother avoids the wife on the many occasions when she is secluded during and after menstruation, childbirth, miscarriage, or the death of an infant, times when the *amau* arrives to provide
crisis-level support. A man's mother avoids his wife so she can provide him
with food and companionship. When a man marries, many of the taboos
imposed during his first initiation shift from his mother onto his wife: he
refuses his wife's produce and again "takes food from his mother's hands."

A young wife is preoccupied with child rearing and often leaves heavy gardening and pig tending to her mother-in-law who, in menopausal middle
age, seems to reach her prime as a food producer (Greenfield and Clark
1974). A newly married man needs pigs to help repay the donors to his wife's
brideprice, often with dividends, and values his mother's output. Freedom
from old taboos, plus a new economic interest shared by mother and son
tend to leave the wife out in the cold.

Yet a woman is entirely dependent on her mother-in-law, as women warn
departing brides again and again. A woman who has the sympathy of her
*kisa anatu*, her husband's own mother, will never be hungry nor without

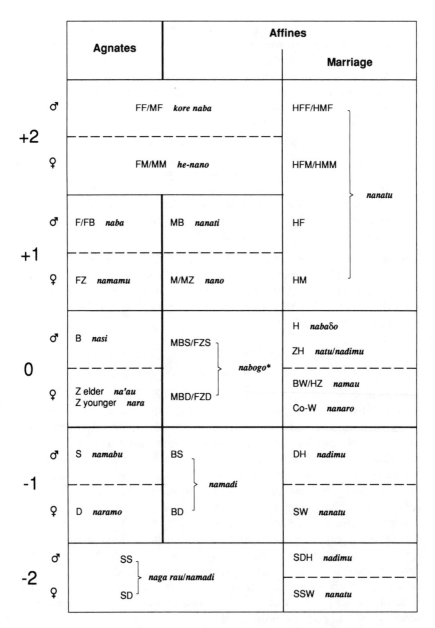

| | Agnates | | Affines | Marriage |
|---|---|---|---|---|
| ♂ +2 | FF/MF  *kore naba* | | HFF/HMF | |
| ♀ | FM/MM  *he-nano* | | HFM/HMM | *nanatu* |
| ♂ +1 | F/FB  *naba* | MB  *nanati* | HF | |
| ♀ | FZ  *namamu* | M/MZ  *nano* | HM | |
| ♂ 0 | B  *nasi* | MBS/FZS ⎫ *nabogo\** | H  *naba∂o* / ZH  *natu/nadimu* | |
| ♀ | Z elder  *na'au* / Z younger  *nara* | MBD/FZD ⎭ | BW/HZ  *namau* / Co-W  *nanaro* | |
| ♂ -1 | S  *namabu* | BS ⎫ *namadi* | DH  *nadimu* | |
| ♀ | D  *naramo* | BD ⎭ | SW  *nanatu* | |
| ♂ -2 | SS ⎫ *naga rau/namadi* | | SDH  *nadimu* | |
| ♀ | SD ⎭ | | SSW  *nanatu* | |

Figure 6. Principal terms of reference for a female ego. (Adapted from C. Hugh-Jones 1979:79)

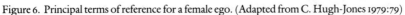

| | | Agnates | Affines | Marriage |
|---|---|---|---|---|
| **+2** | ♂ | FF/MF  *kore naba* | | WFF/WMF |
| | ♀ | FM/MM  *he-nano* | | WFM/WMM  ⎫ |
| | | | | ⎬ *nadimu* |
| **+1** | ♂ | F/FB  *naba* | MB  *nanati* | WF  ⎪ |
| | ♀ | FZ  *namamu* | M/MZ  *nano* | WM  ⎭ |
| **0** | ♂ | B elder  *na'au* <br> B younger  *nara* | MZS  *nanogai* <br> MBS/FZS ⎤ | WZH  *naone* <br> WB/ZH ⎤ |
| | | | ⎬ *nabogo\** | ⎬ *natu* |
| | ♀ | Z  *nasi* | MBD/FZD ⎦ | WZ ⎦ <br> W  *nanaro* |
| **-1** | ♂ | S/BS  *namabu* | ZS ⎤ | DH  *nadimu* |
| | | | ⎬ *namaga* | |
| | ♀ | D  *naramo* | ZD ⎦ | SW  *nanatu* |
| **-2** | ♂ | SS ⎤ | | SDH  *nadimu* |
| | | ⎬ *naga rau/namadi* | | |
| | ♀ | SD ⎦ | | SSW  *nanatu* |

Figure 6*a*. Principal terms of reference for a male ego.

food for her children. According to the rules of *aϑaoina,* the wife is often barred from harvesting or eating her own crops, obliged to leave them for those who contributed to her brideprice and to rely for food upon her mother-in-law. She is always in a supplicant position since the older woman avoids taking food from her. If a man's mother or father were to eat the foods he and his wife rear, they are liable to premature senescence and death. Only in decrepitude does a woman accept food from her son and daughter-in-law: "When my bones are soft, when I am old and blind, then I will eat. 'My son, my *nanatu,*' I will say, 'Bring me the food of your gardens. I will eat the pigs of your hands.'"

A woman taking food from her son and his wife also marks the lifting of the taboo on the couple's commensality. Not until a man's parents are truly old, or until his wife has produced at least five surviving children, do they share the fruits of their common labor, a change celebrated in a rite of second marriage (Chap. 6). For the husband, the rite signals the lifting of an advanced category of antifemale taboos laid down, and progressively revoked, during his various "secret" initiations (see Chap. 9). It also elevates the wife to the status of her husband's partner after long years of service to his lineage.

A woman refers to her husband's mothers and fathers and to his paternal kin generally as *anatu* or *anaturaha* (*anatu* + *raha*/pl.). The term refers specifically to the marriage transaction, designating any woman who reared a pig used in the woman's brideprice or *baϑaϑa* (lit: *baϑa*/woman), or any man who owned such a pig or contributed other valuables. *anatu* is used reciprocally to mean "a woman to whose brideprice I contributed." But between "true" or *kisa anatu,* a woman and her husband's own mother, the term highlights the absence or taboo upon this very relation. A woman neither contributes her own pigs nor accepts payments made on behalf of the wife of her son: "My two co-wives bought my son's wife. Those two can eat her [dowry pork, the products of her gardens, the payments for her childrens' 'heads'] . . . . Not me!"

In accumulating pigs for a brideprice, men name certain women as contributors in the same way they choose caretakers when the animals are born. But the fact that men name individual women as sources of pigs, or that prospective mothers-in-law or co-wives may undermine men's plans, or that brides sometimes run away does not give women significant control over the dispersal of either their pigs or their own labor (see Langness 1974:192). When a woman donates a pig to the payment for the wife of a co-wife's son, or the wife of a husband's brother or of his son, her contribution does give her a claim upon the other woman's produce, labor, and allegiance. At the least, the "other than true" or *amene anatu* relation entitles the older woman to small allotments of food at feasts marking the births of her *anatu*'s children; and at the most, to the designation of "recipient" of substantial portions of brideprice received for the *anatu*'s daughters and of head payments received on behalf of the daughters' offspring. Women take pride in being publicly named in this way, but the recognition is an empty honor in the sense that a woman has little if any say in *redistributing* goods she receives in consequence of the pigs she raised. Women accumulate small sums of money from *baϑaϑa* payments or coffee sales and often complain, even against their own sons, that they cannot choose the brides for whose payments their money is used. During a dispute over *baϑaϑa*, one woman stood up to press her claim for ten dollars out of the hundred received for the daughter of her husband's brother's wife, a woman whom her pigs had helped purchase. She spoke at length but swayed no man present and received nothing.

The network of obligations that *baϑaϑa* establishes among female *anatu* seems mainly to benefit men by organizing women's labor in a way that fulfills men's needs. Men rely upon "mothers" and other women of their clan to rear the pigs they need to acquire wives, and they rely upon sisters to keep them isolated from their wives. During the initial "secret" phases of marriage and female initiation, older women become shrill exponents of men's derogatory rules, impressing upon brides and initiates their duty to protect men from their own damaging habits and fluids (see M. Strathern 1972:172).

## Principles of Marriage and Exchange:
## Avoiding the "Curse" of the Mother's Brother

After pacification, villages increased dramatically in size. Men no longer needed foreign allies for refuge, and village exogamy sharply declined.[13] Women had always encouraged their daughters' liaisons within the village and exerted pressure for them to marry close to home, complaining that daughters were as difficult as sons to rear and ought not to be lost at marriage.

As the term *anatu* itself suggests, marriage rules are inseparable from rules governing exchanges of brideprice, which traditionally consists mainly of live pigs and other valuables like cooked pork or marsupial meat, marsupial furs and Bird of Paradise and parrot plumages, pearlshells, bark for making string, taro, and bananas. In recent years, blankets, tinned fish, frozen meat, and money have become increasingly important. A woman re-

---

13. Of sixty ancestresses who lived most of their married lives in Ubagubi, twenty or 33 percent were also born there. Of twenty-nine middle-aged or old women now living in Ubagubi, as well as twenty-five deceased women in the same age categories, twenty-eight or 52 percent were born in the village. Among the rest, 127 younger married women, ninety-nine or 78 percent were born in Ubagubi.

mains affiliated to her *ababana,* her father and other paternal kinsmen, all her life, but her brideprice compensates them for their loss of her as a wife. When the wives of the *ababana,* the bride's "mothers," formally mourn her departure, they express deep regret over consuming her brideprice as if "eating her pay," or accepting pigs as her replacement, had made it impossible now to take her back. Each time she bears a child, their loss is renewed and compounded, and they receive new payments called *arabosu anotu* or "the head of the child" (lit: *arak*/child + *mo*/the + *su*/poss. + *anotu*/head). Head payments, as Gimi explain, are a repetition of the brideprice: "We pay for a wife and when she bears a child we pay her mother and father *again* for the head. First her brother eats her brideprice and then, each time she has a child, he eats again!"

Head payments are made repeatedly throughout a child's early life, varying in size with the importance of the transition the child undergoes. When a child is named, cuts its first tooth, eats marsupial meat for the first time, has its first haircut, is injured, becomes ill or seems laggard in its growth, undergoes the ordeals of initiation or suffers any crisis, the *anatiraha* or "mother's brothers" (lit: *anati*/mother's brother + *raha*/pl.) receive head payments (see A. Strathern 1971:93n). But in the ideal case, the child's *ababana* give the head whenever they distribute pork and other goods, so that the flow of gifts to matrilateral kinsmen seems compulsive, as though "one gives because one is forced to . . . because the recipient has a sort of proprietary right over everything which belongs to the donor" (Mauss 1967 [1925]:11).

Although the child's father and mother's brother are the principals in the exchange, the "true" brothers of both men are also formally included. As in most New Guinea societies, "rights in married sisters and their children are ultimately vested not in individuals but in clans as wholes" (Bowden 1988:275). Glick describes the corporate nature of the transactions for males:

> The avunculate is another phase—a continuation, as it were—of the affinal sib relationship. The relationship begins when sib-villages provide one another with wives and wealth; it continues and perpetuates itself when the children [i.e., sons] of both partners, by expressing devotion to their matrilateral kinsmen, preserve the ties their fathers established. . . . the earliest gifts to a child's avuncular kinsmen come from his father. . . . When a child reaches adulthood he continues to present gifts to these same persons and their descendants. (Glick 1963:51)

Unlike brideprice, the ensuing head payments are recruitment payments.[14] If the *ababana* refuse to offer head payments or consistently de-

14. It might be more accurate to say, as does Bowden for the Kwoma and Daribi, that "[the] bridewealth payment is genuinely a recruitment payment, but it recruits a couple's children to

fault, the *anatiraha* have the right to claim the child as a member of their lineage, to have it live in their compound and work their land and, in the past, if it were a boy, to fight on their behalf, even against the father's kinsmen. When warfare was a regular part of life, defaults by men who had been killed or routed served as the pretext for affines to adopt their orphaned or abandoned children. When two *amau* quarrel seriously nowadays, one may threaten to refuse to "eat the heads" of the other's children, which is like threatening to take custody. When a pig belonging to her *amau* invaded her garden and uprooted half an acre of newly planted sweet potato vines, representing about a week of work, one woman shouted, "I will not eat your child's head! Give it to someone else to eat!" The threat is tantamount to a curse because, outside the context of war, a child reverting to the *anati* implies death: when a child actually dies, custody passes automatically to the *anati*. Before a father can bury his child in his own compound, he has to reclaim it from his wife's brother by providing a satisfactory head payment, a small male pig, perhaps, and ten Australian dollars. When a father is slow to give "the head of his child," or when he offers a meagre payment, the mother's brother threatens to send his wife and mother to "carry the child away" (although, as far as I know, he always accepts the promise of later payment in lieu of making good his threat).

The rationale for "giving the head," indeed, the whole Gimi idiom of exchange, is to ward off the *huꝧikaina* or "curse" (lit: *huꝧi*/curse + *kaina*/talk) of the mother's brother (see Wagner 1967). A child whose *anatiraha* receive a steady flow of head payments will flourish, Gimi say, because "eating the head cools the rage in their bellies." "We kill pigs to give to the child's mother's father and brother, so they will eat them and say to the child, 'I have eaten your head and eaten well! So now grow and be strong!'" As one old woman explained:

> We give our heads to our mothers to eat. We give them to our *ranatiraha* and our *ramamuraha*. If we do not . . . "fuuuussssss!" they will curse us and we will die! If we do not feed our mothers, we will wander in the forest and never rest. We will cry out and circle the bases of giant trees and go mad like the creatures of our dreams.

During a violent argument with his married daughter, one Gimi elder yelled:

> I am your father but you speak foully to me! and without the least hesitation! Don't think you can send me the heads of your

---

their father's clan, not the wife herself. . . . [A] bridewealth payment typically serves not to cancel the wife's membership in her natal group but to transfer certain rights in the woman to her husband's group" (Bowden 1988:287).

children. Because my son and I will not eat them! Send them to
my brother, why don't you? Let *him* eat them! [The elder and his
married son then spat on the ground to give his words the force
of an oath.] . . . Are you *my* child, I wonder? Or are you really
my brother's child whom I only reared?

But the power of the mother's brother and father to curse her children, and
the consequent necessity continually to placate them with head payments,
do not explain the different requirements for sons and for daughters: the
*ababana* make payments for a son throughout his life, culminating in his
death payment, but they stop "buying the head" of a daughter when she
marries. For the neighboring Daribi, Wagner explains the difference in
terms of recruitment to the father's clan. Payments to the mother's brother
cancel or oppose the mother's blood and "redeem" the father's substance,
thereby strengthening the child's tie to his lineage or clan:

> . . . the tie of mother's blood is "opposed" by payments, that
> of substance is "redeemed" or reinforced by payments.
> . . . the redemption of paternal ties becomes a lifelong propo-
> sition. If the payments are not made, the *pagebidi* (mother's
> brother) retains the right to dispossess the father of the child or
> to curse the latter. (Wagner 1967:117; see Langness 1974:206)

According to Wagner, the reason a man stops making payments on behalf
of his daughter after her marriage is simply that she "is no longer a member
of her father's clan" (ibid., 72). But the fact, as Bowden points out, that

> a Daribi woman demonstrably does not cease to be a jural mem-
> ber of her natal clan following her marriage, even if she is opera-
> tionally incorporated into her husband's group through virilocal
> residence, means that Wagner offers no plausible explanation for
> why recruitment payments for a woman should not continue to
> be made to her MB following her marriage in the same way as
> they are for a man. (Bowden 1988:287)

Like the Daribi, Gimi describe the payments to the mother's brother as a
matter of life and death or madness, a rescue from his devastating curse. For
a woman, the project ceases at marriage, as I argue in various ways throughout the book, because, unlike her brother, she cannot take over her father's
role as *donor* of head payments and ransomer of her own life and sanity. She
assumes, instead, the lifeless or "posthumous" role of recipient. A woman
dies when she marries in the sense that she can no longer serve as an object of
exchange, that is, as a child, and cannot assume the male role of donor. Be-

fore marriage, a woman functions like her brother as an object of exchange between her father and mother's brother. But once she marries, her children immediately replace her and her brother by becoming objects of exchange between her husband and brother. I discuss the logic of these arrangements again in Chapter 9.

Another problem with Wagner's explanation in terms of the Gimi is that Gimi women and men deny that a woman contributes blood or any other substance to the formation of her child, making it hard to construe head payments as "opposing" the mother's blood.

> A developing child receives nourishment and protections from its mother's body; but do a mother's body fluids, her blood perhaps, contribute to the actual formation of an infant? Most Gimi men would say not; a child's body arises from semen alone. (Glick 1963:100; see Read 1952:14)

Just as men do, women openly deny that a woman contributes substance to her unborn child. When a Gimi couple is betrothed in close conformity with the ideal, women remark approvingly that the mothers of bride and groom are *amene amau*. A woman wants to marry her daughter to the son of her husband's sister, to "the child of his *amene asi*," women say, because she wants to give her daughter "back" to her husband, since he is the "true source" of her child. At conception, one woman remarked, "The husband pulls a bird out of the sky and drops it into her net bag, into her womb" (lit: *hanu'o;* [*h*]*anu*/fetus + *ko*/bag).

The exclusive role that Gimi accord to semen seems inconsistent with the inordinate stress they place upon head payments as the means to sever matrilateral connections and thus affiliate the child to the father's descent group (see La Fontaine 1975:37). Gimi principles of exchange are designed to counteract not the stated theory of procreation, as I will argue, but other unstated premises enacted in ritual, such as the one expressed in Big Men's feeding arm blood to initiates to replace intrauterine food. In separate "secret" rites, each sex undermines the contribution of the child's father by showing that the bride arrives already pregnant by her own father, already filled with "the head of his child." In Chapter 7 I explore the set of myths which underlies these rites and which suggests that Gimi men and women are not in the kind of accord implied by their direct statements about the role of semen. It is the unspoken arguments about conception, implied in the relations between men's and women's myths, that I treat as the blueprint for rules of marriage and exchange. Looked at in this way, bridewealth and head payments are not merely compensations for the loss of a wife and child but also accusations of mythic incest, charges of improper ownership and intent to kill. By making married women into eternal recipients, the terms of

Gimi exchanges shift blame for the primordial crime away from the father and leave it entirely in the mother's hands.

According to the rule of sister exchange, the movements of women, brideprice, and head payments are entirely reciprocal. When men exchange sisters in marriage, each one gives and receives head payments on behalf of the children. "The pig comes from the head of my child and I cannot eat it," one man told me, pointing to a piglet just given to him by his wife's brother. "It is the head of my child. I will only care for it, and when it is grown my brothers will eat it." The head payments a man gives on his child's behalf are "the same" as those he receives for his sister's child in the sense that both are subject to the taboo of *aʋoina* on eating the produce of one's own hands (see Chap. 6).

But Gimi also say, according to a contrary logic, that the head cannot be returned because "returning the head of a sister's child is the same as cursing it." As one older woman explained:

> We give birth to children and send their heads to our brothers and fathers. They eat the money and the pigs for nothing! without making a return! . . . When my child dies we kill a pig and give it to my brother and he eats it. . . . I give the head of my child to my brother. He does not send it back!

A grandfather's "eating the head for nothing" is what makes the child prosper. As another woman said:

> My daughter Pariba is grown now into a fine young woman. My father has eaten and said, "I have eaten well. You shall grow and be strong." If her *anati* does not eat, Pariba will die. He will say, "Die!" and she surely will. The *anati* is angry and needs always to be given the head. What we give to our fathers for our children's heads can never be returned. It is theirs to eat for nothing.

In terms of the mythic scenario that I treat as part of the logic of exchange, "sending back the head curses the child" because it effectively reinstates the incestuous marriage between the child's mother and her father; it reunites the first woman with her flute, or the giant penis with his severed head (see Chap. 1). In more conventional terms it might be said that, ideologically, wealth flows exclusively to wife-givers; or that marriage is always contracted asymmetrically, even when there is sister exchange and an alliance between the brothers-in-law. "The husband and wife's brother . . . reciprocally exchange a variety of social and economic services, such as assistance with gardening and householding," Bowden points out about the Kwoma. "[But whereas] the husband 'pays' for these services . . . the wife's brother reciprocates (but does not 'pay') with additional gifts of food" (Bowden 1988:275). Gimi men who exchange sisters conduct their mutual relation as if it were one of bilateral inequality. The same contradiction is reflected in the marriage rules and makes sense in mythological terms: it allows each man to avoid the catastrophe of the first marriage, to renounce the sister who was his "first wife" and who "killed the firstborn," yet to take back his sister and bring the child to life.

## *Gimi Marriage Rules*

Gimi describe their marriage rule as entirely contingent upon the "eating" of brideprice and "the head of the child." The payments instate taboos or avoidances in relations that would otherwise revert to incest. When a man does *not* eat his sister's brideprice nor her daughter's head, sister and daughter theoretically remain potential spouses for him and his son. Men and women agree that the children of a "true" brother and sister are "like brothers and sisters" and should not marry. A man ought "to think only of eating his sister's brideprice and the heads of her children . . . not of marrying!" Yet acceptance of brideprice and head payments is always tantamount to the renunciation of "thoughts" of marriage:

> A man says to himself, "I have a son and my sister has a daughter. I shall buy my sister's daughter as a wife for my son so that brother and sister will marry." But a man should say instead to his son, "You will eat the payment for my sister's daughter. She is like a sister to you so you should eat her brideprice—not marry her." . . . When a man eats a woman's brideprice or the head of her child, she becomes his *kisa asi,* his true sister [lit: *kisa*/true or real + *asi*/sibling of opposite sex], and he may never marry her.

The change in custody and disastrous "curse" that ensue from nonpayment of the head thus refer directly to the possibility of incestuous marriage. When a man defaults in head payments for a son, the son becomes a full member of his wife's patrilineage and may then marry a woman who would otherwise be forbidden as a sister. When he defaults for a daughter, the daughter "returns" to her mother's brother as a wife for his son. In the words of one recently married man:

> My father's sister bears a son and a daughter and my father bears a son and a daughter. My father asks for the heads of his sister's children. If his *atu,* his "taboo" [i.e., sister's husband], should say, "No!" then my father will take his sister's daughter for my wife.

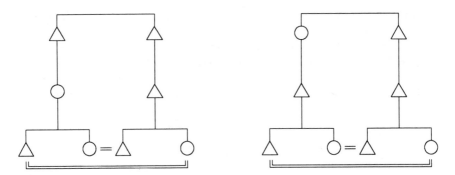

Figure 7. Marriages described by informants as the ideal.

A girl whose head has not been paid off by the time she reaches marriageable age is compelled, according to the rules, to marry her "true" mother's brother's son, a match Gimi ordinarily avoid and consider incestuous. The head her mother's brother did not "eat" becomes the brideprice he will not have to pay:

> My father gave his children's heads to Gana, my mother's [classificatory] brother. I still owe Gana my own head and my sister's head. If I cannot pay him all that I owe then I must give him my sister. Gana will take my sister [as a wife for his son] and pay me no brideprice.

If the "gift of the head" compels a man to disavow the woman he "thinks of first" as a wife for his son, it allows him to select his son's FMBSD, FFZSD, MFBSD, or FFBDD as the ideal wife, a woman one step removed, as it were, from his own MBD or FZD (fig. 7). A man replaces the daughter of his tabooed "true sister" with a woman who most resembles her, the daughter of his closest *amene asi* (lit: *amene*/other-than-*kisa* + *asi*) or the granddaughter, in the male line, of his father's *kisa asi*.[15] Yet, out of 338 mar-

---

15. It has been suggested in a case similar to the Gimi, that of the Iatmul studied by Bateson, that preferences for Z-exchange, marriage to a FMBSD or *iai* and to a FZD—in combination with prohibitions both on true sister exchange and marriage to the true first cousin—are conflicting and call into question Bateson's ethnography (Bowden 1991:228). Bowden counters that both Bateson and his critics may be too literal-minded in interpreting informants' statements as recommendations for marriage to specific genealogical kin when they are, in fact, assertions of general principles of social structure that govern categories of relations. Thus informants may recommend "the occasional marriage with particular categories of relatives, where it is understood that classificatory, not actual, relatives are in question" (ibid., 231). Among the Iatmul, Kwoma, and other Sepik peoples, a preference for FZD marriages need not conflict with a prohibition on marriage to the first cousin if FZD is interpreted as a reference not to a certain woman, or women, but to the idea that the daughter goes in payment for the

riages (including those of ancestors), I counted only four cases of "true" MFBSD marriage, six cases of "true" sister exchange, and seven cases of "true" sister-MBD exchange. In classificatory terms, however, there was high degree of compliance with stated norms. The low incidence of "real" marriages seems to reflect more than the interference of circumstance, sex ratios among siblings, personal preferences, etc. Ideal marriages are rare, it seems to me, because they are idealizations, enactments of impossible or contradictory mythic events. When honored in the breach, they translate *kisa* relationships into *amene* categories of kin, making the transition from real to classificatory relations which is at the heart of the social process (see n.15).

In claiming to take wives from their mothers' groups, Gimi men in most cases make the crucial substitution of father's affine for mother, of male for female. By substituting the mother's brother for the mother and then tracing his ties to ego primarily through the father, Gimi men create an all-male universe of relations as the basis for marriage transactions. As points of departure in finding a wife, a man's parents are two male persona: father-and-father's-sister and father's-affine-and-affine's-sister—who is only sometimes mother's brother-and-mother (see Leach 1961:10). Like a Big Man during male initiation, the mother's brother in an exchange system takes on a silent female role and replaces the real mother, obviating her participation even in the calculations for marriage. The radical deletion of the mother follows inevitably, in my interpretation, from the facts of procreation as Gimi men— and women—have translated them from myth. When men initiate sons and exchange daughters in marriage they put the father in the mother's place and thus create a mythic prehistory that can alter other genealogical connections (see Chap. 9).

---

mother, which in turn reflects "the general principal that the exchange of women between two groups should be balanced over time" (ibid., 232).

Gimi are meticulous and unambiguous in distinguishing "true" (*kisa*) from classificatory or "non-true" (*ameme*) relations, though they designate as "true" relations generated by the system of refuge and male initiation (see above, this chap.). A supposed contradiction between actual sister exchange and the equivalent of *iai* marriage among the Gimi can thus hardly be explained away as my having misinterpreted informants. Though Gimi allow, and indeed prefer, both true sister exchange and marriage to a true FMBSD, instances of such marriages are in fact rare, and even rarer *in combination* as they are often described by informants and appear in figure 7. Analysts who allege incompatibility between sister exchange and close classificatory matrilateral cross-cousin marriage may thus mistake true for classificatory relations in the *general run* of marriages and ignore the often conflicting long-term goals of marriage alliance, especially in the past. The practical need to create and maintain a maximal number of political allies—and debtors—by scattering sisters in marriage is inconsistent with other, mythic requirements to balance the exchange of women. The combination of marriage preferences and injunctions achieves these contradictory ends by instituting a wait of one, two, or more generations to "send back the sister," thus uniting asymmetrical and reciprocal exchanges in a single system.

# PART ONE

Cannibalism and the Rites of Death

# THREE

# Gimi Cannibalism in History and in Myth

The symbolism of Gimi mortuary ritual is based upon myths of cannibalism. The structure of the rites rests upon the premise that women mourners have already stolen and eaten the corpse. In the past, some Gimi, especially women and children, did eat the dead *during* the ritual so that, in a particular limited sense, ritual and myth once coincided with reality.[1] The relation among the rites, myths and past practice of cannibalism is similar, in one way, to the relation among rites of marriage, myths of incest, and cases of incest. The rules and rites of marriage are tied to an ideal and unvarying mythic scenario; and, in a direct sense, marriages enact myths of incest (see Chap. 9). But the celebration of marriages hardly indicates the frequency, or even existence, of incestuous practices. Incest occurs among the Gimi, as among most peoples, and men and women make a clear distinction between specific instances and myth.

Unlike real incest, however, real cannibalism probably always occurred within a ritual context. The celebration of mortuary ritual might thus have coincided with the actual consumption of a corpse, although there is no way to know how often that happened, what proportion of corpses were eaten, how many men, women, and children regularly took part, etc. But the lack of correspondence between an instance of ritual and the actual devouring of

1. Some Gimi women assert that men regularly ate the dead. In other Eastern Highlands societies, Berndt reports that men and women alike practiced cannibalism (R. Berndt 1962). Yet my fieldwork suggests that Gimi cannibalism was associated mainly with women and children. The epidemiology of kuru, a neurological disorder found among the Fore and among some Yani River Gimi who have exchanged wives with the Fore, also suggests that women and young children were the main practitioners (Gajdusek and Alpers 1972:S19). Kuru is transmitted during the eating or handling of infected human tissue and has an incubation period of twenty years or more. The pattern of kuru's disappearance after cannibalism ceased suggests that females often contracted the disease as adults but that the afflicted males were younger, indicating that males were exposed to kuru mainly as children who shared their mothers' meals (see Lindenbaum 1979:26, 1983:102).

a corpse has no bearing, it seems to me, on the past reality of cannibalism. If Gimi descriptions of cannibal practice are to be doubted, then their every account of their life and history must also be called into question.

## A Menace to Public Health

According to the Gimi, Australian officials made sanitation a main priority. On the first patrols, they ordered people to build outhouses and stop defecating in the open and to use less pig fat and more water on their bodies. They also prohibited eating the dead on the grounds that exposing corpses, which was an essential preliminary to the practice, was a menace to public health. In 1974, a woman of about thirty-five recalled:

> In the past when a man died we carried him to his garden. . . . The women stayed on the ground and wept while the men made a bed [or platform] and placed it high in a pandanus tree or in a stand of bamboo. Men lifted the man onto his bed and built a roof of dried leaves over him to keep off the rain. . . . We used to put dead men in trees, but you whites came and said, "When a man dies . . . dig a hole in the ground and put him inside."
>
> "If you expose the body," the government said, "flies will eat it and spit into your food and make you sick!" We bury our dead now and cover the opening.

In ceasing to expose the dead, and in renouncing the cannibalism that ensued, Gimi seem to have been moved less by threats of illness than by the desire to help dead relations achieve an afterlife, which was always the main goal of mortuary ritual. When white men began to arrive in their territory, Gimi explain, they realized that those of their dead they did not eat might go to Australia, a "land of the dead" beyond the horizon, and eventually return as white men. As one woman explained:

> You see, when a man dies, that is not the end of him. He exists. If we do not eat him he may come back with changed skin. Before white men arrived we didn't understand this and so we ate the dead. Then white man came and explained . . . [that] a man can go to stay in Australia and come back. . . . We realize this now so we don't *want* to eat him!

Gimi remember an early patrol that arrived in the midst of a war. Besides trying to stop the fighting, the Australian officers railed against eating the dead and against shooting Birds of Paradise which were then disappearing from more densely populated areas of the Highlands. To the Gimi, the jointly issued prohibitions had a deeper rationale. Both white men and Birds of Paradise were believed to "house" the *kore*, spirits of dead relations. By eating the dead and killing birds, Gimi surmised, they had been keeping the *kore* inside Gimi territory so they could not "fly" to Australia. Unwittingly, they had restricted the movement of ancestral spirit, "closed the road" along which black ghosts and white men traveled, impeding the return to their Gimi birthplace.

The notion that a person might survive death by "changing skin" is also part of traditional Gimi belief. According to one tale, men once had the option of molting like snakes and living forever. But through arrogance and thoughtless haste, they lost the option of shedding their skins and ended up with the same fate as giant tree ferns. The tree fern grows in a coil like a snake but is rooted in the ground and, after putting out a single new shoot at the base, withers and dies.

> "When I die, I change my skin!" the snake told the fern. But the fern said, "When I die, I die completely." "No!" replied the snake. "One can change!" When a snake gets old and sees his skin is wrinkling, he gets rid of that skin entirely. The skin over his whole body—even his eyes and teeth—rots and disappears, and a new skin appears!
>
> That's how a snake does it, and, if the fern had done likewise, men who die would not be finished completely. They would sleep for a night or two and get up again, take off their old skins and get rid of them. . . .
>
> Instead, we die like ferns. The fern that comes out of the ground and unfurls is the same one that dies, and a man dies like a fern. . . . When a new shoot appears—when his child is born—he's finished. Its the beginning of the end.

A snake discards his outer layer and then lives on in himself; his inner being endures (see Paul 1982:101). But a man has to reproduce himself. He can live on only in a child, only by giving rise to a whole other person who drains and depletes his inner being and then replaces him entirely. The birth of a man's child instigates his mortality just as the appearance of a new spore signals the demise of the giant fern (see fig. 8; also see Kelly 1976:42, 49).

But *if* a man were able to shed his skin like a snake, the new skin, the underneath skin, would probably be white because that is his inner color, the color of semen. Semen is white; a newborn child is white (because it takes hours for melanin to migrate to the surface of the skin); and the underlayer of skin that appears when a corpse bloats and the epidermis splits is also "white." Indeed, "turning white" is a Gimi euphemism for decomposition.

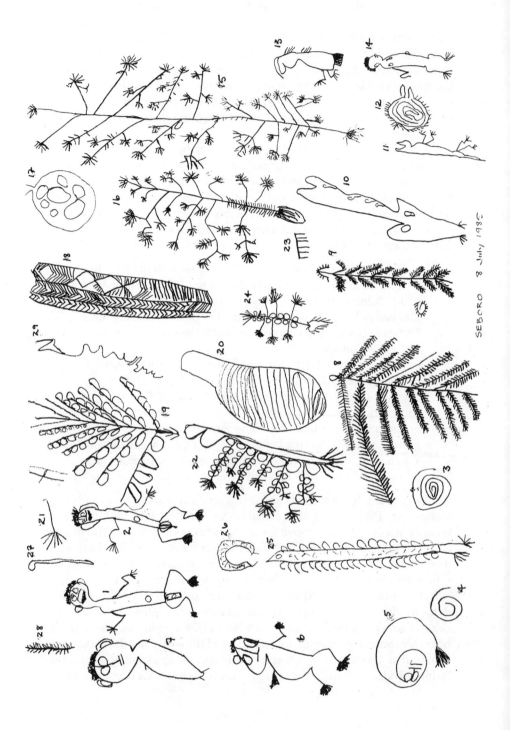

SEBORO 8 July 1985

When a child dies, the mother remains secluded with it for days, wailing, attempting to nurse it, telling it to "wake up! wake up!" In her chants, she pleads with the baby to "stay black":

> Child of mine, I told you not to die!
> But you did not hear me!
> You did not listen! . . .
> Stay black now. Stay as black as you are.
> But you won't listen! . . .
> Soon you'll be a white one!

White men's determination to end cannibal practices and to stop the killing of Birds of Paradise, in the view of some Gimi, stemmed from a covert self-interest, a wish to protect their own freedom of movement, that coincided with the Gimi desire for an afterlife. In the first period of contact, women point out, few whites appeared in Gimi territory. But as the years passed and Gimi continued to bury their dead, white men arrived in increasing numbers. Patrol officers were followed by missionaries, medical personnel, agricultural advisers. The escalating presence of whites in their midst, women remark, is itself a kind of proof of their compliance with Australian demands.

Figure 8. *The Fern and the Snake* (1985), a drawing by Robese, a young Gimi man. Robese drew from right to left and then described each item in the following words, beginning with the last-drawn figures: "[1] Man. [2] Woman. She wants a child and the man has sex with her. [3] The child is starting. This is the man's penis inside the woman's belly. The man is making the child. [4] The child is forming. [5] Look. It's really beginning. [6] The two hands and the two legs are started. [7] [An earlier stage of fetal development showing the tips of limbs as they start to emerge from the body core.] [8] Wild fern [*kore beheϑa;* lit.: *kore*/wild or ancestral + *beheϑa*/fern, an uncultivated green that Gimi say was once eaten with the dead]. [9] Hoop pine [*mane;* tree inside whose trunk Gimi traditionally lodge the bones of the dead]. [10] Frog [*huba*]. [On the night of conception, Gimi women say, an ancestral spirit enters the woman and she dreams. If she 'sees' a frog or other water creature in her dream, she will bear a daughter. If she sees a bird alight on a branch (like the one the artist shows in [13]), she will bear a son.] [11] Lizard [*kou*]. [12] An insect [*nimi kuru*] that sleeps inside a burrow on the bottom of a river. [13] A bird [*korokio*] that sits in the branch of a tree [see item 15] and eats the fruit. [14] The *kore baϑaha* [lit.: *kore*/wild or mythic + *baϑaha*/woman] who lives in the mountain and hides herself in a cave when men enter the forest. [15] A tree [*raho*]. It has no story. [But see item 13.] [16] Another tree [*fare*]. [17] A bird's nest filled with eggs [*nimisu amu';* lit.: *nimi*/bird + *su*/poss. + *amu'*/nest]. [18] Tattoos [*hugu*] [worn by women and men]. [19] A plant [*ϑIgu*] that grows in the ground and bears fruit [lit.: children]. [20] Net bag [*ko*] to carry the child that is growing [depicted in items 3–7]. [21] Arrow [*kiso*]. [22] Fruiting plant [*haϑi*]. [23] Another tattoo [*hugu*]. [24] Papaya. [25] Centipede [*hegiϑabe*]. [26] Another net bag. [27] The woman's menstrual blood leaves her body. [28] Another fern [*beheϑa*]. [29] [Abandoned attempt at a python showing its enormous mouth.]"

## *Who Were the Cannibals?*

Some women say that men regularly ate the dead. "When I was the age of *P* [a girl of about ten years], I saw a man eaten," one woman of around thirty said in 1974. "Everyone, men and women, gathered to cut him. [Gesturing on her body], one man cut this part, one woman cut this part, another woman cut another part. . . . First the man! The pigs came later." Yet, while women declare that women and men ate the dead together, their own accounts of particular cases make male participation seem the exception rather than the rule.

In men's view, cannibalism was entirely "women's idea." "Our mothers tells us, 'A man was the sweetest thing!'" In 1974 a man of about twenty-six said that, when he was the age of a boy I judged to be five or six years old, his mother had given him the flesh of a Big Man, one of the last men in the village to have been eaten:

> All the women were gathered with their children to eat the man. "You are still a small boy," my mother said to me, "so let me give you this." And she gave me some meat. . . . And because I ate it I have beaten every man I ever fought! . . . When a strong man died we ate him so we could defeat our enemies. . . . The boy who ate a man grew quickly. He grew into a man who could fight and clear gardens with the strength of the one who died.

In 1975, a man of about twenty-eight recalled that when he was a child of five or so he had wandered into a house filled with women who were breaking open charred bamboo cooking vessels.[2] The women had teased him good-naturedly about his "small size" and offered him "a penis" to make him grow into a big man. He was told afterward, he said, that the bamboos were filled with the flesh of his father's sister's husband.

Some men state flatly that men were never cannibals. Uninitiated boys were allowed to consume their own fathers and elder brothers, but strong taboos enjoined initiated boys and men, especially the deceased's own age-mates, from eating his flesh. Clan elders and fight leaders sometimes ate pieces of the liver to "fire their bellies" for revenge. The only other men who might partake of an adult male corpse were paternal kinsmen of very low status, or who were very old, or very distantly related and lived in other compounds or villages. No male of any age ever ate any part of a woman—not

---

2. According to men's statements and the indications of kuru (see n.1, this chap.), males participated in cannibal meals mainly as infants or young children. When based upon childhood experiences, men's recollections often seem to be interspersed with imaginary elements, which may explain certain contradictions (see n.8, this chap.).

her own brother nor her own mother's brother nor, most tabooed of all, her own sons.[3]

The only closely related, initiated man in his prime who was not expressly forbidden to eat a man was his *anati*, his mother's brother. "Part of the brother-sister relationship," Berndt says of neighboring Kamano, Jate, Usurufa, and Fo:re peoples, "implies that a sister will give deceased children to her brother for eating, and this is extended too in the classificatory sense" (Berndt 1954–55:173). Some Gimi men mention—always briefly and in passing—the exemption of the mother's brother from the male taboo on cannibalism (e.g., see below, this chap.; also Chap. 10). But this exception to the rule seems to have been an assertion of rights of a different order, giving the mother's brother, and maternal kinsmen generally, the leverage to extract death payments—to "eat the head" instead.

"When a man dies, the men who live feel a great hunger," one man remarked. "Their hunger is for him, for the one who died." But men who yearn for a fallen comrade should fast and intensify their hunger, so it drives them to find the killer. Women are unable to divert their grief, according to men. In the past, when men carried a slain comrade to his garden and installed him on a platform in a tree—that very day, men say—his "mothers and sisters" pulled him down and ate him. "A man's sisters were too sorry for him to let him to rot," another man named Tonaku explained:

> A brother or sister is like no one else. If you were to die here, now, at this very moment, your brother would come to you. He would take your fingers and toes into his mouth and swallow the juices that ran from your nose. It matters less to a man when his brother dies because a brother is the same as a man. A brother has the same body as a man. But when a sister dies, a man feels another kind of grief. Another kind, another kind!

Women also connect intense sorrow with hunger for the deceased, saying their cannibalism both alleviated their own pain and spared the dead the agonies of decomposition. In the past, they declare, "women would not have left a man to rot":

---

3. The worst insult one Gimi man can hurl at another is, "Eat your mother's vagina!" (*anosu aðesena ona;* lit: mother's + crotch-thing + go-and-eat), or "Eat your mother's [menstrual] blood!" (*anosu kora ona*). When a man falls ill, other men whisper that his wife may have laced his food with her menstrual blood or with the combined secretions of herself and her lover, forcing him, unaware, to "eat the meat of her vagina." A man who becomes sick is probably a cuckold, men say, one whose wife secretly made him "eat her" so she could be rid of him and marry her true love.

We [i.e., our mothers and grandmothers] took pity on him and put him into our bamboos and ate him! One woman took one part, another woman took another part, another woman took another part. . . . We cut him again and put the pieces into an earth oven. . . . When a good man died our bodies ached with hunger. We ate him and the pain cooled.

But women also mock their feelings for the dead. In the ritual theater performed as late-night entertainment at weddings and initiations, women put on skits that lampoon the cannibal meals of the past. Theater is the only occasion when women participate in rites held inside the men's house. On the night a group of male initiates were interned, I squatted with other women outside the door and watched the following playlet performed by men and women in the long central corridor of the men's house.

Near one of the fireplaces a lone warrior appears. On his shoulder he carries a wounded comrade, a dummy made of two net bags joined at their openings, held rigid by a plank of wood, stuffed with dried leaves and encased in bark. One end of the dummy is tied with a vine to make a neck and a warrior's headdress of black cassowary plumes is fastened to the head. Branches attached to the sides of the dummy suggest arms and legs.

The warrior is pursued by three enemy, men whose faces are concealed by veils of dried banana leaves. The three crouch behind the central poles of the men's house and take aim at the dummy, firing arrows into the wounded man and crying out, "Spring from which well the waters of Mount Hana!" and "I am the father of the *kebao* flute!" [As a male spectator later explained, "When a man shoots a man or a pig he rejoices by raising the name of his clan mountain. He sends the *auna*, the spirit, of the one he kills to swell his clan's reservoir. He calls out the name of his flute so men far and near will know who has taken a man's life!"]

The three enemy hoot and shout and fill the dummy with arrows. The warrior holds them at bay for a while but is then forced to abandon his comrade. He lays the dummy on the floor, cursing the enemy, crying "Drink my semen!" [figuratively, "You are women!"], and disappearing into the darkness offstage. The three enemy close in and fire more arrows into the corpse, calling out the landmarks of their clan forest and chanting "Blood! O glorious blood! Blood! O glorious blood!"

A line of four women players brush past me and the other wo-

A battle scene from a performance of ritual theater showing one of the enemy being shot full of bamboo arrows. In a moment, he will fall as though mortally wounded and then be lifted by a comrade-in-arms. Scenes like this one, in which the enemy is portrayed by a live actor sheathed in protective layers of banana stem, are a variation on those in which the enemy is represented by a stuffed dummy.

men spectators crowded at the door, and enter the men's house waving bundles of cordyline and shouting "Hurrah!" and "Revenge is sweet!"[4] The women dance onto the scene in jubilation and surround the dummy, shoving aside the armed men. Suddenly their songs and gleeful shouts turn to sobs. Joy over their husbands' victory turns, in an instant, to despair over the death of their brother. Still waving cordyline in triumph, the women

4. One of the women players is descended patrilineally from a man who was shot by ancestors of the actor playing the lone warrior.

cry "Woe! Woe is me!" and throw themselves with loud thuds onto the floor. They take bamboo knives from their waistbands and pull the dummy in opposite directions, tearing it apart, dragging innards [dried leaves and strips of bark] over the floor or flinging them into the air.

The four women leave the men's house and then return, and the scene changes from the battlefield to a garden where they have carried the corpse for cooking. The four hold wide bamboo tubes and line them with ferns, parsley, watercress, and other "wild" greens, the only kind that can be cooked with human meat. Amid their wails, the women begin to fight over choice parts.

FIRST WOMAN: "The head is mine!"
SECOND WOMAN: "The leg is mine!"
THIRD WOMAN TO THE FOURTH WOMAN [who is holding her]: "Let go of me! Let go! *I* want the shoulder!"
ALL FOUR: "Greens! We need more greens!"

Angry exchanges now entirely replace the cries of sorrow. Each woman accumulates a small pile of "meat and innards" and pulls at choice parts, accusing the others of stealing: "Don't try to make off with that! Put it down *right here* and we'll divide it!" Turning to a man in the audience—which is now filled with laughter—one woman says, "Be a good chap and make me a knife. I want to eat the penis. I've taken the head already!"

FIRST WOMAN TO THIRD WOMAN: "*namau* [sister-in-law]! Take what you want! Fill your net bag. I am not a greedy woman. . . . Fill your net bag and put it on your head and be off!"

From the audience, the First Woman's own mother-in-law shouts: "I say, *you* take it! It's *you* who are the hungry one!"

THIRD WOMAN TO FIRST WOMAN: "You are the kind of woman who really likes to eat! Leave it for me! Leave it for me! Please [lit: I'll eat your vagina]!"[5]
FIRST WOMAN TO A MAN IN THE AUDIENCE: "Please [lit: I'll eat your penis]. Tell her to let me have it!"

---

5. I translate "I'll eat your vagina"/"I'll eat your penis" rather inadequately as an emphatic form of please. It is an idiomatic expression, sometimes used in ordinary parlance, to express great deference or an unlimited offer of service in exchange for acceptance of the request being made. Gimi insist that its meaning is wholly metaphoric. (See n.3, Chap. 1.)

THIRD WOMAN TO FIRST WOMAN: "Please leave it!"
FIRST WOMAN TO THIRD WOMAN: "I'm your *amau* [i.e., a woman who gives you food], not a woman who takes food from you! So have it! Take what you want!

The audience roars with laughter at the women's self-mockery and invention, appreciating their rapid asides filled with double entendre and allusions to current entanglements. The players repeat their exchanges three or four times, varying each reprise. Then they gather up the piles of "meat," the filled net bags, and the charred bamboo cooking vessels, and place them on their heads, quarreling hilariously as they file out the door of the men's house into the night.

Although both sexes describe the cannibal meal as a frenzied outpouring of feeling, in reality it appears to have been governed by certain conventions. Men report that only certain knowledgeable senior women made the first cuts and divided the corpse into large sections. Other women carried the sections to separate corners of a garden and cut them again into smaller pieces, each woman distributing the pieces among her husband's mother, sons' wives, sisters, and sisters-in-law. A woman might have partaken of her own son, some women allowed, but she left the cutting to her co-wives, daughters, or daughters of her co-wives. "His mother ate the penis," one woman said, "and his wife ate the stomach and head." Among the women likely to have consumed a man who died in his prime were women of his father's clan, his mothers (*anoha*) and brothers' wives (*araha*), his real and classificatory sisters (*asiraha*) and daughters (*aramofa*), his father's real and classificatory sisters (*amamuraha*), his wife's mother (*aðimu*), and the wives of his sons (*anaturaha*). A special category of women called *faba baðaha*, literally "nothing women" (lit: *faba*/nothing + *baðaha*/woman), also came to eat a man in his garden or were later given cooked pieces of his flesh. The ties of *faba baðaha* were not primarily to the deceased but to the principal women mourners. When a woman received the meat of her husband's brother or mother's brother, for example, she was generally required to share it with her brother's wife or husband's mother, making that other woman *faba baðaha* in relation to the deceased.

## Who Was Eaten?

The only person no one ever ate, men and women usually agree (but see below, Chap. 10), was a firstborn of either sex because "the firstborn child is the same as menstrual blood." Men also say that enemies were never eaten. After a skirmish, warriors threw enemy corpses into rivers where their own kinsmen could retrieve them. But if ritual theater depicts even a partial truth about the past, it suggests that the victors' wives sometimes claimed the corpses the men discarded, perhaps because among the enemy dead were the women's clan brothers.

One old woman recalled that her husband had summoned her to help him retrieve his father, a man named Omanua, after he was killed in a battle outside the neighboring village of Vami. There had been a struggle to recover the body, and she remembered the affair vividly, she said, because it coincided with the first flight of an airplane over Gimi territory.

> "Your *anatu* is shot!" my husband called to me. "Come!" And the two of us went to bring back Omanua. The Vamians tried to take him, but we brought him here. . . . We took him to Casuarina Tree Place [a compound at the outskirts of the village] and started to cut him. I was cutting his leg . . . and other women were cutting other parts [when] . . . "*bobobobobobobo,*" we heard his cries coming from a pool in a stand of wild sugarcane. Omanua was crying out from the water!

Hearing the sounds of an airplane overhead, the women in the midst of cutting Omanua thought his *auna* had "flown" out of his body and taken refuge in a pool nearby, as the storyteller's son-in-law explained. The bamboo knife used to "open" a corpse, the *kane hugu* (lit: *kane*/corpse + *hugu*/knife or incision), absorbed the person's *auna* and, on the night after a cannibal meal, sometimes flew over the village, making implosive, engine-like sounds. The women mistook the roar of the airplane for "cries" of the *kane hugu,* though they were only starting to cut Omanua, and thought that his *auna* had dived into the pool. The old woman continued:

> We ran away from Omanua! We ran up Mount Ugami as fast as we could! When the crying stopped we came back down and began to cut him again. We carried him up to the main part of the village and . . . while we were eating him he began to cry out again! . . . An airplane was flying in the sky above us! "*bobobobobobo*" came from behind the mountain ranges, from all around us! It was Omanua who held that creature. . . . Omanua made the airplane come. (See fig. 9)

Men say that Big Men, orators, and fight leaders were eaten more often than ordinary men. All the cases of cannibalism I recorded involved the consumption of an adult male, a finding reflected in my descriptions by the presumption that the deceased is a man. Men report that women were only rarely consumed and that women of importance, wives of Big Men and knowledgable leaders of women's rites, were preferred to other women. "When a very nice woman, a very good woman died, women sometimes ate her, but they never gave a morsel to their sons!" one man remarked. Women should not have been eaten, men say, and when they were, because "women insisted," some of the ensuing rites of *ruhu* were eliminated or reduced in scale. It was a situation over which men claim to have had little control.

Yet, in 1983 when the wife of a Big Man died and her body began to decompose after several days, men remarked that if her *anaturaha*, the women married into her husband's patrilineage with pigs she had reared, had allowed her, by not eating her, to have reached such an unsightly state in the past, her husband would have been furious. Such comments indicate, in striking contrast to men's direct statements and women's own burlesques, that cannibalism was not entirely "women's idea" nor merely the result of women's loss of self-control.

Women themselves imposed restrictions upon the consumption of a female corpse. When a woman died, women recall, none of her real or classificatory sisters (*araha*), nor her age-mates (*be'a 'aθa*), nor the wives of her husband's age-mates, nor her *kisa anatu*, her husband's own mother, ever ate her. When the deceased was a young married woman, the *anoha* and *amamuraha* who arrived from other villages to "eat her head" sometimes stayed to share the cannibal meal with her *anaturaha* and *imiuraha*.

### *"Eating the Head" Instead*

The fact that a mother's brother, alone among a man's adult kinsmen, was once allowed to eat him may indicate not that he usually participated in a cannibal meal but that he, or the *anatiraha* and *abogoraha* generally, had to be compensated for having that right preempted by unruly women.

When a man's maternal kinsmen received word of his death, they set out for his home, the men armed and the women covered in yellow clay and ashes. The men charged into his compound, swinging axes and bush knives. They cut down bananas and cordyline plants, uprooted coffee trees, pulled out fence posts, and threw themselves into pig wallows or pools of mud while the *ababana,* or paternal kinsmen, "sat silently and stared at the ground" as convention dictated. To end the rampage, a man of the deceased's patrilineage "tied a pig to a stake at the compound's entrance. The pig was the head of our brother and killing it cooled the fury in their bellies. If we had no pig for the *anatiraha* to shoot, then we had to fight."

A young married woman named Sabaro described the current practice:

> When a man dies we put him inside the house of his wife or his mother and his *abogoraha* come crying. His *ababana* tie up

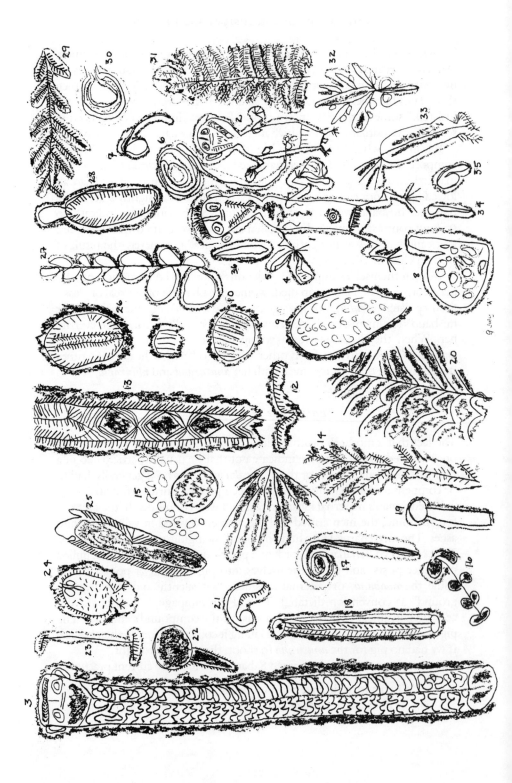

pigs and his *abogoraha* shoot them to cool their bellies. When an *abogo* thinks of his *abogo* who has died, his stomach gets hot! We give him the head to cool his insides.

Describing a scene I regularly observed, another woman named Rekona continued:

> The *abogoraha* arrive covered in mud and wailing and shoot the pig we tied to a stake by the road. They carry it into our compound and we lay bank notes on top of it and give these, too, to the *abogoraha*. "Your stomachs are hot," we say to them. "Your livers [i.e., insides] are stirred with terrible longing for him. So take the pig and the money we give you and eat them! They will make you cold again and you can go home."

When a woman dies, it is her own paternal kinsmen, rather than her mother's, who stage the ritually pro forma demand for her head; and it is her affines, rather than her paternal kinsmen, who contritely offer pigs and bank notes. In either case, the head payment is intended to "cool the bellies" of the deceased's kin and end their furious search for the corpse.

Nowadays head payments purchase the right of burial, the right of "fathers" or "husbands" of the deceased to keep the body in their own territory and possess the *auna* for the posterity of their own clan. Women emphasize that a husband's *amagaraha,* his classificatory sisters' sons (lit: *amaga*/sister's

---

Figure 9. *The Story of Cannibalism* (1985), a drawing made and described by Robese. "[1] Woman. [2] The man who died. [3] The dead man covered up in a bark cloth [*furu*]. [4 and 5] The woman takes her net bag [4] and bamboo knife [*hugu*] [5] and goes to the man. She comes to cut him down the center of his chest [lit.: *hagurihi*]. [6] The intestines [*hara hara*] are removed from the man. [7] An ax [*rukuru*] is used to break the bones. [8] The cut-up parts of the man are placed in a wooden bowl [*usi*]. [9] . . . loaded into a net bag [*ko*] . . . [10 and 11] . . . placed into bamboo tubes [*riϑi;* viewed endwise] and cooked. [12] Kneebands [*kisigi;* worn by both sexes as a sign of mourning]. [13] Dance shield [*keruba;* see Chap. 9]. [14] Ferns [*beheϑa*] are eaten with the man. The parts of him are wrapped in *beheϑa* and loaded into the earth oven . . . [15] Stones are removed from the bottom of the earth oven. [16] Beans [*omatoba*]. [17] Another ax used to cut the man. [18] Headband [*oroba'*]. [19] A creature [*kiϑoba'*] that nests on the ground. [20] Leaves of breadfruit [*isou*] eaten with the man. [21] The dead man's blood. [22] A creature that lives near the river. [One of the "wild meats" eaten with the dead; see item 24.] [23] Ax of the ancestors [*tagIϑo*]. [24] An echidna [*kuiyaru*]. [25] The dead man's fore-skirt [*maro;* used to make *agesagena;* see Chap. 5]. [26] Belt [*amukui;* worn by the ancestors and linked to a neck collar by a centerpiece that extends up the chest; also used for *agesagena;* see Chap. 5]. [27] Wild fruit [*haϑi*]. [28] Another wild fruit [*amoϑi*]. [29] Leaf of *amoϑi.* [30] Women's menstrual blood. [31] More *beheϑa.* [See item 14.] [32] Wild fruit [*bupuina*]. [33] Bloodsucking leech [*hipo*]. When a man goes into the forest, the *hipo* gets on his hands and all over his chest and eats his blood. [34] Bamboo knife [*hugu*] [used only to cut human flesh]. [35] One of the dead man's bones. [36] Another *hugu.*"

(*Top left*) A group of *ababana,* or paternal kinsmen, arrive from another village after the death of one of their daughters soon after the birth of her first child. The women enter their affines' compound ahead of the men, running and shouting in a rampage, while the affines (including the two men in the *right foreground*) stand idly by, as is ritually prescribed.

(*Bottom left*) Men of the dead woman's father's clan roll in pig wallows when they arrive, wearing the mud that clings to them as a badge of rage and sorrow.

(*Above*) Outside the house where the dead woman lies, one of her "mothers," a woman married into her father's clan, confronts her husband's brother. In keeping with both ritual protocol and her own anger over the death, the woman demands to "take her daughter back." The affines' conventional response is the offer of head payments, cooked pork, money, and other valuables that will "cool the bellies" of the paternal kin.

son + *raha*/pl.), to whom they give their daughters in marriage, are also his *anumona* (lit: *anu*/fetus or spirit child + *mo*/the + *na*/thing) and will "eat his head" when he dies:

> When my husband dies . . . the sons of his *amene asi* will cover themselves in mud and clay and come crying, "Our mother is dead!" . . . The *anumona* will attack my sons! They will draw their bows and shoot our pigs one after another after another.
>
> My sons will tie up many pigs for the *anumona* to shoot and give them money. The pigs and the money are my husband's head. As soon as the *anumona* receive the head of their mother, they clear out! They run back to their own houses to eat.

The ritual confrontation between a dead man's own sons, his *amabuha* (lit: *amabu*/son + *ha*/pl.) and his sisters' sons or *amagaraha,* will be more than a mock battle, women add, if the latter have been remiss in providing the heads of their own children over the years:

> "If you look after him well," our sons tell his *amagaraha,* " . . . if you send him meat whenever you kill a pig, if you give him the heads of your sons when you take them into the men's house, then you will eat his head when he dies. Otherwise you can cry and cry but we will not give you his head." (See Brown 1961; Bowden 1988)

In the past, head payments seem to have had the significance of compensating the rampaging maternal kinsmen, or paternal kinsman in the case of a woman, for the fact that the corpse was missing. "The very day a man was lifted into a tree he was cut," men say. "The very day men carried him to his garden and left him there and said, 'Let him rot,' his sisters and mothers said, 'He must *not* be left to rot!'" Paternal kinsmen seemed tacitly to permit, or even encourage, "mothers and sisters" to act out cannibal impulses, thereby obstructing those impulses in their male affines, offering them head payments after the fact, so to speak, "cooling their bellies" with other food once they had made sure the corpse was no longer available for eating.

### The Feast of *ruhu*

Men describe the cannibal meal as orgiastic and chaotic. Women "stole" corpses off platforms and ate them in a kind of frenzy, they say. But such statements ought not to be accepted literally to mean that Gimi practiced cannibalism in the manner of women's burlesque nor entirely without ritual, as has been suggested (Lindenbaum 1979:22). What men's remarks and women's ritual theater indicate, it seems to me, is that cannibal ritual was designed to *enact* utter greed and disorder, to represent a phase of non- or preritualized existence (Gillison 1983a). Unlike women's burlesque, the historical meal was apparently not a free-for-all: specific categories of women were assigned to handle, cut, and even consume a corpse. But these conventions did not alter the symbolic truth of women's theater. When women "seized the corpse" and consumed it "out of men's sight," they took back what men had renounced and "left to rot," undoing the bargain men had struck among themselves. But women did this, I contend, as *part* of the ritual, acting in unspoken collusion or fulfillment of men's demand.

The following account of the treatment of a corpse and the celebration of *ruhu* in the past is a condensation of one man's description but summarizes information given by several. In 1974, Uarafu, a man of about thirty, reported:

> In the days when a man was eaten, he wasn't kept long inside his mother's house [see below, Chap. 4]. After he died, he slept there only one night, and in the morning men carried him outside. . . . They laid him [naked] on a mat of dried pandanus leaves and carried him to his garden [where] they lifted him onto a bed in a pandanus tree or in a stand of bamboo, supporting the bed with poles if they had to. They built a roof to keep off the rain and made a ladder [for men to climb when it came time to retrieve his bones].

The residents of several compounds assembled to watch the removal of the deceased from his mother's house and followed the bier in a procession to his garden. Once the dead man was installed in a tree and the crowd had dispersed, those who intended to eat him went back and "stole" the corpse.

> Everyone came to watch a man being lifted onto his bed. While the others returned to their compounds, the women— and the men, too[6]—who wanted to cut him went away and hid. When the men who had carried him to his garden were back in the men's house, the ones in hiding started to cut him. . . . They hid so that no man would *see* them and say, "Oh! I think they want to cut this man!" . . .
>
> The women were ashamed, and, while the men were returning to the men's house . . . and [while the older] children, too, were coming back to their houses, they went secretly to cut bam-

---

6. The addition of "and the men, too" was prompted by my interrupting to ask if men did not sometimes join the women at this stage, since the informant had earlier allowed, again with my prodding, that some men were cannibals. Without my interruption, cannibal men drop out of the narrative.

boo [for cooking vessels], to collect ferns and parsley and breadfruit leaves [and other uncultivated greens cooked with human meat] and to gather firewood. Only young children went with their mothers and ate the dead.

To make the preparations for the cannibal meal, the women "tricked" their husbands, lying to them about where they were going. Uarafu continues:

> When the men returned to their house, their wives tricked them, saying, "I'm going to the garden now. I'm going to my garden. . . ." That's what the women told their husbands, but instead they all went to the garden of the dead man. The women had sealed their talk and made a pact among themselves. . . . They climbed the ladder and pulled down the man and laid him at the base of the bamboo. There they cut him and loaded the pieces into their net bags and came back to his house.[7] They brought him back to his house and cut him again and divided the pieces among themselves. . . .
> The husbands all thought, "My wife has returned with food from her garden." The women did it secretly so that *no man heard them*. "We're going to cut this man," they decided, "and we don't want a single man to hear us or find us or tell the others so that they beat us. Let's be quiet!" they said to each other. "Let's keep it secret!" If the men had said, "Go ahead and eat," the women would just have eaten him. But the men who buried him (*sic*) said, "We will *not* eat him." That's why the women sealed their talk and deceived the men.

After the women had surreptitiously pulled the man off his garden platform, cut him to pieces, loaded the pieces into their net bags and carried them back to his mother's house, they were "discovered" by their husbands.

> Their husbands entered the house and saw them eating. "So! You are eating!" they cried. "Who pulled this man down and cut him?" And the women answered, "That woman, that woman, that woman climbed the ladder and pulled him down and we cut him."

7. Elsewhere I mistakenly reported that women carried the stolen corpse back to "the men's house" and remained secluded there for the duration of their meal (Gillison (1983a:36 ff.). Informants made continual references to the dead man's "own house" which I mistook for his men's house. Women remained (and still remain) in seclusion with the corpse inside the house of his wife or mother. During the various rites which immediately follow a man's death, his close agnates treat his mother's house as his own house or "womb" (see Chap. 4).

"Alright," said the men. "Eat him!" And when you have finished eating, that woman, that woman, and that woman, whoever among you *cut* this man, your pigs shall be killed!" . . . And
the women who had pigs got up and said, "Yes, we will kill our
pigs."

And so when the women had eaten the man, we held a feast.
We killed pigs and celebrated *ruhu*. That is when the women
came out of the house. The women were gathered inside the
house and slept there and didn't come outside until we held
*ruhu*.

Men describe women as having brazenly conspired against their husbands
and cut a man to pieces; yet they say they punished the women only by interning them and killing their pigs—pigs which belonged in reality to the
men and which the men would, in part, give back to the women as the
second course of their meal. In light of the lethal punishment handed out to
a woman who even inadvertently laid eyes on a flute, the treatment of cannibals seems to have been incongruously mild.

Ronomi, a man some three or four years older than Uarafu, recalled that
it took women several days to eat a man and several more days to "sleep off"
and digest him. It was not until dawn of the fifth, sixth, or seventh day after
the men had made their discovery, he reckoned, that they began to kill pigs
for *ruhu*. Uarafu remembered:

When the women had finished eating, we asked them, "Have
you women *completely* finished?" It was wrong to start to kill pigs
while some part of the man was yet uneaten. . . . It was wrong
to eat the man and the pigs at the same time.

Men killed five or ten pigs that belonged to the dead man's
sons and brothers. . . . They killed the pigs of these men and
butchered them.

When the *ababana* had cooked their pigs, they summoned the man or
adolescent boy who had been secluded with the cannibals and asked him to
name the women who had partaken of various parts of the deceased. According to Ronomi:

There was always a man who went to watch. A nothing man.
A small man. A man without a name [i.e., of low status], like
Damabu or Remota or Batekatepu. And a boy, too, went to
watch the women and to help them break firewood and to heat
the stones for the oven. A Big Man like Kenoba or Operada
would never have gone to watch the women! The women and
the man without a name ate the man inside his mother's house
and slept there for three or four or five nights.

When the dead man's brothers and sons had killed their pigs, they called the man who had watched the women and asked him: "Which one ate his hand? Which one ate his leg?" And the man who had watched answered, "That woman ate the hand. That woman ate the leg." . . . And to the woman who had eaten the man's hand men gave the hand of a pig. "Does that satisfy you?" they asked her. As she took the meat, they called out her name. And she answered, "Yes. I am satisfied."

If, as sometimes happened, no man or boy had been secluded with the women and none could report on the conduct of their meal, the paternal kinsmen called upon one or more of the senior women:

"Who ate his head?" we asked. And one woman, a woman who had watched closely, said, "That woman ate the head." And we said, "Alright. Give her the head." And we gave her the head of a pig.

"Who ate his back?" And that one woman spoke out: "She ate the back." And we gave her [part of] the backside of a pig.

"Who ate his hand?" And the woman said, "That woman ate it." And so we gave her the hand of a pig.

"Who ate his other hand?" . . . We gave the two hands to two women and they took them and then we asked, "Who ate his leg?" And the woman who watched well said, "Oh, that one ate it." And so we gave her the leg of a pig.

"Who ate his thigh?" And the woman who watched answered, "Oh, that woman ate the thigh." . . .

"His chest, who ate his chest?" "That woman ate his chest." And we gave the chest of a pig to the woman who had taken his chest.

"Who ate his rib cage?" "Oh, she did." And so we cut a pig's rib cage down the middle and one woman came and took one side of it.

"Who ate the other side of his rib cage?" And that one woman got up and said, "Oh, that woman ate his rib cage." And we held out the other side of the pig's rib cage and she came and took it.

"His intestines, who ate his intestines?" And one woman came forward and we cut the [braided, roasted] pigs' intestines and handed her a section. "Who else ate his intestines? And to the woman who stood up and came forward we gave another section of intestines.

"His heart, who ate his heart?" "Oh, that woman ate it." And we gave her a heart.

"His lungs, who ate his lungs?" "Oh, that woman ate them." And we gave her lungs together with some meat.

"His liver, who ate his liver?" "Oh, that woman ate his liver." And so we gave her a pig's liver and some meat.

"Who ate his stomach?" we asked. And the woman said, "That woman did." And we gave that woman the stomach of a pig. And then we asked, "Who ate his feces?" "Oh," said the woman, "His wife would not throw away his feces! You wanted to eat every part of him" [she said to the wife]. "So you would not throw away his feces. They were something to eat."

"His penis, who ate his penis?" we asked. "Oh, that woman did." And we gave her the penis of a pig.[8]

"His testicles, who ate his testicles?" "That woman and that one did." And so we cut testicles from the pigs we had butchered and gave them to the women. They were for the women. And that was it. Finished!

Men needed many pigs to match the parts of one man because several women were likely to have partaken of a single limb or organ. "The heads and limbs and ribs and backsides—all the bones of the pigs—and the meat and the innards . . . we gave to the women who ate the man. . . . Good men [i.e., men with names] carried the food" and handed a portion to each of the women as a Big Man announced her name and formally ended her confinement.

The paternal kinsmen held in reserve the pigs' whole splayed "skins" as head payments for the *anatiraha* and *abogofa* who had meanwhile arrived from other villages "crying and covered in mud" (see above, this chap.). They also gave head payments to coresident *abogofa*, men who had removed the corpse from the house, carried it on a litter to the garden, helped build the platform and lodge it in a tree, butchered pigs, cut firewood, dug ovens, etc. The *ababana* followed each presentation of meat with the same rhetorical question they had asked the women, "Are you satisfied?"

> For the men who cut down trees and made the fence [around the pandanus tree or stand of bamboo where the body was exposed] we cut meat. . . . On their account we asked, "Who took him and carried him?" "Oh, that man took him and carried

---

8. Another man told me categorically, "The penis was never eaten. It was buried at the base of a bamboo. And the vagina was never eaten. It was buried at the base of a bamboo or a white pandanus. The women ate only the meat on the bones!" These statements contradict the testimony of a third man, cited earlier, who claims to have been invigorated all his life by having eaten the penis as a small boy.

him." And we gave meat to them, too. . . . We gave them the "head."

We gave the "head" to men who came to see us from other places and had covered themselves with mud. Of each one we asked, "Are you satisfied?"

When all the *ruhu* pigs had been distributed and the mourners had dispersed, the widow remained in seclusion. "She alone of all the women did not come outside." She remained inside the house and received a special allotment of meat:

> From one of the *ruhu* pigs we took the head and the whole intestine and the heart and the liver and the lungs and we gave them to the dead man's wife. . . . We handed them to her son, or to her younger brother if he was still uninitiated, and sent them in to her. . . .
>
> She asked her child, "Who gave you this meat?" And the boy answered, "Oh, *he* gave it to me and I brought it to you." And the mother said, "Alright, eat it." All her children ate part of the pig, and later she married the man who had sent it to her.[9]

### Dead Warriors and Delicious Parrots: Why Women Hunger for Men

Women say that their grandmothers pitied the dead and wished to spare them the agony of decomposition. When a warrior fell, women surrounded his body and sang, "Come to me, come to me, lest you rot on the ground." But women also associate cannibalism with anger, not only in the broad parodies of ritual theater but also in threats to "eat" young children who misbehave and in public insults to other women. When one woman accuses another of adultery, she calls her a *kore baðaha*, a "wild woman" (lit: *kore*/wild, spririt or ancestral + *baðaha*/woman), who flies over the village at night and swoops down to "eat men." She describes her vagina as a "stinking black hole," a filthy swamp encrusted with sores and infested with insects. In insults, women imply that the female appetite for men stems not only from pity but also from rage and sexual desire and that it is directed at the living as well as the dead.

---

9. The rules of widow inheritance give first choice to the deceased's co-initiates, those who "saw the flute for the first time" when he did and are his "true brothers," both close patrilateral cousins and distant affines (see Chap. 2). "A widow follows the flute," men say. A man's actual brother was prevented from acquiring his wife by the rules of bride purchase: anyone who contributed pigs to a woman's brideprice and was her *anatu,* including her husband's elder brother, was forbidden to take her as a wife. A purchaser could never a husband be. Reciprocally, a man could not inherit his elder brother's wife because she had contributed to the purchase of his own wife and was, therefore, his "mother."

In men's myths, a cannibal is usually a *kore baðaha,* a rapacious widow eternally in pursuit of a new husband because she devours every man she marries. Her prey are tired warriors, "old men" perched in trees like flightless birds—and exposed corpses.

> An old man climbed a yellow fruit tree. He made a ladder and went up the tree, leaving a boy on the ground. As he climbed, he spied an old enemy, a man with whom he had fought many battles, already ensconced in another yellow fruit tree.
>
> "Comrade!" he cried as he climbed to the top of the tree. "Yes," answered the other man. "I have arrived!" "Why have you come?" the other man asked. "I have just come [i.e., come in peace]," he said.
>
> A widow climbed the ladder in pursuit of the old man. "O delicious parrot! O delicious parrot," she sang as she climbed higher. "Who are you?" she asked him. "And who are *you?*" the man replied. . . . She carried a long sharp stick and thrust it up the man's anus, burying it deep inside him until it came out his mouth. "Ahhhhhh!" he cried. "What are you doing? I want to talk to you!" "But I am not listening!" the woman said. Before he died, the man gasped, "I came to shoot the parrot that eats the yellow fruit of the tree!"
>
> "O delicious parrot! O delicious parrot!" the widow sang happily. Her husband had died the day before, and she wondered, "Where shall I find another?" Then she found that man [in the tree] and took him for a husband!
>
> The widow climbed the other tree. "O delicious parrot! O delicious parrot!" she sang. . . . Hearing her song, the old man called out, "Come up here!" . . . "Get up here fast," he said to himself, "I'm going to kill you! . . . You cannot simply kill my comrade and get away."
>
> Up and up and up she climbed until she saw him above her. "I have come to hear what you have to say," she said. But the man went down the tree to where the boy was standing and, without so much as a greeting [lit: without saying even, "Are you staying? Are you leaving?"], got a stick. . . . [while from above he still heard] "O delicious parrot! O delicious parrot!"
>
> He climbed back up the tree and saw the woman sitting there. Up and up and up he climbed and, when he was higher [than she], she thrust her long sharp stick up his anus, burying it deep inside him, and he died. Her husband had put himself above her and she thought, "I wanted to marry this man but—what do you think?—his skin was all wrinkled!"

She pulled him down out of the tree and cut him into small pieces and fed them to her fatherless children. . . . That is how women used to finish off us men!

That woman would have killed man after man after man until there was not one of us left. And when she went in search of a husband, whom would she have found? She would have looked in tree after tree after tree until she came upon the boy standing on the ground. . . . So would the *kore ba ϑaha* have reduced our kind to a single boy had we not uprooted the wild grasses and wild banana and planted them, closing her way into the wild.

To find a husband, the "wild woman" climbs a tree like a hunter in search of "delicious parrots." But the bird she finds turns out to be wrinkled and old and to have "put himself above her." She kills him in a fury—without listening to a word he has to say—and makes herself again into a widow. Left to her own devices, the *kore ba ϑaha* would finish off every man in every tree, leaving only the boy standing at the base, a "bird" who may be flightless—uninitiated and without sexual prowess—but who is also un-wrinkled and truly "delicious". Had men not taken the steps they did, the *kore ba ϑaha* would have killed every husband and married the boy at the base of the tree, a boy she had made "fatherless" like her own sons.

The myth concludes with a standard refrain, describing how men cur-tailed the limitless appetites of "wild women" by uprooting wild grasses, a symbol of woman's pubic hair, and the wild banana, a plant whose fibrous stem sorcerers use as a substitute for the "soft rotten inside" of a vagina, and by planting them inside the settlement. "We keep women out of the wild," men say, "by marrying them with *ba ϑa ϑa* [brideprice]." Unrestrained by marriage, men's myth alleges, women would act out insatiable desires and turn bad just like unattended plants that grow overabundant and spoil in the forest.

The characters in men's myth have obvious counterparts in *ruhu*. The vet-eran of many battles who climbs the fruit tree on a ladder is like a dead war-rior being lifted into a tree in his garden. The boy he leaves at the base of the tree, in a position to observe what happens above him, is like the boy or man of low status whom men sent to watch women's cannibal meal. And the *kore ba ϑaha* who impales every man she "marries," cuts him to pieces and feeds the pieces to her children, is like a caricature of cannibal mothers, especially the widow who feeds her children meat supplied by the man who intends to be her next husband. Whereas the mythic widow finds a husband and feeds him to her children, the ritual widow finds a husband by "eating his meat" and sharing it with her children, accepting as an engagement present parts of pigs already identified with the body of her dead husband.

The association of the mythic widow with the actual widow, and with other women mourners, seems to have extended as well to men related to the deceased through women, that is, to the maternal kinsmen who came afterward to "eat his head." The women and the matrilaterally related men—the female and male "mothers" of the deceased in the Gimi idiom—behaved in similar ways and evoked similar, ritually mandated responses from the "fathers." The women's "theft" of the corpse and the maternal kinsmen's rampage were each permitted by the *ababana*. By remaining ignorant of women's plot, the *ababana* allowed the corpse to be stolen; and by refusing to protect their compound and property they allowed the *anatiraha* to work havoc. Yet, in each instance, the men who were the victims of these crimes became indebted to the malefactors: though "mothers and sisters" ate the man, the *ababana* had to supply a second course to their meal; and though the *anatiraha* ruined their compound, uprooted trees and fences, burned houses, etc., it was the *ababana* who made reparation by "giving the head" and inquiring solicitously in each case, "Are you satisfied?"

The conventions of *ruhu* demanded that the participants adopt attitudes and enact sentiments that were at odds not only with their ordinary secular relationships, in which men stayed inside their houses while women prepared and served food, and affines stayed enemies, but also with the events of *ruhu* itself. The rage and desperation of cannibal women and of matrilateral kinsmen, and the resignation of the *ababana*, were poses that seemed to correspond not to the logic of what transpired during the ritual but to the attitudes of mythic counterparts, to the fury of the widow in search of "delicious parrots," and to the powerlessness of the impaled warriors, or of the boy who stood at the base of the tree and could only watch the couple in the branches above him. Viewed in these terms, the feast of *ruhu* ended the mythic era of "wild" marriage and defeated the *kore baðaha* by instating brideprice, substituting head payments for the men—and boys—she preferred.

Interpreted in light of men's myth, women's supposed "theft" of the corpse staged a return to mythic beginnings that preempted the basis of kinship and served men as pretext to celebrate *ruhu*, a feast that repaired the catastrophe of women's act by substituting pigs for human flesh in a precise redoing of the cannibal meal. Men put back order, as it were, by curtailing women's appetites with a second course of new meat, a payment for the head of the deceased that was tantamount to the invention of brideprice. But to tame wild women, to uproot wild grasses and the wild banana in the context of ritual, the *ababana* had to placate not only the women themselves but also their paternal kinsmen, presenting male affines with the "skins" of pigs whose "bones and meat and innards" they had already given to the women cannibals.

*Chapter Three*

## The Flight of the Torrent Lark: Women's Counterportrait
## of a Cannibal

When the events of *ruhu* are considered in terms not only of men's myth of Delicious Parrots but also of a myth women tell about the origin of cannibalism, the reasons for placating the *anatiraha,* and the complexity of women's ritual motivation, begin to emerge. In women's account, the *kore baꝺaha* is not a harridan but a beautiful girl. And the "wrinkled old bird" ensconced in a tree is not a noble veteran of countless wars but the girl's own father who "tricks" her into marriage. In revenge, she kills their child and presents it to him as his evening meal. She kills the firstborn, acting not out of mere appetite like the widow in men's myth, but to annul an incestuous marriage, a marriage without brideprice. She kills her child to feed her husband, treating *him* as the cannibal. When he tries to shoot her, she changes into a Torrent Lark and escapes into the forest.

> A woman bore and reared a beautiful daughter. Men wanted to marry her. "Marry me!" one man said. "Marry me!" said another. "Marry me!" said another. All the men said, "I want her!" She was a beauty, one of a kind.
>
> Mother and daughter lived in a house in the forest. One day the old woman spied a possum in a tree and she called out to her husband to shoot it. An ugly old man came instead and shot the possum. While he was still up in the tree, he gutted it and emptied the feces into a narrow bamboo tube. He tucked the tube behind his ear so it was hidden in his hair.
>
> The man climbed down the tree and said to the two women, "Soon it will be dark"—although darkness was not close. "There is no time to reach your house in the light," he said. So the three of them went to sleep in a lean-to with a roof of dried sugarcane leaves [i.e., a hunting lodge or assignation site].
>
> The two women ate the possum and fell fast asleep facing each other. The old man slept with his head lost inside the buttocks of the beautiful girl. During the night the old woman awoke. She blew on the embers of the fire and saw her daughter and the man. "Oh!" she cried, "This man sleeps with his head in my daughter's buttocks!" She looked again and saw feces in the man's eyes. She woke her daughter: "You have defecated in his eyes!" she cried. "While he slept you defecated on him!"
>
> The girl awoke and looked at the old man. He had spread the possum feces on his face and over her buttocks. She thought she had done it in her sleep. At dawn her mother said to her, "You must marry him." And they were married.

The girl became pregnant and, because she was a story-woman, a *nenebaϑaha* [lit: *nene*/story + *baϑaha*/woman], she bore a child in no time. One day the old woman came to help the couple weed their new taro garden and overheard her son-in-law singing to his child:

> I got you from the feces of a possum, the feces of a possum.
> The feces of a possum gave me my son! . . .
> Not by pleading and pleading—but by feces [and feces]!
> —Did I get a son!

Hearing the ditty, the old woman knew that the son her daughter bore was the child of a trick. "You tricked us with possum feces," she thought and told her daughter. "I am sick at heart [lit: my stomach is broken]," her daughter said. "I married a rotten man."

The young wife took her baby out of her net bag and laid him on the ground. She went down to the lower reaches of the river and found leaves of a ficus tree—leaves that are black on top and red underneath. She tried them on as if they were the tail feathers of a Torrent Lark, a *neterebuϑa*, and they fit well. She took more ficus leaves and put them on her chest, first on one side, then on the other. They were like the feathers of a lark. Without difficulty, she flew down to the river estuary and back to its source high in the mountains.

When she was sure she could fly, she killed her son and prepared an oven. She peeled taros and bananas and tied greens into bundles and . . . placed her child on his side [i.e., in the fetal position] at the bottom of the oven. She added arm bands and knee bands and covered him with food on all sides and closed the oven.

That is how it is told.

When the cooking time was over, her husband arrived and said, "Why don't you empty the oven?" But she said, "You do it. I worked hard to fill the oven. So now you empty it." And so he did.

The husband unloaded the layers of food, going deeper and deeper into the oven. He took a bite and said, "What I eat doesn't taste sweet to me." Finding an upper arm band he cried, "Ah! What is this?" "Oh," said his wife, "I carried the food in the bag I use for the baby."

The husband continued to unload the oven, going deeper and deeper and deeper. . . . "I see the child's knee bands!" he exclaimed. But again his wife said, "Never mind. I used the child's net bag to carry home the food." The man went deeper and deeper into the oven until he saw one wrist band . . . then another . . . but he said, "You used the child's net bag." "Yes," the wife said. "Now just eat!"

At last the man saw his son, his body shriveled like a suckling pig, the hands and feet curled so tightly that the anklebones and wristbones protruded through the skin. "*ki'3oooooome* [lit: *ki'3*/guilt, remorse]!" he cried. "My child!"

The old man went into the house and tightened his bow. He was going to kill his wife. But she had already attached ficus leaves to her hips. She jabbed a ripe red pandanus fruit with a long stick and the oil gushed out noisily, covering her body. She climbed onto the fence and then leaped in a single bound to the top of a stand of sugarcane, and from there to the roof of the house. Back and forth, back and forth, she moved [trying to take off]. . . . In a moment she was crying "*netere, netere, netere*" and flying to the river's edge. Her husband tried to shoot her, but she had flown away.

One man who helped me translate this version of women's myth commented:

Originally men got wives without brideprice. Women went into the forest, spotted marsupials, and called out to men to come and kill them and give them to women to eat. Men came when women called and tricked them into marriage. But after we uprooted the wild banana and wild grasses and planted them, we married women with brideprice instead of tricks! Brideprice did away with the *kore ba∂aha*. She is gone forever. She is the Torrent Lark who lives on the shore.

Some men, he added, still use tricks to marry women:

When a man is attracted to a girl of a distant place . . . he opens a vein inside his elbow and fills a small bamboo tube with his blood. He hides the tube in his rear skirt and arrives at the girl's house to spend the night. When they have finished their love play and she is fast asleep, he pours his blood into her skirts so it runs between her legs. After a while he wakes her and asks her to fetch a light. . . .

"What's this?" he exclaims when she comes back. "Something of yours is all over me!" He smeared the blood on himself, too. The girl is terribly ashamed because she thinks the Moon has killed her for the first time. She wakes her mother, "Oh, mother! The Moon has killed me!" she cries. And her mother says, "He is your *abogo*. You must marry him."

That is how some men still use tricks to get a wife from a distant place.

A man tricking a woman into marriage is "the same," my translator allowed, as the Moon killing her. Both "men" act while she is asleep or unaware.

In the *nenekaina*, the Moon comes to earth in the guise of an "ugly old man." The old woman calls for her husband, but the old man shows up instead and she accepts him unquestioningly. Even when he tells an obvious lie, saying it is nearly dark "though darkness was not close," the old woman and her daughter agree to spend the night with him in a hunting lodge, the site of assignations, and they eat the food he kills, behaving in conventional Gimi terms as his wife and daughter. The daughter marries the "old man," the Moon, and he produces her first menstruation in the form of "trick" feces. But after bearing a child, she reverses the situation and herself provokes the flow of blood, using her stick to jab the ripe red pandanus fruit so the oil gushes over her and enables her to take off on a flight of liberation. In the end, the old man discovers his son at the bottom of the oven, knarred and shriveled like a suckling pig, and cries out "*ki'3!*" He is now the recipient of a gift of meat and the one filled with remorse. He married "without brideprice," stealing sex from his own daughter, "losing his head inside her" while she was unaware and a child, still sleeping with him under the same roof. "Theft" connotes adultery in everyday parlance: an adulterer is literally a "thieving man," an adulteress a "thieving woman." In myth, where everything that happens happens for the first time, "theft," or "marrying without brideprice," connotes incest.

### The Concept of Guilt and Trading of Blame in Myth

The Gimi notion of *ki'3* is similar to our concept of guilt. As one man explained:

> When you are a child and your mother spanks you, and you feel the pain, and you think a long time about what you did to make her angry, and you cry because you are sorry, that is *ki'3.* . . . When you fight with your husband, and go over and over in your thoughts what happened between you, and you cry because you are filled with regret, that is *ki'3.* . . . *ki'3* is what you feel afterward.

*ki'3* is used idiomatically with *aobaE*, the verb that expresses feeling, sensation, body need, or hunger. For example:

| | |
|---|---|
| I am hungry for sweet potato | *mihi naobaE* |
| I feel like smoking [lit: I hunger for tobacco] | *sobo' naobaE* |
| I feel like/have the urge to urinate/defecate | *abe/are naobaE* |
| I hurt [lit: I feel pain inside my skin/body] | *naupi nasisi naobaE* |
| I miss/am lonesome for my son/my mother | *namabu/nano'z naobaE* |

While one may hunger for food or tobacco or feel the absence of a relative, one doesn't lack pain or urine but is rather discomfited by an excess and moved to expel it. Sensations, needs, urges, feelings, and desires arise either from the loss of what should be inside or in contact with the body (e.g., food, tobacco, mother, etc.), or from the wish to expel what originates there (e.g., urine, feces, heat, cold, itchiness, pain, etc.). According to the usage of *aobaE,* to feel is to feel deprived or about to be deprived, to miss or sense the imminent loss of part of oneself, to have need of *bodily* reparation. To eat or satisfy any craving is thus *to get rid of an absence,* to repair the lack of food, to put back something—or someone—who arose as part of the self and was expelled or lost.

The Gimi self depicted by the multiple uses of *aobaE* encompasses objects, states, and relations of the external world. The acts and feelings of others, my mother hitting me, my husband's anger, etc., originated inside me—and are my fault—in the sense that they are the offspring of things I did, the consequence and replication of deeds that escaped me with the same inevitability as my own urine or sweat. I can mitigate my suffering, and undo the pain and injury others inflict, by putting back what I lost, repairing my own depletion, refilling myself, *replacing the contents of my body* to "cool" the hot ache of guilt and loss. "Their bodies ached from hunger so they ate the man and eating him made them cool," women say of their cannibal ancestresses. "I hunger for the man who died," one woman said, explaining why women, especially widows, still blacken their faces and cover their bodies with clay and mud to "hold the spirit" of the deceased (see below, this chap; also Chap. 5). "I put on *nini* and *abiare* and the *ki'z* stays in my stomach."

In women's myth of the Torrent Lark, the one afflicted with *ki'z*, the one presented with a cannibal meal is not the new wife but the trickster-husband. Yet women's tale is not a simple inversion of men's story of Delicious Parrots. It seems to exonerate the *kore baðaha* by portraying her as a beautiful girl tricked into marriage, but it also implicates the mother by implying her complicity with the old man. At the very outset he tells an obvious lie, saying it is nearly dark "though darkness was not close" and suggesting the three sleep together in a tiny lodge lovers use for assignations, giving immediate cause for suspicion. By showing that the mother has reason to know about the father from the start, the women's tale hints that she colluded with him by offering her daughter, letting him sleep with his head "lost in her buttocks," and then insisting they marry.

Women's myth of the Torrent Lark speaks to men's myth through certain structural parallels. The ugly old man, beautiful girl, and murdered baby on the ground replicate the tired warrior, cannibal widow, and boy at the base of the tree. By adding the old woman to the nuclear triad of man-wife-child, the women's tale identifies the "old man in the tree" as trickster-father. It expands the men's version by suggesting *why* every husband turns out, upon close inspection, to be old and "wrinkled" and "on top" and, therefore, why the *kore ba ϑaha* is always enraged. Analyzed in terms of myths of both sexes, women's ritual fury, frenzy, and appetite derive not from simple grief nor a wish to spare the dead a slow decay, as women declare, but rather from the logic of an incestuous drama, a mythic first marriage that drove woman to murder her husband—or his child—out of a complex mix of guilt and revenge. By presenting cannibal women with a second course of pork, and then offering the "skins" of the same pigs to their paternal kinsmen, the deceased's *ababana* attempted to restore order—not simply by organizing in retrospect a chaotic first course—but also by undoing the incestuous marriage that precipitated it. The *ababana* offered to placate women in a collective, mythic sense for their fathers having "tricked" them into marriage and made them menstruate; for men having "stolen wives" and married them with possum feces instead of the real meat of brideprice.

In terms of women's myth, the rampaging *anatiraha* are ritual counterparts of trickster-fathers, stand-ins for the Moon or primordial husband who cried "*ki'ʒ*" because—though his wife killed and cooked the child—he is secretly to blame for knowing all along and *not paying*, for giving her feces instead of "the child's head." When the *ababana* distribute the "gift of the head" to *anatiraha* to assuage their inordinate grief and convince them to end their rampage and "go home," in this sense, they attempt to buy off the first husband, to persuade the old man to stop tricking the girl into marriage so that she, in turn, will stop converting their firstborn to "Moon's blood." In the logic of women's myth, the deceased's "fathers" treat his "mothers" and "mothers' brothers" collectively as substitutes for the original parents, providing them with the inducement to stop marrying and "killing their firstborn" so that the child—who was the deceased—can come to life in a forest afterworld. I return to these themes in Chapter 4.

### The Aftermath of ruhu

Though Gimi no longer practice cannibalism, women still go into seclusion when a man or woman dies, and men still summon them by name at the end

A performance of ritual theater depicting the retrieval of a Big Man's skull by his mother and his wife. According to the play's scenario, the man's wife had given birth to a child, prompting him to hunt marsupials for the *ϑau*, or naming ceremony (see Chap. 8). But his enemies were lying in wait inside the forest and shot him. When he did not return home, his mother and his wife set out to look for him and came upon the hunting lodge where he had slept. Suddenly, from behind a tree, his wife spotted his head, which was singing by itself (*upper left*). She took off the net bag on her head, inside which lay her newborn child, and handed it to her mother-in-law. Then she reached down to take hold of her husband's animated skull (*lower left; upper right*). With her child back on her head, she gathered up the rest of her husband's bones (*lower right*)

and carried them back to the settlement where his kinsmen killed pigs and prepared to celebrate *ruhu*.

The three women players cover themselves in the gray clay of mourning and use the fibrous root of a fern tree to represent the Big Man's skull. The woman holding a rope of vine attached to one end of the root plays the part of the dead man's singing ghost, and she manipulates his "head" as if it had a life of its own. The woman in the center of the four images plays the widow. The third player (sidelined *lower left* and *upper right* and not seen in *lower right*) is the dead man's mother.

of a week or so, presenting each one with "matching" portions of cooked pork. Women coat their bodies with thick layers of gray or yellow clay and blacken their faces with a mixture of fat and soot to "hold the *auna* on their skins." Some women tear the deceased's clothes and net bags and use the shreds to make armbands, kneebands, skirts, and turbans. After a man decomposes, his mother retrieves his skull and wears it at the back of her head, hanging inside a net bag. Other women make neck amulets of his hair, teeth, and finger joints. In the same way as men accuse women of having stolen the corpse and eaten it alone "without ritual," they say the mourning decorations are "entirely women's idea," "something only women do" when men are not around.

In the case of a man, the *ababana* celebrate an elaborate series of rites in the year following death, each designed to remove women's decorations and each conducted like a lesser version of *ruhu*. Men assemble the mourning women and have them sit in a row, calling each one by name and presenting her with cooked meat in exchange for her divesting herself of the dead man's clothes, burning the clothes and consigning the ashes to a clan-owned river; removing the blackening from her face; handing over bundles of the dried spines of ferns she consumed, together with red pandanus, during a symbolically cannibalistic meal (see Chap. 5). Time and again, in rites held over the course of a whole year, men compel the mourning women to give back the man they surreptitiously absorbed or put on.

The implication of the entire series of death rites, as I suggest in Chapter 5, is that the *symbolic* act of cannibalism makes women lose their individuality, makes them share with the dead not only an appalling smell and appearance, and an immobility due to a moratorium on garden work, but also a creeping anonymity. By announcing women's names in rite after rite, breaching what is ordinarily a strong taboo, men make women publicly accountable, giving them back an identity as guilty party, making them subject to a new order in which they give up one mythic identity and take on another: in exchange for men's gift of other meat, women give up the leaves of the Torrent Lark and collectively assume the whole blame for death in accordance with men's myth.

The yearlong series of death rites, in which men buy back women's decorations and other sacred residues of their symbolic meal, precedes or coincides with the transportation of the bones into special niches of the clan forest. "Only men can take the bones," one woman told me. "And when men take the bones into the forest they don't come back in a hurry!" They decorate skull and jaw with red cordyline and lodge them in the forked branch of a tree, or set them in a row beside other "large bones," like femurs, inside a cave at the source of a river or waterfall. In the past, men say, women dried finger bones in the sun, ground them to powder, and used the powder to make a blood pudding. But nowadays, and in the recent past, men bury these "small bones" at the base of a bamboo or pandanus or other "wild" tree with red blossoms. Bones of the legs, arms, and torso are traditionally placed in the hollow crevices of trees or stuffed inside the trunk of a hoop pine that has been stripped of bark. After inserting the bones, men put back the bark and encircle the trunk with vines.

When Gimi first started to bury the dead, women say, men took pains to "clean" the bones by building a drying rack near the grave, exposing the bones to the sun and rain until all the mud and adhering flesh were gone, and then placing them in the rafters of the dead man's house. Women complain that men do not bother anymore. "They bury the body and forget the bones. I feel so sorry for the man. I get his bones myself and bring them to his house."

As bones decompose over the course of years, they release the spirit held in their porous or hollow cores. Men associate bones with the penis and consider marrow, nasal mucous, and gray matter to consist of *aðuso*, the same glutinous light-colored stuff that generates semen. "When a man ejaculates, the *aðuso* in his head and in his bones flows into his penis making it hard as a bone," one man explained. "A woman pulls out all a man's *aðuso* in the moment he ejaculates. And when he loses his semen, he loses all his *aðabuna*, his strength [lit: *aðapu*/bone + *na*/thing]." Bones house a man's spirit after he dies in the same way his penis once held semen: their disintegration is like a slow but endless ejaculation. The caves, niches, and interior spaces of the clan forest where Gimi men traditionally carried their kinsman's bones symbolize the female interior: in the imagery of male initiation songs, the hollow cavities in tree trunks where marsupials nest stand for "wombs" or "vaginas"; the fork of a branch is a woman's "crotch," men reveal, and the red flowers of vines that cling to it are "like menstrual blood." The dissolution of a man's bones enriches his clan forest, giving rise to new life forms in the way semen engenders life in a woman's body.

But the female orifices of the forest exist inside male bodies: the trees where hollows form, the mountains where caves lie hidden, etc., are monumental phalli (Gillison 1980:170). Though men name woman's anatomy in discussing initiation songs, their other remarks suggest that the songs evoke birth as a moment of ejaculation, as the sudden flight of a flock of birds, startled by a hunter's arrow, out of a sunlit treetop, as the unexpected emergence of a stream or river from a mountain cave, as the explosive ripening of fruit in the upper branches of a giant tree, etc. The gigantic formations of the surrounding rain forest represent ultimate evolutions of male ancestral spirit. Life in the "wild"—which is the source and essence of human existence—is the issue of dead Gimi men, the material result of their bones decomposing inside the niches of ancient forebears. But living men have to guarantee this cyclic issuing forth by transporting their comrades' bones into clan forests. When women stole a corpse and ate it, in these terms, they took everything with which to regenerate life-in-the-world and made it disappear inside their bodies. The consumed man's sons and brothers initiated the yearlong series of exchanges, in this sense, in order to buy back from the women all of life in the visible world.

In the past, men claim, their ancestors exposed the dead in trees to allow the flesh to rot and be washed away by the rains. When men installed a corpse on a platform, they say, they intended to let it rot and to retrieve the cleaned bones two or three months later, climbing the ladder and using sticks or special tongs to lift the "hot" remains.[10] But the thing men were forced instead to buy back from women was a superior product. The bones of a man women had eaten—or even handled, as I argue in Chapter 4— were a potent concentration of his spirit, the digested essence of his being, which would not have existed had the women left him in peace on his platform. In the sense that *ruhu* was a jointly constructed show of conflict between the sexes, it also concealed their common interest in preserving and elevating male spirit (Gillison 1980:161).

The importance of connecting Gimi myth and ritual is not simply to demonstrate that characters in myth have ritual counterparts or vice versa, or even that the motives of mythic characters explain the proforma attitudes and emotions of ritual actors, that the rage of the mythic widow applied both to cannibal women and to *anatiraha* who demanded to "eat the head," or that the helplessness of dead warriors translated into the required passivity of the *ababana*, etc. What I argue eventually is that, in determining the ritual scenario, the logic of mythic sentiments also provides the motivating premise of Gimi marriage and exchange and explains why women and men say that brideprice and head payments are "the same." The purpose of "feeding angry women" and handing over head payments to rampaging *anatiraha*, in these terms, is to enter woman's mythic prehistory and cancel her devastating first marriage. While the marriage is no more than a myth, its deadly consequences are as real and recurrent as menstruation, miscarriage, and death itself.

According to men's account of Delicious Parrots, death is the consequence of women's cannibal desires. While it seems that Gimi women sometimes ate the dead in the past, especially the corpses of kinsmen killed in war, mortuary rites treat women mourners, then and now, as if they had all

---

10. One woman told me that, in the past, after women had pulled a man down off his "bed," cut him, and eaten him, they placed his bones on the platform to "trick the men" into thinking he had not been eaten.

been cannibals at some unseen time, as if, like the *kore ba ϑaha,* they had impaled the warriors, murdered the firstborn, cut off the giant penis, etc. The mourners' identification with the first woman is expressed in their loss of individuality, symbolized in the ritual when they blacken their faces, don the deceased's relics, and forfeit their own names. At the end of the mourning period, men give back the women's names and present them with head payments in exchange for residues of the dead. But men's reinstating gift is also an accusation: it purchases the head woman severed and stole, the firstborn child she turned to blood, etc. The ritual intervenes in the mythic scenario and delays the terrible outcome, in this sense, by converting the premise of woman's guilt—articulated in different ways and to different degrees in the myths of both sexes—into the social basis of female identity. Men invent themselves as fathers, and guarantee the continuity of life, by shifting the whole blame for death onto women, defining wives and mothers as those who cut off the head in a fury, and fathers as those who undo women's crime and give the child new life by rescuing the severed "head," carrying it into the forest, and putting it into circulation among ancestors and men. I return to these themes in the next chapter.

# FOUR

# The Death of a Man in His Prime

## Posthumous Adventures of a Man's Spirit

When a man is near death, his cohorts carry him out of the men's house to the house of his mother, if she is alive, or to his wife's house, and lay him on a mat beside the fire. His mother, wife, and sisters, including his father's brothers' daughters, begin a wailing vigil and laying-on of hands, stroking his head and body and swatting away flies with cordyline wisks. If the man lingers, "his mother gets up and says, 'Pull out the stone and let him die!'" as one man described it. "She takes a stone from around the fire to open the way for his *auna*. His *auna* wants to go to Australia and the stone blocks his way."

At the moment of death the women cry shrilly and press closer, running their hands over his torso, lifting his arms and legs and squeezing his joints, and caressing his fingers. They bend forward to kiss him one at a time and then sit upright, their heads moving up and down like birds drinking from the rim of a fountain. The mother stands up and dances beside his head, shaking her hands and lifting her feet in tiny frenzied steps. She kneels to kiss his face and then cradles his arm in hers, rocking it in time to the women's shrill chants. In the hours that follow, the dead man's age-mates, brothers and father's brothers—but not his own father—come to kneel among the women who surround his body. "You only sleep!" the men chant. "Stop playing with me! Stop trying to fool me! Come Back! Hear what I say! Come back!" Before the men leave, one or two place bank notes on his chest to sustain his *auna* on the journey to Australia.

Soon after dark on the night following death, the men order the women out of the house. They move the corpse next to the wall so that the top of the head nearly touches it and then leave the hut, sealing the doorway in the traditional manner by stacking planks across the opening and lashing them together with vines. The men bring a bamboo pole about nine feet long which they have "emptied" by rupturing or removing the interior lateral sections. The pole is covered with dark green cordyline leaves and has a "mouth" at one end indicated by a clump of red and orange foliage. The men tear a hole in the wall of the house adjacent to the head of the corpse and insert the "mouth" end of the bamboo pole until it almost touches the fontanel. A few men roll tobacco leaves into crude cigarettes and blow thick puffs of smoke onto both sides of the long protruding end of the pole. "We blow and blow and call out his name and our smoke enters the bamboo. 'Come inside, you!' Come inside and show us! Show us the man who killed you!"

After some time, the *kore riϑi* or "ghost bamboo" (lit: *kore*/ghost + *riϑi*/bamboo) begins to vibrate. "The moment the [dead man's] *kore* enters the bamboo . . . it gets terribly heavy and starts to shake!" Five or six men pull in unison, and as they dislodge the pole from the wall of the house they let go of it and pile on top of one another, forced to the ground by the gyrations of the *kore*. A moment later, two men pick up the stilled bamboo and place it on their shoulders so it rests between them. A ritual expert, who is also the deceased's classificatory father, begins to prance beside the pole, his tiny, mincing steps recalling the mother's dance beside the head of the corpse. He holds an arrow to whose tip is tied a clump of cordyline leaves that hide a wad of the dead man's hair pulled out from above his fontanel. The expert dances parallel to the length of the bamboo, passing the arrow-wand above it as he makes his way slowly toward the mouth. As he approaches the end, he charges forward and touches the mouth with his wand. "Arise!" he cries in a hoarse whisper. "Arise! You are no small boy who has died! Tell me who worked sorcery against you. Take me to the house of the man who killed you! Show it to me! Come outside of your mother's house and enter the bamboo!"

Still prancing, the spell-sayer backs away and makes a new approach, tapping the mouth of the *kore riϑi* with his wand and repeating his commands. But the pole lies motionless between the shoulders of the two younger men. The spell-sayer lights a cigarette, fills his mouth with smoke and blows it into the mouth of the bamboo. Everyone stands back as if he expects the pole to erupt in movement, but it lies still and the spell-sayer continues his efforts. He rubs the red end of the bamboo with the tip of his wand, smokes many cigarettes and blows the smoke into the pole to fill the hollow chamber. Afterward, he calls the dead man's name and incites his *kore* to revenge.

After ten minutes or so the pole begins to vibrate, and, if the movements do not quickly become stronger, one of the men holding it is replaced. Then the pole shakes violently, pivots in a circle, and heads off with a crash into a nearby fence or stand of wild sugarcane. The men reel backward, moving exactly as if they could barely hold an object propelled from within. Armed men run behind the *kore riϑi* in a V-formation while others run alongside it carrying flares, hooting and shouting war cries as they climb the steep, rocky paths that connect the compounds of the village. On a ridge or in a muddy clearing, the men may stop suddenly, alternate carriers, and change course. As the *kore riϑi* and its armed escort move erratically through the night, compounds become deserted and silent. People stay out of sight, the men say, because they know the bamboo will not hesitate to kill the one it seeks:

> The bamboo moves with great speed because it doesn't want the killer to get away! If it finds the man . . . it crashes into his house . . . and smashes his eyes and nose and kills him. No one can hold the bamboo then because the dead man's *kore* is inside it!

The *kore riϑi* makes an accusation by returning three or four times by different routes to the same compound and turning in circles outside the same house. The men holding the pole rush at the house, making a loud, imploding hiss like a war cry, but back off at the critical moment because the bamboo falters, "realizing" the man it seeks is not inside his house—put to flight, no doubt, by one of the *kore riϑi*'s earlier appearances. After leading the men on several circuits of the village, the *kore riϑi* returns to the house where the corpse lies. Men lay the long pole on the ground and dismantle it, destroying the leafy decorations so they cannot fall into sorcerer's hands. Like any decorations or exuviae, both of which are called *autaisana,* literally "body-leavings" (*au*/body or skin covering the body-surface + *tai*/dir. + *sa*/poss. + *na*/thing), the leaves men tied onto the *kore riϑi* are invested with the dead man's *auna* and can be used by a sorcerer to work new spells against other members of his clan or lineage.[1]

---

1. Codrington describes a similar practice in the Banks' Islands:

> After a burial they would take a bag and put *make*, Tahitian chestnut, and scraped banana into it. Then a new bamboo some ten feet long was fitted to the bag and tied with one end in the mouth of it, and the bag was laid upon the grave, the men engaged in the affair holding the bamboo in their hands. The names of the recently dead were then called, and the men holding the bamboo felt the bag become heavy with the entrance of the ghost, which then went up from the bag into the hollow of the bamboo. The bamboo and its contents being carried into the village, the names of dead men were called over to find out whose ghost it was: when wrong names were called the free end of the bamboo moved from side to side while the other was held tight, at the right name the end moved briskly round and round. Then questions were put to the enclosed ghost, "Who stole such a thing? Who was guilty in such a case?" The bamboo pointed itself at the culprit if present, or made signs as before when names were called. This bamboo they say would run about with a man who had it lying only on the palms of his hands; but, it is remarked by my native informant, though it moved in men's hands it never moved when no one touched it. (1891:211–12)

Chapter Four

## *How the* kore riϑi *Works*

One of the men who accompanied the *kore riϑi* on its nighttime excursion told me the next day that the pole was impelled by his kinsman's *auna* as if "he had only gone to sleep at night and dreamed," as if his *auna* were exploring the village as it often did during dreams. On the night after his death, men of his lineage constructed the *kore riϑi* so they could follow his dreaming *auna* and see what —and whom— it saw while he lay "asleep" inside his mother's house. *auna* is the life force that motivates people, pigs, and other sentient beings including the *kore* or ghost. It arises in the head and moves in the blood to the heart, producing pulse and heartbeat. *auna* fills the lungs, liver, and other organs with "wind" and is exuded in breath, voice, sweat, tears, intestinal gas, feces, urine, semen or vaginal secretions and in every *autaisana* (see Kelly 1976:37 ff.). During dreams and at death, *auna* leaves the body through the fontanel and "flies" toward the forest. The dreaming *auna* embarks upon a journey that the dreamer sees while he sleeps, sometimes entering a bird or marsupial and moving above the village. A person's *auna* is like an errant "child" or *anu,* literally, "fetus" or "spirit-child." It has appetite and curiosity, men say, "the same as a man":

> When you go to sleep at night your "child" is inside you the same as your *auna.* It's like breath, like the air that moves inside your body. At night, it goes out to wander. You sleep and forget the things around you. . . . You die because your "child" has deserted you and gone away! You sleep deeply until the moment it returns. Then you feel hungry and wake up.
>
> When you go to sleep at night you go outside yourself. In the morning, a woman doesn't wake her husband. She waits until his "child" returns. . . . And a man doesn't wake his wife. He doesn't caress her while she sleeps nor come near her bed nor raise his voice. He lets her sleep until her *auna* comes back into her head and settles again in her heart. . . .
>
> Your child is like a man [i.e., a person]. Do you get hungry? Well, it gets hungry too . . . and goes out at night to look for something to eat while *you* go to sleep. When your child goes away, you are wrecked . . . wrecked completely and cannot stay awake.

Death is a permanent dream-journey: the *anu* or *auna* departs in the last breath which is exhaled—not through the nose or mouth as any other breath—but through the "opened" fontanel. Once the breath passes through the fontanel it can never reenter the body. When a man is seriously wounded or at the point of death, his comrades knot the hair above his fontanel to stop his breath from "running away." They cover the knot with a piece of bark and press the bark in place by wrapping the head with vines. As death nears, however, the *auna* becomes increasingly volatile. The last breath passes through the remedial barriers of knotted hair and bark with the same inevitability as a child is born. A man's fontanel is literally his "first mouth" (*forita'ara*/first, front or vanguard + *asa*/mouth), as a second ritual expert explained:

> When a man is about to die, I cover his first mouth. . . . That closes the passage. . . . When a child is born we cover the head. Do you know why? Because of the way we are born, because of the way we come out of our mothers. Women have us inside them. And then we come out *here* [gesturing to his crotch]— and we don't come down legs first! We dome down *head first.* . . . That's why, when a man is about to die, I put bark in his hair and close his first mouth. . . .
>
> Our hearts have breath in them. When a man's breath tries to leave him it cannot get out because I have closed the exit. Other men don't know how to do this . . . so many good men die for nothing!

When a man is near death, the breath in his heart rises to his fontanel and tries to escape. The fontanel, once the soft, pulsating spot on top of a baby's head, is "like a vagina" (*kagora asa,* lit: *kagora*/vagina + *asa*/mouth), the expert reveals, because it is the first part of the body to enter the birth canal. While a person is alive, breath fills the body and pulsates invisibly "under the skin" in much the way an unborn child moves inside the mother's belly. But breath deserts the body at death, "slipping out" the fontanel as a child emerges "head first" through the vagina, leaving the body bereft and unalive, in the postpartum condition of a mother. The body lies motionless, with eyes closed, as if the person were merely asleep and lost in a dream while the escaped breath, or *auna,* "flies away." But just as a newborn clings to its mother, the *auna* or animating "child" returns to hover about the body, hoping to gain reentry and permeating the hair around the fontanel. By attaching fontanel hair to his wand, the spell-sayer tries to attract the deceased's departed "child," enticing it to enter the "mouth" at the top of the *kore riϑi* as a newborn cleaves to its mother, filling her emptied, exhausted body with movement and life.

The fontanel is called the "first mouth" for another, less esoteric reason. During the months of gestation, it functions as a mouth, as the site where the fetus takes in nourishment. According to a myth men tell, the first Gimi man was born "unfinished," without eyes or a mouth. He ate like an unborn child, blindly tossing food into his gaping fontanel. The food fell whole through his head into his stomach, jostling the membrane that covered his mouth cavity—so his mouth pulsated like a fontanel. Nourished in this way, he grew quickly into a giant. But being blind, he soon toppled and fell, cutting open the mouth at the bottom of his face. When his second mouth formed, it, too, became surrounded with hair. "After we are born, after we come out of women," the expert added, "we grow bigger and bigger and the skull closes in . . . until the opening at the top closes completely. But the first mouth remains the escape route of our spirit . . . the main route of our death."

The associations men make with the *kore riði*, their discussions of *auna* and of dreaming, comparisons of fontanel, mouth, and vagina, allusions to the "unfinished" first man, etc., suggest that they construct the *kore riði* as a kind of mythic fetus or "first man"—a hollow, faceless giant with a wide open "mouth" at the top—and use it to replace the body from which the dead man's "child" departed too soon and "unfinished." Luring the *auna* into the bamboo pole thus seems like an attempt to reverse the *auna*'s fatal exit through the fontanel by inviting it to reenter a different "first mouth," undoing a premature birth-into-death. Indeed, men's explanations of how they entice the dead man's *auna* into the *kore riði* recall their descriptions of inducing actual birth.

As men instruct the newly married: once a man has "placed" his child inside his wife, he has to abstain from sex to allow it to "sleep" undisturbed in the womb. But at the end of the pregnancy he returns to induce the birth. If a man does not have sex with his wife "one more time," men say, the child would "stay asleep and die inside the mother." He inserts his penis to "wake" the fetus and "move its head into the vagina":

> . . . the child stays inside the mother a long time until it's finished growing. Then the father enters her once more. You know the way it is with birds? The way some eggs are abandoned and rot without hatching? We don't want that to happen, so we *finish* the child. We go into the mother and wake it. . . . We don't want the child to lie in one position thinking, "I'm in my house," and go on sleeping. . . . So we move it!
>
> If the father doesn't go into the mother one more time, there is no way for that child to be born. No way! . . . His penis makes space for it to lower its head into the vagina.

The "finishing" ejaculation also closes the fontanel and "makes the child shiver," filling it with the strength to be born.

> When the mother's belly is tight, the father goes to her at night while she is asleep and says, "I have come to finish the

child." The woman lies like this [in the fetal position, as the informant demonstrates]. The man does not get on top of her because, if he did, the child inside her would die. . . . He does not *touch* her belly: he enters her from the rear so she does not even *see* his penis! . . . He moves in a little way at a time until he touches the baby and his wife says, "You've touched the child in me. Now back off." . . .

The child is right there, lying at the exit. If the father's penis touches the child's head, the child will be ruined. So he ejaculates at the entry to the vagina. . . . His semen enters the woman and she dies [i.e., swoons]. . . . The semen goes into her—not into the child! It closes the child's first mouth.

Many of the rites surrounding the *kore riϑi* seem to allude to the literal process of placing a child inside the mother and returning to induce the birth. Men and women both use a woman's house to refer to the womb, as did one of the men just quoted, speaking of the "house" where the unborn "sleeps." Men, in particular, often say that "woman is our house." The act of carrying a dying man into the house of his wife or mother is easily interpreted, in this sense, as depositing the child inside her. Later, when men evict the women mourners and reposition the corpse so that the head abuts an inner wall, they continue to treat the man as a fetus, maneuvering his head to a closed exit so it is poised in the antenatal position. By then leaving the hut and sealing the corpse alone inside it, men close the mother's body, as a pregnant women is "closed" after months of sexual abstinence. When they tear a hole in the wall opposite the doorway and insert the *kore riϑi* so it "nearly touches" the dead man's fontanel, according to this analogy, they copulate with the mother "one more time" to wake the child and "make it shiver" with life. They insert the pole gingerly, and at the back of the house, because a man ought to enter his wife cautiously from the rear when he "finishes the child," being careful not to wake her nor make direct contact with the unborn head. The billows of tobacco smoke men blow onto the bamboo to rouse the deceased's spirit may be compared, in this light, to the final infusions of semen which, released "just at the mouth," just at the entry to the vagina, gently wake the child and induce birth.

The smoke from all our mouths goes into the bamboo and enters the house right where the *kore* is. . . . The man is dead and his spirit has left him, but not completely. . . . You don't see it— nor do we—but it's there, very near.

Men's exegeses of the *kore riϑi* suggest that it serves as a substitute for the deceased's own lifeless body, an emptied vessel into whose "first mouth" his *auna* can be enticed to return. In a less direct sense, the men's statements also indicate that the *kore riϑi* stands for the mother's body; that it serves as a replacement for the womb the dead man quit prematurely and into which he can be lured back by the ministrations of an anxious "father." But according to the comparison I have just drawn between the order of the rites and the process of inducing birth, the *kore riϑi* also embodies a giant penis—an association men themselves did not make. A phallic interpretation of the *kore riϑi* becomes irresistible, however, when the details of the ritual, including men's exegetical allusions to a gigantic but "unfinished" first man, are interpreted in light of women's myth.

### *The Giant Penis's First Night Out*

According to women's *nenekaina*, the first man was ordinary in size, but he possessed a giant penis with a life of its own.

> Once a penis was an enormous thing. When the man went to sleep in the men's house, his penis went about by itself. It didn't know women. Women lived in women's houses.
>
> When the man was hungry, he went into the forest. He took his dog and coiled his penis like a rope of vine, bundled it into a net bag and hung the bag around his neck. . . . Inside the forest, he let his penis out of the bag and, like a dog, it stalked and killed marsupials. . . . When day was done, he slung the marsupial his dog had killed over his shoulder and wound his penis into a pile of coils, leaving the marsupial it had killed at the head. Then he loaded his penis [with the marsupial inside] into the net bag and came home to sleep.
>
> While the man slept inside his house, this penis of his got up and went out alone. Just the penis! It went into the woman's house. The woman was sleeping, and the penis approached her. It touched her here and there. . . . but she was fast asleep. It moved over her body but could not find the vagina. The penis lifted her string skirts, still looking, and slid between her thighs. The man slept. The woman slept. The penis came alone.
>
> The penis came in search of the vagina but, alas, it was closed. There was only a tiny opening . . . and the penis thought, "There is none." Then he smelled the vagina and again tried to enter but could not. He ate a part of the hole to open it and then went inside and ejaculated. His fluid opened the way so the whole penis could enter. An enormous thing went into the woman and she awoke. The man still slept.

A performance of ritual theater depicting the hunting exploits of the first man with the giant penis, represented by the figure on the right carrying bow and arrows and wearing a heavy twisted cord hanging from his waist. Behind the cord, also fastened at the actor's waist, is a net bag like the one the first man used to carry his penis. The player on the left on all fours is the dog who stalked marsupials beside the giant penis. Though here played by a male actor, the part of the first man is often taken by a woman.

The woman took the penis in her hand and went out of her house. A stem of sugarcane was growing beside the door and she cut off a section and a half. Holding the penis, she walked to the man's house and went inside. She saw him asleep and placed the sugarcane next to his penis and cut it to the length of the cane, throwing the huge severed portion into a river.

The man awoke with a start and the woman said: "That was a heavy thing you carried about with you. When you wanted to copulate with me, you did not get up. You didn't even leave your house! You slept here and sent your penis. That was not right. So I did you a favor!" . . .

"That's alright," the man said. Other men saw his penis and cut theirs the same. . . . That's why men's penes have the same markings as sugarcane.

There are several striking similarities between women's myth of the first sexual encounter and men's description of the actual act of "finishing the child." In both accounts, the woman does not "see" the penis because her back is turned or she is asleep; and there is great concern about the extent of penetration. When inducing birth, a man is careful not to "touch" the un-born head lest he "ruin" the child. In women's myth, "an enormous thing entered the woman and she awoke." She cut off the penis, turning it to men-strual blood. "When the woman cut off the man's penis," one man com-mented while translating a version of this myth, "the Moon killed her for the first time. . . . Moon's blood is blood of the penis. A woman's blood is really the blood of a man." Tracking marsupials by scent and killing them, he ad-ded, is another metaphor for the first coital act, for "turning semen to stink-ing blood." From the point of view of women's myth, men's instructions to other men on how to induce a live or "finished" birth seem designed not to enrage the mother so she is roused to "cut off the giant." If a man goes too far into the mother and touches the child or wakes her, if she sees his penis, men seem to suggest, she will cut it off in anger; that is, the child will be stillborn.

When I discussed the myth with women, I asked why the heroine was angry. Several pointed out that she was "asleep" and that the man "tricked" her by not leaving his house. When I asked the meaning of a trick, one woman responded by repeating the myth of the ugly old man who used pos-sum feces to trick his wife into marriage (see Chap. 3). In terms of her com-parison, the woman carrying the penis back to the sleeping man and then cutting of the "head" are analogous to the beautiful girl killing her child and presenting it as a feast to her oblivious husband. In both stories, the heroine is violated and takes revenge: she gets the penis or child from a man, reduces it to blood, and hands it back to him. But comparison with the Torrent Lark myth also introduces the element of collusion. Though the ugly old man "tricked" the girl into marriage, she —or her mother— might have known his intentions all along since "darkness was not close," as he said it was. Like the woman whose husband came to "finish the child" and entered her from the rear, she might have been half-awake and said, "You've touched the child in me! Now back off!" The accounts of men and women imply, on the one hand, that deep penetration or direct contact between the giant penis and the unborn child is itself lethal: the penis would "ruin" the unborn by letting ejaculate enter its still-open "first mouth," etc. Yet both sexes also imply women's complicity in what happens inside her body.

When we examine the ritual details of the *kore riϑi* in light of the various myths and exegeses of both sexes and of men's instructions on inducing birth, the rite seems to enact a multiplex myth of first coitus: moving the corpse beside a "closed" wall opposite the door, opening a hole in the wall beside the head, inserting the *kore riϑi* with tentative, groping movements, cajoling the deceased's spirit to enter the pole, the pole suddenly "awakening," coming to life as an independent being and setting out upon a wild chase to find a "closed house," etc., all seem to refer to mythic events and to recapitulate *this* death as if it were the very first, the death of the firstborn, the "first appearance" of menstrual blood, etc. But there is a kind of double identification in the ritual: the corpse sealed alone inside the mother's house seems to represent both the sleeping first man and his penis's severed head, both the distant Moon and the firstborn trapped and "unfinished" in the womb. As a ritual object, the corpse condenses the scenario of women's myth, combining the giant's departure from his house with the catastrophic return, and thus embodies both cause and effect, both perpetrator and victim. In the sense that the corpse possesses this double identity, the men who manipulate it and who wield the *kore riϑi* replay women's myth with a new outcome. The *kore riϑi*'s wild hunt for the killer can be interpreted, in light of women's myth, as enacting both the giant penis's search for the vagina and the woman "carrying the penis" back to the house of the sleeping man. But if the route of the *kore riϑi* plays out women's myth, it also *reverses its direction,* carrying the penis the woman carried back to the man's house back to *her* house.

One of the ways, it seems to me, that the *kore riϑi* "searches out the vagina" is by finding and accusing an affine or matrilateral kinsman, a man related to the deceased through women. In cases I recorded, the *kore riϑi* arrived two or three times, by different routes, outside the house of the dead man's "true *abogo,*" his mother's brother's son, or of a close affine, a man he addressed in life as "my taboo." In locating the house of a matrilateral kinsman, the *ababana* who carry the *kore riϑi* seem to respond in advance to the accusation the maternal kinsmen will make when they charge into the dead man's compound, as convention dictates, and vent their fury against the *ababana* for having "taken bad care of the sister's child" (see Chap. 3). The *ababana* deflect the indictment of the *anatiraha,* using the *kore riϑi* to turn away the hand of blame, retracing the route of the mythic penis from the dead man's house back to the house of the woman—back to the house where she copulated with her "first husband." In the combined terms of the ritual and women's myth, the *ababana* fix the blame for death by carrying the giant penis back to the house of the mother's brother, naming *him* as the one who surreptitiously married the mother and "cursed the child."

## The Morning After . . .

Later that night, men dismantle the *kore riði* and unseal the door of the house, allowing the women to resume their vigil around the corpse. As morning nears, women arrive from other compounds. They are the deceased's *amamuraha*, his father's own and classificatory sisters who are often also the wives of his mothers' brothers; *anoha*, wives of his father's clan brothers; *asiraha*, his sisters, or daughers of his father's clan brothers; *araha*, wives of his own clan brothers; *aramofa*, daughters of his clan brothers; and *anaturaha*, wives of his sons and other women to whose brideprice he contributed. His mother, widow, sisters, daughters, and own sons' wives emerge from the hut to welcome the women with displays of grief. They move into the midst of the enclosure around the house and sit down apart from one another, digging their hands into the muddy ground, stacking the mud beside them and rubbing it into their hair. When the wife of a Big Man from another village appears, the widow or mother may acknowledge her arrival by leaping across the enclosure in a crouched position, landing on the wet ground with sickening smacks as other women scramble to clear rocks from her path. Later on, the important guests give counterdisplays by leaping across the same strip of muddy ground.

The women from other compounds and villages crowd into the hut to wail with the others, surround and caress the corpse and swat away flies with bunches of cordyline. From time to time one of the deceased's age-mates or clan brothers pushes his way through the women to whisper in the dead man's ear or place a few notes on his chest, adding to the fund his *kore* will need to buy food for the journey to Australia. The women mourn in shifts. Some attend the corpse while others crouch in the low doorway or sit outside around a fire, reheating cooked tubers of sweet potato brought by girls of other lineages, nursing children, and searching for lice in the strands of their skirts or the heads of older women.

Early on the day after the *kore riði* made its rounds, the man it accused arrives at the dead man's compound armed and alone and covered in the mourning clay of the maternal kin. By late morning, other representatives of local enemy clans and most of the deceased's own clansmen fill the center of his compound. Just as they did the night before, men of his lineage send the women out of the house where he lies and seal it closed. Again they tear the wall opposite the doorway, this time hacking open a large hole. The men uproot a part of the fence that surrounds the house and create an enclosed space in front of the hole. The deceased's mother, father's sister, and the senior wife of a Big Man of his clan move to the side of the house where the men have torn open the wall, leaving his widow alone in the mud or embracing one of her *amau*. Other women cover their heads with net bags or blankets and station themselves behind an already existing fence near the sealed doorway.

On the other side of the house, one or two men crawl through the low jagged opening and pull out the lower half of the corpse so that it protrudes from the house. The deceased's own father or son and a Big Man of his clan flank the body. The Big Man takes hold of the dead man's penis and leans into the darkness of the hut to whisper in his ear. A line of some forty men, *ababana* and certain close *abogofa,* stand behind the new fence, about ten yards opposite the house, with axes raised to their shoulders and arrows poised to shoot. Another line of about a dozen men, mostly *abogofa* who have been summoned by the *ababana* as prime suspects, stand ready to approach the corpse. After twenty minutes or so, the Big Man lets go of the penis, giving the signal for the trial to begin. The long line of armed men stamp their feet and give out war cries as the suspects come forward one by one. Each man walks slowly past the line of warriors, lays his weapons on the ground and walks alone to the corpse. He takes hold of a big toe or the whole top of the foot, and gingerly slides his thumb into the arch. "Defecate!" the suspect commands, addressing the corpse by name. "If I have killed you, defecate now!"

In the days immediately after a man dies, the search for his killer centers upon his corpse because it is still the principle site of his *auna,* which is nowadays the sole witness to his death: "We used to fight with arrows. We killed one of our enemy and our enemy killed one of us. . . . But white men have come and stopped our wars so now we cannot *see* who kills us." The *auna* still residing in a corpse can accuse the man who holds his foot by releasing a tiny drop of urine or particle of feces or whiff of intestinal gas—a possibility in tropical conditions. When certain of their enemy come forward, bystanders shout *"fa! fa!"* ("Shoot! Shoot!"), and men say the line of marksman would shoot to kill if the Big Man watching the corpse were to give the command. But no corpse ever "spoke" when I was present. After about half a minute, the Big Man signals the suspect to let go of the foot and the next man approaches.

Allies of the main suspects stand together on the sidelines, armed and ready to retaliate. One man recalled a trial at which his clansman Sapiau was falsely accused of killing his classificatory sister's son:

> Everyone was shouting *"fa! fa!!* . . . Kill Sapiau!" . . . "If you shoot our clansman," we cried, "we are all here and wait-

ing!" Sapiau covered his eyes with his hand. . . . A man who has worked sorcery doesn't go anywhere near his victim's house because he might be asked to hold his foot. But a man who closes his eyes doesn't care how close he gets!

If the corpse had released urine while Sapiau held it and they had shot him, we would have said "You have shot your mother while she held you. . . . Into whose body did you send your arrows?" we would have asked them. "What man did you look in the eye? . . . You looked into the eye of your spirit-mother and shot 'her' in the flesh!"

Men refer to a guilty man as a "spirit-mother" because he is a matrilateral kinsman. But his participation in the trial may itself give him a "maternal" identity by situating him in women's myth. Approaching the dead man's house and grasping his foot puts each suspect in a position like that of the first woman who "carried the penis" back to the house of the sleeping man. I return to this interpretation of the trial in a moment.

When the line-up of suspects is over, senior paternal kinsmen examine the corpse and probe any wounds. Other men put back the fence, pull the corpse back inside the house, replace the cut-out section of wall, and unseal the door. Women resume their vigil once again while men gather on the other side of the compound to listen to speeches. A Big Man of the deceased's clan consecrates a variety of cordyline to his name, forbidding men of the village to plant it or wear it as rear-skirts. With oratorial flourish, he announces his intention to quit this village of secret enemies. Soon, he vows, he will send an advance party of young men to clear gardens near his clan's ancestral home. And when his clan departs, they will carry with them the bones of their murdered son. "You men do not speak the truth!" he yells, referring to the trial's inconclusive result. "Some of you worked sorcery and killed this man!"

### The kore riði *and the Mythic Debate*

The only way to prevent more deaths in the deceased's lineage or clan is to name the killer and interrupt his plans. But the only way to know the killer's identity is to *see him in the act* of killing which, except in open war, is impossible. A sorcerer cannot be seen in the ordinary sense because he works in secret. His deed is knowable only after it is done so that it always has to be repeated and reviewed through ritual (see Part 4). Rites surrounding the *kore riði* and the trial attempt to fix blame by arranging for the dead man himself—first through the *auna* that leaves his body and then through the *auna* that remains inside it—to name his killer. The ritual recreates the mythic circumstance in which death originates, and which is therefore the ultimate cause of every death, as the essential context of accusation: the rites show that the man dies *because* his penis's journey of discovery ended up where it began, because he was carried back to the house of his mother.

The mythic first marriage or copulation to which men's rites allude is not a unitary event, as I have repeatedly stressed. It contains male and female versions, manifest and latent contents, articulated and unarticulated implications—as well as retaliatory trips back and forth between the houses of woman and man. By carrying the *kore riϑi* and holding the trial, according to my interpretation, men enact unspoken contents of their myth that are overt in women's version. The morning after the *kore riϑi*'s excursion, *ababana* again vacate the mother's house, seal in the corpse, and tear open the wall. But rather than attempt to extract the man's "heavy" vibrating *auna,* they pull out the lower half of his corpse. And instead of using the *kore riϑi* to carry his *auna,* or animating "child," away from his body, they demand that a line of suspects approach his body and "carry it back." In this interpretation of men's rites based upon women's myth of the giant penis, the *kore riϑi* performs the penis's initial exuberant voyage of discovery, and the subsequent trial enacts the deadly return. Looked at in these terms, the trial, in which suspects approach the corpse and take hold of the foot, arranges for one man after the other to "try out" for the part of primordial woman as she grasps the penis, carries it back to the sleeping man, and cuts it off.

A man intent upon proving his innocence grasps the foot with eyes closed to show "he has no fear how close he gets." By blinding himself, the suspect seems to situate himself in a different myth, or in a different part of the same myth. With eyes closed, he has "only a mouth" in his head and is "unfin ished." He resembles not the first woman, embarked on a tour of revenge, but the first man who, according to men's myth, was born in a fetal condition and ate through the hole at the top of his head. In women's myth, the "unfinished" first man is no fumbling babe but a self-motivated penis who uses his "top mouth" to smell out and "eat the vagina." When the blind suspect takes hold of the corpse protruding from the torn wall of a woman's house, it seems to me, he claims the innocence of the "unfinished" man in men's myth or of the penis on its maiden voyage in women's *nene.*

In alluding to women's myth, men's performances reverse or "cut off" its meaning, keeping intact the articulated surface content of men's views, reasserting men's side in the mythic debate with women. Men treat the corpse like a fetus "asleep" inside his mother; and the bamboo pole like the father, or father's penis, who "returns to mother to finish the child" and induce birth (see above, this Chap.). But in tearing a hole in the wall of the mother's house and inserting the *kore riϑi,* and in the conduct of the trial, men also seem to refer to exploits of the giant penis in women's myth, to the penis invading the women's house and body while she slept unaware, etc. The same gestures, in other words, enact both the penis's heroic rescue of the "sleeping child" and an untoward invasion that rouses the mother to kill it. In the sense that the *kore riϑi* plays out these conflicting myths, I suggest, it overturns the one and reinstates the other. Once the *ababana* entice the *auna*, or "unfinished man," inside the *kore riϑi*, they run with him *away from* "his own house" to the house of his killer, who is his mother, in the sense that the killer is generally reckoned to be an affine or close matrilateral kinsman.

In using women's myth to establish the ultimate context of accusation, men's death rites imply that, whatever man was the actual agent of death (and the findings in this regard are usually inconclusive; see Chap. 11), the real blame lies generically and collectively with mothers. Men perform women's myth in order to blame them, enacting their protest as the pretext to override it. The ritual search for the killer shows the cause of death as *not* the going-out but the coming-back—as the result not of what man began but of what woman ended, of her fury, her slaying the firstborn and starting to menstruate. Men's trial of return attempts to put the killer in *her* place—to catch him red-handed, as it were. By demanding that their enemies line up and hold the dead man's foot, the *ababana* try to place the guilty man at the scene of the crime. To shoot a suspect while he holds the foot, men say, is to "look into the eye" of the spirit-mother and fill her body with arrows. The act of *killing in secret* makes a mother of the perpetrator so that, at the level of myth or final cause, woman is always to blame: the corpus delicti is always discovered inside her house.

### *"Remnants" of Cannibalism*

In the first days after a man dies in his prime, or even before old age, his wife or wives, his own sisters and brothers' wives, grown daughters and sons' wives, and even certain daughters of his father's brothers cut off the tops of their fingers. Although a man's mother is his chief mourner, she rarely amputates part of a finger because, as a woman of at least middle age, she may have already lost the top halves of her index, middle and little fingers on account of the deaths of her father, husband's father, husband, brother, husband's brother, and especially of her own young children (see M. Strathern 1972:95). Except for the deceased's mother and paternal grandmother, all the women of his compound are supposed to share a meal that includes these severed finger joints. On one occasion, I was told that bamboo tubes lying in an open fire contained finger parts, but I did not look inside the tubes nor examine what the women ate. Women say they cook the joints, skinned and boned, with uncultivated greens in separate bamboo containers. "We put the blood [and the finger] in bamboo and cook it," one woman told me. A woman is careful to avoid eating her own part and that of any other woman severed on account of her child—joints of her son's widow, for instance, or of other daughters-in-law or her own daughters. But she is obliged to partake on other occasions of those of her *amau* and *anatu*.

Women associate the sharing of *aϑa'ora*, "the blood of our hands" (lit: *aϑa*/hand + *kora*/blood), with other kinds of cannibalism:

> When a man died we took a bamboo knife and cut him and stuffed him into bamboo. . . . Women used to eat men when they died but we don't anymore. . . . Our mothers cut Benoi and his wife, Taneoigi, who is now an old woman, ate him.

Taneoigi's son recalled that, as a boy of five or six, he had been with his mother and other women and children during a cannibal feast. "The women gathered to eat the man," he said, "and when they had finished they ate each other's *aϑa'ora*." Using the bamboo knives they had used to cut the corpse, the women made slits across veins on the backs of their hands and let the blood drip onto leaves, folding the leaves and inserting them into bamboo tubes for cooking. When the *aϑa'ora* was cooked, Taneoigi's son remembered, women gave it to their *amauraha* to eat.

When a man dies nowadays, women say, they may eat the *aϑa'ora* of one of his sisters or the *nakora*, literally "elbow blood" (*na*/elbow + *kora*), of a brother, son, or parallel cousin. "All the women get excited and say, 'Give us the blood you shoot,'" a man named Petoma said. "Meduna shot Tehamaoga and all the women ate his blood. They cooked the blood in a banana leaf and ate it with tinned fish. Only the women ate Tahamaoga's elbow blood, but if there were a man who wanted to eat it, he could have. It's up to the man himself." But in general, a third male informant insisted, "men do not eat blood. It's something only women do. Men let blood inside their elbows and women eat it. But when women cut their hands, men do *not* eat!"

## The Rites of Divination

### *Singing the* auna *into the Forest*

When a man dies in his prime, Gimi say, his *kore* is enraged and becomes hypervigilant, floating like an omnipresent "eye" over the village, pulling the unwary into suddenly turbulent rivers and stirring up the wind. In the immediate aftermath of death, the *auna* feels banished and unfinished and clings to its body and old haunts, taking refuge at first in things that traverse forest and settlement and fill them with danger. As one man recalled:

> When Bobanima died, a wind began to blow. It was his dream—not ours. His *kore* dreamed of the wind. Before he died, he said, "When I die, a terrible wind will blow and send trees crashing down . . . so stay out of the forest."

Throughout the night after the *kore riϑi*'s excursion, and for four or five more nights, men and women crowd into the hot, reeking hut where the corpse lies and serenade the *kore*'s *auna*. To make their environment safe, to be able to cross rivers without slipping and drowning, to cut trees and vines without mishap, and to find plants and prey, the living have to entice the dead into the deep forest.

> When my father and mother die I will sing to them, "Go into my forest, stay at Kobiratibi. When other men come, hide the birds and marsupials! But when I arrive and call out to you, throw birds and marsupials before my eyes. Let me shoot them with ease!"

Over time, *auna* penetrates the deep forest and is gradually transformed entirely into *kore*, taking up residence in giant trees, high mountain caves, and every kind of wildlife. A hunter says, "The *kore* takes you into the forest and you kill what it shows you. You think you are killing alone, but the *kore* has called you and goes with you." Waterfalls are called *kore abe* or "ghost urine," a euphemism for semen, because, like mountains, giant trees and other forest monuments, they represent ultimate transformations of personal *auna* into *kore*. But in the days and nights following a death, men and women have to cajole the *auna* into the forest.

The mother and father of the deceased take turns leading the crowd in songs that flatter and glorify the *auna* by identifying it with splendors of the clan forest. "Papuan Lory washing its tailfeathers at the top of the waterfall, . . . King of Saxony [Bird of Paradise] delighting in the fruit of the *ubiϑa* fig, . . . lovely leafed taro growing at the base of the red pandanus, . . . yellow bamboo shining on the mountainside, . . . red orchids overhead," they sing in separate songs, "these are none other than *you*, my child!" "Sweet brother," a man sings to his sister's uninitiated son, "you looked for a place to stay but found none! Be the Pesquet's parrot perched on a branch of the *fakiϑa* tree! Arise in myriad shoots of red lilies that cover the forest floor!" For a young married woman, the crowd sings wedding songs that compare the bride's beauty to wild flowers, birds, and other treasures, sending her *auna* into the clan forests of both her husband and her father.

*Dispelled from the Vicinity of the Corpse, the* auna *Enters the Clan Forest and Hunts Marsupials, Repeating Exploits of the Giant Penis*

During the period of nighttime singing for a man, his age-mates and close *abogofa,* including those most suspected of killing him, go into the forest to capture live marsupials. They also collect bark and vines to build a rough shelter at the edge of the compound "out of the sight of women." Each day for a week or so the hunters supply marsupials to certain of the dead man's *ababana* (but never his actual father), his *anatiraha,* and his fathers' *aturaha* or *abogofa,* elders and ritual experts who remain secluded inside the shelter to interrogate the animals. "When a man dies his *auna* enters marsupials but only stays with them for a day [i.e., a matter of days]. Then it wanders in the forest, entering birds and mountains and headwaters. But the *auna* goes first to the marsupials."

The *auna* of a newly dead man or woman is like a child who, having been forced to leave its mother, shut out of the "vagina" at the top of the head, as it were, seeks a new "house" in the forest. "We are not born out of holes in trees or rocks but come from this 'house,' from our mothers," a man named Rabofa explained. Men say that a marsupial is like a woman, and they attribute most of their taboos against eating marsupials to the fact that they are "covered in female pubic hair" and give off an odor "like menstrual blood." Certain species, as men point out, also resemble the unborn on account of the quality of skin beneath the fur, the tightly curled "hands" and "fetal posture." In women's myth, we may remember, the giant penis stalked marsupials by day and woman's vagina by night: killing a marsupial and enfolding the carcass "at the head" was parallel to entering woman's vagina and being cut off at the head. The *auna* penetrating marsupials, in other words, seems to have the significance of the spirit returning as a firstborn child to mother and, less overtly, of the penis finding the first woman.

Like the *kore riði* and the corpse itself, marsupials are vessels for the dead man's spirit, "houses" that lodge his rage and therefore can identify his killer. Each day, the hunters deliver five or six live animals to the specially built enclosure, leaving them in an anteroom from where they cannot see the activities of their elders. Each marsupial is placed inside a bamboo cage and interrogated in turn. One of the elders holds out a piece of raw sweet potato, skewered on a stick, and recites a series of enemy clan names. To induce the animal to eat at the right moment, another elder holds over its head the same arrow-wand with the deceased's hair that was used to entice his spirit inside the *kore riði.* A third man, meanwhile, repeating other procedures used with the *kore riði,* puffs on a tobacco pipe and blows billows of smoke over the marsupial's body, inviting it to bite when it hears the killer's clan name. When an animal does take a bite, the men continue to interrogate

Inside a specially built enclosure, a ritual expert holds two of the five or six live marsupials that are hunted each day of the weeklong divination period. Each animal will be "questioned" by various methods about the identity of the killer.

Elders interrogate a marsupial inside a cage of *pitpit,* or wild sugarcane. One man holds out a raw tuber of sweet potato as another (*foreground*) wields an arrow wand to whose tip is tied a clump of the deceased's hair pulled out from above his fontanel. Both the hair and the marsupial "house" the dead man's vengeful spirit: by bringing the two into contact while reciting a list of enemies' clan names, the interrogators try to excite the marsupial to bite into the potato the moment it hears the name of the clan to which the killer belongs.

Ritual experts open the earth oven and inspect the leaf packets containing grubs that were tied to the marsupials' limbs before cooking. The men consult one another on the condition of each grub since, if one survived the heat of the oven, it would indicate the guilt of the clan "named" by the marsupial to whose limb it was attached.

it by holding out new pieces of sweet potato and reciting names of lineages and compound sites that belong to the "bitten" clan, hoping the animal will bite again and reveal further details of the culprit's identity.

When thirty or forty marsupials have been interrogated in this way over the course of a week, the elders kill them and pull out their fur, literally, *ari'aθa* or "hair." Marsupial fur exudes the dead man's *auna* in the same way as did his hair while he was alive, and pulling it out imbues the elders with his anger. "The men who pull out the marsupials' fur want to work sorcery and take revenge. . . . Pulling out the fur makes them hot." In order to "stay hot," the elders have to hide their identities, abstain from sex and refuse foods that women have handled or that have female characteristics, like sugarcane or greens "filled with water," red pandanus fruit "like Moon's blood," and mushrooms that "smell like vaginas."

After the marsupials have been killed and denuded, they are questioned again by new methods. Men gut each animal and attach live grubs or caterpillars to the four limbs. The insects are wrapped in layers of leaves that, as the men note, serve as both food and "home." As an elder encases each whitish, wriggling grub and prepares to tie the package to a marsupial's "hand" or "leg," he whispers the name he spoke when that animal took its last bite. When all the marsupials have been dressed in this way, they are placed in an earth oven. After the cooking, the men carefully open and inspect each package to see if any grub survived the heat. An insect that lives even for an instant, as the experts take great pains to determine, points to the guilt of the clan "named" by the marsupial to whose limb it was attached. When all four grubs are motionless, as is almost always the case, they nullify that marsupial's accusation. The elders and experts who perform the oracle afterward eat the marsupials and grubs. The deceased's own father, age-mates, and brothers, specifically his father's father's grandsons in the male line, are forbidden to eat any of the contents of these ovens or even to watch the proceedings.

By wielding the *kore riði,* conducting the trial, serenading the corpse, hunting marsupials and using them to divine the name of the killer, men harbor the dead man's rage and deploy it to fix blame. They orchestrate the movement of *auna* from corpse to bamboo pole to forest and back into the bodies of clan elders. But men's elaborate and time-consuming efforts are highly inconclusive, as far as I can tell. The only certain identification seems to be the eventual death of the culprit or his close relation. Divination rites may indicate the neighborhood of guilt, but only death or serious illness can pinpoint the actual perpetrator. A sorcerer's identity, like any knowledge, is always ex post facto: it has to happen and be seen to have happened before it can be accepted. A sorcerer, or his close relation, has to die before he can be known and, even then, doubts may linger: if the next death in enemy ranks is a woman or child or man of small account, then the *ababana* may not know if the killer is the woman's husband or husband's brother, the child's father or father's father, etc.

Knowing who is to blame for death, which is the essence of Gimi knowledge and understanding, is always a confrontational process. In public discussions of sorcery, Big Men allocate guilt among their affines by constructing conflicting histories of the region (see Part 4). Each orator finds a compelling way to connect the deaths in neighboring hamlets over the last several decades, and to link past triumphs and routs in war, establishing a pattern of vendetta that shows his own clansmen to be the current victims. Only men can be blamed for deaths because women do not practice sorcery, as they did not fight wars. Women have no "names" and cannot be held accountable. Men are responsible for the demise of individuals, but the consequences, like the crimes themselves, are ambiguous. The same illness or death may constitute evidence of proper vengeance or unprovoked aggression: the injured party is always likely to be a secret perpetrator, his current suffering the just reward—and proof—of past misdeeds (Evans-

Pritchard 1976 [1936]). Like men's public memories, male-perpetrated facts are highly negotiable. Women are left out of the mundane arena to commit crimes in myth, a realm where blame is as irreparable as the missing ends of their fingers or the loss of menstrual blood.

## Burial and the Celebration of *ruhu:* The Gift as Accusation

On the morning of burial, the dead man's affines, his *abogofa* and *aturaha,* dig his grave amid the banana plants or coffee trees at the edge of his garden. Then they go back to his compound and reopen the hole in the wall of his mother's house while his paternal age-mates and kinsmen, who are forbidden to touch the corpse, stand aside and watch. The *abogo* pull his body through the low, jagged opening and tie it to a litter. The man whom the *kore riϑi* accused crouches on the ground nearby wailing loudly, his face and hair heavily caked in yellow clay. Women emerge from the other side of the house, leaving through the regular door, many with heads and faces covered in pale grey ash. The dead man's mother races back and forth behind the men who remove the corpse, stabbing the ground with her long pointed digging stick and thrusting out her chest on which hangs a net bag stuffed with his clothes. "Don't take my son away!" she screams, waving her arms as if to disrupt the work of the pallbearers. "Let him stay! Let him stay inside my house!" Unheeded, she kicks one of her daughters who is sobbing on the ground beneath the litter. A man's closest female relations, his sisters and father's sisters and his wife's mother—but not his widow who remains mostly out of sight—and one or two of his *kisa abogo,* sons of his mother's own brothers, display their grief as his body is carried away, the men wailing as freely as the women.

The dead man's brothers and age-mates stand with arms folded, stoically apart, and remain in the compound while the *abogoraha,* including the officially suspected killer, carry him to his garden, followed in a procession by his mother or grown daughters, sisters and fathers' sisters, and older men of the patrilineage. Inside the grave, Big Men conduct an autopsy, covering the dead man's eyes with dried leaves and instructing one of their wives to handle his swollen corpse so they can examine wounds and probe orifices, looking for evidence of a sorcerer's work (see Chap. 10). Afterward, the mother retrieves the pandanus mat on which her son has lain and which is filled with his juices. Other women kneel and weep behind the fence the *abogoraha* have built around the vault. In the far distance stand the paternal kinsmen, watching their affines close the grave and plant cordyline amid the fence.

For days or weeks after the burial of a young or important man, maternal kinsmen continue to arrive from other villages covered in thick layers of *abiare,* the ochre or gray clay that "holds his *auna* on their skins." The men halt at the entrance to the compound to allow their wives to precede them. The mud-covered women kneel outside the dead man's house and give out a long, synchronized wail, waiting for the appearance of his mothers, sisters, and wife's mother—but not his widow who stays in seclusion. The women sob as a chorus, each visitor caressing, commiserating, and weeping in the arms of her own *amau.* From time to time, the dead man's mother or sister raises her voice above the rest to rasp a solo lament or cry in a duet with her *amau.* At the end of the required display, the *anatiraha* enter houses where the *ababana* ceremoniously wipe off the *abiare* and feed them chunks of cooked pork or roasted fat to "cool their anger." When the *ababana* are hard-pressed by large numbers of mourners, they may send word to distant affines asking that they come unadorned. But the *anatiraha* rarely comply.

When the man died, his distraught *auna* "flew back" to his *anatiraha.* Like the gyrating *kore ri θi,* the ravenous marsupials and, in the past, the cannibal thieves themselves, the *anatiraha* are filled with the angry spirit of their murdered child and serve him as refuge of first resort, as vessel and vehicle through which he himself may speak against his killers. The *anatiraha, kore ri θi,* marsupials, and corpse serve, in this sense, not just as realizations of mythic characters or objects but as condensations and concealments of whole mythic episodes: their rampages, furious appetite, or flatulence "accuse the father"—as did the beautiful girl who killed her child in women's myth. And, like her, they evoke his response. By wiping off the layers of clay and feeding the *anatiraha,* by running with the *kore ri θi* through the night, by conducting the trial, and by hunting marsupials and subjecting them to tests, it seems to me, the *ababana* turn away the child's accusation, conveyed in the various maternal vessels, and discover the guilty man within the mother's own ranks, in the person of her "first husband."

The essential method of shifting blame to the mother's side is to give back the incriminating evidence. When the *anatiraha* conduct their rampage, when the *kore ri θi* starts to vibrate, when the corpse lets go of a drop of urine or feces or intestinal gas, the movement is like an incriminating gift that the recipients, the *ababana,* hasten to return. When the *ababana* wipe the mourning clay off the *anatiraha* and feed them chunks of cooked pork, they conduct an exchange: they divest them of the *auna* "held" by the mud, replacing a moving part of the deceased with "killed meat" that is called "the head of the child." The *ababana* replace the child that moves—the one who is alive and on the attack—with the one they killed, giving away meat like the marsupial the giant stalked. Every rite of divination is inconclusive and men's guilt is eternally undetermined, in these terms, because men can *exchange it away:* they can divest themselves of the corpus delicti by repeatedly offering "the head of the child" and condemning the recipients in their stead.

The aftermath of a death.

Some two weeks after a man's death, a week or more after burial, the *ababana* celebrate *ruhu* formally to end women's confinement and to "send home" the *anatiraha*. When the deceased is a Big Man and attracts many foreign mourners, or when his lineage are recent arrivals in the village and few in number, close coresident affines assist the *ababana* in mounting the distribution by hunting marsupials and handing over pigs owed as future brideprice. The man whom the *kore ri ϑi* or marsupial rites accused, as well as those less publicly suspected, are also likely to contribute meat to the *ruhu* distribution in order conspicuously to align themselves with the dead man's clan brothers.

Those who have pledged to contribute meat cook it in their own compounds and arrive about midday in the compound of the *ababana*. Men carry metal pots of rice and gutted pigs trussed on poles. Their black-faced wives, many of them sisters of the deceased, balance huge loads of sweet potatoes, taros, bananas, greens, and whole gutted marsupials. Women of the dead man's clan sit in small groups outside his mother's house, grooming one another, netting string bags, and stuffing scraps of meat and vegetables into bamboo tubes which they lay over small open fires. Some of the arriving women, especially the wife of the man marked by the *kore riϑi*, approach these groups and give out piercing wails. In the main part of the compound, other clanswomen empty the shallow oven pits of charred, wet refuse, wrap greens around slabs of cooked pork, peel taro, tapioca, and bananas, and fetch firewood and water. Men chop wood and make fires to heat rocks for the ovens and to singe the hair off the whole uncooked pigs.

Older men butcher the pigs on thick beds of ferns and leaves. They make the first cuts at the corners of the mouth, beginning a Y-shaped incision that opens the animal's underside down the middle and creates two flaps, facilitating the removal intact of lungs, heart, kidneys, liver, rectum, and womb. When the pigs are gutted, women carry the intestines to a nearby stream, remove the feces, wash the casings and braid them for roasting. The butchers section the limbs, rib cages, tails, backbones, necks, and lower jaws but leave the singed hide in its entirety. The procedure creates four categories of meat: the whole "skin" with head attached, "bones" with some meat adhering, "meat," and "innards." The apportionment of these cuts when I was present corresponded to what Gimi said transpired in the past when cannibalism was still practiced: "bones" and "innards" were distributed to women and coresident affines, and the pigs' splayed, fat-saturated "skins" and "meat" were reserved for foreign matrikin.

After the women finish tying greens into bundles, peeling tubers and filling bamboo tubes with bananas, ferns, and scraps of meat, they join the deceased's close relations and become spectators, watching the men cut pigs and prepare the earth ovens. Men remove burning timbers that lie across the pits so that rocks piled on top of the wood fall into the ovens. Using split branches as tongs, they pick out burning embers and place de-stemmed banana leaves over the smoldering rocks in the bottom of the oven, lining the sides with more green leaves and ferns.

Separate ovens are used to cook the *ababana*'s own pigs and to reheat cooked pork, whole marsupials, and red pandanus fruit donated by affines. Food grown or reared by certain affines is set aside for women and children of the dead man's clan: "When a woman's friends give her food, she can eat it," a woman named Bobau told me, referring to pandanus brought from another village by two of her "true *anati*," her own mother's mother's brother and his son. "But men are not women's friends. When men eat, women and children do not!" Sorcerers who have succeeded in killing a man try afterward to reach his children with "poisoned" food, Bobau explained, using the grandmother and other women as unwitting conduits.

"Perhaps a man of Vami killed my son!" the mother thinks. So she doesn't eat with the Vamians [i.e., doesn't eat food they raised] because if she or her daughters or any woman of his clan eat food from Vami, her son's children will get very sick.

Men arrange whole marsupials and wrapped sections of pork beneath layers of vegetables. A few senior women sit behind them, handing over bundles of greens and criticizing the men's placements, gesturing and shouting excitedly that the meat will not cook thoroughly. Men heed some of this advice and then close the ovens, piling on more ferns, green leaves, and earth and, as a final layer, the soggy, charred linings of previous ovens. When the pile is bubbling hot, one man inserts a stick at the center to create an opening, and others pour in water from nine- or ten-foot-long bamboo poles, covering the hole quickly to seal in the steam.

After about an hour, the senior women squat around the steaming mass and begin to pull off the outer layers while the men keep their distance. The women spread the contents of the oven on the ground, picking at the food and eating morsels as they work. Elder men cut the meat into small pieces and hand "the first piece" to the dead man's sister. She takes it to the house where he lay and places it on the roof, offering it to his hovering *kore*. "When the *kore* eats the *auna* of the marsupial [or pig], there will afterward be plenty of meat for everyone," a man named BoϑaEha allows. As another man, Rifeko, says:

> The dead man's *kore* will eat this food and say, "How well I have eaten!" And so there will be food for us all. His *kore* is angry and, if we let him stay angry, there won't be enough food. Some of us will get nothing to eat! We give food to the *kore* and say, "Don't be angry." And afterward there is plenty because we gave some first to his *kore* to hold.

The *kore* has already sent fierce winds to endanger the hunters and afflicted his brothers with wounds or maladies like the one to which he succumbed. When Bobanima impaled himself on a fence post and died, apparently of tetanus, three of his father's brothers' sons developed shooting pains in their chests and were unable to open their mouths. Each realized that he had unwittingly provoked the dying man's wrath: one brother ignored his request to stay at his side the night he died; another did not return from the village where he had gone to buy rare ingredients for a medicine; and the third did not kill a pig for the medicine. The third brother killed the pig after Bobanima died and gave the meat to his wife to offer the *kore*. Arriving at the dead man's door, the wife said: "My husband wanted to kill this pig to make your medicine. But you died and he let it forage in the bush. You have made him sick so we killed the pig. . . . Eat it now and take back his sickness."

After the initial offering to the *kore,* men salt and apportion the meat. Women sit on the sidelines or inside their houses, out of the afternoon rains, while Big Men consult conspiratorily on the distribution. They direct younger men to cut huge banana leaves into forty or fifty plates, one for each woman, and to fill them with chunks of meat and fat, bananas and taros. While the men work, the women assemble and sit cross-legged in two long rows outside the dead man's house. On some occasions, men set out empty leaves in front of the women and then fill each one with food, crossing and recrossing the compound like waiters. At other times, the Big Men call out women's names, and as a woman's name is announced one of the men carries her allotment across the compound and places it on the ground in front of her or directly into her hands.

In every death rite I witnessed, and in *ruhu* of the past according to informants, some women included in the distribution were referred to simply as *faba baϑaha* or "nothing women" (lit: *faba*/nothing + *baϑaha*/woman) because they had no significant tie of kinship to the deceased, having been given by a female relation his tattered remains to wear or, supposedly in the past, his flesh to eat. According to past ritual convention, women descended willy-nilly upon the corpse, too grief-stricken, angry, and excited to notice or remember who ate what part of the man. Men, therefore, had to assign a boy to watch them or, if there were none around, to rely upon the report of an older woman who had her wits about her. In the sense that women in general didn't know—or weren't supposed to be in a condition to know— what they were doing when they ate the dead, all were treated as *faba baϑaha.* The current practice of announcing women's names at the end of *ruhu,* when they accept men's gift of meat, suggests that the names have been withheld until then and seems to express the same loss of identity that cannibalism engendered. I return to this important point in the next chapter.

Once the women are formally named and fed, the distribution of head payments to foreign matrikin begins. About six to a dozen men who represent those from other villages entitled to "eat the head" have sat since midmorning in a secluded corner of the compound, their heads bowed, and their backs to the proceedings in a ritual gesture of hostility. A Big Man of the deceased's clan finally acknowledges them:

> We have killed pigs and bought rice and cooked them and give them now to the women and to our enemies. Our gifts make our enemies rejoice so they will work new sorcery against us. We give too much food! We make our enemies too happy! "We

The distribution of a head payment to one of the women mourners at the conclusion of *ruhu*.

ought to kill another of them," they will say to themselves, "so they will make us another fine feast!"

Gimi associate death with anger and anger with hunger. Divination rites are based upon the fury and voracity of the dead man's *auna:* the *auna* inside the marsupial attacks the sweet potato the moment it "hears the killer's name." The hunger of the dead is a constant menace. During the butchering of *ruhu* pigs, the *ababana* offer the *kore* the very first raw piece so there will be enough meat to distribute to the assembled mourners, suggesting that, if the *kore* is not placated, he will devour the meat beneath their hands. The *abanana* feed the *kore* for the same reason they "give the head" to the *anatiraha* and once provided "a second course" to cannibal women: to dispossess the recipients of what they would—or already have—devoured in utter fury; to take back something that was taken illicitly, in fantasy, or in the mythic past, and may, as a consequence, permanently disappear. By responding to the secret meal with a ritual feast, giving the myth tangible form, the public offer of the head appeases the rage, temporarily at least, and thus undoes its consequences.

But head payments carry the benefits and risks of any ransom: they induce the recipients to release the one they hold hostage but also incite them to steal again. The uterine tie that makes a man's *auna* fly home to his *anatiraha* and gives them the status of chief mourners also makes them the beneficiaries and prime suspects in his murder. Immediately after a death, the *ababana* accuse the *anatiraha* and conduct elaborate rites to identify the killer in their ranks. But throughout the rites of divination, and culminating in the distributions of head payments at the end of *ruhu,* they begin to shift the blame away from men entirely. In the next chapter, I describe the small-scale versions of *ruhu* held during the following year, when men again, in rite after rite, publicly name women and present them with head payments. Unlike the *anatiraha,* the women can make no eventual return because they cannot initiate exchanges. They are left holding men's gift and become eternal possessors of rage and deadly appetite, the ones to whom *ki'ʒ* is permanently affixed.

# FIVE

# The Death of a Man, Part II: Women Convert the Man to Decorations

On a morning a week or so after burial, women in mourning cover each other's faces with *nini*, a mixture made by adding powdered ash and carbon to *ϑarI*, the combination of pig fat and pandanus oil women use to coat new bark-string skirts and to make their skins glisten on festive occasions. Sitting in the midst of the open compound and holding up pieces of broken mirrors, the women smear the pitch black mixture over their faces, carefully filling in creases and wrinkles. Then they cut each other's hair, making a pile of the "leavings" to discard in a river or fast-moving stream. After one success, sorcerers are likely to strike again in the same clan and to attack other married men, perhaps by ensorcelling strands of their wives' hair. The mourners coat their shorn heads and bodies with *abiare*, the white, gray, or ochre clay collected in pigs wallows, riverbanks, and landslips. Later the same day, they put on *agesagena*, literally, "fat-soaked things" (*age* or *hake*/pig-belly fat + *sa*/from + *ge*/? + *na*/thing), making armbands, kneebands, tattered skirts, and turbans from torn pieces of the dead man's or woman's clothes and net bags, and then smearing them with pig fat to seal in the *auna*. Around their necks, the women pile strands of grayish white *kareta*, the beads of Job's Tears.

All the women born or married into the dead man's clan—his father's sisters, his true and classificatory sisters and daughters, the wives of his fathers and brothers, etc.—and his wife's mother, the wives of his age-mates and cross-cousins, especially the wife of the man suspected of killing him, and, sometimes, his father's sisters' daughters, are expected to "put on *nini*." His widow, mother, sisters, daughters, and sons' wives, women who are expected to cut off the tops of their fingers, also wear the completest coverings of *nini* and *abiare*, the heaviest layers of *agesagena*, the most strands of Job's Tears. The widow's *agesagena* are made of the bags she used to carry her husband's food from her gardens and include small netted envelopes, hung around her neck, that contain his hair and teeth. The dead man's mother, sister, daughter, father, and brother may also wear these tiny sealed amulets

After the death of a young married man, the women of his father's clan cover their faces with a black mixture called *nini* and cut each other's hair.

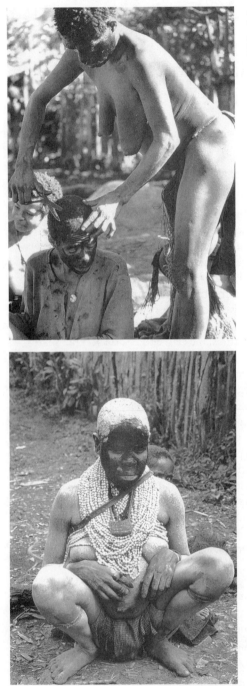

The widow crouches with her son peering over her shoulder. Her newly shorn head and body are caked in gray clay and her face is covered in *nini*. Around her neck she wears strands of Job's Tears and an amulet containing her husband's hair or teeth. Her kneebands and ragged skirt, made of her husband's torn shirt, are the first *agesagena*. The top of the middle finger of her right hand has just been amputated and bandaged with a leaf and vine.

The dead man's mother with his eldest son. The mother wears necklaces of Job's Tears and her son's jaw encased in netted marsupial fur. The small net bag hanging from her head (of which only the strap is visible) contains her son's skull.

The immediate family of a man who died in his prime. An elder brother (i.e., the son of the deceased's father's elder brother) opens his mother's net bag to reveal the deceased's skull for the camera. The dead man's own younger brother stands on the left, wearing an amulet of the deceased's hair. The brother's pregnant wife is beside him.

of teeth or hair; and his close kinsmen (father, brother, father's brother, father's sister's son, etc.) may blacken their noses with *nini* or slash their earlobes, letting the blood dry conspicuously on their cheeks and shoulders.

Men and women agree that putting on the deceased's *autaisana* or "leavings" was entirely "women's idea," something "only women do to cool their stomachs." "The women's stomachs were hot from longing for the one who died, so they put on clay and blackened their faces," one man remarked, virtually repeating women's explanations for cannibalism. Like cannibalism, decorating the body "cools the sorrow in the belly," eases the pain of loss by attaching the deceased's *auna,* holding his smell, keeping the image of his face before one's eyes. *nini* and *agesagena* also serve as protection from the *kore's* free-floating wrath by sustaining the wearer's guilt: "I put on *nini* and *abiare* and *rasi* [ashes]," one woman explained, "and the *ki'3* stays in my stomach" (see above, Chap. 3).

In the past, some men say, a man or woman was eaten one or two days after death. Women say they acted quickly to spare the dead the humiliation of decay. Nowadays, however, a dead person is caressed and serenaded for five or six days and nights and then buried once decomposition is well underway. If a man were to be buried before he began to decompose, men calculate, women could not put on mourning disguises for a month or so, not until, at the slowed rate of decomposition inside the ground, his body had reached a suitably disintegrated state. The corpse's coming apart seems to be the prerequisite for women's decorations, suggesting that the delay in burial is designed to give women mourners time to "dismember and ingest" the body by different means and through other orifices, taking him in with their eyes and nose and through the pores of their skin. The sort of "cannibalism" practiced by women nowadays seems to occur by contagion, in the same way as pallbearers, grave diggers, fence makers, and other maternal kinsmen who touch the fluids or inhale the smell of the corpse automatically incorporate the *auna.*

Women's elaborate mourning disguises, their mutilated fingers, shorn heads, heavy coatings of light-colored clay, blackened faces, ragged skirts, armbands, kneebands, and turbans made of the deceased's torn clothes and net bags, amulets of his hair and teeth, and his mother wearing his skull in a net bag at the back of her head show they have "taken him apart"; show that the women who looked after him when he died ingested his life-force and attached it "on the skin." The effect of women's decorations is not only to make them look and smell like the dead but also to make them unrecognizable and anonymous. Like corpses, women in mourning appear all alike because their faces are covered with *nini* and blacked out. For about a month after an important death, no one of the deceased's clan should clear garden land or plant, and no one in the village should light a fire in a garden.

Mourning women thus resemble the dead not only by their ghastly odor and appearance, and loss of individuality, but also by their inactivity. Collectively, they become *faba baϑaha*. They lose their kinship with the deceased, and hence their social identity, as I argue later, because *he*—or his *auna*—cannot see their faces or know their names.

During the year following *ruhu*, in a series of attendant lesser rites, men bring the women back to life, as it were, and restore their identities by divesting them of the deceased's spirit, buying back the *auna* that still resides in their body coverings and in certain relics of the *ruhu* and later feasts. At *niniusina* (lit: *nini*/blackening + *usi*/dish + *na*/thing), celebrated some two to six months after a man's death, women gather to remove the *nini* from their faces and to receive men's gifts of meat in the manner of *ruhu*, sitting in rows and having their names called one by one. At *beheϑabaϑa* (lit: *beheϑa*/fern + *ϑabaϑa*/spine), the mourners burn the dried central spines of ferns that were cooked in the ovens of *ruhu* and *niniusina* to symbolize the uncultivated greens once cooked with human flesh. At *agesagena*, women burn their ragged clothes and replace them with new ones, officially ending the period of mourning. *niniusina* and *beheϑabaϑa* are ideally celebrated on consecutive days but may be held months apart, or in separate rites for the women of different compounds, depending upon the importance of the deceased, the number of women mourners, the resources of the *ababana*, etc. *agesagena* is usually held much later, a year or longer after *ruhu*.

### niniusina and beheϑabaϑa

*niniusina* is like a scaled-down version of *ruhu*. There are fewer outsiders and the ovens are usually filled with marsupials instead of pigs, perhaps twenty or thirty animals cooked whole, and many varieties of *beheϑa* or ferns. The women stuff their mouths with ferns as they begin to unload the ovens, pulling the long central spines dramatically between spaces in their teeth. Men cut plates from banana leaves and, as always at these affairs, complain about women's chattering and order them to quiet their children and keep the dogs away from the meat. Once senior women have emptied the ovens, men take over, cutting and apportioning the cooked meat. "Cut it small!" commands the chief butcher, holding up a piece of exemplary size.

Women sit cross-legged facing each other in parallel rows. Two women of the deceased's clan move up and down the central aisle to perform the *niniusina*. One woman removes the *nini*, using a small loop of bamboo to lift off a token fleck from the nose or forehead of each woman, and collects all the flecks in a leaf. Her cohort stands behind her, holding an *usi*, or wooden bowl, filled with chunks of cooked meat and fat. The moment a fleck of *nini* is removed, she places a piece of food directly into the woman's

Women eat ferns or *behe ϑa* as one of the requirements of mourning, using their teeth to tear leaves off the long central spines. They will save and collect the dried spines and later turn them over in a bundle to men of the deceased's lineage in exchange for payments of cooked meat.

Mourning women sit in long lines during *niniusina*. A senior woman uses a small loop of bamboo to remove a speck of blackening from the forehead of each mourner. Another woman then takes a chunk of cooked pork or fat from an *usi* or wooden bowl and places it directly into the mourner's mouth. On this occasion, a metal pot lid is used instead of an *usi*.

After the token removal of *nini*, men place a banana leaf "plate" in front of each mourning woman and fill it with luxury foods like cooked marsupial, rice, banana, taro, and yams.

mouth. When the two have moved up and down the rows, attending in this way to each of the women, and then to themselves, they sit down at the end of one of the rows and the men set out banana-leaf plates in the aisle. A Big Man who directs the distribution calls out each woman's name in turn. As a name is called, other men, who are the waiters, fill the woman's plate with sections of cooked marsupials, bananas, taro, and rice. Though naming is a regular feature of these rites, it is always startling to hear the Big Man announce women's names because of the taboo in everyday life upon saying a person's name in his or her presence.

Black-faced women are not the only ones to be named publicly and to receive allotments of meat after *niniusina*. Distantly related women who wear no *nini,* maternal kinsmen from other villages, and a few young men who "ate *beheϑa* with the women" are included in the distribution. On one occasion, men announced the name of an unmarried man, adding: "He is a young man who ate our father's *beheϑa*. When all the women were eating, he sat down with them and ate *beheϑa* too."

> When a man dies, women eat *beheϑa* because it's not good food. They wouldn't eat sweet potato or sugarcane. They eat only the leaves of the ferns. The spines they keep in reserve and put away inside their houses. . . . A man can eat *beheϑa* with the women but not if he is the [dead] man's own age-mate! Age-mates are the ones who call his sisters to bring the *beheϑabaϑa* when its time to take off the *nini.*

Though I saw women—but never men— eat ferns out of the ovens at *ruhu* or *niniusina,* I did not observe the meals of ferns and red pandanus women say they gather "in the forest" and eat "out of men's sight":

> We gather *habi, miϑu, ba'aϑa, baϑo'eparo, na'efabo* [varieties of *beheϑa*] and remove the leaves and keep the spines, the *dabaϑa*. . . . When we ate a man we ate *beheϑa.* We gathered *nasu* [wild greens, including ferns, parsley, watercress, and edible grasses] and cooked them with the meat. We put the man's skin into bamboo and his bones into the oven. . . .
>
> When a good man dies we do not gather *remu* and *hore,* the things we planted with our hands. We do not go to our gardens. We eat only what grows by itself. We gather ferns and eat them in the forest.

The dozen places one woman named as current sources of ferns and wild greens for *beheϑabaϑa* were fallow gardens belonging to nearly every clan of the village, some completely overgrown and reverted to forest, others with sections still being cultivated. After gathering wild greens, women say, they collect red pandanus from semi-cultivated groves in low-lying river estuaries. Then they return to the compound to prepare an evening meal of the "wild foods." The next morning, and for four or five more days, women go back into the "forest" alone or in small groups to gather *beheϑa*.

> The first time Sabaro went to get *beheϑa*. We ate it and slept. The second day I went. We ate up all the *beheϑa* I had brought and went to sleep. In the morning, Anoikinan went and brought back *beheϑa*. We ate it and slept. The next morning Tabe went and got *beheϑa* and we ate it all and slept. Eafi . . . Monuota . . . *kore*-Taneoigi [naming all the women of a compound] . . . Boabu, Baruke and Buru [two co-wives and their husband] brought red pandanus and *beheϑa* and cooked them in an earth oven and gave them to us and we all ate and went to sleep.
>
> We ate and ate and ate and slept and slept and slept. We were too sad to go to our gardens. . . . We took some of the spines to the dead man's mother. After that we didn't eat *beheϑa* any more. It was over. Finished.

I commented to the women that the number of days spent eating *beheϑa*, and the intervening nights of sleep, reminded me of men's accounts of cannibalism, especially the delay in starting *ruhu* until the women had completely digested or "slept off" their meal. My comment prompted only the demurral that it took "only a day or two" to consume a man. Men, as we have seen, directly connect *beheϑa* with a person, attributing human mortality to the fern's foolish disregard of the snake and men's ensuing inability to "change skins" (see Chap. 3). In the past, an old woman named Nubimi told me, women often caught a snake and cooked it with the ferns "because we were sorry. We ate the snake in sorrow for the man. . . . Our bodies ached with hunger so we ate . . . and our pain was less." As in rites surrounding the *kore riϑi*, one sex here seems ritually to enact—but decline to put into words— ideas or associations that are direct and explicit in myths of the other sex.

Though I was not present when women consumed ferns in the marathon manner they described, I did see the huge piles of dried spines they kept in reserve. The women presented a token bundle to the dead man's mother "for his father to burn" and stored the rest inside the house of a Big Man. When it was time for *niniusina,* they fetched the bundles of *beheϑabaϑa* and carried them to the compound of the deceased, making a pile on the periphery.

Before dawn of the morning after *niniusina,* after token specks of *nini* have been removed from women's faces, several sisters of the dead man and wives of his brothers set out for the upper reaches of his clan forest, carrying with them some of the meat they received the previous day, the leaf-wrapped packet containing the specks of *nini,* and the bundles of *beheðabaða.* At the source of a river, or amid a stand of white pandanus, the women make a fire to heat the cooked meat and to burn the *nini* and *beheðabaða.* The thin spines are very dry and burst into flame. When the flames "reach highest," the women throw water on the fire to make it "die" and then bury the soaked ashes amid the pandans' aerial roots. Sometimes they let the fire go out by itself and rub the ashes onto their thighs or throw them into the river. "We throw away the ashes and we cry," the women say. "We burn the *beheða* beside the river of our father."

While the women are in the forest, they remove the rest of the *nini* from their faces as well as the layers of *abiare* and "hide" them with the ashes, burying all the "leavings" amid pandanus roots or casting them into the river. Afterward, several older women set leaf plates in a row and fill them with the reheated meat, mimicking the style of distribution at *ruhu* and *niniusina.*

> We burn the *beheðabaða* and bury the ashes. We hide them completely and put the meat in our mouths. We bury the *beheðabaða* and come back to eat. And when we have eaten, we go back to our houses.

Before returning to the settlement, the women examine themselves and each other to make sure they have removed every particle of clay and blackening, searching their bodies with the care and scrupulousness of midwives at the end of a birth making sure they have washed away every trace of parturitory blood.

### *agesagena*

A year or so after a man dies, his clan celebrate *agesagena* to end the period of women's mourning. Until this final rite, women who are betrothed cannot be sent to their husbands, and the widow cannot remarry because "the *auna* of her husband's *kore* inside her *agesagena* would kill the new man." Her husband's age-mates and men of his clan (but not his own brothers) who wish to claim her vie for the right to supply the meat that will "remove her *agesagena*": "The woman thinks, 'I have no pigs and you kill a pig to raise the name of my husband. Then you are the man I shall marry'" (see Chap. 3n.9).

Women describe *agesagena* as a repetition of *beheðabaða.* "We burn *agesagena* the same way," they say. Before dawn of the day after a feast celebrated in the compound, a small group of women climb high into the clan forest to the source of a river, carrying with them the tattered net bags and other mourning garb. They burn bundles of *agesagena* and bury the ashes amid pandanus roots or cast them into the water.

When we burn the *agesagena*, we get rid of all the leavings. We burn the *kareta* [widow's beads] and the *maϑo* [the (dead man's) loincloth] and the *koata* [net bags he wore or that his wife and mother used to carry his food].

We all fetch rocks and heat them to make the earth oven. We gather parsley and ferns and leaves and bring them to the river's edge. Some of us burn the *agesagena*. Others make the oven and reheat the meat. . . .

We take off our *agesagena* and get a knife and cut the meat into pieces. Then we line up the banana leaves and divide the meat. We give meat to that woman, that woman, that woman and that one. . . . Then we put on new string skirts and return to our houses.

Men describe *agesagena*, the eating of *beheϑa*, the wearing of *nini* and *abiare*, and especially cannibalism itself, as practices women invented and undertook on their own. "Women alone had the idea of making *agesagena*, of tearing up net bags to make skirts and of afterwards making new skirts," men say. Women decorate each other without ritual, men insist, exactly as they "stole the corpse" in the past. Men characterize *ruhu*, and the subsequent feasts of *niniusina*, *beheϑabaϑa*, and *agesagena*, as their response to what women did by themselves, out of men's sight, without "songs or names," attributing to women the kind of priority and independence the first woman had when she created—and plugged—the flute.

In the rites surrounding death, the essence of all women's illicit acts and unnamed inclinations lies in the *symbolic* theft of a corpse: even when women did not actually consume the dead in the past, their mourning garb rent the man asunder and attached him "on the skin." Women absconded with the corpse in the sense that they tried to make it disappear *as part of them*. They cut the man to pieces by tearing up his clothes and net bags, making amulets of his teeth, hair, and small bones, reducing him to items of decoration and attributes of themselves. But in the process of disassembling the man, dispersing his parts and putting them on, women's faces "blacked out" and they lost their own identity.

The anarchy of the cannibal meal, and even the meal itself in many instances, were deliberate fictions, as I have emphasized, dramas of confusion and emotional abandon concocted by both sexes as the pretext for men to celebrate *ruhu* and the subsequent death rites as impositions of male order and control, presentations of a second course that blamed women for the theft and dismemberment and divested them of the spoils. The "other meat" men distributed, the pig's "head" for the man's head, the pig's "arm" for the man's arm, the pig's "leg" for the man's leg, etc., was not merely the replication of the deceased as an object but the recapitulation of his entire demise, the enactment of a myth of how he—like the firstborn—was reduced to pieces and devoured by his mother. In rite after rite, men give women back their names and identities as mothers (as I show in a moment) by presenting them with head payments, second-course replacements for the mythic "head of the child" (see Chap. 3). The payments unattach what women stole: in exchange for the head, women burn the *behe ðaba ða* and the *agesagena,* wash away the *nini* and *abiare,* and consign the dead man's *auna* to the clan forest. But the "child" women surrender is not alive. In order to rescue it and bring it to life, in order to make the child's head available to other consumers, men also have to present head payments (meat taken from the same animals) to the cannibals' fathers and brothers, entering into alliances with their "first husbands."

In traditional Gimi society, women were forbidden to handle knives or axes. The butchering of animals and allotment of meat at feasts were, and are still, exclusive prerogatives of elder Gimi men, symbols of men's superior judgment and right to dominate women. The public division and distribution of head payments to waiting women stands in opposition to women's secret act by demonstrating men's ability not only to share food but also to *remember* and *name* the recipients in an orderly way. But if *ruhu* was, and is, a play on women's greed and unruliness, then so are women's predawn trips to the headwaters to burn the *behe ðaba ða* and *agesagena* mockeries of men's daylight achievements. Women respond to men's response to their supposedly illicit deeds with similar acts of repetition: having been publicly feted, women return before dawn to the forest, going back to the place and time of the original cannibal meal. There they again eat alone and "out of men's sight." But this time women "line the plates" in imitation of men's improved version of their chaotic first course. They perform "a pallid imitation of male ceremonial . . . [that is itself] symbolically imitative of direct . . . activities of women" (Mead 1970:258). Women's forest rites seem to undo the undoing of their subversion and thus to counteract men's ritual intention. Looked at in this way, Gimi death rites are a series of ploys and counterploys, an unspoken acting out of conflict whose course and outcome the sexes understand in advance.

### Blaming the Mother

In a society governed largely by kinship, or by rules expressed through the idiom of kinship, in which participation in group activities is based upon careful genealogical reckoning (as my lists of ritual attendance clearly show), it is remarkable that at death "nothing women," women without a significant tie of kinship to the deceased, put on mourning decorations and "eat *behe ða*" and, in the past, supposedly participated in the cannibal meal. At death, it would seem, a woman's inclusion in ritual is calculated not simply according to an assigned kinship status but also according to the myth of what she did secretly in concert with other women, of how she acted as part of a faceless, unruly mob. Women's collective guilt and depersonalization are expressed in the onerous garb that make all the mourners look and smell like a decomposing corpse. But they are also expressed more subtly in food taboos. Food brought by mourners from other villages is dangerous, men and women say, because it may have been raised or owned or tasted by men who ensorcelled the deceased and therefore permeated by their will, imbued with malevolent *auna*. If women of the dead man's clan—his widow, mothers, fathers' and brothers' wives—and even women of affinally related clans—his sisters and fathers' sisters—were to eat this food, it might attack the dead man's children but leave the women themselves unharmed. In the logic of these prohibitions, women's bodies serve as conduits, as unmarked vessels through which a sorcerer can reach his victim. But if women are treated, in this sense, as passive and anonymous, as empty objects that men can manipulate, how can they also be regarded as the underlying cause of death and destruction?

There is a dramatic contrast in the kinds of things men and women do, or consider important, when someone dies in his or her prime. Among the close male relations of a man, there is often a rash of illness, prompting each to review in obsessive detail his last contacts with the deceased, to confess old quarrels and debts and indifference to final requests. The ailing kinsmen are filled with self-reproaches and offer belatedly to make amends, usually by killing pigs to "feed the *kore*" (see Chap. 4). Women do not often fall ill, nor do they reproach themselves, nor are they accused by others of failing in their devotion or of ignoring opportunities to care for the deceased. Women, as individuals, are rarely targets of the *kore*'s wrath. During the period when men succumb to sympathetic pains and maladies and search their memories for past misdeeds, women sever the ends of their fingers and put on mourning disguises. A woman's guilt seems to be unrelated to her own character or actions, to anything she did or failed to do, so that she can do little to erase it or mitigate its extent. While men fall ill and make amends and recover, women seem to be blamed collectively for crimes of their mythic past. Mourning blacks out women's faces, as I have suggested, in the sense that their whole garb, the *agesagena, nini,* and *abiare,* and the required self-mutilations, symbolize the deadness and lack of individuality that ensue from their commission of a mythic crime. Men and women seem to agree that women, or primordial woman, did something that "caused her to be classified with all other women under one general concept" (Simmel 1955:180, quoted in Rosaldo 1974:28). A Gimi woman is passive in this sense, yet culpable.

If *ruhu* and the rites that follow it enact a dispute between the sexes, a trading back and forth of blame based upon the shared fantasy that death and cannibalism arose in their first union, in incest and the onset of menses, then the outcome of the whole mortuary sequence substantiates men's position, imprisoning women inside a myth men created or, more accurately perhaps, inside a version of women's myth that men appropriated and altered to suit themselves. In men's myth of the first marriage, the wife is a rapacious widow and her husbands, or potential husbands, are innocent and "delicious" victims, parrots perched in trees, whom she impales with a stick and devours or feeds to her orphaned children (see Chap. 3). After a death, men are unable to identify their wives. They cannot see the terrible thing women have done and are, therefore, in the terms of their myth, defenseless. A man who cannot see his wife—because she is blacked out in mourning—is in the position of a "delicious parrot" sitting in a tree: he may be overtaken from below and behind; he wants to "talk" to his wife, but she is "not listening." He cannot *speak her name* because he is—or is about to become—her husband, her meal, a dead bird in the next tree. Covered in *nini* and *abiare*, bedecked in the dead man's "leavings," mourning women all become the cannibal widow of men's myth.

If women's disguises signify their guilt in the terms of men's myth, then they also contradict women's own myths according to which it is the wife—not the husband—who is defenseless, asleep, and approached from behind. In women's myth of the Torrent Lark, for instance, the wife is not a widow but a virgin. Her husband is an ugly old man who "loses his head inside her buttocks" (Chap. 3). In revenge, she kills their child and hides it at the bottom of her oven, cooking it like a suckling pig. The argument put forth by women's myths is that if woman created the first cannibal meal—if she provoked the "first appearance" of her own menstrual blood—she did it because she was raped and tricked into marriage by a man like her father. Treating the mourners as rapacious widows hides their identity as virgins and new mothers, as the mythic woman who cut off the giant *because* he raped her, or as the beautiful girl who killed her firstborn *because* her husband created the child out of feces instead of "real meat." *ruhu* and the rites that follow it enact the dispute between men's and women's myths in a way that spoils women's excuse by denying the presence or even existence of a father. According to men, everything women do in the event of death is entirely their own idea.

But the initial phase of mortuary ritual—the part men say women carry out on their own and "without ritual"—seems instead to have been orchestrated by men in conformity with their own myth. Women's cannibalism, extravagant attentions to the corpse, and ensuing disguises appear to enact men's own fantasies of the first marriage, the time when woman "had the flute"—or wielded the stick at the top of the tree—and the only man alive was a "small boy." Mourning women are unrecognizable and cannot be named, according to the logic of men's myth, because the first woman devoured every grown-up witness. "She finished off every man in every tree! . . . killed man after man after man until she found the boy standing at the base." Not to "see" the mourners' faces, to take away their identity and clan affiliation and turn them into *faba baϑaha,* in these terms, is to void their status as wives, to deny that they have living husbands who are the source of their appetite, rage, and guilt.

Ironically, women's ritual anonymity helps the *ababana,* the men who conduct the rite, to ignore the mythic father and to identify themselves with the deceased by adopting the posture of mute spectator, like the boy left standing at the base of the tree. Men stage *ruhu* as the repetition of a cannibal meal that no man saw and no man could prevent. The sole witness—the one upon whose testimony they reconstruct the original partition of the corpse—is a boy (or a man of low status or a woman with her wits about her) who watched the women (see Chap. 3). In the terms of men's myth, listening to the boy (or his counterpart) was like listening to the boy beside the tree, the one who survived, like Jonah in the whale, to tell the tale of his terrible adventure. Calling in the boy as a witness was like reviving the firstborn child in women's myths and hearing *his* side of the story—a side that contradicts women's version of how he died.

If the initial phase of mortuary ritual enacts men's myth of incestuous marriage, then it also enacts the concurrent death of the firstborn. Women's behavior around a corpse is chaotic and subversive in this light because it recapitulates *male* fantasies not only of incest but also of birth, an event in which a man can have no cognizant role, in which the mother is the only adult, the only one fully present, the only one able to see and hear. From the perspective of the deceased as firstborn child, no man was present when he died—when his mother began to menstruate. Because a woman is sole witness to the "first appearance" of her blood, or the birth of her child, men's myths seem to say that she alone possesses sexual appetite and is hungry for a mate. "I already have a wife," the old man tells the widow, attempting to halt her advances. "I am not hungry," he might have said. "I am satisfied and have no desire." As a story of copulation recounted by the unborn, by one ensconced in the womb looking up at the "head" of the giant penis, men's myth of Delicious Parrots describes first menses as an event women instigated by themselves. When men say that cannibalism or mourning decorations are "entirely women's idea," from this mythic perspective they express their own wish not to see the father, not to acknowledge his role in the child's creation and death, and to treat the murder weapon—the vicious "stick," giant penis, lust, greed, appetite, etc.—as if it were owned and invented entirely by the mother.

But if the first phase of mortuary ritual may be construed as an elaborate denial of the father, a bid to make mother the sole author of death and desire, it also plays out the humiliating circumstance of men's birth, a fantasy of incest in which their mothers devour them unaware, while their eyes are still closed. In the second phase of the death ritual, in *ruhu* and the ensuring rites of divestiture, men repeat the mythic incest with themselves in control, looking into their mothers' faces, in retrospect as it were, compelling the mourners to take off the *nini*, discard the disfiguring *agesagena*, etc., so they can publicize the names of those who would impale them on sticks and sexually devour them. By using the boy as their witness and providing replacement food, the men most closely identified with the deceased, those most likely to share his fate, redo his demise with a new outcome. Through the eyes of the boy, as it were, the *ababana* watch the rapacious widow in the midst of the first marriage and offer her something else to eat. They invent brideprice and head payments to replace the boy at the base of the tree and allow him to escape her.

Interpreted in light of myth, *ruhu* is a rite that identifies the mother by establishing her guilt, enacting the mythic moment when the murdered firstborn child, revived as the boy in men's myth and then played in ritual by the deceased's paternal kinsmen, looks into his mother's face and realizes who she is. Men calling out the names of women mourners has the significance, in these terms, of the corpse himself bearing witness to woman's primordial crime; as if the murdered boy lying at the bottom of her oven, or the giant's severed head, were to speak and accuse his killer. Like the first woman who owned the flute, cannibal women behaved as if they were self-sufficient and inaccessible, as if they were alone and had no husbands—no grown or cognizant men—to stop them from fulfilling unruly desires. If the firstborn child had opened his eyes, he would have seen his mother cutting and devouring him. He would have caught her in flagrante delicto and known she was his mother. He would have seen the face of *faba baðaha* and known her name.

But if *ruhu* is interpreted as the child's first sighting of his mother and understanding of her guilt, then it, and the subsequent rites of *niniusina, beheðabaða,* and *agesagena,* also represent the ensuing recognition that, contrary to first appearance, the mother is *not* alone; that the father exists inside her and appears on the skin; that a mother is not an anonymous woman, after all, but one who secretly possesses the father. *ruhu* and the later rites buy back the spirit of the deceased, divesting the mourners of the man they ingested and surreptitiously put on. But in de-manning the women, reducing them to an unadorned, nonmythic state, the rites inevitably acknowledge the father's presence. To right the wrong of their own birth and first marriage, men have to redo the myth in the ritual present—and thus acknowledge the father's role. When the deceased's paternal kinsmen distribute a second course to women mourners, they give a kind of recognition to women's myth by showing they indeed possess the "head" the giant penis hunted and killed. The presentation of head payments and announcement of women's names at *ruhu, niniusina,* etc., are like accusations of theft: they expose the women who dismembered the man and misappropriated his parts. Yet in identifying the mother as she appears in their own myth, men also implicitly recognize the father as he appears in *women's* myth, as a giant who stalked marsupials and invaded woman's house to "eat the head." As a bid not to return, not to reenter the house the giant invaded, men's offer of a second course and purchase of an escape are also tacit acknowledgment that they once were there; that they, too, attended the death "between woman's thighs" and are at fault.

In the sense that *ruhu,* or any Gimi rite of exchange, corrects or alters the myths of one sex, it both affirms and overrides myths of the other. The manner in which the *ababana* present women mourners with head payments both acknowledges the father and at once removes the signs of his presence. With the gift of the "head," the *ababana* both display the meat the penis killed—admit the father ventured inside the mother—and create a new exit in the mother through which he irrevocably departs. Before a man is carried to his garden to be buried, or installed on a platform in the past, his corpse is pulled out of his mother's house through a specially made opening. Men seal the doorway and tear open a hole in the opposite wall, altering the design of the house, I suggest, as if to modify the mother's body; at once repeating the giant's first invasion and closing that hole through the creation of a second exit, a second mouth that is impossible to reenter. The second time a man leaves his mother's house, so to speak, he moves feet first out an opening into which he cannot return. When women burn the *behe ðabaða* and *agesagena,* wash the *nini* and *abiare* from every crevice of their bodies, and consign the "leavings" to a river deep inside the clan forest, they give the deceased the same kind of irrevocable second send-off, discharging him from their bodies through new orifices. The rites celebrated the day before, in which women accepted men's gifts of "other meat," created new exits in their bodies. Once women "eat the head of the child," they are compelled to release it in a new way, to let it out a second exit through which they cannot take it back. Gimi mortuary rites reveal how the child died and establish who the mothers were so that men, or their *auna*s, can make a permanent escape and achieve immortality in the forest.

The whole series of Gimi death rites suggest that the social definition of motherhood, and the basis of kinship, stem from a male fantasy of incest. When a man is born, when he emerges from his mother the first time, according to this fantasy, he cannot see her face or speak her name. He recognizes his mother entirely by what she *does* to him—by her "killing" him at birth, hiding his corpse at the bottom of her oven, etc.—things she does to induce her menstrual flow and become a mother. The first time a child sees his mother, she is in the midst of cutting him and starting to menstruate. The father seems to be missing from the scene although, paradoxically, he is entirely present, lurking inside the mother and hidden from view—like the plug in the flute. To the newborn, the mother *appears* to act alone and to hold the penis or "stick" by herself: her fury seems spontaneous and unprovoked. As long as men keep the fantasy of the father's absence, in other words, they maintain the idea of the mother's guilt and use it as the pretext to arrange a second escape.

In the father's absence, men are obliged to take out of women's hands—and houses—the thing they keep turning to blood. The means of dispossession, the means of opening women's bodies and acquiring what they stole, is to offer them the "head of the child" as replacement, to present a second course in exchange for the digested remains of the first. Women seem to accept men's gift in the spirit in which it is given, as an accusation of theft, as showing they ruined the child they took from men and cannot send it back. Women's participation in mortuary ritual thus seems to represent more than compliance in a male game and to express women's own fantasies and wishes, the subject I next explore.

# PART TWO

Women's Work and the World They Hide

# SIX

## "Songs Hold the Spirit": Garden Magic, Blood Songs, and the Nature of Women's Work

When I began to spend days in the gardens, the women quizzed me about my identity. Nupa, a woman of about my age, decided, because of our rapport and the relation between Samantha and her elder daughter, that I might be a sister who had died as a child. As we sat together in the shade at the edge of her garden, she gave her baby daughter a plantain and then broke off a piece and handed it to me, deliberately making the child cry. She had named the baby after her father and addressed it as *natu,* "my taboo" (*n*/my + *atu*/taboo), a term equivalent to "daddy." In a playful gesture, she lifted her daughter's arm as if to strike me. When I responded in kind, she pleaded mockingly on the baby's behalf: "Don't hit me! I am your father!"

Months after this exchange I realized that I was regarded as a woman of the village who had come back from Australia, the land of the Gimi dead. I had returned home with my husband and daughter, yet, curiously, we refused to name our relations in the village, forcing people to calculate our ancestry by keeping careful track of who visited our house most often, shared our food most freely, made us laugh most easily. Our white skin and "cargo" showed that we transacted with the *kore,* spirits of the dead, who provided us with access not only to material wealth but also to heightened insight, giving us the ability to see our invisible trading partners and to know the past (see Burridge 1960; Lawrence 1964; Worsley 1968). Mysteriously, we were reticent to describe a world that was inaccessible to other Gimi, yet intimately tied to them. For this reason, perhaps, I was rarely told things directly. I had been in the field nearly two years before I even knew women's myths or *nenekaina* existed, and it took me another year or so to connect them to the major life-crisis rituals, to female initiation (*haro;* Gillison 1987), rites of death (*ruhu*), birth (*ϑau;* Chap. 8), marriage and male initiation (*kuta* and *apina;* Chap. 9).

But it was nearly nine years after I began to study *nenekaina* that I realized their relation to the many lesser rites of women's daily lives. Women invoke the "secrets" of the *nene* in *nasobakaina* or "food talk," the cryptic spells and songs they recite during nearly every phase of gardening and pig rearing, and, in the *korabak* and *hibosubak,* the "blood songs" and "Moon's songs" they sing to end their periods. In 1985, Monuato, an elder ritual expert, told me that the whole meaning of "food talk" lay in the *nene.* "All our talk comes from the *nene,*" she casually remarked, presuming from our years of discussion I was well aware of the link. "Whatever we say and sing to our sweet potatoes, yams, bananas, taros, pigs—to all our food—is in the *nene.* That's the mother of our talk, the source of our magic." "Those who know the meaning of *nene,*" another woman added, "know how to speak to food and how properly to divide it." Women's garden magic, and its elaborate connection with the *nene,* highlight the unreality of men's claims that women tend to do things "without songs or names."

Women hear garden magic all their lives, as infants slung in net bags across their mothers' backs, as three- or four-year-olds beginning to work in the gardens, and as mourners at women's funerals (Chap. 8).

> We care for pigs with song and we plant sweet potatoes, greens, wild sugarcane, everything, entirely with song. . . . We sing and our songs hold the *auna.* . . . Songs make the woman's *auna* and the *auna* of her pig or plant into one. . . . That is how food grows and gets bigger.

A girl is not given spells of her own until she is initiated and married. During the initial secret phases of female initiation (*haro*) and marriage (*kuta*), a woman "receives" spells from older women. Before pacification, a girl was often married and sent to live in her husband's settlement before she had reached menarche so that she received a first set of instructions from her *anoha* or mothers when they celebrated *kuta* before her departure, and a later set from her *anaturaha* when she began to menstruate and underwent the ordeals of *haro* before actually cohabiting with her husband. In ritual terms, a woman's marriage is the cause of her first menses: during *kuta,* she "loses the flute" and then celebrates her initiation (see Chap. 9). Today the order of *kuta* and *haro* are usually reversed because women tend to marry later, some years after menarche, and to find mates within their own villages. But young women still "forget most of what they hear," as the older women complain, and are still subjected to a second ritual of instruction.[1]

Food talk is "secret" and shared only among close classificatory mothers

---

1. When a woman marries within the village, she may take up residence in her husband's compound before she starts to menstruate or before her father has assembled the pigs for her initiation. To celebrate the rite, she and her affines convene in her father's compound.

A Gimi woman alone in her garden.

and daughters and between mothers- and daughters-in-law.[2] A married woman samples, discards, combines, and invents her own formulas, repeating only those that seem to work, until she has assembled a unique repertoire. Men have their own songs for male crops like bananas, sugarcane, and pandanus, but "a man follows the mouth of his wife" when he speaks to his pigs. Men also learn pig spells from their mothers and sometimes serve as links in transmitting them to wives or daughters, but men are not privy to women's magic. As one woman said:

> We take the girls inside and give them spells to make food grow, to rear pigs and to plant new gardens. We give them songs to get rid of the Moon's blood. We close our doors and men do not hear our songs and stories. . . . The spirit of *kuta* and of *haro* is the spirit of food. . . .

Early in the evening of the first night of *haro* or *kuta*, the two initiates or brides—a pair of *amau*—are escorted to the house of one of their mothers and seated side by side on a pandanus mat before the central fire. Women tell them that a wife who sulks and does not repeat the spells for pigs, who does not "hide her blood," work tirelessly in the gardens, and help her *anatu* in unsolicited ways will soon be outdone and replaced. The women pile wood on the fire, building it to an enormous heat, and tell the initiates that their sweat will rid them of menstrual blood. "When the Moon's water hits [a woman's] legs, we cook her [i.e., celebrate *haro*]. We cook and cook the girl but give her no water to drink."

Describing her own *haro* some fifty years before, Taneoigi recalled thrashings and scoldings. Two of her *anatu* sat on either side of her, kept her constantly awake and refused to let her drink for four days and nights:[3]

> "This is how you will plant food in your gardens!" they told me. "You must talk to your plants to make them grow. . . . When your back aches and sweat is pouring from your brow . . . you will work! You will work while the sun beats down on you . . . and not even *think* of finding a cool place or sitting down!"

2. There is a hierarchy of secrecy in which spoken spells are valued over song. Women talked about their spells, but when I asked to record them they usually sang songs instead. After one or two women gave me recitations for sweet potato and taro, I was confronted by their angry *anaturaha* who said that my "taking" the spells would make them loose their efficacy.

3. Like a male initiate, a woman is attended throughout her ordeal by a chaperon or *ahamo* (lit: *aha*/same + *mo*/the), one who has the "same name" (see Chap. 9). The *ahamo* is an *anatu* (but not the *kisa anatu*; see Chap. 2). Since co-initiates or brides are usually *amau*, their *ahamo* are likely to be their mothers as well as mothers-in-law.

At the end of her ordeal, emptied of her own sweat and the Moon's "water," the initiate will be presented with a bamboo tube containing water drawn from her husband's clan river (Gillison 1980, 1987).

Between the harsh warnings, the women crowded into the stifling hut recite the songs and chants that accompany virtually every aspect of gardening. A woman "speaks" to her sweet potatoes while she loads the vines into her net bag, gathers loosened earth into mounds, tunnels her hand into the centers of the mounds and inserts the ends of the vines, "straightens" the vines she leaves exposed, "cleans" the mounds by removing weeds or other debris, etc. (see Malinowski 1922:59; 1965 [1935]). To introduce a song for taro, Darebaro says, "I gently wipe the earth off the new shoots and sing this song. The taro hears my song and comes up, up, up out of the ground!" The songs flatter and inspire each plant to grow big and delicious, comparing the beauty of its new shoots to the plumage of a Bird of Paradise and the ease and speed of its growth to the rush of water over a fall or the slithering of an eel out of one's grasp.

### Sequel to the Giant Penis: The kore baðaha's Second Marriage

One reason I did not connect women's fertility magic with their myths is the striking difference in tone. It did not occur to me to link songs and spells filled with resplendent images of the forest with tales of incest, murder, and cannibalism. Another reason I did not associate "food talk" with *nenekaina* was that I did not hear the myths recounted during the rites I attended, although the women say that they are traditionally repeated during the initial secret phases of marriage and initiation. Like the rites themselves, *nenekaina* are mainly concerned with the origin of menstruation.

The following *nene* about the sorry fate of a widow, and eventual triumph of her daughter in marriage, is the second of a series that starts with the Giant Penis (see Chap. 4). The myth can be heard, on a nearly explicit level, as a reply to men's myth of the Widow in Search of Delicious Parrots (see Chap. 3) and to *ruhu* itself. Like the Giant Penis and Torrent Lark myths (see Chap. 3), it seems to shift blame in the vicious cycle of mythic accusations. This version of women's myth is a combination of two of the more than thirty renditions I collected. The marauding giant or trickster is portrayed here by the ghost of the dead husband, a "wild man" or *kore bana*, with an ax blade protruding from the middle of his forehead.

> Once there was a widow. Her husband had just died and left her with a daughter and infant son. "You two stay here," she said to her orphaned children. "I'm going to collect ferns for the *behe-ðabaða*. Stay here and watch that banana tree! If you hear the

ripe fruit falling, if you hear the banana cry *ororo ororo,* you will know I have been killed." She told her children to listen and watch the banana and went off to the place where her husband had been sharpening posts for a fence. The fence stood half-built and the garden was half-cleared.

Up and up and up she climbed, following the river to its source. She collected *beheᵭa* along the way and caught frogs, wrapping them in leaves and stuffing them into her net bag. As she climbed higher, collecting more *beheᵭa* and catching more frogs, she saw debris of a dead tree being carried downstream. Approaching the source of the river, she came upon an old man who was hacking open the tree to take out grubs. The woman watched him thrusting his forehead into the tree. "Old man," she said, "I see you're collecting grubs."

"Who are you, old woman? Why have you come?" he said. "I left my children at home and came to the place where their father was sharpening stakes for a fence," she replied. "I've come to gather *beheᵭa.*" "Go ahead," he told her. "But if you come with me I'll show you where you can dig yams, too."[4] He said this to her and the two of them went off together.

"There are frogs under the raincover inside your net bag," he said to her as they walked along. She gave him the frogs and he ate them. "You have more frogs in your net bag," he said, and she gave him the frogs and he ate them. "There are frogs inside the bamboo container you use for making fires," he said, and she gave him the frogs and he ate them. "You've hidden more frogs under the *agesagena* on your head," he said to her. And she gave them to him and he ate them. "You've hidden frogs in the *agesagena* you wear as a rear-skirt," he said to her, and she gave him the frogs and he ate them. And the two of them continued on their way.

Having eaten all the frogs the widow had collected for her children and hidden in her mourning raiments, the *kore bana* killed the widow, thrusting his long stick up her anus.

---

4. Yams were once included in brideprice. A yam is "like a vagina," men say, because, eaten raw, it makes the mouth pucker or purse. A yam is also associated with the buttocks. To a lazy wife a man may say, "What's the matter? Your ass turned into a yam [i.e., become a heavy and immovable object]?" But the yam is also a symbol of a man's hairy anus, a connection men rarely mention. Discussing the symbolism of objects and qualities, Gimi men often refer to a woman's sex or anatomy but tend to be hesitant, oblique, or silent in making associations with the male.

When they arrived at the place with wild yams, the *kore bana* told the widow how to dig. "If you raise your rear end and put your head to the ground," he told her, "you can break the yams in half easily." So the widow raised her buttocks to the sky and dug up yams while the old man went off to clean his sugarcane. He had hidden a long stick amid his sugar and, as he stripped dead leaves off the cane, he pulled it out. The stick was blackened and encrusted with the guts of other old women. He thrust the stick into the old woman's anus, pushing it all the way inside her until it came out her mouth and penetrated the soft ground. She shuddered and died in a spasm.

The *kore bana* ate the widow's insides but saved the rest of her to make a disguise, fitting himself with her head, arms, legs, breasts and mourning attire.

He pulled his stick out of her anus and licked it clean. He downed every morsel of blood and feces and then cut the widow to pieces. He cut off one hand and tried it on. It fit him well. He cut off the other hand and tried it on. It fit him well. He cut off one leg below the knee and tried it on. It fit him well. He cut off the other leg below the knee and tried it on. It fit him well.

He cut off one breast and tried it on and it fit him well. He cut off the other breast . . . he cut off her head at the neck and tried it on. . . . He put on the *agesagena* from her head and her *kareta* and they fit him. . . . Then he put on the *agesagena* that covered her rear . . . and the *agesagena* that covered her vulva . . . and what was left of that old woman he cut up and ate. He ate her up without a trace and set out for her house.

Disguised as the widow, the *kore bana* went to her house to "trick" her children.

"Are you two here?" he called out when he arrived at the house. "We're here," the children shouted back, "but we've been very worried. We heard the banana cry, 'ororo ororo.' . . ." "I've come back and I'm fine," the *kore bana* said. "I wonder why the banana fell? . . . I've brought you *beheða* and a rat to eat. I'll heat some stones in the fire. . . ."

"I'm thirsty," the *kore bana* said to the daughter, who was already a young woman. "Go to the river and fetch me some water," he ordered. "But I don't drink the water from that river, nor from the river beyond it, nor from the river beyond that one, nor from the river beyond that one, nor from the river beyond that one. . . . " While he was saying this to the girl, he broke open the base of the bamboo container.

He handed her the bamboo. But as she was about to leave she saw that the bottom was open. "You've given me a broken bamboo," she said. "If the bamboo won't hold water," he told her, "then say to it:

> *ne'e na'ate a'e na'ate ne'e ure na'a ure* [literally, with added onomatopoeia of the sound of water filling bamboo, "I'll drink, you'll drink, I'll eat you," or, loosely, "If you won't drink the water, bamboo, then I shall eat you! So better filllll up!"]

"Say to it, 'Fill the space between two marks [on the bamboo].'" The girl went off to the distant river and repeated the ditty many times, but water still leaked out of the bamboo.

While the girl went to fetch water for the *kore bana*, he murdered her infant brother.

> While the girl was away at the river, the old man heated stones in the fire. "Open your mouth," he said to the boy, "I want to give you a rat's liver." The baby opened his mouth and the old man tossed in a hot stone and killed him. He wrapped the corpse in bark cloth and placed it in the overhead rack for drying firewood. When the sister returned, she asked, "Where is the child?" "He's sleeping inside my net bag [literally, "Let what is hidden stay hidden," an idiomatic expression that means, roughly, "Never disturb a sleeping baby"]." The old man said this and fell fast asleep.

While the *kore bana* was asleep, the girl discovered her brother's corpse in the rafters and realized the old man had murdered her whole family.

> After returning from the river, the girl sat down and began to twist string. Death juice from her brother's nose dripped onto her thigh, but she wiped it away thoughtlessly. Another drop fell and she wiped it away. Another drop fell onto her thigh and she picked it up with the end of her finger and smelled it. She smelled a corpse and looked up and saw her brother lying on the overhead rack. She stoked the fire to get a good look at the old man and saw his penis beneath the *agesagena*. "You are not my mother!" she realized. "You tricked me! . . . You killed my father and ate him! You killed my mother and ate her! Now you've killed my brother and put him here!"

The heroine took her brother's corpse out of the rafters and set out in search of a husband, killing the *kore bana* as she departed.

> She wrapped her brother tightly in bark cloth and put him inside her net bag together with the string she was twisting. She took the dog and a lighted firestick and left the house. She put the child and the firestick on the ground and sealed the door [i.e., by laying planks one on top of another]. . . . Then she set fire to the house. As she was leaving, she commanded the fire:

> "As I cross the first ridge, burn one of his testicles until it explodes! As I cross the next ridge, burn his other testicle until it explodes! As I cross the next ridge, burn one of his thighs until it explodes! As I cross the next ridge, burn his other thigh until it explodes! As I cross the next ridge, burn his penis . . . ! As I cross the next ridge, burn his stomach . . . ! . . . burn his one arm . . . ! . . . burn his other arm . . . ! . . . burn his nose . . . ! . . . burn his eyes . . . ! . . . burn his head . . . !"

> She said all this to the fire and it consumed the man inside the house. "*ki'3 oooooome!*" he cried out as he died. The girl heard him and shouted back, "I have seen you! I have seen you! I have seen you!" Carrying the baby inside her net bag, she set out to find her *true* husband, the man who would marry her with brideprice.

After crossing many ridges, the girl found her true husband. She told him what had happened to her family and handed him her brother's corpse.

> "If you see the man who will marry [lit: buy] me," she said to her dog, "come back wagging your tail. If you see another man, come back growling [lit: speaking with your teeth clenched]." The dog went off and came back wagging its tail. She sent him off again [as one translator added, to be sure it was not another trick!], but the dog returned a second time wagging its tail. The girl saw smoke coming from a garden rain shelter [lit: lean-to with a roof of dried sugarcane leaves, i.e., an assignation site]. There she found the man who would pay her brideprice.

> "Why have you come?" her true husband asked her. "An old man killed my mother and ate her. Then he tricked me and I thought *he* was my mother! He killed my baby brother and I have brought him inside the net bag on my head." "Alright," he said. "Put the baby down and stay here." The man went away

and cut the top off a hoop pine and hollowed out the trunk. Down and down and down he gouged out the tree. He dropped in a stone and the echoing "*nu nu nu nu nu nu*" told him the depth. "I have finished," he thought, and went to fetch his wife. "Make a fore-skirt," he told her. "Make a waistband, kneebands, wristbands, and a net bag and I will make upper armbands, anklets, and belts." The two of them made these things with the string she had brought.

The newlyweds put the dead baby and the decorations they had made into the hollowed tree and the boy came back to life, changed into countless birds.

Her husband threw all the decorations into the tree and the baby boy too. Then he replaced the top [lit: head] of the hoop pine and closed it. "I am going away," he told his wife. "After I am gone, wonderful sounds will come out of the tree. But don't go near it or hit the trunk." . . . When her husband had gone, she heard the beautiful sounds he described. "I want to see what's inside the tree," she thought and got a stick and hit the trunk.

"*ko ko ko ko ko ko*," cried Count Raggi's Bird of Paradise as it flew out the top of the tree and headed for the mouth of the river. All the Birds of Paradise, lorikeets, Hornbills, red parrots, green parrots, and eagles flew out of the tree and dispersed. Some were red as flame and others were black as smoke. Some flew down to the water's mouth and others flew high into the mountains to the river's source.

By finding a true husband, the heroine gave up her existence as a *kore baϑaha* or "wild woman." Yet she was able to liberate her brother/son so that he could enter the forest. As one woman remarked:

The *kore baϑaha* gave her brother to her husband and he put the boy deep inside the tree. If she had not hit the trunk with her stick, birds would still dwell upon the ground. It is because of what the *kore baϑaha* did that birds live in the air.

Some elements of the myth have conventional meanings that emerge in comments women and men make in recounting or translating this and other myths. "A frog is a woman," Gimi say, on account of the way it squats. A pregnant woman's dream of a frog heralds the birth of a daughter, and *ubabo* or Frog (lit: *huba*/frog + *bo*/the) is a female name.[5] The old man eating frogs from every crevice of the widow's raiments is like a foretaste of the thoroughness and rapacity with which he will devour her—just as her *agesagena* and search for *beheða* indicate that she has already eaten him and that he is a ghost. The frogs or "little women" in the widow's clothes also reverse the idea that *agesagena* represent pieces of the man (see Chap. 5). The *kore bana* killing the widow is posthumous retaliation: he uses the same weapon and the same orifice to impale her as the widow in men's myth used to slay old men in trees. The *kore bana* eats the widow and becomes like a woman who has eaten a man: he looks like a woman but has a man hidden inside. As part of women's own pedagogic tale, this initial episode portrays the consequence to a woman who does *not* participate in the culminating exchanges of *ruhu*, does not accept the "gift of the head" and divest herself of the man she devoured or put on. A widow who keeps wearing *agesagena*, keeps searching for *beheda*—a woman who keeps the man, as it were— herself becomes a *kore badaha*. She goes back into the wild to search for a new husband but finds the old one, the *kore bana*, and is impaled in revenge for the unexpiated crimes of her "first marriage."

"The old man, the *kore bana*, is the Moon," one Gimi elder told me. The child he kills and places on the rafters, the dead baby whose nose leaks "water" onto the girl's thigh, is the symbol of her first menstruation, he said. "When the girl carries the dead boy to her husband," he continued, "she carries the Moon's leavings, the Moon's filth." The *kore bana* is the counterpart of the giant penis or ugly old man who tricked the girl into marriage; and the dead baby in the rafters, leaking "water" from his nose, is another version of the giant's severed head or the cooked boy at the bottom of the oven. As a sequel to other *nene*, this story shows that a woman need not carry the dead issue of her first marriage *back* to her first husband but can transport it to a new man and bring it to life. "The husband loads the baby and the decorations into the hollow tree," a man translating the myth remarked, "because everything comes from the man. It is his penis, his semen, that makes the baby. He puts in red decorations, red flowers first . . . because first comes the dead child, the Moon's blood, just as flames come underneath smoke. Red is first because blood is the first child. Black is on top and alive, rising like smoke!"

At the start of the myth, the tree is not hollow or packed with new decorations but rotting and filled with grubs. The *kore bana* opening the tree with his ax-forehead to remove the delectable grubs seems to repeat in advance

5. Most Gimi names are marked for gender, but a few women give their daughters the names of their fathers and brothers (see above p. 155).

his thrusting his stick into the old woman's anus and then licking off her blood and feces. It also recalls the trickster placing his head in the sleeping girl's buttocks so feces "filled his eyes"; and the giant penis blindly eating his way into the girl's "closed" vagina. The decomposing tree filled with delicious food thus presents an image not only of the widow, of a spoiled old woman at the end of her reproductive life, but also of the heroine when she starts to menstruate, when she is rotting yet delicious, death-ridden but filled with life. This image of the heroine is repeated in the broken bamboo and in her endless journey to fill it. The rivers she passes symbolize the great length of her dalliance with the giant penis who furtively broke open her bottom and made her menstruate. Though water leaked out, she was able to hold it inside the bamboo, just as she was later able to carry off her brother's corpse and bring it back to life.

Most of these associations lie close to the surface of the myth. At this more or less overt level, it was possible to discuss the myth's dramatic repetitions and to establish connections between the series of rivers the girl passes, or the mountain ridges she later crosses in search of a "true husband," and the reach of the giant penis; and between the several lists of body parts—those the *kore bana* cuts off the widow, and those the girl "explodes" in the fire— and the distributions of head payments at *ruhu*. Only rarely did discussions with informants delve into characters' motivations. One woman made a "free association" between this myth and the myth of the Torrent Lark. In the earlier tale, the heroine's mother blows on the embers of the fire and sees the old man with his "head inside her daughter's buttocks." She sees "feces in his eyes" and insists they marry, in effect condoning the incest. Here it is the heroine who awakes and stokes the fire. She herself "sees the penis" beneath the *agesagena*. She sees her father hiding inside her mother and realizes his guilt. By opening her own eyes, she is able to escape her mother's fate. In the Torrent Lark myth, the girl kills the trickster's child in his absence and later gives it back to him cooked like a suckling pig. This time she rescues the child *he* killed in *her* absence and delivers it to a new man. By finding a "true" husband, she gets to keep her father's child. She keeps the dead part of his penis and escapes his reach, outdistancing her endless desire, exploding her own repetitive wish for her father.

The girl entrusts the new man with the Moon's murdered gift, and he buries it deep inside the tree. Though he forbids her to touch the tree, or to look at what he put inside it, he goes away and lets her do as she pleases. The reward of her heroic escape and search for a real husband is that she gets to "keep her father's stick" and use it for life. Like a man who blows into his own "bird" or flute, she is able to "finish the child" *by herself* and to launch it into flight. This Bird of Paradise *nene* is like a female version of the Flute myth, as we will see in Chapter 9.[6]. But what is its connection to garden magic? How does an understanding of this Bird of Paradise myth help women "speak" to the plants and pigs in their care? Let us first look closely at the magic itself.

## The Dyadic Mode of Production: A Gimi Woman's Magical Relation to Plants and Pigs

### Garden Magic

When a woman sings to her pig, she names the intimate details of its existence, mentioning the grubs it likes to forage or the stagnant pond where it likes to wallow. She revels in the smoothness of its coat and the way it slides through her hands. In one song, Geroka urges her shoat to grow as fast as a slimy eel or hairless skink slips out of her grasp. "'That's how I want you to get big in my hands,' I say to my pig, 'so I cannot even hold you!'" Each main verse or *anobak* (lit: *ano*/source or mother + *bak*/song) is preceded by four or five repetitions of *are*, a highly rhythmic wordless chant that delivers the song's ineffable message. "The *are* is the song of the *auna* itself," women say. "We sing the *are* first to hold the pig's *auna* so it can hear the *anobak*."

| | | |
|---|---|---|
| *are* | *ayeyi aiyo ayayi aiyo* | |
| *anobak* | *onepisa maϑo* | [You] eel of the river, |
| | *usurupa titi maϑo* [rep] | Slimy eel sliding out of my hands. |
| | *otipabisa hegiroro* | [You] skink of the garden compost, |
| | *oʒ3 baEpaE* [rep] | So white and hairless and smooth! |

In the *anobak*, a woman flatters her nurtured object with ordinary words, referring to it as some dramatically prolific, fast-moving, or beautiful thing. Whenever her task requires a delicate touch or steady hand—when she tugs at taro shoots to coax them out of the ground, aligns sweet potato vines above a mound, holds a taro bulb with one hand while loosely gathering earth around it with the other—the accompanying *anobak* tends to be short and repetitious like *are*, calling the plant by its intimate variety name, telling

---

6. One of the main aims of the book is to show how men's myths and fantasies play into a different female fantasy based on the female Oedipus complex in which the primary attachment to the father needs to be addressed or resolved before a woman can marry. In comparing the Oedipal triads of women and men, I focus upon the father because both sexes seem to grant him primary importance and to collude in masking his pivotal role, although men go farther than women in this direction, often marking the father's presence by his too-apparent absence. The Oedipal triad, of course, also includes the mother who receives less than her due in the present analysis. Gimi women possess other myths, which I do not include here, that concentrate upon the mother-daughter relation.

it to sit comfortably in the ground, extolling its potential for growth. "I hold the base of my taro [lit: *ina*]," Morukareka explains, "and gather earth around it and sing to make it grow into an enormous thing."

| anobak | *ϑoa ϑoa birio* [repeat] | Sit down and cross your legs |
|---|---|---|
| | *kahoibe kahoibe birio* | In my garden at Gaho, |
| | *ina kanama birio* | You *kanama* taro of mine! |
| | *ϑoa ϑoa birio* [repeat] | Make yourself at home in my garden. |

"'Cross your legs and get comfortable here,' I tell my taro. 'You are the taro of Gaho . . . you are the taro of *my* garden and no other!' I say this to my taro and it grows big in the place where I plant it." As Geroka gathers earth to create a mound around her taro, she addresses it in Chimbu as *mena*, telling it to notice the boundary markers of her garden and grow to reach beyond them.

| anobak | *u ϑi ϑi u ϑi ϑi a ϑi ϑi* | Big thing! Big Thing! . . . |
|---|---|---|
| | *ϑaba ϑaba bia kagano?* [rep] | Do you see the boundary markers? |
| | *u ϑi ϑi u ϑi ϑi a ϑi ϑi* | Big thing! Big thing! |
| | *mekonimena bia kagano?* [rep] | *koni* taro of mine, do you see the markers? |

To plant yams (lit: *hago*), Monuagiaru breaks up the ground with her digging stick and makes a mound of loose earth, inserting a cutting of the vine at the center. With both hands extended flat, she pats the mound and sings softly:

| anobak | *gabuo gabuo gabuo 33* | Go down! [Take root!] . . . |
|---|---|---|
| | *hago amenanipe gabuo* | You *amenani* yam of mine. |
| | *uruo uruo uruo 33* | Then arise, arise (little shoot) |
| | *onek makipe uruo uruo 33* | 'Til you reach the headwaters of the River Maki! |

"I say to the mother yam, 'Go down [take root] and send your little one up to me. Let your first shoot arise to reach the headwaters of the River Maki!'" When Monuagiaru removes dried growth to expose new suckers of *hore*, a cultivated form of wild sugarcane, she addresses her plant as a Pesquet's Parrot that has just molted, urging it to send out new shoots as proudly as if they were magnificent tailfeathers.

A woman's success as gardener and pig herder depends upon the constancy and quality of her intimacy, upon her ability to "join her *auna*" with the *auna* of each plant or pig by convincing it of her exclusive attachment. All garden magic employs the first-person dual or "we two" form of the verb

(McBride and McBride 1973), and most spells conclude with the refrain, "I speak of no one else, to no one else, but *you*, my darling taro, sweet potato, green vegetable, pig, etc." A woman inspires growth by beguiling her charges, telling each one, again and again, in effect, "Do it for me. Do it because you are mine and no one else's!" Addressing an unplanted bundle of sweet potato cuttings, one woman sings, "What garden shall we two [plant ourselves in] today? Where shall we two be off?" [7]

Entering a taro and yam garden requires special purification. After menstruating or having sex, a woman stands at the fence and recites a spell to "hold the dirt inside her vagina" so that it will not "fall to the ground" and kill her tubers. Penota speaks to new plants from outside the fence, telling them, "I've just come to hold you for a moment."

> I stand at the gate of my garden and sing to my taro, "I'm coming! I'm coming inside to hold you for just a moment. . . ." And then I touch the new shoots and pull them up gently and sign, "Come up! Come up to look at your mama!" I sing and I hold the leaves and my taro grows into an enormous thing.

Like a child, each tuber of taro, yam, or sweet potato possesses a "nose," "anus," and "skin covered with tiny hairs." When the women of a compound open a communal earth oven, each one recognizes her own plants, partly by their position in the oven but also by the shape and bodily features of individual tubers (see fig. 10).

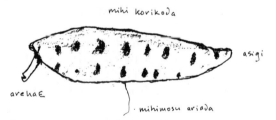

Figure 10. Human features of the sweet potato. Legend: *mihi korikoϑa*/sweet potato of the *korikoda* type; *arehaE*/anus; *mihimosu ariaϑa*/the sweet potato's hair; *asigi*/nose.

7. Gimi women's dyadic involvement with plants and pigs raises issues of body boundaries that have been explored in some attempts to formulate a female psychology.

> Women's biosexual experiences (menstruation, coitus, pregnancy, childbirth, lactation) all involve some challenge to the boundaries of her body ego ("me"/"not me" in relation to her blood or milk, to a man who penetrates her, to a child once part of her body). (Chodorow 1974:59)

In consequence, it has been suggested, women may tend to see themselves more in terms of relatedness to others than men do (see Bardwick 1971; Bakan 1966).

1

Within a woman's repertoire of magic, there is a hierarchy of modes of utterance that places *kaina,* or "talk," above *bak,* or "songs." Spoken spells are more powerful and secret than incanted ones and incanted spells are more potent than songs. In the critical business of planting, incantations usually come first. While inserting sweet potato cuttings in the centers of mounds, Monuato implores each tuber to grow as big as the giant echidna (lit: *kuiyaru*), becoming so heavy no other woman could lift it:

> *kimi kimi fore fore ba ϑahabo*
>> Women of Gimi! Women of Fore!
>
> *keke isa ϑa rakai teberebemosu kemo teberebemosu haupi*
>> There—truly!—within the roots [lit: *au,* body] of the huge *rakai* tree and the huge *kemo* tree
>
> *ame behetarinema kuiyaru ame behetari kono*
>> Sleeps the giant [long-beaked] echidna.
>
> *kimi kimi fore fore ba ϑahabo*
>> Women of Gimi! Women of Fore!
>
> *arame ibi aume kagagate ini marahama!*
>> Unearth [lit: uncover with your digging sticks]—if you can!—[the giant who sleeps there] and look at him! [So heavy is he, you have to] leave him where he lies!
>
> *kage aboa amupa faba*
>> That one [I speak of, that echidna too big and heavy for any woman of Gimi, any woman of Fore, to lift] is none other than *you* [my sweet sweet potato]!

"I say to my sweet potato that no woman of Gimi, no woman of Fore, could pick up the echidna who sleeps amid the tangled roots of the huge *kemo* tree. He is too heavy for them to lift! too big for them to carry away! 'That is no echidna!' I say to my potato, 'And that is no *other* sweet potato! It is you, my very own. You are the giant sleeping there!'"

A woman who wants her plants to proliferate may draw an analogy in her recitation to an animal that produces many young at a time. To plant a new sweet potato garden, a women obtains vines from an established garden, reciting one spell as she cuts the vines and another as she loads them into her net bag. To fertilize the cuttings as she places them in her bag, Tabe names the wild turkey that builds its nest in a mound and lays its eggs one at a time, wandering off after each egg and returning to deposit another. Tabe commands her vines to produce tubers inside her mound the way the bush turkey lays its eggs, "one after another after another without end." In her taro garden, she reminds her plants that they are "none other than" a great boulder of her husband's clan mountain breaking into a cascade of rocks as it plummets into the headwaters of the river that flows above her garden.

A woman's spells and incanted utterances have a special efficacy, and heightened intimacy, because in them she plays with the images she invokes, repeating and alternating the first syllables of key words like "big," using her whim, and modulations in her voice, to create a unique and powerful non-sense. In the following spell for sweet potato, I omit some of the spell-sayer's dazzling invention and reduplication of syllables. Like the spell that named the giant echidna, it is recited while inserting vines into the tops of mounds.

> *nimi rufuni kafuni fure ϑa*
> > Feathers of the Black Sickelbilled Bird of Paradise
> *tape are bime ifafame bome bime ifafame bagi bime ifafame . . .*
> > cover the heads of men who fill the men's house to overflowing.
> *ikinibisa kuhabi fore ba ϑaha namatabi akata bagate*
> > Women of Fore! In my garden at Ikini, asleep in their house,
> *aba bagate bebekera arubome behetarai kono*
> > are crowds [getting bigger as fast as]
> *aregosubo bobo kaina homiriba*
> > the buzzing gets louder when flies converge on a pile of dung.
> *ro amupa kage*
> > [These feathers that cover a man's head, these feathered heads that crowd into a men's house, these buzzing insects that converge on new dung] are none other than you [sleeping and getting bigger inside a mound in my garden]!

To encourage her vines to be prolific, the spell's author explains, she compares the mound where she inserts them to a man's head adorned with Bird of Paradise plumes, to a men's house crowded with men during an initiation, and to a fresh pile of pig dung swarming with flies.

These images of mounds, like those that invoke the mounded nest of a bush turkey or the maze of aerial roots used by an echidna, are also images of the spell-sayer's pregnant body. During the recitations of "food talk" and planting instructions older women give to a bride on the eve of her departure, they tell her that she will make gardens "out of yourself." "You cannot be lazy!" they warn. "The sweet potatoes and pigs you rear come out of you [lit: *auatatia*/a thing out of you; *au*/self, body, or skin covering the entire body surface as manifest aspect of the person + *atatia*/thing from or out of]. . . . When you care for something, it is your own self you produce [lit: put out]." A woman "joins her *auna*" with the objects she cultivates by communicating with them as intimately as she communes with her unborn child. Her spells issue invitations to her new plants to come inside and increase in the autonomous way a fetus gets bigger during the long "sleep" of gestation, while her husband avoids her, leaving the child inside her "mound" to enlarge undisturbed (see Chap. 7).

The more potent incantations become, the more they seem to recede from ordinary meaning. As spells increase in efficacy they tend to become shorter and more repetitious, to be spoken rather than chanted, and to include words or phrases in dialects of Gimi or in other languages like Chimbu or Kafe that the spell-sayer herself does not understand. The more "meaningless" a spell, the closer it is to pure mumbo-jumbo even for the spell-sayer, the more faithfully it expresses the singularity of her bond with the nurtured object and, therefore, the more powerful it is as ritual communication (see Bloch 1974). A litany that has no conventional meaning, that cannot be translated or explained and is inexpressible in any other form, approximates a private language, binding speaker and object by giving voice to the uniqueness of their attachment. Potent magic is often spoken because speech is less patterned than song or chant, its cadence and rhythm more tied to idiosyncrasies of the speaker's own voice. By employing words in other languages, or nonwords of the kind a mother whispers to soothe her child, the gardener conjures a closed world like the one inside her body, a world where two *auna*s can unite.

## *Pig Magic*

A pig (*ugunu*)is more valuable and difficult to rear than a vegetable, which may be why songs and spells for pigs are shorter and more esoteric than those for plants and far harder to collect, being shared only among a woman's own daughters and daughters-in-law (see n.2, this chap.). In the same way women have songs to accompany the smallest routines of gardening, they have songs to assist with virtually every task of pig rearing: songs to summon a pig home at dusk after a day spent foraging in an abandoned garden, songs to subdue the pig while the "mother" slips a leash over its leg, etc. By far the most numerous spells are those to encourage a new pig to grow.

A woman takes hold of her shoat, feeds it a specially cooked tuber of sweet potato, and starts to sing. In her other hand, she holds a smooth, oblong stone covered in soft ash and rubs it over the pig's back. The stone, called

Holding a smooth oblong stone or *kari* in her right hand, a pregnant woman rubs ashes over the back of her young pig and recites a spell to induce growth.

*kari*, looks like a part of a pestle (see R. Berndt 1954). Women say they un-earth the *kari* while clearing their gardens and that they are fragments of the "penis" of the giant *higi*, a creature who inhabits the forest and makes infrequent sorties into women's gardens. Holding a *kari* and rubbing ashes along her pig's spine, an old woman named Taneoigi chants "*robu robu meso rega makaso.*" She knows the meaning of none of the words, she says, except for *robu*, the Gimi name of a giant tree.

Part of the secret of pig recipes lies in the order in which they are recited.

Often, the powerful spoken spell is sandwiched between an incantation and a song. After her chant, Taneoigi gently pulls her pig's limbs and utters a spell whose only "name," she says, is *kabo,* a fast-ripening cucumber (lit: *rukura*):

> *imifai amafai okafaga rukura kabo fegimoro fagimoro.*

After repeating the phrase eight or nine times, she takes the pig in her lap and sings a song exhorting it to grow with the effortless speed and abandon of a river rushing headlong down the mountain and casting detritus along its course.

> *onek abini ugunu moro ara ϑa ko ϑa*
>> My pig is tossed like flotsam in the current of the River Abini.
>
> *utunu ugunu moro ara ϑa ko ϑa*
>> My black pig is tossed by the water . . .

Women rarely perform pig or garden magic without using their hands, rubbing the back of a pig with the *kari* or gently pulling its limbs, tugging at new shoots of taro, shaping earth into mounds, etc., as if their hands, too, were magically life-giving. "I care for my pig by singing this song and it grows big in my hands," one woman remarked. Every pig "has the hand" of the woman who nurtured it, and, before it is killed, she performs a rite called *aϑamepaE,* literally, to "take back her hand," so she can retrieve the *auna* she instilled over the course of its life and transfer it to new pigs. Her husband, or another man, distracts the pig by tossing a tuber of sweet potato to it while she moves behind it and grasps the hair at the back of its head. She leans over her pig and whispers in its ear, meanwhile moving her right arm, with the hand spread wide open, in a circular motion from head to rump. After she has moved her opened hand several times back and forth over the length of her pig, a man lifts it around the middle and another man clubs the head. If the woman neglects to perform *aϑamepaE,* men say, she will be unable to nurture other pigs. "The new pigs she cares for will not grow." Nor will the pig just killed yield enough meat for the men of her husband's lineage to meet their obligations. "The one who cares for a pig wants to hold on to it," a man named BoϑaEha explained, so the butcher recites other spells to get rid of residual *auna* left by the woman who reared the pig and by her husband.

### *"To Cultivate and to Kill"*

The Gimi language itself links cultivation and death: the verb "to plant," *fa,* also means "to implant," "to hit," "to strike," and "to kill." "To kill a pig" is *ugunu fa,* "to plant sweet potato" is *mihi fa,* "to plant a new garden" is *ϑo fa,* "to strike a tree" is *ϑa fa,* etc. And "to menstruate," which is at once to become fertile and to deliver a dead child, is *hibo fa,* literally, "to strike" or "to be struck by the Moon" (*hik*/Moon + *mo*/the + *fa*). To make pigs and plants flourish, a woman beguiles them with songs and caresses. But her most powerful inducement, her ultimate weapon, so to speak, is the promise to eat what she nurtures. "I give the talk to my greens and they come up abundantly," Taneoigi brags. "To my greens and sweet potatoes I say, 'You sleep there and grow big as a rock. . . . Get that big," she says, gesturing with her hands, "and I'll eat you!" "'Listen to me,' I say to my yam. 'Hear my song and grow big enough for me to dig up and eat!'" In the words of another woman:

> We women make food grow by singing and talking. There is no other way! We hold our pigs and make them grow into food that is sweet and delicious to eat.[8]

Garden magic is the ritual expression of a mother's love. The vital incentive for growth seems to lie in her undivided attention. Yet a woman's tender care always hides a sinister motive in the sense that she cherishes her pig or plant to turn it into food. She intends every object she nurtures to end up dead and devoured. Through song and spell, a woman associates her nurtured objects with her unborn child, with the life that "gets big while it sleeps" inside her, and with the newborn she cradles in her arms. When garden magic is tied to *nenekaina* which women say is its "true source," a woman's plants and pigs take on the further identity of the *nene* child, the child the "wild woman" murdered and cooked like a suckling pig, or the head of the giant she severed and threw into a river. In the terms of *nenekaina,* a woman's plan for her loved ones is that they eventually suffer the fate of her firstborn.

The link between garden magic and *nenekaina* suggests why women possess no spells for children. I elicited great laughter by asking women if they had magic for infants: "Spells for plants, spells for pigs, spells for new gardens, of these we have plenty. But what to say when we make love to our husbands, *this* our mothers did not tell us!" Responsibility for the growth of children after weaning rests entirely with men (see Langness 1974:205–6). Certain Big Men know spells to make weak or sickly children grow, women told me. But in an explicit sense, the whole system of head payments and of

8. A woman's ritual promise to eat her pig or plant is a "lie" in the sense that, throughout most of her married life she is forbidden to eat much of her own produce. See *a ϑaoina,* below. Yet, like Melpa women, Gimi women are associated with the desire to eat the pigs they nurture. "'We women want to rear pigs for eating. . . . We look after them. Men think only of shells and money, but women think they rear the animals to eat them later. . . . the flesh of pigs is sweet'" (M. Strathern 1972:137). Despite this general ethic, Gimi women seem to consume less meat than men (see Chap. 11 n.2).

male initiation rites is designed to this end. *apina,* the first stage of male initiation, is the ultimate growth ritual for boys. Its aim is utterly to reverse women's spells of incorporation by removing boys from their mothers' houses and from every type of contact with women (see Chap. 9).

Men begin to intrude upon the mothering bond after weaning at about three (see M. Strathern 1972:173). Up to that time, mother and child share an intense physical closeness. My strongest impression among women was created by their incessant fondling of infants. Holding her sick child, a woman agitates it gently in her arms, burying her mouth in the baby's neck to whisper sweet nothings. Infants evacuate freely into the laps of mothers and grandmothers (whereas a man reflexively avoids contact with a child's feces). The unflinching mother does not disturb the flow of her baby's movements, enhancing its sense of bodily continuity with her. Women feed their infants until they refuse the breast. Indeed, as the baby grows, it is sometimes the mother who insists upon continued contact, interrupting her toddler's play repeatedly to offer the breast.

Masturbation is another pacifying technique. With a baby girl, the mother or *amau* holds her hand over the vulva and shakes it vigorously. She may kiss the vagina, working her way up the middle of the body to the lips and then inserting her nipple (often when the child has given no sign of discontent). With a boy, she kisses the penis, pulls at it with her fingers and takes it into her mouth to induce an erection. Several women may pass a baby boy back and forth, each one holding him over her head as she takes a turn sucking or holding the penis in her mouth. When the child then pulls at his own organ, the women, greatly amused, offer squeezes and pulls of their own. Such ostentatious shows of affection sometimes seem like bids for dominance among women, especially during a feast, when older women may take the baby boy from his mother. Girls are rarely fondled in this public way or by more than one woman at a time.

### Blood Magic

In the early 1960s, fundamentalist missionaries effectively halted the construction of menstrual huts, the rough shelters that were built on the outskirts of a settlement for the seclusion of menstruating women. Menstrual huts had three names. They were called *kamiϑama* or "flute house" (*kamiba*/flute + *nama*/house), *keterama* or "house of shame" (*kete*/shame + *nama*), and *arega* or "toilet" (*are*/feces + *ga*/place). In the past, a menstruating woman spent the four or five days of her period in a menstrual hut, enduring a loneliness in the early years of marriage that symbolized her general alienation. During *haro,* her mothers-in-law taught her laments to pass the hours in seclusion:

O mother-in-law of mine,
I am the woman you bought,
    alone in my menstrual hut.
You bring me no food and I chew *hagui* [an intoxicating leaf]
    in hunger and in pain.

O father-in-law of mine,
I am the woman you bought,
    alone in my menstrual hut.
With no sweet potato to eat I chew *kiba* [an intoxicating nut]
    and am filled with woe.

One older woman recalled how she felt the first time she heard the song:

> When I was a girl, I heard that song and wondered what to
> do, what to think. But I did as I was told and planted sweet po-
> tato and gave it to my *nanatu*. . . . When I hear this song even
> now, I cry . . . I have made many gardens but the soil here is not
> so good. I would have liked to go elsewhere and married another
> man. But I stayed. And I have enjoyed my gardens. And I know
> that in another place there is no other sweet life.

A woman confined to her menstrual hut walked to her gardens along specially cut paths. She crouched outside the fence and used sticks to reach between the posts, unearth tubers of sweet potato and load them into her net
bag. When she returned to her hut, she used other sticks to unload the tubers, tongs to bury them in the hot ashes of her fire, a ladle to retrieve them,
and twigs to wipe away the ash. Even today "a [menstruating] woman never
holds the sweet potato she eats. She skewers it with a stick." She avoids bamboo shoots and greens and other foods that are too slippery to hold between
sticks or whose copious juices would dislodge the blood beneath her fingernails and carry it into her mouth. "If our hands touch our food," women
say, "we will grow weak and sicken and die."

Nowadays a menstruating woman remains inside her house within the
compound, or retires to her "pig house," and goes to a river or stream several times a day to wash her hands with soap. To absorb the menstrual flow,
she inserts a wad of soft tree moss or the sapling bark she shreds into
string—a practice recalled in the *nenekaina* by the boy's "nose-water" dripping onto his sister's thigh as she twists string (see above, this Chap.). She
uses only her left thumb and index finger to insert or pull out the tampons,
reserving her right hand for preparing her husband's food.[9] Immediately

9. Women collect tree moss in the forest by dislodging it with sticks from low-hanging
branches and carry it to their houses hidden under their skirts. Women of a compound, including mother- and daughter-in-law, freely share their moss, women say. "A woman says, 'Are you
fine?' I answer, 'Yes, I'm alright.' She adds, 'My blood is running down, give me some [moss].'"

after removal, a blood-filled plug of moss or shredded bark is intensely "hot" and must be left to "cool" before it is discarded in a deep latrine or fast-moving river, a place where it will be beyond a sorcerer's reach or neutralized by the flowing water. A woman's menstrual blood is as closely associated with her *husband* as is his own semen, nasal mucous, feces, urine, hair, etc., and a sorcerer who steals her blood can use it to cast a fatal spell over him. "If you are careless with your blood," women warn their new daughters-in-law ad nauseum during initiation rites, "your husband will fall ill and we will know why! We will see what you have done!"

Before a woman can cook her husband's food or return to her garden after a period, she has to "expel the Moon." Unless she purifies herself each month, her songs and spells will be ineffective. Vestiges of blood that dry beneath her fingernails, and in the crevices of her vagina, will wither any plant she touches, poison the food she cooks, and ruin the fertility of the ground that "passes between her thighs."

During the seclusions of a woman's initiation and marriage, which last four or five days, like a menstrual period, she learns "blood songs" and other methods to end the monthly flow and rid her body of bloody traces. "You must seal off the blood," her elders tell her during *haro*. "Hide the blood! Hide it well!" they intone. "No man or child should ever *see* it!" The women spit into the palms of their hands and wipe their buttocks and thighs with exaggerated gestures, showing the initiate how to make sure no drop of blood "appears" outside her body. "A woman puts in the moss . . . to fool everyone! So no one will ever *see* her blood and make her ashamed. We hide the blood well," a young woman called Revakione told me. "If a woman's father should ever see her blood running down her legs, or staining her bark-string skirts, he would get sick and be as ashamed as she." Monuato remembered:

> Our mothers built menstrual huts and stayed inside them the whole time. . . . When a woman's blood stopped and she wanted to return to the compound, she cut a section of sugar-cane and planted it beside the hut. As soon as a leaf had dried she removed it [to monitor the new growth], and when she saw that the cane had grown a little she said to herself, "My blood must be completely gone. I can go back to my house." And she went back to cook food for her husband.

"When it was time for a woman to return to the compound," Napusi added, "she sang to warn her husband to stay away:

| | |
|---|---|
| *nama namapiti* | We come from the house [of blood]. |
| *yi abao iii* | Move up out of our way, |

| | |
|---|---|
| *runugi ooo* | You marsupials. |
| *yi abao iii* | Move up out of the way of |
| *keterama* | Us who return from the house of shame. |
| | |
| *nama namapiti ganaune* | We come from the house [of blood]. |
| *ru abao iii* | Keep down out of our way, |
| *kabuso iio* | You possums. |
| *ru abao iii* | Keep down out of the way of |
| *kora namapiti ganaune* | Us who return from the house of blood. |

This is a song our mothers sang when they came back from the [menstrual] huts. We still sing songs to warn our husbands, "Stay away from us!" "When you make a fire," our mothers tell us, "say to your husband: 'Blow on the embers yourself.' If you blow on his fire," they tell us, "his skin will turn to dust."

The idea that a man's skin will dry out, that he will turn pale and fall ill from eating food cooked in a fire tended by his wife right after she menstruates, is linked in women's myths to the fate of the *kiri* or python. Men say that the entire species is female because their mouths can expand to encompass whole wild pigs, cassowaries, tree kangaroos, and even people. When the victim is human, men say, the *kiri* swallows it in the fetal position. The *kiri* can decapitate prey with a single blow like the first woman who cut off the giant's head. But the *kiri*'s great length, and habit of encircling prey, make it also resemble the mythic giant himself.

The following *kiri* story was told to me by a girl who had just had her first period:

The *kiri* coiled herself around the branch of a tree. She sent her children to the ground, telling them to fetch insects for her to eat, and went to sleep.

Fire erupted along the edge of the River Kaho and traveled higher and higher, moving up the side of Mount Doba. The fire pursued the *kiri* to the top of the mountain and she awoke. The mother slid out of the tree to search for her young but the fire consumed her. All of her children died in the fire except for one who had descended into the roots of a tree. That one alone was spared. She climbed onto the branch of a tree and sang:

If the *kiri* moved along the ground,
she would turn to ash.
But she stays inside the house of shame,
crying "*ki, ki, ki, ki, ki . . . .*"

The *kiri* went up to the headwaters singing this song. She went into the high forest and never comes down to the river estuary.

When I repeated this myth to a man some years after I first heard it, he remarked:

All the snakes died in the fire except the one who escaped to the mountain top. That snake is like the penis of the Moon. . . . It comes down from the mountain [once a month] and strikes the woman inside her menstrual hut. . . . If the snake had stayed on the ground, it would have turned to ash and women would not menstruate.

In this man's view, the sleeping python who sends her young to the ground is like the Moon who throws his penis out of the sky and puts out the fire between woman's thighs, causing the first menstruation (see Chap. 7). In the context of women's Giant Penis myth, the mother python who goes to sleep after sending her young to fetch insects is like the first man who lies asleep while his penis wakes up and goes wandering. Insects are an overt symbol of woman's pubic hair so that, like the hungry penis who awakes in the night, the descending snakes set out to "eat the vagina." And like the penis, the snakes are "cut off," consumed by fire, reduced to dust. Like the primordial giant in women's other story, the *kiri* suffers a great loss: only a small part— only a single offspring—survives; and that one is bleeding inside the house of shame.

Menstrual blood is really "a man's blood," Gimi say. It is "blood of the penis." Both sexes treat a woman's menstrual or parturitory blood as her husband's "leaving," as much a missing part of him as his own semen or feces or sweat. A menstruating woman possesses something she *took from a man* in the same way mythic woman became filled with the giant's blood after she cut him down to size (see Chaps. 1 and 3). She cut off his head, killed his child, and got *his* blood "in her hands," giving her the power to reduce the rest of him to soft bone and ash and to pollute whatever she touches, including her own food. Like a woman who ate a man and covered herself in mourning regalia, like the Torrent Lark who killed her son, like the python who sent all her young into the fire, the menstruator "looks like a man": she has a bleeding penis and knows how to "fly." She is a "wild woman" and lives alone outside the settlement.

In the days when Gimi women retreated to menstrual huts, a woman often ended her confinement by burning odoriferous leaves in a slow fire. The "sweet smell" filled the hut and drove away the blood's foul clinging odor and debilitating *auna*. When the fire went out, she rubbed the cold ash, together with her own spittle, over her belly, hips, and buttocks, "drying her skin" to seal in the blood. "I wipe ashes over me to stop the [flow of] oil," said a woman who still performs this rite. "I dry my skin so it will hold the blood . . . I make my skin as dry as ash." As she rubs her mid-section, she chants *korabak*, addressing her blood, or the Moon, as "you" in the same intimate terms she speaks to her plants and pigs. She tells the blood to "stay inside."

"I have my own name for the Moon," Monuato told me. "I call him *kaba heroba*. It is the name my mothers used." Spitting onto her hands and wiping her hips, she sings:

| *are* | *aiyau aiyau eyau* |
| | *aiyau aiyau eyau* [repeat] |
| *anobak* | *kerobare kerobare kaba herobare* |
| | *kerobare faba kerobare* [repeat] |

I make the blood stay inside so I cannot see it. . . . Today the man above looks at me. I sing this song and tomorrow he is gone. . . . "*faba*," I say to him, "Nothing. You are nothing. Finished!" *keroba* is the name of a stone. I call the Moon "stone" and make him go away.

Monuato repeats the *are*, rubs more ash on her body, and sings a second verse, referring to herself as a "dusty," dry-skinned tuber of *mura* taro:

| *anobak* | *ki ϑi ϑi ki ϑi ϑi kaba mura ki ϑi ϑi* |
| | *ki ϑi ϑi kaba mura ki ϑi ϑi* |

A wife who is a "dusty taro," whose skin is utterly dry, cannot lose a drop of fluid, as the singer explains. Unlike the "leaky bamboo" in women's myth (see above, this Chap.), a dry *mura* taro is a perfect container that holds every drop of "water" a man deposits. But in retaining the Moon's "water," in making it disappear inside her, a dry-skinned woman also dries up the Moon: she turns him to stone or, in the imagery of the python myth, to ash. If a woman could turn the Moon to stone or dust, she could stop his filling her with blood—and so stop his blood from leaking out.

*korabak* and other purificatory rites are designed to make a woman's blood disappear in apparently opposite ways—by expelling it from every crevice, driving out even the blood's foul odor, and by holding it inside her body. In another song, Sabaro replaces the Moon with Makaru, the name of her own husband, and refers to herself as leaves of red cordyline (lit: *haori* + *bo*/the), as one whose redness is "only a shine." By naming herself "red cordyline," Sabaro says, her song holds the blood safely inside her so it cannot leak out and harm her husband. Her song makes the blood stationary and innocuous so it gives her skin a beguiling "red light."

anobak     *kini ϑa kini ϑa haoribo kini ϑa*
            *kini ϑa kini ϑa makaru kini ϑa . . .*

I sing this song to stop the blood! My song says to the blood, "You cannot come outside! You have to stay inside me!" . . . "I am like the leaves of *haori*," I say to my husband. "My blood is just the color of my skin. It is only the shine."

## "A Woman's Blood Is the Water of Her Brother's Nose"

During female initiation, late on the first night of internment, when the singing has faded and many of the women crowded into the sweltering room have dozed off, the leaders of the rites stage a surprise performance of ritual theater to give new life to the proceedings and to demonstrate how a woman ought properly to "look after" her blood. Some fifteen minutes before the play begins, two older women, prominent among those who have led the songs and instructions, discretely leave the house to collect materials for costumes and props. When they return, they send out the children and instruct several women to guard against eavesdroppers. One woman circles the outside of the house and another stands outside the door.

The play is staged around the central fire, which is the only source of light in the room, and is set inside a menstrual hut, sometime in the past.

> The two performers sit cross-legged before the fire. They wear ceremonial bark cloth fore-skirts and huge rear bustles of poinsettias and red cordyline leaves. They hold sticks for "handling" menstrual blood and the green twigs whose bark women shred to make string and to use as tampons.
>
> One of the players stands up and pokes one of her sticks between her legs to dislodge some of the poinsettias from her bustle. Red petals drift to the floor and she crushes them with her heel, mixing her "blood" into the earth "to hide it from the eyes of all men," as a woman in the crowd explains. She uses one stick to scrape "blood" off the insides of her thighs and the other to hold her fore-skirt out of the way.
>
> The second player stands, and the two women together go through the motions of "cleaning" their lower bodies, using one stick to scrape and scratch their buttocks, inner thighs, and calves, and the other to hold up their skirts so they do not come in contact with the "blood." Each one "buries her blood" by digging and twisting her heel into the poinsettia petals she has let fall to the floor.
>
> "My husband is calling me," the first player says. "Let's go

back to the compound." But the other woman sits down and picks up a twig to scrape off the bark: "I still have blood in me," she says. "I'll stay here and make string." "I want to go back to my husband," the first woman repeats. "I can't go," the other one insists quietly. "I still have blood."

Using her sticks, the first woman gathers the crushed blossoms into a pile and carries them to the door. Appearing oblivious, the other player takes a handful of ash from the fireplace and spreads it liberally over the inside of her thigh, preparing it in the usual way as a surface for rolling shredded bark into string. After the first player leaves the house, carrying her "blood" between sticks to the river, the woman by the fire stands up and again cleans her lower body.

Minutes later, the first player reenters the house and addresses her cohort: "Look at my vagina," she says, pushing her hand into her vulva. "All the blood is gone! I'm going back to my husband." Unimpressed, the other woman gathers up her "blood" with sticks and says, "Mine is not finished. I'm staying here to make string."

The two players repeat their interchange three or four times and then together trample the remaining poinsettias, digging the red petals into the earthen floor of the house.

As the play ends, women in the audience begin to sing softly. In separate verses, their song names each of the bride's or initiate's brothers and close patrilateral cross-cousins. "What the Moon kills," the first performer explained to me days later, "is blood from our brothers' noses. Those boys give us their blood." A woman's brother is the "true source" of her firstborn, another woman added. He is the red Lorikeet in women's secret song:

> From the nose-blood of Harato [the bride's older brother],
> Comes the *hane* Lorikeet-child, the *baϑa* Lorikeet-
> child. . . .
> From the nose-blood of Borua [the bride's younger brother],
> Comes the *hane* Lorikeet-child, the *baϑa* Lorikeet-
> child. . . .

Red Lorikeet is the name men use for an adolescent male after his nose has been bled for the first time at the end of *apina* (see Chap. 9). In secret initiation rites of their own, Gimi men let blood from their noses to rid themselves of accumulations of female blood that dull their skins and sap their strength. In the days of war, a man bled his nose regularly by sharply inserting and withdrawing a plug of stinging nettles, creating a "hot" blood-soaked wad like a woman's tampon. Menstrual blood infiltrates a man's body, men say, not only during sexual intercourse, when particles lodged in the vagina may invade the head of the penis, but also during ordinary contacts, especially while eating the "food of women's hands" (see Read 1952, 1965; Hays and Hays 1982, etc.). But though men speak of closeness to their wives and children and to women in general as the source of pollution, their secret rite refers to a myth of incest. When a man expels the "Moon's blood" from his nose, he "sends the blood of his sister back to his sister. The man wants to get this blood out of his body! 'Let the blood of my sister go back to my sister,' he says."[10]

By naming the red Lorikeet, women's secret song seems to answer men's secret rite, sending the bride's blood *back* to her brother's nose. When I asked the second performer in women's play to explain the concluding song, she paraphrased it in the words of a bride: "The blood of my brother's nose is in my body. When I get rid of it, a real child, a beautiful red Lorikeet, will lie inside me." The idea that a bride has to get rid of her brother, or his blood, in order to produce a "real child" recalls the climatic incident in women's *nenekaina* (see above, this Chap.). After the Moon or *kore bana* murders the heroine's brother, his corpse drips "nose-water" onto her thigh. She kills the *kore bana,* rescues her brother's corpse and carries it to her "real husband," and together they transform the dead boy into countless beautiful birds. Interpreted in light of the myth, the performer's comments on the play's concluding song suggest that a woman becomes pregnant by *actively* expelling the "Moon's leavings," annihilating the primordial father, killing the killer inside her and carrying his bloody traces to the river. Though women's song names the bride's brothers as, collectively, the "true source" of her blood, their myth, and the songs a woman sings alone in her menstrual hut, or carrying out ablutions beside a river, suggest that her blood, and her brother's "nose-water," derive from their father the Moon.

At the end of women's play, the two performers repeat that a woman is not fit to return to her husband simply because she has stopped bleeding. The use of tampons leaves vestiges of blood in her hands. After every period, women tell the bride, especially in the early years of marriage, she must wash her hands with red lilies and other wild red flowers, rubbing the petals to extract the red juices that will carry away the blood she cannot see. She must scrape beneath her fingernails, using the stiff, dried spines of ferns to lift out hidden "dirt." Crouched beside a river, scouring her hands, one woman sings of the *konime* taro, calling her sex a "hairy" taro root inflated with "red Lorikeet's nose-water." By naming the blood's "true source," she says, she can send it away.

10. It is certainly true, however, that, outside the context of ritual, a man is endangered less by his sister's blood than by the blood of an affine.

*koraϑebao koraϑebao ii* [repeat]
    *kora*/blood *ϑebao*/you ["she calls the blood," notes a
    translator]
*nimi baϑa baϑI nimimosu asigipisa baϑao onek nene*
    *nimi*/bird *baϑa*/Papuan lorikeet *nimimosu*/the bird's
    *asigipisa*/nose-from *onek*/water
*koraϑebao koraϑebao raraneba raranebao ii* [repeat]
    *raraneba*/finish!
*ina konime konimesu aupisa baϑa onek*
    *ina*/taro *konime*/type of taro *aupisa*/body-into
    *baϑa onek*/Papuan lorikeet-water
*koraϑebao koraϑebao raraneba raranebao ii* [repeat]

O blood! You blood!
Water from the nose of the Papuan Lorikeet,
O blood! You blood! Stop flowing
Into the *konime* taro. Lorikeet-water,
O blood! You blood! Stop flowing!

"The blood of the bird's nose enters the root of the taro," the singer explains. "It goes inside the taro's skin. Something of men's goes into
women. . . . Our vulvas are like the hairy roots of taro bloated with red
Lorikeets' blood."

Like a refrain between the songs, and an amen at the end of each set of
instructions, the leaders of the rites intone: "*fanaume!* Take care [of your
husband's semen]! *feteore!* Hide [your menstrual blood]!" A new wife is
likely to be careless of her husband's welfare not only in the way she handles
her blood, forgetting to purify her hands and contaminating his food, but
also by allowing his semen, or their combined sexual fluids, to "fall to the
ground" and into a sorcerer's hands. Well past midnight, when the singing
again fades, the leaders of the rites command another performance. The following playlet was described to me by a newly married man from a neighboring village who said he had watched it as an adolescent peering through
a hole in the back wall of a woman's house during an initiation. Responding
to my show of mild surprise, he said: "When we celebrate *apina,* women
hide just the same and hear us." But then he quickly added that women did
*not* see the flutes. "Men are strong and command, 'You must not look!'"[11]
    I give his account of women's drama instead of my own (though I was
present at similar performances) to illustrate the high level of interest and

---

11. Traditionally, the Gimi language does not distinguish between seeing or looking and
knowing. To hear (lit: *feo*) something is not to understand or know (lit: *a'a'o*/see) it. The
Melanesian Pidgin word for "know," *savi,* is now used by Gimi speakers and conjugated as the
verb, *sabeo.*

accurate knowledge some men have of women's affairs. Morukareka and Regeno are leaders of the rites. Inside the woman's house there is a "room" or "nest of sugar," a raised platform surrounded by a wall of sugarcane constructed by the initiates' *ababana* to hide the girls from view during the subsequent public portion of their initiation (Gillison 1987).

I looked through the wall and saw Morukareka and Regeno get up [from amid the crowd of women sitting on the floor]. Morukareka went inside the room. She took off her skirts and put on a man's fore-skirt and rear covering of cordyline. Regeno kept on her woman's skirts and lay on the floor near the fire. The two of them were about to teach something to the girls!

Regeno was "asleep" and Morukareka said, "I want you." But Regeno—who was the woman—answered, "No, I don't want it." The women made the fire burn high beside her. Morukareka, who was the man, said, "You are lovely. I want you now." "No!" Regeno insisted, but Morukareka kissed her on the mouth. "Go away!" Regeno cried. But Morukareka took off her fore-skirt and cordyline and took off Regeno's skirts and lay on top of her. . . .

Afterward Morukareka got up and put on her skirt and left Regeno sleeping. Then Regeno got up and picked up her rear-skirt [upon which the two of them had lain] and wiped her vagina and abdomen and all around the insides of her thighs. She rubbed her *kagora ano* [lit: *kagora*/vagina + *ano*/body-water or fluid] and Morukareka's *abara ano* [lit: *abara*/penis + *ano*] until they disappeared into the cloth. Regeno sat cleaning her vagina and said, "I'm getting rid of my husband's semen. I don't want a sorcerer to kill him!" She didn't let a drop of semen fall to the ground.

Morukareka came back into the room. "I want to do it again!" she cried. The first time they showed the initiates how a woman should look after her husband's semen. The second time they showed them what happens when she doesn't! Regeno went to sleep again and Morukareka lay on top of her. But "he" got up right away and said, "Your vagina is too wet. . . . " Regeno rubbed her vagina with her rear-skirt. "That's better," Morukareka said, and "he" had sex with her. When they were finished Regeno didn't get up and remove her husband's semen. So it fell to the ground.

A sorcerer [a third woman performer] had been watching them all the time. Regeno and Morukareka left [the area around

the central fireplace] and the sorcerer came and took the semen. . . . On the sidelines, Morukareka asked Regeno, "Did
you get rid of my semen properly?" "Yes," she replied, "You are
my husband. What do you expect?" But she had just left it
there. . . .

"Ahhhhh," Morukareka sighed, "I feel sick." The sorcerer had
stolen his semen and was heating it [over an imaginary fire on
the other side of the room].

Morukareka's brother [a fourth woman player] arrived and
asked Regeno, "Haven't you lost something?" "No," she replied. "Really?" the brother said. "I think you have. Your husband
is dead!"

Then Morukareka got off the floor [where she had been lying
"dead"] and said, "This wife killed her husband with his own
semen. She killed him! When you go to your husband, you must
find the semen that falls to the ground and carry every drop back
to your own house or throw it into a river. If you do not, you'll
lose your husband for nothing. You won't have him long!"

The sorcerer did not just happen by. According to dramatic convention,
he is the woman's lover, an adulterer or *uꝗabana*, literally a "thief"
(*uꝗa*/steal + *bana*/man), who waits in hiding for the chance to take her husband's semen. "Run away from *uꝗabana!*" women shouted during the rites
I attended. "Look after your husband well!" they intoned. "If you have sex
here and there, with this man and that one, you'll kill him!"

After the performance, the eavesdropper reported, Morukareka and Regeno continued to instruct the brides:

When the Moon kills you and your husband demands sex,
you must be strong. Tell him the Moon has closed you up completely. . . . Tell him while the Moon is still with you the opening is small, and a man who tries to enter you will hurt his penis
and get sick.

It is a woman's responsibility, as older women warned the brides again and
again in my presence, to protect her husband even when he protests, to prevent him from penetrating her while she is menstruating or when her vagina
has either an excess or lack of lubrication, conditions that would cause his
semen "to fall to the ground" and into a sorcerer's hands. It is woman's duty,
even in the face of her husband's forceful opposition, to shield him from the
other man—whether sorcerer or Moon—by making her body a perfect vessel, one that leaks neither semen nor blood.

At the end of *haro,* when the leaders bring the pair of exhausted initiates out of seclusion, they subject them to a test of fidelity. Each is made to grasp wiry, deep-rooted *imperata* grass with her toes, uproot it and toss it into the air: if the grass lands in front of her, she will be a true wife and "take care" of her blood and her husband's semen; but if the grass falls behind her and out of sight, she will seek adulterous liaisons and ruin her husband's health.

### Blood and Ambivalence

Women's secret rites, blood songs, pedagogic plays, etc., are pervaded by a contradiction. All are based upon disposing properly of menstrual blood, upon making the blood—and, in the past, menstruating women themselves—disappear in the interest of their husbands' safety and well-being. A wife is responsible for protecting her husband even by rejecting his demands for sex which, both sexes say, he sometimes pressed inside the seclusion hut. But the methods she uses to dispose of her blood, and of her husbands' semen, suggest that she is ambivalent about which of her husbands she really prefers—second or first, man or Moon, reality or myth. Some "blood songs" are designed to get rid of the Moon by "drying" and "closing" the singer's body, sealing in the blood, turning her into a seamless vessel, a "dusty taro," etc. But a woman may sing these songs of retention while performing ablutions or burning odoriferous leaves to *expel* the blood's every vestige and odor, to get rid of unseen traces in her hands and skin and drive the blood back to its "true source in men's noses." A woman "gets rid" of the Moon in apparently opposite ways, attempting both to discharge the Moon's "leavings" and invisibly retain them. She disposes of her husband's semen by similarly discrepant methods. She either throws it into a river or "carries it back to her house," rubbing it into her skirts and skin until it is absorbed and disappears.

According to myth, theatrical performance, and song, and as announced by the very term "to menstruate," a woman bleeds each month because she "kills" or is "killed by" the Moon, because she married an ugly old man and a trickster, because the Red Lorikeet lodges his bleeding "nose" in her vagina. In various ways, women convey the idea that a woman's blood is the residue of a *fantasied* incest, that every bride was married a first time to a disguised figment of her father or brother. But during the marriage ceremony women also attribute menarche to penetration by the real first husband. While tying on the many layers of a bride's new skirts in the moments before she leaves for the groom's compound, her mothers whisper into the bark strings, implanting spells to deaden the groom's desire and thus delay the onset of menses. "Who will enter her now and make her bleed?" they utter aloud after imparting their secret formulas.

When we send a girl to her husband we close her vagina. "If
your husband enters you all the time, you will soon menstruate
and get pregnant. We will close your vagina," we tell her, "so he
doesn't get too many erections!"

Men can be just as literal minded:

The penis breaks the [hymen] and makes the blood
flow . . . like a wound. The vagina of a virgin is not open. . . . If
a man doesn't have sex with a woman the Moon cannot kill her.
A penis opens the vagina so the blood can come out. . . .

After translating the Trickster myth, we may recall, one man remarked
that some men still use tricks to marry women who are reluctant or who live
far away. He described how an anxious suitor let blood from his elbow and
poured it into his lover's string skirts and onto himself to fool her into believing she had menstruated for the first time and spilled blood on him. "She
was terribly ashamed and married him because she thought the Moon had
killed her!" (see Chap. 3). Even if more bravado than fact, such accounts reveal that Gimi believe first menses may be induced by actual penetration.
Insisting that a man, not the Moon, "kills a woman for the first time" directly contradicts the myth. But denying the role of the Moon is also a way
for men to appropriate it. Men use their own exploits to insinuate themselves in the myth and thus substantiate it, proving that a woman cannot
menstruate without a man. Rather than undermine the myth, men's and
women's occasional denials of its overt premise validate its underlying truth
by linking the mythic circumstance with everyday experience.

Women's instructions to brides and initiates are always contradictory in
this sense. When they recite spells into a bride's skirts to deaden the groom's
erections and delay her first period, when they warn that ingesting her own
blood will debilitate or even kill her, when they tell her that her blood, fallen
into a sorcerer's hands, has the same power to transmit harm to her husband
as his own semen or other "leavings," they convey the idea that the blood's
"true source" is outside her body and other than she. But in myth, incantation, and song, in ways that are perhaps more powerful than harangue,
women also suggest that the blood is the residue of a fantasy, a union with
the Moon that occurred as the figment of her own desire. Women's blood
magic implies that a woman can keep her desires secret—keep them harm-
less and unreal—by hiding their monthly discharge. Using ash and spittle to
"dry" her skin, commanding her blood to return to her brother's "nose," she
can reclose her body. But if she is careless and leaks her blood into the visible
world, the forbidden mythic relation it embodies will also be transformed

into a dangerous reality: her tie to the Moon, her life as the *kore baꝺaha* and secret possessor of his penis, may then threaten her living husband.

Women's obsession with getting rid of the *sight* of blood by both washing it away and "hiding it well" seems to express a contradictory wish to keep both "husbands," to protect the living one yet harbor the Moon or red Lorikeet. By commanding her body to "hold the blood" as a leaf of red cordyline holds its color, the menstruator attempts not only to shield her living husband from danger but also to lock in another who would destroy him, thus exposing one husband to the other, creating, within the hidden precincts of her body, the very danger her spells are supposed to avoid. When she seals her body and makes the Moon disappear, as the mythic fire swallowed the python, leaving nothing but bone—or stone—and ash, a menstruating woman keeps the Moon as her "first husband" and secret love. She appropriates his deadly power and becomes a snake like him, reversing the ostensible intent of her magic.

Whereas men exchange sisters in marriage, a woman conducts—and may refuse—an exchange of husbands at the level of substances within her own body. Blood magic gives her control over a realm men cannot see.

The other husband a woman hides is not always a fantasy nor wholly inside her body, as we have seen. The real men women insert into their myths are not only their own husbands but also sorcerers and adulterers. A sorcerer is apt to trail a married couple to their garden or into the forest, hoping to catch them in a tryst, a danger women dramatize for brides and that men impress upon grooms. A sorcerer stalks a couple and watches them from behind a tree, men warn. When he grows impatient, he recites a spell to excite the husband's desire: "'You will have sex with your wife *now*,' he chants in a secret language. . . . So the man has sex with his wife while the sorcerer watches. He sees where his semen falls and takes it! That man is hardly sick, he dies so fast!" Implicit in the sorcerer's presence is the notion that he was summoned by the woman's desire. Men say that sorcerers are lured mainly by dissatisfied wives:

> A woman looks at her husband's penis. If it's big, that's fine, but if it isn't she finds one that is! . . . "When we get old," women tell younger women, "our skins sag and our vaginas shrivel like the bark around a knot in a tree. . . . If your own husband doesn't satisfy [lit: fill] you, then find a man who does."

Even when a woman is not menstruating, even when her mythic first husband is in retreat, her body is still dangerous on account of the "real" adulterers and sorcerers who trail her. A woman is always inhabited or shadowed in this sense, pervaded by the presence of a previous, unseen, or illicit "hus-

band" who threatens her own husband—whose safety she has the responsibility to protect by keeping herself "clean," ridding her body of the
residues of Moon and man. But the tasks of purification that follow menstruation, sexual intercourse, and childbirth—the blood songs, hand wash-
ings, cleansing rituals, etc.—are pervaded by a sense of futility. Regardless
of how meticulous a woman is, her touch is always contaminating to a degree because *aðarena,* the filth of her hands (lit: *aða*/hand + *re/*? +
*na*/thing), is "well hidden":

> The Moon kills us so we cannot prepare red pandanus. . . .
> We use our hands to stop the blood so men tell us not to touch
> pandanus. "We don't want to eat the bloody filth beneath your
> fingernails," they tell us.

*aðarena* also refers to babies' feces. "Men don't want [our children's feces] in
their food so they prepare their own pandanus," women say.

A Gimi woman can never get rid of *aðarena* because, like Lady MacBeth,
she cannot wash away her guilt. The infinitesmal amounts of feces and
blood—dead aspects of the child—that remain ineradicably in her hands
are residues of things she did not only in life but also in myth. *aðarena*
remains not only because she actually menstruated and cleaned her child but
also because her mythic counterpart killed the firstborn or had a part in the
death. A menstruating woman is like the beautiful girl who—seeing that
"darkness was not close," realizing the old man was a trickster—married
him nonetheless and then killed the child in revenge or left him to do it while
she was away. She is like the orphaned girl who, having heard the "*ororo
ororo*" of the falling banana, having seen for herself that the bamboo was
broken, went for a walk across distant ridges, leaving the *kore bana* to murder her infant brother while she was fetching water. Looked at in terms of
the *nenekaina,* as women themselves recommend, their blood magic parallels the project of the mythic heroine. Rites that both expel and retain menstrual blood are like the efforts of the *nene* girl to escape her ogrish father, to
explode and annihilate his every part, yet to keep the vestiges and carry them
to her "true" husband, presenting him with the child in whose death she
colluded (see above, this Chap.).

Woman's fertility rests in this sense upon the maintenance of her mythic
guilt and ambivalence. A woman has to "hide her blood"—to retain in her
hands and vagina vestiges of the mythic child she killed—in order that she
have it there to dispose of. Emptying and purifying her body, like hollowing
out the mythic hoop pine, are the crucial first stage of conception, the very
method of producing live birds. A woman's reproductive life starts with
menstruation, and her initiation begins with blood songs and menstrual
theater, because killing is the essential prerequisite for life. A woman has to

kill the father inside her, kill her firstborn, in order to take it to her husband, in order to acquire the stuff she needs to cultivate new life, to make it "get big in her hands" and "between her thighs." The initial eviction is thus always deliberately incomplete: she makes her crime disappear, but also makes sure to hold onto the traces.

### The Singularity of Magic and Devotion

If menstrual blood is both deadly and fertilizing, then its ambivalence makes the quality of a woman's nurturance unpredictable and initially unknown, something that has to be established by experiment at the start of her marriage. Ritual leaders warn that a menstruating woman should sleep apart from her pigs. "When the Moon kills us we put our pigs to sleep in their stalls. . . . If a pig ate the blood it would not grow." Yet they also advise a newly married woman to tie her first pigs to her bed in the main part of her house. If these pigs prosper, she should keep all her pigs close to her, letting them "eat" her blood and secretions. But she has to protect her pigs from the leavings of other women:

> I let my pigs sleep with me but if another woman comes into my house and sits on my bed, I say, "Don't sit there! My pig will eat your vaginal fluid and get sick. Go sit somewhere else. Move! Or the dung flies will bite you in the ass!"
> If you put your pig in its stall by the door, other women will step over it as they enter and leave your house and the pig will spoil. Keep your pig with you, where you eat and sleep, and it will grow fast and strong. . . .

While a woman's secretions may sometimes benefit her pigs, they are invariably harmful in direct contact with her plants. Once inside her garden, a woman is careful not to step over any plant, literally, to "place it between her thighs" (*aramiti ϑa ho; arami*/thighs + *ti*/in + *ϑa*/? + *ho*/do).

> If we step over new taro it will die inside the ground. . . . If we step over yams they will become covered with hairs [i.e., root fibers] and spoil. . . . If we have sex and let our taros and yams smell our vaginas they won't grow into good food.

In the same way as a woman's congress with Moon or adulterer may ruin her husband, her relation with the Moon or any man may endanger her plants and pigs. The fantasied incest that produces a woman's menstrual blood and makes it poison to her husband extends, in the presence of other third parties, other love objects, to all her sexual relations and secretions. "Dirt" lingering "between a woman's thighs" endangers her taros and yams, in this sense, because it embodies other attachments, both fantasied and real, and thus spoils the singularity of her devotion. Purifying herself at the garden threshold gets rid of the residues of other bonds, or keeps them hidden, thus renewing her undivided attention.

Women equate the capacity to make things grow and flourish with the talent for unmediated attachment, for speaking "of no one else, to no one else, but you, my dear," for "joining the *auna*" with the *auna* of a new plant or pig, incorporating it like an unborn child, etc. But as a woman's own songs and spells vividly reveal, removing the "dirt" also means keeping it hidden. In fertility magic, a woman conjures a self-contained dyadic world that, from its inception, includes traces of a forbidden other love. Indeed, that suppressed third element—her tie to the Moon or adulterer in relation to her husband, her tie to any man in relation to her nurtured object—is the secret of her success, for it is mainly by getting rid of the contamination of other desire, purifying herself at the garden gate, that she establishes a nurturing attachment.

A successful mother and gardener only promises the communion of I and thou. The idea that motherhood originates in the "first appearance" of menstrual blood, and that the blood belongs to the Moon, means that a woman is never sole author of her fertility; that, despite the intimacy of her magic, she is never really alone with her child or nurtured object. The life-giving bond she invokes is already enmeshed in an invisible prior relation, a fantasied copulation with the Moon or actual defloration by his living stand-in. Through spells and caresses, she invites her plants and pigs inside a self that (like a flute) only *appears* to be empty but that is already occupied—or just vacated—by Moon or man. She endows her nurtured objects with the capacity to "fly out the head of the tree" by conjuring a relationship that seems to exist in isolation, seems to exclude the father, only because he went away.

At the end of a pregnancy, after months of sexual abstinence, a man returns to his wife "to finish the child" and induce birth. In women's myth, the heroine herself "finishes the child" by hitting the tree with a stick and releasing all the birds. Yet even in women's own myth, the woman acts as her husband's surrogate and uses *his* stick in the sense that he tells her what she will hear, what she will be tempted to do, and then invites her to do it by going away. Without some kind of husbandly intervention, without at least his vicarious presence, men and women seem to agree, life cannot occur. In the permanent and unqualified absence of a real husband, the object a woman nurtures, the child she invites inside her, will die in consummated dyadic union: it will revert to the Moon's blood, to murdered food, to a corpse dripping from the rafters, etc. The unspoken message of women's own myths and songs is that a woman's *uninterrupted* nurturing is lethal. The notion that her blood and sexual secretions are ambivalent, that she sheds blood as the *kiri* sheds its skin yet retains imperceptible vestiges, implies that, despite every effort, a woman cannot divest herself of certain fantasies; and that, left to run their course, these fantasies may have tangibly fatal results.

## *aϑaoina:* Food Taboos and Other Antidotes to Women's Magic

An elaborate system of food taboos and exchanges within the patrilineage protect both sexes from the dangers produced by the incessant contact between women and the foods they produce. The crops and pigs a woman addresses in song, holds in her hands, "passes between her thighs," etc., are polluted by the blood that remains ineradicably in her hands and vagina. Gimi say that a woman's own nurtured objects and those of her firstborn children are "the same" as her menstrual blood and that, therefore, neither she nor her husband may eat them. In the words of one man, BoϑaEha (see fig. 11):

> Teba does not eat the first pig Bobau [her firstborn daughter] rears because it is the same as Teba's own first blood . . . and the same as Bobau's. It's as if the Moon killed Bobau and she bore her first child who is that pig. Teba cannot eat that pig. Nor Bobau. Nor Beaku [Bobau's father]. Teba and Beaku copulated and bore Bobau. She was their first: she is like Teba's blood. Deo is their second. Teba and Beaku can eat the first pig of their second-born child . . . or of their third.
>
> If I were to eat the first crop of a garden made by my firstborn son I would lose the strength to work. But I take food from my son's *fiϑa,* from his old gardens. . . . When my first child plants a garden or raises a pig my wife and I don't eat it because it is the same as [my wife's] blood. Our first sex made that child. It is as if the Man [i.e., the Man Above] had killed her and made her blood run.

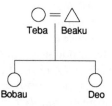

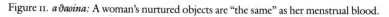

Figure 11. *aϑaoina:* A woman's nurtured objects are "the same" as her menstrual blood.

Throughout most of a marriage, the rules of *aðaoina* prevent a couple from eating the first fruits of their combined labors, especially pigs the woman rears and the first crop she produces on land her husband cleared and fenced. During male initiation, Big Men explain *aðaoina* to novices, warning them to avoid foods "like a wife's menstrual blood," foods they will one day engender by their own "fathering": "When you become a father, when you bear a child by 'going between the thighs' of your wife, you must not eat the pigs she rears there [lit: places between her thighs]."

Women give similar instructions to a bride on the eve of her departure, warning her not to eat her own produce because it is "the same as her first blood," as deadly to her as *aðarena,* the "filth of her hands." In the past, when a woman was initiated, she was beaten with lengths of sugarcane by her *anatu,* women of her husband's lineage who had reared the pigs for her brideprice and who, on that account, had a claim on her labor. "'Plant sweet potato! Plant greens!' my *anatu* told me, '[But] eat them and you will die!'" Monuato remembered. "I planted beans and maize for my *anatu* to harvest . . . and I ate what my *anatu* planted." Slapping her fist into her palm to recall the beatings she had received some thirty-five years before, she repeated her *anatu*'s warnings:

> "You must not go to your brother's house. You must not visit your mother. You must stay here with us and plant new gardens and care for pigs. Listen to us! Watch what we do and follow our ways. Tend pigs and your gardens but do not eat the food. And do not give it to your husband! First your *anatu* shall eat!"

"Only my mother and her co-wife give me food," a young married man explains. "I don't eat from the hands of my wife. The men who bought her must eat first. It is they who take food from her gardens. When she plants *fiða,* a second crop, I take it. Otherwise I eat only the food of my mothers' hands." In the first phase of his marriage, a man turns over to his lineage all the pigs he receives in exchanges with his affines. These pigs, like the ones his wife rears, are "the same as the head of his child." "I cannot eat a pig that comes from my child's head," Rudoi explains. "I will rear it and when it is grown I will give it to my brothers to eat." If a man becomes ill, his sister's husband may be the first obliged to kill a pig for him. But neither his sister nor her husband eat any part of that pig, even if it were reared by others. As part of an affinal exchange, "it is the head of their child."

Counting dramatically on her fingers, Monuato says that after a woman bears a fifth surviving child, her husband's father celebrates *habarena omenaha* (lit: *habare*/cutting + *na*/thing [i.e., marriage] + *ome*/do *naha*/we eat), a rite like a second marriage, after which she and her husband may together eat the products of her gardens:

> After a fifth child, a woman can eat from her own garden. They cut [i.e., marry] her again and send her to her husband. Her husband's father gives her husband red pandanus fruit and says, "You two can eat from your own gardens now." And the couple give the pandanus and taro and bananas, together with a pig the woman raised, to their mothers [i.e., to the wife's female *anaturaha*].

The relaxation of the taboo on a couple consuming their own produce after the birth of a fifth child is short-lived. As soon as their firstborn is betrothed and marries, they are subject to a host of new restrictions. A man and wife may not partake of any item of brideprice or wedding payment received on behalf of their firstborn daughter, nor may they eat the first pigs or crops she raises, nor food from the first plantings of her other gardens, nor pigs received as payments for the "head" of her firstborn child, etc. Often, the couple abstain as well from the heads of her other children and of firstborn children of other daughters. A couple who are still young and vigorous when their firstborn child matures, and have begun to eat from their own gardens, may extend the prohibitions of *aϑaoina* to other children. "A man thinks, 'I bore four children. I will not eat their pigs nor the food of their new gardens. But I have a fifth child whose produce I will eat because I am already old.'" Women say that a woman, too, thinks of eating her own pigs only when she is already a grandmother many times over.

A woman may attend the initiations of her firstborn daughter and of the wife of her firstborn son, but she absents herself from the concluding feasts on pain of death. She and her husband do not participate in the feast that celebrates the birth of their firstborn son's firstborn child nor, if the child is a girl, do they share in her betrothal or brideprice pigs. A couple eat none of the pigs reared by the wife of their firstborn son; nor the first plantings of her gardens; nor the meat the son traps or shoots; nor the red pandanus, banana, and sugarcane he cultivates in his orchards and gardens. When a woman's co-wives or other sons' wives eat these foods, she leaves their company. "This is part of *aϑaoina*," a man explains. "It's the same custom. The mother runs away because she has to give sweet potato to her son." But she also runs away to protect her own life. "I would die fast!" Monuato told me, if she were to eat part of an eel her eldest son trapped. "When my firstborn shoots a bird or traps an eel, or when his wife rears a pig or makes a new garden, neither I nor my husband eat the food. The two of us stay away so we may live and live . . . and see our grandchildren marry." "When our firstborn bears its first, this we two shall not eat," one man said. "That is the rule of *aϑaoina*."

Gimi fertility magic and food taboos are based upon a rampant generaliz-
ation, a tendency to root all productive endeavor in myths of cannibalism,
incest, and death. The fruits of a marriage, the plants and pigs the woman
rears, the birds and marsupials her husband shoots, the cassowaries and eels
he traps, foods their firstborn and other children cultivate, rear, or hunt,
etc., are all linked to menstrual blood, as if the blood issued directly from a
myth, as if it were the doomed firstborn, the boy woman buried at the bottom of her oven or abandoned on her walk. Until a couple have borne five
surviving children, their own food is like death unto them, a death they
avoid by surrendering the fruit of their loins to the patrilineage, repudiating
the incest, infanticide, and cannibalism of their own mythic past. By submitting to the injunctions of *aϑaoina* and the rules of *anotu nao,* a couple for-
swear their own firstborn and consume the heads of others instead.

In women's myths, the first couple are often partners in crime: she kills the
child to obliterate the incest he instigated. Woman's guilt is shared, miti-
gated by the fact that her first marriage derived from a "trick," from the
Moon disguising himself in her mother's clothes, from the giant invading
her house while she slept unaware, etc. According to the logic of *aϑaoina,*
the true husband is *also* the mythic husband, implicated by the real sexual
relationship with his wife in the "appearance" of her menstrual blood and
misdeeds of her mythic past. "Our first sex made that child," BoϑaEha said.
"It is as if the Man [i.e., the Man Above] had killed her and made her blood
run."

During the prime years of a marriage, the husband forsakes his wife's produce and takes food instead from his mother and sister, shifting onto his
wife the taboos that prevented him as a youth from "taking the food of his
mother's hands." The wife becomes the mother; and the husband's ability to
isolate himself from her shows again her greater guilt, her willful desire to
"hold the Moon's dirt."

# SEVEN

## Theories of Conception: Alternative Outcomes in an Intrauterine Scenario

Women cultivate food gradually and laboriously, building mounds, transplanting vines, weeding, caressing pigs, "joining their *aunas*" at every stage through song, touch, and flattering allusion. They use magic to instill a kind of growth that is the reverse of their method: by naming birds, waterfalls, giant trees, and other spectacular forest life, they invoke a place and state of being in which the multiplication of forms is swift, abundant, and without apparent effort. Nearly all the foods women produce appeared first in the forest, which Gimi call *kore maha*, literally, "ghost ground" (*kore*/wild, ancestor or ghost + *maha*/ground), and all are sweeter in their original wild form. The first sweet potato, *kore mihi*, grew to fruition within days, arising spontaneously above a man's grave. As one man recounted:

> Once upon a time a man buried his father at Lufa. That night he dreamed that sweet potato vines were growing on his father's grave. In the morning he went to look and there they were! He cared for the vines and they grew very long and he replanted them. This is the same sweet potato that now grows everywhere in Unavi . . . in Gimi, in Chimbu, in Goroka.
>
> By the time women uprooted the first tubers, they were big and heavy and filled with sap. The sap spilled over the women and they couldn't wipe it away. The women couldn't get rid of the sap because it was strong stuff! . . .
>
> How delicious they were, those very first sweet potato! A man from here went to Lufa and tasted one. . . . "What is the name of this wonderful food?" he asked. "Ah! That's *kore mihi*," the Lufa man replied. . . . The man from here asked for the vines and brought them back and planted them.

Wild things, *korena* (lit: *kore*/wild + *na*/thing[s]), grow without attention from the living, without the input of women's *auna*, because they are animated by *kore*, ghosts of the Gimi dead. Nonhuman life originates, paradoxically, in the innermost regions of the human body: the *auna* or "child" that animates a person in life, and fills the organs with "wind," flies out the fontanel at death and embarks upon a dreamlike journey, taking refuge at first in the wind, rivers, and marsupials, and later entering Birds of Paradise, giant trees, mountain caves, and every form of forest life (see Chap. 4). Death and the movement of *auna* through the fontanel (which men compare to a "vagina") is like the birth and dissemination of inner being. As *auna* "flies" away from the body, it is dispersed, depersonalized, and eventually transformed into ancestral *kore*.

All the foods and valuable materials that Gimi take out of the rainforest— bamboos for bowstrings, arrowheads, flutes, necklaces, carrying and cooking vessels; vines to tie fences and house walls; bark to make string for carrying bags, clothes, and ornaments; black palm for bows; Birds of Paradise; marsupials; medicinal leaves and plants; nuts, mushrooms, hearts of palm, and other delicacies— are gifts from the ancestors. Ancestors create these goods in a way radically different from the living mode of production. While a woman converts her *auna* to food gradually, sending it into plants and pigs through a repetitive process of singing, cajoling, and caressing, a corpse projects *auna* instantaneously, in an ejaculatory release from the head, penetrating new life-forms and reaching fruition automatically. Like products of the wild, white men's cargo arrives fully formed and complete, revealing no hint of the effort with which it was assembled or the process by which it grew. Our access to cargo identified us ipso facto with the Gimi dead.

After the death of a young married man, I took my place among the women mourners and was confronted by his mother: "You sit here and talk with us but you hide what you know. My son has just died and you have seen him but you don't say to us, 'I have seen your child.'" That evening one of David Gillison's guides explained her anger:

> White men and women return to Australia at night and meet our dead there. That is how you get cargo. The trousers, shirts, radio, tarpaulin, car, tinned meat and fish you have were not made by you. White men did not make those things! Black men who have died made them. Their *kore* send them to you to give to us. "Take this cargo to my birthplace," the *kore* tell you. "Give it to my mother and father. Give it to my wife and children."
>
> But you whites take the cargo and hide it from us or ask us for money. *kore* deliver their cargo at night. They arrive at your house and enter your bedroom. That's why you ask us to leave when you go to sleep.

Cargo is created in the *effortless* manner of all original life-forms, like the first sweet potato vine that grew overnight above a man's corpse, or like the mythic penis—as long and convoluted as a vine—that roused itself and ventured into the night, leaving the first man fast asleep. Women uprooted the first tubers when they were *already* enormous in the same way the first woman awoke and cut off the giant after he had penetrated her. And just as the giant's blood filled the vagina so did sap from those first sweet potatoes "spill all over the women" so they could not wipe it away. Women's work begins, we see again, only after she "uproots" the first man and is inundated with his fluid. Like pregnancy, cultivation originates in—and reverses—the "wild" mode of production. Wild forms of life are the forever-more-varied-and-delicious precursors of cultivated species in the same way effortless nights of copulation precede difficult months of pregnancy and child care.

Gimi calculate the sexual division of labor and ownership of resources according to these cultural facts and fantasies, assigning men and women tasks that seem to repeat or expand their mythic roles in copulation, gestation, parturition, and antenatal attachment (see Yanagisako and Collier 1987:39). Women have daily responsibility for tending gardens and pigs because they are deemed capable of magically extending motherhood to other objects. Through songs and spells, a woman internalizes her charges, joining her *auna* with the *auna* of her plant or pig in the way a pregnant woman or new mother attaches her child. But her talent for dyadic connection, her power to conceive a child and to make things grow—the wellspring of her *auna*—originates in her menstrual blood, a thing she stole from a man and therefore possesses only temporarily. A woman has to surrender her children and the foods she nurtures because, like her blood, they are illicit possessions, things she took without exchange and keeps on loan.

Men own the land and the pigs and monopolize production outside the settlement where plants and animals arise spontaneously and are obtainable without repeated exertion or the gradual infusion of *auna*. Men alone have the right to hunt game and fight wars, reaping precious meats and skins and enemies' souls in single acts of killing. Shooting extends the male reproductive role by "opening" closed bodies and liberating the *auna* or "child" woman captured and held illegally inside her "house." Shooting with bow and arrows is magically creative because it achieves the swift release and dispersal of life-force, giving rise "overnight" to complete new forms. If women are the final cause of entropy, senescence, and death in the Gimi scheme of things, then men are the whole source of spontaneity and life.

### The Man Provides the Whole Child

Both sexes state that a child is created entirely from *hato* or semen and that it remains part of the father, connected to him in the same way as his other "leavings," until it is weaned at about two-and-a half years. To make a child, men explain, a man has to copulate with the mother many times in order to "fill her womb." During orgasm, the *aʋuso* in his bones and head, the glu-tinous, light-colored stuff that constitutes bone marrow, nasal mucous, gray matter, etc., flows into his penis and "shoots" white *hato* into the woman (see Paul 1982:114). Once he installs the child over the course of weeks or months, he refrains from sexual relations for the rest of the pregnancy, leav-ing the child to sleep and "get big" undisturbed.

A woman's bones, nose, and skull are also filled with *aʋuso*, men allow, but she has no organ in which to collect it, convert it to *hato*, and discharge it during sex. Whereas a man has a penis through which he loses *hato*, a woman has a vagina and womb, a "fetus bag" (lit:*[h]anu ko; anu*/fetus or spirit-child + *ko*/bag), to "pull out" and retain it. "The moment a man ejac-ulates the woman pulls all the *aʋuso* out of him," a man named Rabofa ex-plains. "When a man has sex he loses *aʋuso* from every part of him: it rushes from his head and bones into his penis. . . . A woman steals *hato* from a man and keeps it."

Asked to describe conception, one woman said, "A man goes into a woman and his *hato* enters her belly and makes the child." In response to my probing, another insisted, "A woman's belly is empty. . . . It doesn't *make* anything." With each ejaculation, the husband creates another part of the fetus. The woman continued:

> A man's *hato* makes the bones and the flesh, the face and the limbs, every part of the child. . . . Nothing else can do that. Only a man's *hato* can make a child . . . and make it get bigger. [Responding to my query . . . ] What does the mother give? Her belly is there. It doesn't *do* anything. A woman has nothing to give. . . . Before a woman is married, she cannot bear a child. A man buys her and gives her to her husband and her husband puts his *hato* into her belly and makes the baby.

When I asked women what happens to their menstrual blood during preg-nancy, they said, "It's there with the child, lying beside it, and comes out when the child is born." Might the child eat the blood? I persisted. "Never," the women responded in horror, "because the eyes and mouth are *closed* and blood cannot enter the mouth! A child is born *clean* with skin as clear and smooth as the backs of your hands."

But according to men's myth, we may recall, the first father did know how to "finish the child." He did not "return to the mother" at the end of preg-nancy to have sex with her "one more time," and the child was born incom-plete, its mouth wide open—a gaping hole at the site of the fontanel (see Chap. 4). Food fell through the fontanel directly into the stomach, men's myth says, and the child grew magically into a giant. According to women's myth, the creature with an open mouth on the top of his head who "gets big" with impossible speed is not a child but a penis. Women's heroine completes this monster by cutting him down to size (see Chaps. 1 and 3). The myths of both sexes describe the end of pregnancy as unfinished business but differ over which sex ought to "finish the child" and by what means. That argument, I suggest, lies at the heart of Gimi ideology of production and exchange. It unfolds as part of an intrauterine drama that starts with a confrontation between man and Moon at the inception of pregnancy.

### Defeating the Moon

When men advise the newly married, they speak of a man's duty to copulate many times with his wife, perhaps thirty or more, over a period of weeks or months. When a man "goes inside" a woman the first time, he is not "thinking about putting in his child." To make her pregnant, he has to go back and "defeat the Moon," stopping the Moon's monthly visits by matching or outdoing his persistence. Women are reluctant to bear children, men complain, because they would rather consort with the Man Above.

> It is always the Moon who takes a woman the first time. During the nights when there is a full moon, all the women run off and . . . the Moon has sex with them all and makes their blood flow. The Moon is like a man. A menstruating women says to her husband: "I am sleeping with the first man in my life so go away."
> . . . The Moon doesn't let up! He has sex with women all the time. He kills them all the time, all the time. . . . You are a woman and you know. *He* is your true husband, your first husband, and *we* are the adulterers.

The Moon "opens the way" into women and closes it to everyone else, making women inaccessible, keeping them all for himself. The condition of a menstruating woman is like that of the virgin in men's myth whose vagina was on fire. One day, a small boy put out the fire.

> He led the woman up a mountain and had her lie down beside a lake. He picked up a stone and climbed to the top [lit: head] of a tall tree and cast the stone into the still water. The water splashed the woman, and she shivered and opened her thighs. The water entered her vagina and cooled it. The boy put out the fire between the woman's thighs and opened her passage. . . .
> The stone was inside a very, very long net bag that hung around the boy's neck. When he threw the stone into the lake he

didn't throw it away completely! He kept it inside the bag. When the fire was out, he pulled up the bag and got back the stone.

That boy was the same as the Moon. The Moon threw his penis out of the sky and had sex with the woman. . . . He put out her fire and took back the stone. The Moon says, "I am the one who opens her passage." And we say to the Moon, "You are the one who enters first, and we are the ones who come after."

In this male version of the first coitus, the first man is represented by the tall tree or the Moon, a dominating but still and distant figure whose deeds are performed through the surrogacy of the small boy. As in men's myth of the "unfinished" man, the child is identified with a giant and his actions seem to replicate—or invert—erection and ejaculation on a monumental scale (see Chap. 4). As *hato* rises without interruption and emerges from a hole in the head of the penis, so in the "unfinished" first man does food enter a "mouth" at the top of his head and fall unimpeded into his stomach, causing magical enlargement. A similar phallic trajectory seems to be created here, too, when the boy climbs the huge tree, casts the stone from the top, and the stone falls into the lake, splashing out the woman's fire. The boy-with-the-stone resembles a miniature or clonelike version of the giant, a humunculus who rises through his enormous length and exits alive and splashing, as it were, but dies in the fall to earth, landing lifeless as stone in the cold lake between women's thighs. Unmoving or stagnant water is an overt symbol of menstrual blood, and "stone and blood" is a Gimi term for stillbirth or a retained placenta. When the boy at the top of the tree pulls up the net bag around his neck and retrieves the stone, in these terms, he portrays the Moon reabsorbing his own spent and lifeless seed.

If the boy's retrieval of the stone depicts the Moon taking back his own ejaculate, it suggests that, in falling to earth, *hato* "died" and that the giant used his urethra as a "first mouth," filling his head with the blood of his own firstborn. If this is, indeed, part of the submerged imagery of men's myth, then it contradicts men's direct statements about the exchange of fluids in the immediate aftermath of climax. When men describe sex in nonmythic terms, they say that relations with a woman are always polluting, to a degree, because particles of menstrual blood remain in the crevices of the vagina, combine with other secretions during sex, and invade the head of the penis. After a woman "pulls all the *aðuso* out of a man" and leaves him empty, men say, her fluid inundates his penis and "makes him sick":

> We men continually give up to women something that is ours, and we grow weak and old before our time. . . . But the blood of women enters men. . . . The moment a man ejaculates and is empty, a woman's fluid enters him and makes him sick. . . . It's

poison to men. The fluid women have ruins us. It bends our backs and makes us old.

Interpreted in the context of men's pollution beliefs, the boy climbing the tall tree, throwing down the stone and pulling it back, never letting it out of the net bag around his neck, presents an image of semen rising through the penis, cast out from the head, killed in the fall, *and reabsorbed.* In men's myth, the poison blood, the "blood and stone," originate not inside the woman on the ground but inside the head of the distant and unmoving giant.

If the underlying premise of men's myth seems to contradict men's own statements about the source of menstrual pollution, it also seems to coincide with women's myth of the Giant Penis, recalling the giant's exploits when he was let out of the bag around the man's neck, when he shot the marsupial and coiled it at the head of his enormous length. That night, the giant ate his way inside the "closed vagina" and was cut off, his head filled with the blood of his own severed self. Taken together, men's and women's myths and secular accounts of conception imply that ejaculation may both produce life and pull it back. During orgasm, a man gives up the very marrow of his bones to feed the unborn, to give shape and substance to fetal organs and limbs, etc., but, especially the first time, when he is not "thinking about putting in his child," he is likely to turn around and "shoot" it, to reduce it to "dead meat," or menstrual blood, killing the life he engendered and pulling it back inside his own head.

During the very first coitus the penis automatically revokes the life it sends out, pulls back the stone, shoots the marsupial and envelops its dead weight at the head, etc.: it lets go of nothing and stays enormous. When men say that the Moon is their forerunner, that he "opens" a woman and then "closes" her again, according to this interpretation they mean that when a woman menstruates, or is premenarcheal and a virgin, she is utterly possessed by the first man. Her vagina is "on fire" and a danger to ordinary men, in these terms, not because she is alone or has never copulated but because she has never stopped, because the first coitus is interminable. The Man Above is still inside her, hidden from view, and would "burn and break" the penis of any other man.

> When a man wants sex with a woman and the Moon is killing her, he doesn't go near her. . . . He stays away because that is the law. Because she is with her other husband. . . . A man who enters a woman then will die because the blood will get on his body and his hands. He will put his hands in his mouth and swallow the blood and cough without stopping. When he tries to climb a mountain or lift something heavy, he will just collapse and die.

> When a woman says, "Go away" [because she is menstruat-
> ing] and a man goes into her, he is sticken that very moment be-
> cause he contracts another man's germ.[1]

A man who penetrates a menstruating woman encounters her "other husband" and is inundated with blood, reduced to "stone" like the firstborn,
"turned to ashes" in the conflagration between her thighs. The Moon seems
a distant figure, merely part of the scenery, but he is also inside the woman
pulling back his issue, making sure no man or child escapes him or sees the
light of day.

According to women's myth, the first woman awoke from her sleep with
the Moon and cut him off (see Chap. 3). She evicted the giant penis and
made life possible. But in men's view the culture hero is the "small boy," and
his part is played in real life by the husband. Men characterize a husband's
work in cultivating unborn life, in ejaculating time after time until he "fills
the womb" and installs his child, as a kind of engagement with the Moon, a
battle with a prearranged truce.

> When a woman gets pregnant, it isn't only a man who's had
> sex with her, the Moon has had sex with her, too. The first time a
> man goes into a woman, the Moon gets rid of his semen. And
> the second time, too, the Moon gets rid of it. By the eleventh or
> twelfth time, maybe, a child lies sleeping in her. And then the
> man asks his wife, "Shall we have sex again?" And his wife says,
> "I already have the child."
> But the husband says, "I haven't had sex with you enough
> times to make you pregnant. I think you are stealing [i.e., com-
> mitting adultery] with another man." And the woman says,
> "Yes, I have the Man Above, too." . . .
> When a real child sleeps inside a woman, the Moon doesn't
> kill her anymore . . . [but] his semen stays in her and heats (lit:
> cooks) the child to make it grow. The Moon is not enough to
> *make* the child! But he holds it. His semen stays on the side,
> keeping it hot. When the child is about to be born, it pushes out
> the blood. That's why children were born in menstrual huts. Be-
> cause the blood of birth is the Moon's filth.
> A man waits until his child is grown [i.e., weaned at two-and-
> a-half or three years] to go back to his wife. But by then the Moon
> is back, too! By then she is married again to her other man.

---

1. The word "germ" and its meaning were introduced by Australian patrol officers and District Health officers who framed their demands that Gimi bury the dead and dig latrines in
Western theories of contagion and disease prevention (see Chap. 3).

The Moon or other husband in women's myths is a father figure, as we have seen, an ogre, trickster, or giant penis who seems to symbolize the enormity of incestuous desire. But the Moon may also take the live form of a woman's husband, uniting the fantasy of the "first time" with actual sexual experience. The rules of a *ϑaoina* seem to be based upon this equation, assimilating the conjugal relation, and everything it produces, with myths of incest (see Chap. 6). But husband and Moon are mainly adversaries. Men associate the Moon with the sorcerers and lovers who lurk around married women and visit them in their menstrual seclusion. For a woman, the Moon's main living counterpart is her real or classificatory father, the man who controls her fertility throughout much of her marriage.

### The Men in the Moon

When a woman wants to prevent conception or hasten menopause, she returns to her natal compound or village to ask her father or father's brother, or any of the senior men who "ate my bridewealth and my children's heads," to perform sterilizing spells. After the birth of a child, she asks her father to "close" her so she does not become pregnant again too soon. Her father invokes the Moon, instructing him to visit her until further notice because "when the Moon kills her, he closes her up. . . . and her husband's semen falls to the ground." Her father prepares a *rakukusa,* or medicine, of barks and leaves and, after she eats it, knots the hair above her fontanel or pinches her lower abdomen (as explicit substitute for the labia) and kisses his "closed" thumb and forefinger.

A classificatory brother of Bobau's father performed such a rite after the birth of her second child, a second daughter, and then died without undoing his spell, leaving her unable to conceive, she said, and eventually unable to menstruate. Bobau was content to have no more children, but her husband wanted a son. In an effort to "open" her body, she borrowed the spell-giver's jawbone from his widow, who kept it in the rafters of her house, and circled medicinal leaves above it as she pleaded with his *kore* for another child. Then she ate the leaves. But her efforts have been unsuccessful, as her brother explained, because when a spell-sayer dies without "opening" the woman, she is "closed forever."

> When she has sex with her husband, his fluid goes into her but falls out again . . . because the womb is closed. There is no space for a child.
> Only the Moon can open the passage. . . . If the Moon stops killing her she is completely closed. You see, the man who gave her the *rakukusa* is dead . . . so she cannot bear a child. Absolutely cannot! . . . If that man could touch her with his hand, if

he could hold food and give it to her to eat then, only then, might she conceive.

A woman's father possesses spells to make the Moon close her body and exclude her husband's semen and other spells to make the Moon retreat. If the father dies without having performed the latter spells, then the Moon, too may die inside her, or cease to come and go, taking with him the true husband's chance to arrest his visits. When a young married woman is childless, her husband's relations may accuse her of having eaten potions her father rubbed in his armpit or *sagana*, literally, a "crotch," and demand that she return to his compound so that he may "open her vagina." When I suggested that Tomaba, a man with two wives but no offspring, might himself be incapable of "placing a child" inside a woman, women were emphatic. "No," they replied. "There is nothing wrong with Tomaba's semen. His wives have eaten their fathers' contraceptives."

A woman can call upon the Moon to foil her husband's efforts without traveling to her father's village. "A strong woman doesn't get pregnant in a hurry!" men complain, because she has the power to dream night after night and exclude her husband's seed. To conceive a child, a woman has first to dream it, to "see" a bird or frog or other ancestral incarnation of the fetus in a dream. On the night of conception, her *auna* leaves her body by the usual route, but ancestral *kore* also enters her head—which is why her father knots the hair above her fontanel. A woman cannot conceive a child without first "seeing the *kore*" in her dream, as Monuato explained:

> A woman cannot simply conceive a child. She has to dream it first. Gasarika has never had a child because at night she never dreams of a bird or frog. . . . If I dream I am holding a frog, or if I see a creature of the water, my husband will have the same dream and I will give birth to a daughter. A man follows his wife in such things. I dream and my husband follows me. The *kore* comes at night to trick me and goes away. Then he comes back to trick my husband. First he wakes me. Then he comes back to wake my husband.

A dream is a kind of "trick" or copulation with the ancestral *kore*. A woman who dreams continually, who is always filled with the *kore*, is as barren as one who never dreams: in different ways, each prevents her husband from defeating the first man inside her.

A woman relies upon her father, both as a living man and as an ancestor, or dream, to prevent pregnancy *and* to open the way for it. In matters regarding her fertility, her husband consults his own father. A man's father tells him where to find contraceptive fruits in the clan forest. "If you give her this," our fathers tell us, "the Moon will stop killing her." The husband gives the fruits to his mother or sister to administer to his wife, intending to stop her periods, or to prevent a pregnancy, mainly to protect himself from the sorcerers who are drawn to her during menstruation and in childbirth, looking for a discarded tampon or pieces of afterbirth to use in spells against him (see Chap. 2). Sorcerers are "lonely men," men without wives, who trail the wives of other men to get close to the *men*—while the men themselves are absent or off guard. A sorcerer waits in hiding to steal a drop of "fallen" semen or blood or a piece of a child's corpse, "leavings" that represent dead parts of the husband, parts he cast off without awareness, parts of himself he "forgot" inside his wife.

Men regularly accuse women of plotting against their husbands so they can marry their amours. One man repeated to me what he said was an old woman's confession to him about how other women operate. Her use of "I" was merely illustrative:

> "If I really wanted to kill my husband and marry another man," she told me, "I would seduce him on the road. 'Let's do it here.' I would say . . . and his semen would fall on the road and I would leave it there. . . . Or I would tell the man who wants to kill him to keep watch at a certain spot and I would sweet-talk my husband into having sex with me there. 'Watch us,' I'd say [to my lover in advance], 'I'll put his semen aside [so you can come afterward and take it].'" . . . That's how women can get rid of husbands they don't want.

A woman may concoct *ha ð ana,* a special poison, with her lover, men say. "If my wife didn't like being married to me," BoðaEha hypothesizes to explain the origin of *ha ð ana,* "she would find another man she liked better. She would have sex with him in secret and keep the "water" (lit: *ano/* fluids) they make together. She would smear it on my food and I would eat it. The *ha ð ana* would stay inside my belly and I'd start to cough and get very thin and my belly would swell because I could not excrete it. Soon I would die and my wife would marry that man. . . . That is how Mugiri died and how Sataibua [another of BoðaEha's clansmen] *now* is dying!" A woman who has no lover but is dissatisfied with her husband, perhaps because he insists upon anal intercourse, can use her menstrual blood alone to get rid of him. "When she wants a new husband," BoðaEha continues, "she takes blood from her moss and puts it in his tobacco or sweet potato or cooks it with greens and gives it to him to eat. . . . His bones go soft, his skin shrivels and soon he dies."

Do women actually devise or carry out such schemes? A few young wives boasted to me of seeking liaisons, and some women admitted to succumbing with pleasure to the advances of other men during weddings and initiations, occasions when there is general sexual license. Women's enjoyment of sex is revealed in songs they sing magically to induce erections and to plead with men to penetrate more deeply, imploring the beautiful red Lorikeet to enter completely into "the mouth of the bamboo." Women also have songs that ridicule men, describing the moment of ejaculation as the bursting of a boil, or likening the penis to a rat, a creature absurdly small to "fill" a woman.

Though I never heard a woman say she wanted to be rid of her husband, or that she would use her lover or her own blood to ensorcel or poison him, women constantly accuse each other of harboring such intentions. When a man announces that he intends to take another wife, his present wife may inform him that his paramour is promiscuous, bound to be careless with his leavings or to convey them to a sorcerer. When the prospective co-wife is a widow, other women publicly accuse her of having slept with many men since her husband died, saying that she will pollute the next one with semen the others have left behind. "If only she had come [to my husband] when her husband died," one woman objected, knowing that no widow can remarry for at least a year, not until her husband's *agesagena* have been removed. If a widow is chaste, she embodies the undiluted jealousy of her husband's ghost; if his brothers and patrilateral cousins exercise their right to cohabit with her during the year or more of her widowhood and thus moderate her husband's wrath, she then harbors the brothers' residues. No matter what a woman does or does not do, her behavior is interpreted to reveal her insatiable nature, to show that she is eternally "hungry for men" like the *kore baðaha*, anxious to kill off her husbands and lovers and replace them with new ones.

### The World Inside Woman's Body

When I asked men how a child was conceived, they told me that *hato*, the culmination of a man's *aðuso* or body substance, accumulates in the womb during many acts of intercourse and "makes the whole child" (see Ferenczi cited in Paul 1982:109). The womb merely "houses" the growing fetus. Women state that "a woman's belly is empty," that "only *hato* can make the child," seeming to agree with men that a woman contributes no substance of her own. But such statements, reflecting the often uncomprehending terms of my questions, fail to convey the complexity of the procreative act and its inherent antagonism.

In giving up *aðuso*, a man sacrifices part of himself to make a child. Part of him "dies" or "turns to blood" inside a woman. He suffers a little death which is the origin of his mortality and fragile fern-like existence (see

Chap. 3). A woman is a thief, men say. She "steals *hato*" in the moment a man ejaculates and then lets it "fall to the ground" where a sorcerer may steal it again. Men compare the interior of a woman's body to a marsh or *neki maha*, literally "mad ground" (*neki*/mad or insane + *maha*/ground), a place that absorbs and decomposes what a man leaves behind, fatally mixing his "leavings" with those of men who preceded him.

In various overt ways, women seem not merely to accept the blame men invest in their sex but to embrace it, taking upon themselves the duty to protect men's welfare as if the threat stemmed from woman's own nature and men risked life and health every time they ventured inside their wives. Instructions older women give to brides and initiates portray the younger women as impetuous, careless, unreliable, seductive, promiscuous, in league with sorcerers and the Moon, and in need of constant supervision, constant reminders to "clean" their vaginas. The elders' threats and warnings are entirely in keeping with what men say, presuming a wife to be unworthy to house her husband's gifts. But as I talked to women individually and studied their myths and secret songs I saw that, in agreeing with men that semen provides the whole content of intrauterine life, and in accepting the link to the Moon that men assign, women do not simply disavow or condemn their own role. A man injects *hato* and installs his child by doing battle with the Moon, stopping his monthly expulsions, binding him in the womb, etc. To the extent that a woman is tied to the Moon, and to adulterers and sorcerers who haunt her movements—to the extent that she is linked to a wicked man, fantasied or real, who holds the place of her father—she, too, can have an active role in defeating him and making way for a living child. In women's Bird of Paradise myth, the heroine explodes the ogre who devoured her mother, transports her murdered brother to a husband, and takes for herself the role of "finishing the child" (see Chap. 6).

In the following *nenekaina*, the heroine again assumes an active role. When the story begins, a mother and father have already gone into the forest to hunt marsupials, leaving two little boys at home alone. Hunting marsupials is a standard Gimi metaphor for getting a baby. The parents going to sleep when they return from their expedition into the forest underscores its sexual meaning. The giant who invades the house while the parents are away is portrayed here by two men, signifying perhaps that, as a mother of living children, the heroine has already succeeded in dividing the giant penis and has achieved, together with her husband, a measure of control over the Moon's comings and goings.

> The two men came down into the valley, one coming from RakItI, the other from Abini. "*ðoreðoreee mora kinasooo ðoriðe!*" sang the one. "*kirekire sasa ðorireee!*" sang the other

coming down the opposite side of the valley. They met at RuyIpi where the little boys had been left at home alone. . . .

"Where are your mother and father?" they asked them. "Why are you here all alone?" "Our mother and father have gone into the forest to hunt marsupials," the boys replied. "When they return with the kill, what will you give us?" the men demanded.

"When they bring back the marsupials," the boys offered, "you can eat the head." "But we don't like the head," the men said. "Then eat the arm and shoulder," the boys offered. "But we don't like the arm and shoulder," the men said. "Then eat the other arm and shoulder," the boys offered. "But we don't like the other arm and shoulder," the men said. "Then eat the leg," the boys offered. "But we don't like the leg," . . . "Then eat the other leg," . . . "Then eat the rib cage," . . .

The boys finally offered the tail, but the two men said they didn't like the tail and hit the boys. "We don't like you!" they cried. They beat the boys and took off in different directions.

The two boys were crying, tears falling from their eyes, mucous running from their noses, when their mother and father returned from the forest and asked, "Who beat you?" "A man from over there and another man from over there came down here and beat us. We didn't know them," the boys said. "We couldn't see their faces." The mother and father went to sleep and, in the morning, returned to the forest.

"*ϑore ϑoreee more kinasooo ϑoriϑe!*" sang the one coming down from RakItI. "*kirekire sasa ϑorireee!*" sang the other coming down from Abini. . . . They came singing down the mountainsides and met at RuyIpi. "Where did your mother and father go?" they asked the boys. "They went into the forest and left us here," the boys answered. . . . "And when they bring home the marsupials, what will you give us?"

"You can eat the head," the boys offered. "We don't like the head," the men said. "Then eat the arm and shoulder," the boys offered. "We don't like the arm and shoulder," the men said. "Then eat the other arm and shoulder," the boys offered. "We don't like the other arm and shoulder," the men said. "Then eat the leg," the boys offered. "We don't like the leg," the men said. "Then eat the other leg," . . . . "We don't like the other leg," . . . "Then eat the rib cage," . . . "We don't like the rib cage," . . . "Then eat the tail," . . . "We don't like the tail," . . . "Then eat the liver," . . . "We don't like the liver," . . . "Eat the lungs," . . . "We don't like the lungs," . . . "Eat the kidneys," . . . "We don't like the kidneys," . . .

The mother and father came back from the forest and asked, "Did they come again and beat you?" "They did," the boys replied. "I am angry [lit: my stomach is not right]," the husband said. "*Whose sons* do they come to fool with?" He took his spear and his wife took her digging stick and they said to their children, "You stay here." The two of them went to lie in wait and play a trick on the two men.

"*ϑoreϑoreee mora kinaso ϑoriϑe!*" sang the one. "*kirekireee sasa ϑorireee,*" sang the other. . . . They came down the mountains and met in the valley and asked the boys [what they had to offer]. The boys offered the liver and the stomach . . . and the husband whispered to his wife, "I am going to kill them now!" He grabbed his spear and she took her digging stick and off they went. The husband shot the one and the wife broke open the head of the other and they killed them both.

We bear children and leave them alone in the house. If we do not kill the intruders they will come inside while we are gone and fool with our children.

Like the giant penis and the "unfinished" first man, the intruders in this myth are faceless: the boys hear their melodious arrivals and feel their beatings but say to their parents, "We could not see their faces." The boys' sensing the intruders' rhythmic incursions yet being unable to see their faces suggests that the house where they have been left alone is the womb, a dark place far away from the head of the giant penis, as far away as the bottom of a valley from the Moon, or from the mountaintops where the pair begin their descent. The repeated, part-by-part recitations of marsupial anatomy recall the successive ejaculations that nourish the fetus and bring it into being limb by limb and organ by organ (Gillison 1987). When the intruders are identified with the giant penis, their outrageous demand for marsupial meat becomes comprehensible as a demand for compensation, a demand that the boys, or their parents, replace food that the intruders have already "shot from the head." Interpreted as part of an intrauterine drama, the pair's demand for meat becomes an attempt to recuperate what they have lost, to take back parts of themselves sacrificed to gain entry into woman's "house."

The faceless angry men are not strangers, in this sense, but the boys' original fathers. The marsupial meat, offered "head first" and part by part, identifies the interlopers as maternal kinsmen, as those entitled to "eat the head of the child." Their repeated refusals and beatings of the boys they "do not like" represent the curse of the mother's brother and the catastrophe that ensues when head payments are not made or accepted, prompting their own father to ask, "*Whose sons* do they come to fool with?" The intruders' implied threat to the boys is to take back their lives as the Moon pulled back the

stone. The repeated listing of marsupial parts, the repeated offers and refusals, thus refer not only to the installation of a child in the womb but also
to head payments—and to the second course of a cannibal meal (see Chap.
3). They reveal the implicit logic of Gimi exchange by suggesting both the
nature of the mother's brothers' demand and the consequences of default.

When mother's brothers are unrecompensed and left to carry out their
inclinations, women's myth suggests, they return to the mother's house to
"eat" her children, refusing to be dissuaded by any substitute. As a last en-
ticement, after the men have refused every other part, the boys "offer the
tail" in what is perhaps a homosexual allusion (see Chap. 1). The beatings the
men then administer fill the boys' eyes with tears and their noses with mucous, implying both pain and sexual arousal in the sense that a "snotty nose"
is a euphemism for the arrival of semen at adolescence. Unplaced with
other food, as it were, the mother's brothers are inclined to *re*incorporate
the boys into the head of their penis: in lieu of head payments they would
remarry the boys' mother, invade her unguarded house, and sexually devour
her boys. They would turn their own emissions to blood and repeat the incest of red Lorikeets (see Chap. 6).

The cruel intruders are hard to evict. Each time the parents go off into the
forest, each time they are transported in love making, the men return to
make mischief. They return to "fool" with children who have been "left
alone," a reference to the required period of sexual abstinence during pregnancy when the father is supposed to leave the child to "sleep" undisturbed
in the womb. The fact that the intruders always arrive when the parents are
away—when the man is on a hunting expedition inside his wife—suggests
that the pair's intrusion also recapitulates the parent's escapade; and that the
giant penis also belongs to the true husband, whose failure to abstain from
sex during the critical period of gestation risks miscarriage (see Chap. 4).

The pair of faceless men thus stand not only for the mother's brothers but
also for the father himself, for his own mythic penis. In this sense, the parents getting rid of the intruders is like breaking themselves away from them,
like dividing the giant into separate persona. Indeed, the couple's retaliatory
stroke—shooting one man and "breaking open the head" of the other—
recalls the decapitation of the giant in women's other myth. Here we see that
the penis is partitioned, that the invaders become plural and acquire
"wounds" or *asa* (lit: mouth, cut, wound, fissure), literally "mouths," as the
consequence of refusing other meat, refusing to transact the boys to life.
Their wounds suggest that they devoured the boys as they implicitly threatened, filling their heads with their own blood (and repeating the image in
men's myth of the boy who pulled the lifeless stone back into the head of the
tree). In the sense that the ambush symbolizes the onset of menses and killing of the firstborn, it shows that destroying the invaders is the same as de-

stroying the boys. The couple sacrifice their firstborn, in these terms, as a way to separate themselves from the primordial father, making it possible from now on to "bear children and leave them alone in the house."

Typical of a second stage or cycle in women's *nenekaina*, this rendition of the origin of menarche shows husband and wife working together to defeat the Moon, the one wielding his spear, the other her digging stick. Conjugal teamwork was also decisive in resolving the Bird of Paradise *nene:* the groom allowed the bride to hit the tree, causing the head to burst open and release birds of every hue. In the act of "opening the head," the heroine cuts off the giant. But by repeating her deed *with a husband,* she divides the monolithic penis into parts he cannot reabsorb and devour, parts that fly away and take on a life of their own. Analyzed in this way, women's myths contradict many of their direct statements by showing that woman's role in procreation is neither passive nor obstructive.

Whereas women's myths portray the violent annihilation of the Moon, the death of the invaders, the severing of the giant's head, the explosion of the *kore bana*'s every limb and organ, etc., men tend in their own myths to underplay the conflict between first and second husbands or to avoid it altogether by absenting the former, placing him high in the sky or outside the main narrative, representing him as a distant or inert figure like a tree. In order to "fill the womb" and install a child, a man has to stop the Moon, he has to stop the Moon getting rid of his deposits. But rather than kill his predecessor, the true husband forms an uneasy alliance: he holds the Moon in check, keeps him within the womb where he "sleeps on the side," holding the fetus in his "hot embrace," "cooking" it to make it grow. Interpreted in the context of their own myths, men's descriptions of gestation indicate that a man subdues the Moon not by killing or decapitating him, as women seem to prefer, but by giving him the child to hold. The fetus spends the main part of pregnancy not "alone in the house," in this male version, but sleeping in the arms of the Moon (see above, this Chap.). A man who has sex with his wife during this period may be identified with the Moon *before* he was subdued—with the invasive, predatory giant in women's myth. But when a man goes back to his wife to induce birth, to "wake the child" so it does not "stay asleep and die inside the mother," he becomes the true husband by gently dislodging the child from the Moon's embrace—offering the Moon a second course in place of the child he would prefer.

Women's myths suggest that a woman alone may defeat the Moon and may even, in the consenting absence of her husband, finish the child and arrange passage into the world outside her body. But men take a different view, asserting in separate lore that only a husband can use the stick and finish the child. "If a man does not have sex with the mother again," men say, "there is no way for the child to be born! No way!" It will "rot like an egg abandoned in the nest." In terms of women's myth of the singing raiders, men's instructions on "finishing the child" imply that the final ejaculation is an offer of new food. The husband gets the child out alive by "closing the first mouth," preventing the Moon from devouring what he already holds, stopping the raiders from eating boys already in their grasp. He offers them other meat to replace the boys, food equivalent to their own repeated ejaculations. The final "finishing" copulation is thus the prototype of a head payment: it secures the child's release and induces birth by offering the man in the womb other semen, other meat. A head payment offers the Moon or hidden father, in the person of mothers' brothers, the nearest possible thing to what he came for, and so induces his departure.

Men's myths and instructions on producing a child are like a blueprint for social relations in the sense that men concoct exchanges of the head to counteract an exchange that occurred for the first time in the womb and in the primordial past. If women's myths suggest that a man cannot make a child, stop the Moon, rout the cannibal giant, etc., without a wife to use her stick beside him, then men's myths counter that men come to better terms without their wives, arriving at an accommodation that avoids death in their own ranks.

### The Intrauterine Scenario

The terms of Gimi social life and the rules of marriage and of "giving the head" are explicable with reference to complex hypotheses about embryonic life and human prehistory that are implicit in the myths, performances, remarks, and associations of both sexes. Considered together, women's and men's versions of the first man, and rites surrounding the *forita'ara asa,* the fontanel or "first mouth" (lit: *forita'ara*/first, frontal or vanguard + *asa*/mouth), create a picture of conception and fetal nourishment as a magnification and transposition of erection and ejaculation. As semen rises through the urethra and emerges from the head of the penis, so does food enter a mouth at the top of the fetal head and fall unprocessed through the body, causing the child to develop and grow big with impossible speed. The body of an unborn child of either sex is like an offshoot and inverted replica of the penis-during-coitus: instead of discharging food, the urethra works in the fetus as a "first mouth," taking in semen from the "head" of the father. Considered in these terms, the weeks- or months-long process of conception, the repeated copulations in which a man places his child in the womb, feeds it, and provides the substance of limbs and inner organs are like a succession of head-to-head encounters, the equivalent of a hidden homosexual relation between father and unborn child.

Such a vision of intrauterine life may emerge implicitly from a comparison of the myths of women and men, but it is hardly explicit in men's discussions. Male informants liken the fontanel to a vagina, pointing out that a child emerges "head first" at birth and that the fontanel is the first part of the head to enter the birth canal. On this account, the fontanel functions for the whole of life as a site of exit for the person's inner "child," giving birth to *auna* in dreams and at death (see Chap. 4). If we combine this explicit association with the implicit content of myth—with the image of the fetal body as a giant penis, the fetus's intake of nourishment as an inversion of ejaculation, the fetal mouth as a urethra, etc.—then the notion that the fontanel is a "vagina" would seem to commemorate not only the child's having come out of mother head first, as informants point out, but also the father's penis having gone into mother and touched the child's head. Comparison of the fontanel to the vagina may thus symbolize prenatal sexual contact not only with the mother but also, covertly, with the father, suggesting that men treat the fontanel as the relic of a kind of prenatal homosexuality.

Originally, that contact was fatal. A man abstains from sex with his wife during the main part of pregnancy so his penis does not touch the child or rouse it prematurely, disturbing the sleep of gestation and inducing miscarriage. According to the intrauterine scenario I am proposing, the "homosexual" link between father and child was lethal at first. The first fathering, the first exchange between the Moon and the unborn, ended in the child's demise because *there was no exchange:* the Moon "pulled back the stone" and the mother leaked blood. The child's first nourishment, its first "eating of the head," provoked a furious response: the first time the child ate the head of the father's penis, the father retaliated by eating the child. He reabsorbed his own issue because it was his first time, too; his first entry into woman. When a man has sex for the first time, he goes deep into the forest. He is lost in ecstasy and has no thought of making a child. But when he comes back to his house, when he awakes from the dream of sex, he feels robbed—tricked—and retrieves the head he lost, making a meal of his own firstborn.

In this interpretation, the Moon pulling back the stone and the intruders rejecting every part of the marsupial and beating the boys represent the father reabsorbing his own ejaculate, refusing any substitute for what he lost without awareness, while his eyes were closed and his mouth was a gaping hole. To repair the theft, the giant father withdraws the child into the *same hole* from which he lost it, filling his own head with blood. The fact that menarche comes before a live birth means, in this image, not only death precedes life, or that the firstborn is always sacrificed, but also that it dies inside the father while he is still copulating and *hidden* inside the mother. The firstborn steals life from a father in the midst of perpetual copulation and is devoured in revenge, pulled back inside the head of the giant. The only outward sign of the giant's presence inside the mother is the reappearing blood of his meals.

If the mythic origin of menstruation is the model for death, then the fantasy of stopping the menstrual flow through repeated ejaculations—ending the Moon's carnage by providing him with another child to hold, giving him another head to eat—is the model for life and social relations. By continuing to "finish the child" throughout the whole of life men create a system of kinship and exchange, repeating intrauterine transfers of substance in exchanges with affines after the child is born, when he or she marries, is initiated or dies. Elders describe the process of placing a child inside a woman as the gradual subjugation of the Moon and establishment of an uneasy truce. The Moon or "first husband" tries to exclude his living successor by closing the vagina, causing the latter's semen to fall to the ground. But a persistent man stops the Moon's visits, stops his amorous comings-and-goings—not by ejecting the Moon as the Moon tries to eject him—but by offering him substitute food, "closing the first mouth and finishing the child." His head payment keeps the old man inside his wife, forcing him to stay hidden and out of sight, a scheme that coincides in certain respects with his wife's own deepest wishes, as we have seen.

According to men's accounts of gestation, the closeted Moon sleeps for months alongside the fetus, heating it in his embrace, helping it to "get big." But the Moon's invisible hold will become permanent—it will turn into a fatal retention or taking back of unborn life—unless the parents intercede. The method of intercession, of inducing birth by compelling the Moon to let go, varies dramatically in the myths of women and men. In a female scenario, woman kills the Moon but carries away his dead residues, transferring them to her "true husband" in order to bring the child back to life. In a male scenario the true husband acts alone and spares the Moon: at the start of pregnancy, his ejaculations merely put the Moon to sleep by giving him the child to hold; to induce birth, the husband goes back to loosen the Moon's embrace by offering him a new head, inserting his stick "one more time" to replace the life the Moon is poised to devour. In postnatal life, the cannibal Moon or giant penis—a woman's own unseen masculine content—is personified by her father and brother and other paternal relations; and the life-promising "gift of the head" becomes the meat and other valuables her husband regularly supplies them.

### A Woman Is Never Empty

Gimi men and women state that a man provides the whole child because only a man can accumulate and transmit *hato,* the life-giving form of *aðuso* or body substance. When a woman is prudent and willing, she retains *hato* and houses the growing fetus but does not herself contribute substance. Her womb is a sterile vessel, in this sense, but is never empty, never devoid, from her husband's point of view, of a hostile male presence. The eternal preexistence of a man inside a woman creates permanent danger in her reproductive organs, a danger that includes her connection with sorcerers. The ineradicable nature of menstrual blood has a kind of parallel in the omnipresence of sorcerers about a woman. When she marries or is initiated, her elders remind her ad nauseum to perform every sort of ablution and purificatory ritual. Their admonitions derive from the same assumptions as men's sorcery beliefs: that a man's leavings tend to remain in the recesses of a woman's body and to empower her, undetectably and with ease, to conspire in his death; and that this deadly adhesion or ineradicability of male substance is the direct consequence of woman's own desires, the result of secret efforts to "close" her body and keep the father (see Chap. 6).

A woman lures the sorcerer as her lover. Or she takes a lover who is neither sorcerer nor co-conspirator and makes *haϑana* from their combined secretions. Or she takes no lover but still yearns for another man and attacks her husband with her menstrual blood: her blood alone incarnates her first marriage to the Moon, her relations to the first man in her life. Even when a woman is careful with her blood and an entirely faithful wife, she becomes a killer when her husband dies (see Kelly 1976:50). Then it is he, or his *kore,* who permeates her sex. Like the Moon's blood or a living lover, he becomes the hidden man jealously lying in wait to kill any man who dares to follow him.

A woman never being empty constitutes both her danger, her "badness" or guilt, and her fertility: the other man a man encounters inside his wife both threatens his life and gives him his only chance to extend it by collaborating to create a child. Like the *neki maha,* the marsh or gully where ferns grow, the woman in whom a man deposits new shoots is unsafe because she is already filled with *kore,* already pervaded by the spirit of an older, more honored, or dead man. The woman is inclined to garner what she holds and be indifferent to the new arrival, letting his semen fall to the ground. The husband, therefore, has to come to terms with his predecessor himself, to feed the Moon directly, submitting his own emissions, putting his own head into the old man's mouth to make the child. A man's conquest of the Moon is thus also a capitulation: he donates his own substance so his rival will surround and heat the sleeping fetus but not eat it. The second husband only seems to displace the first: actually, he makes peace with the old man inside his wife and feeds him regularly, keeping him satisfied and out of sight.

According to my analysis of Gimi myths and secret rites, both sexes interpret menstruation and childbirth, and certain aspects of infant anatomy, as the visible aftermath of a relation that men, or their penes, sustained in the womb, signs of a hidden homosexual relation that at first kept the second man, the giant penis-child, unborn, imprisoned in the womb. Men's descriptions of the mandatory first appearance of menstrual blood, of the child passing through the birth canal head first with open fontanel, etc., suggest that they view the process of conception as a series of head-to-head confrontations, the first of which "killed the child." The first "shootings" produced no new life because the first husband was like Chronos, an insatiable, monolithic giant who devoured his every offspring. According to women's myths, woman took the initiative in cutting him off. But in the view of men's myths, the giant was stopped only after one of his own offspring escaped *and came back with other food,* food that merely resembled the giant's severed head. A man conceives his child, in these terms, by closing the Moon's mouth. He "feeds" the Moon his ejaculate during many copulations so that, eventually, the Moon will stop "eating his head" and allow it to fill the womb and become a child. When a man goes back to his wife to finish the child, he makes a final submission of semen to satisfy the Moon's gargantuan hunger, making sure the Moon doesn't "pull back the head" at the last moment. By satiating the Moon, the husband stops the cannibalism and induces between Moon and fetus the kind of soporific embrace a woman extends to nurtured objects. The one who mothers a man's unborn child, in this sense, is not his wife but the mythic father he divides and conquers inside her.

Whereas men assign to the father a uterine role, women choose for themselves a more active, phallic part in making the child. According to my reading of women's myths, motherhood begins not while a woman sleeps but the moment she awakes; not while her body serves merely as a house or oven or bamboo tube but when she kills the Moon, cuts off the giant, slays the firstborn, wields the stick and strikes the tree. The heroine of women's myths seals the ogre inside her house and burns his every limb and organ: she destroys the father inside her and uses his bloody parts to conceive a "true child." Whereas a man eventually subdues the Moon with food, creating a second mouth to feed by filling the first, a woman kills the Moon so she can get hold of his dead parts and transfer them to a new man.

Men openly characterize women, and women often characterize themselves, as seductresses and man-killers, attracting lovers—both real and fantasied—to replace their husbands. In reality, of course, it is men who have better opportunities to launch adulterous liaisons and the right to acquire more than one spouse. Why, then, do men blame women as originators of sin and why do women accept the blame, adhering to taboos men set up against them, embracing the responsibility to safeguard men's welfare as if the danger originated in women's own bodies and nature? The implication of men's myths and ritual usages, according to my interpretation, is that they attempt to resolve fantasies of Oedipal encounters and homosexual love by treating them as if they arose—not in men's own relations—but in female anatomy and character. By blaming women, in this sense, men deny their ambivalence toward the father, concealing even his presence by treating it as an attribute of the mother, as the hidden source of her menstrual blood and fertile power. Though women often oppose men's interests, they also acquiesce in the male view. They, too, wish to disguise the mythic father, deny his presence, and treat his might as if it originated in them. Gimi conception beliefs thus often represent a convergence of the sexes' contradictory wishes. The next chapter explores the translation of these beliefs into the rituals of postnatal life, beginning with the exchanges that surround the death and birth of a child.

# EIGHT

# Rituals of Childhood Death and Birth: Men's First Exchanges Outside the Mother

## Death in Childhood

If Gimi interpret menstruation as proof that death is the primary and habitual condition of life, they reach a conclusion much in keeping with common experience. Until the early 1960s, genealogies indicate that as many children died as survived. It is still true that more infants die than older children and that firstborn children have an especially high rate of mortality.

When an unweaned child is mortally ill, the mother takes it into seclusion and keeps a constant vigil, wailing night and day. Wives of her husband's brothers and other women of her compound bring food and sit with her in shifts. As the hours and days pass and the infant's conditions worsens, her *amauraha* arrive from other compounds or hamlets. The moment the child dies, or seems to have died, the mother hands it to another woman and stumbles out the door of her house. She places her hand on a tree stump or other hard surface and, with a single sharp blow from a bush knife, removes the top third of an index or middle finger (unless she has already removed several fingers to commemorate the deaths of other children or male relations; see Chap. 4). She props herself up in the doorway and lets the blood drip into a leaf or tin cup while her *amau* ties a vine around her wrist to stanch the flow and wraps a rag around her head to ease the pain. Later, her *amau* will dress the amputated finger, making a bandage of leaves and bark string. The wounded mother goes back into her house and takes her child in her arms. For the next several days, she remains in confinement, wailing and speaking softly to her baby, placing her nipple in its mouth to wake it and inventing sorrowful chants (see Chap. 3).

When the deceased is an infant born while an elder sibling was still at the breast, an event Gimi regard as a disgrace for the mother, the suspicion of infanticide may arise. On one such occasion, the mother's display of abject grief inspired biting comment from several of her *amau*. " The child was sick for days and still she carried it about with her!" one of them broadcast. "She took it to her garden yesterday in the pouring rain and even walked with it near graves where *kore* lurk! So what do you expect?" another asked sarcastically. Recalling the death of her own child at a similar age, one *amau* said, "When my child was sick I stayed inside my house and my *nanatu* brought me food." Once a child dies, accusations may be laid against the mother, but while it is alive the father is held responsible for the illness. It is he who seeks a cure by searching his memory for the crimes that provoked this retaliation against his child.

## The Guilt of the Father

When a woman announces she is pregnant, during the second or third month, her husband stops having sex with her so the child can sleep undisturbed. He enters a period of sexual abstinence that, except for "finishing the child" and inducing the birth, generally lasts until the child is weaned at two-and-a-half or three years. At the same time as a man forgoes sexual relations with his wife, he stops going anywhere near *neki maha*, literally, "mad ground" (*neki*/mad + *maha*/ground or place), the term for marshes, gullies, stagnant pools, river outlets, and other low, wet "bad" areas. *neki maha* are also steep cavernous ravines enclosed by vegetation and inhabited by fruit bats; alpine bogs filled with insects, giant earthworms, frogs, reptiles, and marsupials; forest depressions where ferns, philodendrons, wild bananas, red pandanus trees, flowering gingers, taros, vines, and other moisture-laden plants grow in profusion. A man's incursion into a *neki maha* in the midst of his wife's pregnancy would endanger the fetus in the same way as his breaking the taboo on sexual intercourse. Merely by treading upon undergrowth, he would damage or kill plants and set their trampled *aunas* on flights of revenge against his unborn child. But even if he avoids *neki maha* during his wife's pregnancies, transgressions he committed there as a youth or unmarried man may come back to harm his children.

Years ago, before BoɗaEha married, he went into a *neki maha* with two married men whose wives were pregnant at the time. They asked him to cut the vines they needed to tie a fence and the walls of a house, but, thinking of the children he would someday bear, he refused and his companions cut the vines for themselves. "The firstborn of one man, a son, died," he told me. "And the first three children of the other, two daughters and a son, died too. It was the vines that killed them." Yet for every occasion when a man was prudent inside a *neki maha*, there are others when he was wasteful and foolish, when he uprooted wild ginger or taro he did not need, idly cut off a lizard's tail or lit a fire to smoke out a rat, possum, or fruit bat, and then, for mere amusement, sent his dog into the cave for the kill. In the moment the animal lost its tail, or died in a trap, or was mangled by his dog, it cursed him

After preparing a bowl of oily red pandanus fruit, a man invites his son and his brother's son to lick his fingers. Although a man is held ritually responsible for the illness of his own young children, his relation with them is often tender and close.

and stole a part of his *auna*, depleting what he could later impart to a child. "The *kore* of the bat is still furious and wants revenge," BoϑaEha explained. "When that man's child becomes sick, it finds its chance."

> When you kill a fruit bat and cook it, it clenches its teeth at you. And when you kill a snake, it writhes on the ground. So if your child dies with its teeth clenched [i.e., with meningitis or tetanus], a bat is taking revenge. And if your child dies writhing [i.e., in convulsions], you know it's a snake.

The flightless creatures and large plants that flourish in *neki maha* can also work sorcery against a man, taking revenge directly against the one who carelessly cut them down or needlessly collected their fruit:

Wild bananas can poison us . . . if we cut them down for no reason . . . our heads and bodies become swollen and heavy and we die. A banana can poison us the same way as a snake or a frog. A man who urinates or defecates or has sex near a *neki maha* may die. . . . A frog may get hold of his *abara ano* (lit: *abara*/penis + *ano*/fluid) mixed with his wife's *kagora ano* (lit: *kagora*/vagina) and eat [i.e., work sorcery on] it. Stagnant water is a sorcerer!

When a man dies in his prime, or even after his first initiation, his spirit surges through the settlement inside turbulent winds or rivers and later takes up residence with Birds of Paradise, soaring through the sunlit upper reaches of clan forests. But the *kore* of young and unborn children—by far the most numerous of those who die and the hungriest—gravitate to *neki maha* because food is abundant there and often spoiled or fermented, "sweet" like mother's milk and intoxicating, literally, "making *neki.*" Still-born children are "held inside the mother." They die like snakes or lizards trapped in caves, and their *kore* are stuck forever in dark, low-lying gullies, ravines, and swamps. Mired in the *neki maha,* incarnated in its convoluted vines and small, slimy flightless creatures, infant and fetal *kore* take revenge on thieves and trespassers, devouring the leavings of those who hunt, gather, defecate, or copulate in their territory (fig. 12).

Some men can tell by looking at a sick man that he was stricken near a *neki maha:*

> I looked at Borua and thought no man had worked sorcery on him. He had gone down to Veresegu to visit maternal kinsmen. Veresegu is a bad place filled with *neki maha.* . . . He urinated and defecated there . . . and killed a snake. The [*auna* of the] snake stole his feces and worked the sorcery on them.

To be cured, the stricken man has to remember where he defecated and name the place, so his kinsmen can go there and bring back leavings of the creature who stole his feces, and collect some ferns. His kinsmen "pull the *negina*" (lit: *neki*/mad + *na*/thing) on his behalf:

> A man who travels to another place and *forgets* where he urinates, *forgets* where he defecates, *forgets* where he has sex, may die. But if he remembers and speaks the name of the place, we go there to collect ferns . . . and he needn't die. We bring sugar-cane [and wrap it in the ferns we find there] and . . . we call out to the *auna* of the worm or frog or snake. The *auna* enters [the fern-encased cane and causes it to "fly" out of the spell-sayer's hand. From a spot near where the cane lands, the spell-sayer

Figure 12. A *neki maha* or "mad ground." A tree-covered mountain and river estuary, typical of configurations in the landscape that Gimi compare with the torso of a pregnant woman.

picks up a partly decomposed, larva-infested dropping of a wild pig or bush wallaby. This ancient leaving, "found" by the creature's *auna,* is the *negina*].

Once we get hold of the *negina,* we take it back to the sick man and hold it above his head and pour water over it. The water [suffused with the *negina*] touches his head . . . and makes him cold and ends his sickness.

A guilty father uses a similar technique to cure a dying infant. He "remembers" the scene of his crime, the *neki maha,* where as a youth, perhaps, he slew the creature whose *auna* is now claiming the life of his child. If the child is firstborn, he is likely to remember having harmed a marsupial because marsupials are especially prone to seize firstborn children. The father sends his brother or age-mate to the *neki maha* to retrieve the animal's dropping or a stone from the entry to its cave, and to fill a slim bamboo tube with water from a nearby river or stream. "The *auna* of the marsupial is angry and taking revenge. Running water from the place where it was killed will cool the child's sickness." The father receives the *negina* wrapped in ferns and the water inside a sealed bamboo tube. He cuts a slit in the side of the bamboo because, he says, "the water must not come out the hole it entered." He carries the bamboo and the *negina* into his wife's house and takes the dying child in his arms. With his mother crouched on one side of him and his wife beating her breast on the other, he holds the *negina* above the baby's fontanel and positions the bamboo tube so water drips from the slit over the stone, or runs down a trough he has opened through the middle of the dropping. "Finish! Finish!" he utters with each drop.

The search for ferns far from home, the invocation of a creature of the *neki maha* like a frog or rat, the father holding a stone above the child's head, making a hole in a bamboo tube, etc., all recall incidents in women's Bird of Paradise myth (see Chap. 6) and show again that men enact women's myths. The father enters the myth, as it were, and becomes identified with the Moon or *kore bana* so that, by altering or correcting the misdeeds of his own remembered past, his performances also change the myth and avert its outcome. The thing he did long ago or far away—before marriage, inside a *neki maha*, on a visit to maternal kinsmen, etc.—immobilized his *auna* because, as he now recalls, he did it on a whim, as an adolescent prank or act of thoughtless greed. Cutting down lianas or killing a bat or maiming a tiny flightless creature inside a *neki maha* as a youth, or with youthful abandon, was like entering a woman for the first time, without a thought of making a child (see Chap. 7). He gave up part of himself without awareness and then angrily took it back.

An unweaned child, one who has barely left the womb, is still attached to the father in Gimi reckoning, still a part of him in the same way as his own leavings. "The state of a male parent after birth is comparable in nature to that of a man after copulation (although intensified in degree)" (Kelly 1976:42). When the Gimi father killed or maimed a fetal-like forest creature, he devoured the spirit of his own child. He behaved like the Moon in the midst of copulation, reabsorbing his own ejaculate, taking back his own issue. His child is hot because he has never let it go. He is still invisibly holding it in his hot embrace, still "eating the head." By dripping water over the baby's fontanel, he attempts to put back the *auna* he stole and "close the first mouth," repeating the *intrauterine* method of head-to-head feeding (see Chap. 7). He cools the child by restoring the full complement of his own substance, belatedly giving away enough of himself to make the child separate from him and establish its existence.

### Rites of Burial

On the occasions when I saw a father perform these rites, the child was already mortally ill and soon died. Early on the evening of the first or second

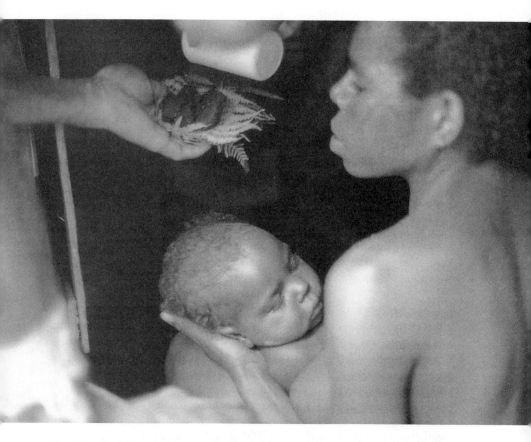

The father of a sick baby girl pours water from a plastic cup onto an animal dropping or *negina* retrieved from a *neki maha*. The water that passes over the *negina* and falls onto the girl's head is supposed to return a part of her life-force or *auna*, lost through the father's own carelessness, and restore her to health.

day following death, the father and the mother's brothers arrive at the mother's house to join the crowd of women in singing to the child and praising the *auna* throughout the night (see Chap. 4). They give the *auna* songs to sing at marriages and initiations so it will not be "left just to look" jealously at the living. They teach the *auna* songs to win love, to bring success at everyday tasks, to ease travel in the forest, locate shelter in a downpour, find a bridge over a torrent and water safe to drink. When a baby girl dies, her mother leads other women in songs of courtship, songs to "join her *auna*" with plants she will never tend and pigs she will never raise, songs to make her pigs fat and bring them home at dusk, songs to find wild shrubs, effortlessly shred their bark, twist the shreds into string, and net the string into carrying bags and ornaments.

To the *auna* of a boy who will never be initiated, his father and his mother's brother dedicate songs of initiation, songs a youth sings to make flowers bloom amid the mosses that cover high branches, songs to make the vines he climbs to pick the flowers cling as securely to the tree as a flying fox, with young hanging from her belly, clings to the smooth basalt walls of a ravine. To a dead boy's *auna* men dedicate the songs of an impatient hunter waiting inside his hide for a bird to pause at the river's edge and take a drink, or to alight on the branch of a nearby palm tree and eat the flowers' seeds, giving him the chance to shoot. His mother's brother may launch into the song of an age-mate dripping with sweat and gazing at him across the fire: "Let's go now to where the Black Sickelbill roams and the yellow bamboo grows. Let's drink the cool, sweet water flowing there!" His father may "give" him a song to rejoice in the wife he will never have, a song the father himself sang to the boy's mother to celebrate their success in rearing gardens and pigs: "Look at us!" he sings, "[you] a stunning red lily and [me] a fine cordyline!"

From time to time during the night the spirit of the one who "sleeps" in the middle of the room responds through the mourners' voices: "I left my age-mate on a ridge and kept climbing the mountain," he sings to them. "Look up! Look up high in the branches. I am the red orchids growing amid the mosses." "Hey, father! Hey, age-mate!" the dead boy cries. "Find me in the branches of the fig tree, I am the iridescent green beetles, . . . the fruit doves, . . . the parrots, . . . the possums you see feeding there."

The hot air inside the hut is filled with smoke and the stifling odor of death. Many in the crowd doze off, slumped across each other or pressed against the wall. When the singing fades, the mother begins a solo lament. "What have you done? What has happened to you?" she cries again and again. "Are you asleep? Why is the house filled with people singing?" Her brother interrupts her and chants over her infant son, "Your mother just bore you. I was ready to eat your head but you died and made my liver hurt." His wife, the *amau*, had gone to another village while the child lay dying. "If only I had come to look at you," the *amau* sings, "if only I had stayed." The shrill, tormented solos wake the crowd and inspire them to sing with renewed fervor.

The vigils continue for two or three nights, during which time the mother's brother is supposed to receive the head of the child. When the father cannot provide adequate payment, the mother's brother agrees to a deferment and arrives with men of his lineage in the father's compound early on the morning of the third or fourth day. The mother's brothers dig and line a grave chamber at the edge of the father's compound. The mother crouches beside it, weeping and singing softly. Her principal midwife, usu-ally the *amau* who washed the child in the river and carried it into the com-pound after birth, now carries the corpse out of the house and hands it to her.

The mother places the child into the grave and, while her brothers cover the opening with sheets of bark and layers of earth, she moves some ten me-ters away to dig a shallow second hole. As soon as she realized her baby would die, she began to collect the leaves she used to wipe away the watery feces, saving them in a net bag. Now she empties the dried matted leaves into the second grave. "The feces and the child are buried in separate places," one main explained, "[because] if they were put in the same hole, the father would get sick and die fast. . . . The stuff that makes the child comes from the man—not the woman! The man gives her the child and she gets preg-nant. She takes what the man gives her and looks after it." While the child's body is part of the father's own supply of semen, the feces are pure breast milk. Burying an unweaned child's feces and corpse in the same hole, men say, would be "the same as mixing his wife's 'water' into his semen."

Combining the child's corpse and feces, so that they decomposed to-gether, would affect the father's health in the same way as a sorcerer working directly on his semen or on a piece of his child's corpse. On the nights fol-lowing burial, men of the father's patrilineage keep watch over the grave to prevent a sorcerer from stealing a part of the child. "The father would die [from a spell incorporating his child's flesh]," men say. "But not the mother." In the past, these men add, "Women ate the child like [i.e., by cooking it in the same manner as] a suckling pig [see the Torrent Lark *nene* in Chap. 3]. They threw the feces in the river and ate the [rinsed and braided intestinal] casings. . . . When the mother [and other women] consumed the child, the sorcerer could not find it. He could not use the child to kill the father."

## After the Firstborn Dies: The Arrival of the True Child

### *Childbirth*

Children were born in menstrual huts before missionaries forbade them. "The white men told us to bear our children beside the river so we could get rid of the blood and the afterbirth [lit: Moon's dirt] and keep them out of sorcerer's hands," the women recall. "Before white men, children were born in the house of shame. Going down to the river is white men's idea."

When a woman's labor begins, women of her compound summon the *amau* who will serve as chief midwife. The *amau* escorts the woman in labor and other women (who are not subject to *aɗaoina*) to a river below the compound or near the forest. At the water's edge, the women spread vines to make a thick bed and gently lower the expectant mother onto her back so that she faces the river, with her knees raised and wide apart. During the long hours of labor, the women reach into the small of her back to massage her and slowly pull bunches of water-soaked vines or stinging nettles across her belly. They sing to pass the time and make a small fire to warm the mother, intermittently searching her head for lice, holding her hand, stroking her brow, feeding her a piece of cooked sweet potato or placing a roll of lighted tobacco between her lips.

If labor is prolonged, as it often is, the *amau* may summon a Big Man to perform a rite that will hasten the birth. The Big Man belongs to the patri-lineage of the *amau's* father and the father of the unborn child. He arrives at the water's edge carrying a stem of wild sugarcane about three feet long. He crouches beside the laboring woman and circles the stem above her belly. Then he hands the cut end of the cane to the *amau*, who crouches on the woman's other side, and holds the leafy end so that its length extends across her belly. The Big Man twists the leaves to grasp the inner core and extracts it quickly, inducing the baby to emerge with the same swift, easy movement. Then he stands, throws the two pieces of sugarcane into the rushing stream, and quickly departs. In the course of a long labor, the *amau* may repeat this rite several times, using another midwife, or the mother herself, to hold the other end of a cordyline leaf.

When a woman's labor is difficult, men and women agree, it is usually on account of the anger of her husband's father's *kore*. Men of his lineage may lately have neglected to offer the *kore* pieces of raw meat before feasts, rousing him from his forest niche and tempting him to take hold of the child. To force him to let go, the women attending the mother go to sleep so they can dream and "see the *kore*." Darebaro told me how her dream of her dead brother-in-law saved the life of his son's child (fig. 13).

> "Ukake is always angry at us!" Baia told me. Then I heard Iapi calling me, "Come here, old woman, come here!" . . . and I went to the place where Botukofe was in labor. She was in great difficulty. . . . During the night we cooked some food. Ukake was with us but no smile was on his face. . . . He was angry that night and took hold of the child . . . I went to sleep inside Bot-ukofe's house and dreamed of him.

When Darebaro awoke, she told her dream to Baia and Botukofe and the child was born. Commented Darebaro's son:

> If Darebaro had not told her dream, Bokutofe would not have had the child. . . . Ukake was hiding [inside her] and holding

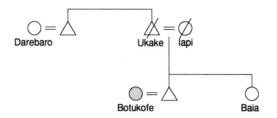

Figure 13. Botukofe's difficult labor.

the child but Darebaro *saw* him. "Darebaro has seen me," Ukake realized, "so I will let go of the child."

Women sometimes reported their dreams to me, especially in connection with the conception or birth of a child, but they were reluctant to discuss the nature of dreaming per se or to speak in general terms about *auna* and *kore*. "That is men's talk," women said when I raised these subjects. "Now we are discussing women things [lit: making woman's talk]." But men referred to women seeing what comes out of the womb as the basis of their capacity to dream, to see with their eyes closed and thus to know what is hidden from view. As Darebaro's son continued to explain:

> Women have a great power on account of seeing us when we are born. Women give birth to us which is why—whatever we do in secret—they can *see* us. If a man makes love to a woman, another woman will say, "You made love to that woman and I *saw* you!" It's a power only women have. It comes from giving birth to us.

The woman in labor dozes from time to time. When she awakes, she rolls onto her front or sits cross-legged, clawing at the soft ground and moaning in pain. Her *amau* embraces her from behind, rocks her and wails in unison. The *amau* says:

> It's hard to bear a child. A woman feels she's about to die and decides never to have sex again—but she does. . . . When my *amau* is in labor I take pity on her and hold her in my arms. I put her head to the ground and hold her chest so she does not roll around . . . and harm the child. She mustn't be allowed to kill it!

When the child is about to be born, the midwives examine the sky. Strong sun heralds the birth of a boy and cloud, shadow or rain announces a girl. "A woman is cold," women say, as cold and damp as the forest floor, and "filled with water" like the marsupials that dwell on the ground and drink from icy streams. The women deliver the baby directly into the freezing, fast-moving river. When a girl is born, the *amau* may register immediate disappointment, exclaiming, "It's not a boy!" The *amau*, or the mother herself, cuts the umbilicus near the middle with a bamboo knife, and someone else wraps the dangling end in leaves. Standing in the river, one of the women holds the baby while others force it to swallow water from a cupped leaf, scrub the head with soap, and wipe the body with soaking leaves. The shivering mother crouches nearby to await the delivery of the afterbirth. The *amau* will rotate it vigorously or stand on it to force out the blood, turning the river into a sea of red. To make sure no drop of blood falls into sorcerers' hands, she and other midwives scrupulously search their bodies and nearby rocks, pulling leaves off overhanging branches and using the sharp edges to lift off even tiny spots.

The *amau* carries the newborn into the compound, leaving the exhausted mother and other midwives beside the river. If it is a girl, men may greet the arrival with half-meant cries of, "Get rid of her!" and "Throw her away!" and the *amau* herself may concur, announcing that she ought to have left the child "under a stone" at the river's edge. Women sometimes say that daughters, especially, are not worth the pain of bearing because "they leave you in a little while." A woman told me that one couple agreed in advance that the wife would kill the child if it were a girl. But the wife's mother attended the birth and took the child. Men accuse women of trying to kill their babies at birth but deny that they ever acquiesce. "This is *my* child! Not a dog nor a pig!" Uarafu said he told his wife when she rejected a daughter born while another was still at the breast. "You cannot give her away unless I say so." But women point out that a mother has subtle ways to kill a baby she does not want, including neglect and exposure (see above, this Chap.).[1]

Inside the mother's house, the *amau* gives the newborn its first breast milk and lights a fire in the hearth. She holds her hand over the flames and presses her heated palm onto the baby's forehead and crown and squeezes the bridge of the nose and nostrils. She repeats the procedure several times to impart the heat of life. Hours later, the mother and other midwives return from the water's edge. They carry leaf-wrapped packages that contain the rinsed placenta and bamboo knife used to cut the umbilicus. "My *namau* will burn the 'fetus bag,'" one mother explains. "She will burn it and throw the ashes into the river so no man can kill my husband." The new mother props herself up against a wall near the fire and takes the child to her breast.

---

1. I have direct knowledge of two cases of male infanticide and five cases of female infanticide in 1973–75. During the same period, there were also several reports of thwarted attempts by mothers to kill female babies.

"A woman doesn't enjoy bearing a child," one of the midwives remarked days later. "But the men who paid her brideprice tell her, 'We gave a lot for you so you must bear . . . '" Another woman named Bobau told me on a different occasion:

> When my second child was born I didn't pick her up. And when my *namau* took her I said, "Get rid of it!" I was in such pain! So she took the baby away, and when the pain eased I saw her feeding my child, and I said, "Give her to me I want to feed her."

When four or more of a woman's children have died less than a year after birth, an occurrence more common in the past, she and her *amau* perform a rite to ensure the survival of the newborn. The mother holds the baby inside the seclusion hut, nowadays a pig house or woman's house, while her *amau* climbs onto the roof and tears a hole in the thatch. The mother passes her infant through the hole to her *amau* who holds it in her arms for a moment and then passes it back to the mother. When the mother receives her child "for the second time," she bites off the top half of its little finger. She will seal the severed joint inside a tiny net bag and wear it as an amulet around her neck for several years, until she considers her child has a firm hold on life.

Like the father's rite of cure, this rite may be interpreted as an attempt to save the child by reversing the denouement of one of women's myths. Interpreted in the terms of women's tale of the Giant Penis, the *amau* tearing a hole in the thatch recreates the giant "eating his way" into the first woman; and passing the child up and down through the tear repeats the giant's copulatory movements. By biting off the top of her baby's finger, the mother duplicates the severing by her mythic counterpart. And by wearing the severed finger for years in a tiny bag around her neck, she keeps—rather than discards in a river—what the first woman cut off in a rage. But in altering the myth, as it were, the mother's rite, like the father's rite of cure, also corrects part of her own reprehensible past. When the mother retains and wears her baby's finger, women and men explain, she makes up for any small amount of her husband's semen that she may have carelessly lost—or deliberately let fall to the ground—during the conception of his child. Like the father's cure, the mother's rite reverses a myth that is at once collective and personal, changing a past that belongs both to the first Gimi woman and to herself.[2]

---

In 1969–72 the sex ratio of Unavi Census Division was markedly imbalanced in favor of males. In the intervening twenty years, the population has dramatically increased while the disparity between the sexes has declined. Female infanticide once may have accounted in part for the imbalanced ratio. Since pacification, the practice seems to have declined both because of efforts by the government and missions to lower infant mortality and because of increased village endogamy which, women say, increases their incentive to raise daughters.

2. The child-passing cure also reverses the culminating rite of female initiation or *haro*. Men

## rakukusa *and* ðau: *The Celebration of Birth and Rite of Naming*

After a Gimi child has survived the first precarious weeks or months of life, the *ababana* celebrate *rakukusa* and *ðau* to mark the emergence from seclusion of mother and child and to give the child a name, a right they acquire from the mother's brothers by offering the first head payment. The mother sings "blood songs" and performs purificatory rites inside her house (see Chap. 6) while the father and his brothers go into the forest to hunt marsupials and collect ferns, barks, liquid-filled fruits, and the leaves of heavy vines and giant trees, ingredients they will use to make the mother's *rakukusa,* a medicine to give her strength and fill her breasts with milk. The one or two oldest men of the mother's or father's patriclan, or, if he is a very old man, the mother's real or classificatory mother's brother, prepare the *rakukusa,* reciting secret spells while they gut and dismember the marsupials and combine organs and limbs with the wild leaves and fruits and powdered barks. Senior men of the father's clan chew salt and leaves and then spit the masticated stuff into the medicine just before it is encased in pandanus leaves and placed on an open fire.

When the *rakukusa* is cooked, the mother emerges from her house. It is her duty to distribute it among the midwives "who cared for my child when it was born and washed me afterwards in the water," and among the five or more *amauraha* who brought her firewood and food during confinement. She may also give *rakukusa* to her own mother and sisters and to certain *anaturaha* who provided for her and the baby, wives of her husband's brothers indebted to her because she reared pigs for their brideprice, or wives of his father's brothers who supplied pigs for her brideprice and have a lien on her labor. Traditionally, *rakukusa* was held near the hut where the child was born and is still sometimes celebrated at the edge of the forest, especially if the father and men of his lineage were short of pigs and hunted marsupials to provide meat for *ðau.*

In the past, women say, a man whose wife had just borne a child killed a dozen or more marsupials, or a wild boar and a cassowary, and carried them back to the settlement. Women's myth describes a new father's preparations for *ðau,* telling how he ventures into the forest and encounters his dead parents who provide him with all the meat he needs to "give his child a name."

---

of the groom's patrilineage, but never the groom himself, climb onto the roof of the hut where the bride-initiate is secluded and tear a hole in the thatch (lit: *haro*). The men insert a huge sugarcane pole, some nine or ten feet long, and repeatedly thrust it through the hole, withdrawing it each time the initiate's chaperons—without the initiate—reach up and try to break off the end. The ritual simulates the first copulation and dictates that the "angry women" inside the hut will win the tug-of-war with the men on the roof by breaking up the enormous pole and "discarding the pieces to rot" in shrubs outside the hut (see Gillison 1987).

Waiting for the *rakukusa* to cook.

His wife had just given birth to a son and the man went into the forest, taking along his dog and a basket of sweet potato. . . . The dog entered the roots of a huge tree and disappeared wagging its tail. The man waited, and the dog returned wearing garlands of wild flowers . . . and led him into a land below the ground.

The two entered a marvelous place filled with hoop pines and casuarinas and cordyline. They kept going down and realized they were on top of a mountain. Below them, they saw an enormous old woman sitting beside a stand of bamboo and a red parrot perched above her among the fronds. They kept going down, and the old woman approached them. She embraced the man and wept. The bird flew off his perch and shook his hand heartily! They were his parents greeting him in the land of his ancestors.

The bird flew away. "Your *kore aba* is going off and will return," he said. The man and his dog sat down and waited. After a while they heard the old man's panting. He was climbing the mountain carrying wild pig, cassowary, and eel, and the old woman went down to help him. Together they brought up the wild meat. It was cut up helter-skelter, and the old man gave some to his son and embraced him. "You are my son!" he wept and went to sleep holding him in his arms. In the morning the old man killed a pig and prepared the greens.

"My wife has given birth to a son and I want to name him," the man told his spirit-father. "Your wife has had a son, you say, and I am sorry, indeed, to hear it!" the father replied, and he butchered the pig for his son. "How shall I carry such a heavy load?" the son wondered. He cut the pig into smaller pieces and filled his nets bags and then made baskets to carry the meat.

"Come here and stand on my foot," his father told him. The old man kicked his foot [launching his son into flight]. The man flew home and unloaded the meat for his wife's *ϑau.*

"Where have you been?" his elder brother asked him. "I have come from the place where mother and father live," he said. . . . "They killed a pig and gave it to me so I could name my child." He told this to his elder brother and gave him the meat to distribute.

A boy was born and *ϑau* was held.

The size and heterogeneity of the old man's delivery, and its swift appearance, are typical of the posthumous mode of production. When men and women die, their *auna* enter the forest and give rise spontaneously—by a kind of ejaculation from the head—to countless life-forms, turning the clan forest into a massive reservoir of food and other resources (see Chap. 7). A Gimi hunter depends upon his paternal ancestors, especially his own dead parents, to "throw birds and marsupials before my eyes." In this *nenekaina,* the hunter and his dog enter a subterranean world "beneath the roots of a huge tree," a place women invoke in garden magic to conjure the interior of a woman's body (see Chap. 6). Like the two boys "left alone at home" in women's other myth (see Chap. 7), the hunter and his dog seem to be inside the womb listening to coitus, hearing the old man panting up the mountain (see Kelly 1976:40). In this interpretation, the wild meat the old man delivers to his son is *hato* or semen; and his deriving it from different animals that are cut up helter-skelter represents the many "shootings" or ejaculations that give rise to the fetus limb by limb and organ by organ.

To acquire the head payment he needs to name and sustain his son, a man embarks upon an adventure in his clan forest that, in the terms of women's myth, symbolizes a reliving of his own prenatal history. To father a child, a man repeats his own conception. He goes back into his mother and is there embraced and supplied with food by his father. But his return to the womb and reunion with his father happen when the old man is already dead. His incarnation as a red parrot perched in a stand of bamboo, with his "enormous" wife seated at the base, suggests that, like the "delicious parrot" in men's myth of the Cannibal Widow (see Chap. 3), he is about to be —or just was—her meal. When the son announces that his wife has borne him a son, his father replies, "I am sorry, indeed, to hear it!" a remark strikingly at odds with the normal pride and joy of a Gimi grandfather, but consistent with the mythic idea that the birth of a grandson signals a man's own demise. It is the paternal grandfather's *kore*, we may remember, who "holds" the child inside the womb so it cannot be born.

"The old man gave some [wild meat] to his son and embraced him," the myth says. "'You are my son!' he wept and went to sleep holding him in his arms." These lines recall the onset of pregnancy when the Moon falls asleep for months, clutching the unborn child in his "hot embrace" (see Chap. 7). But whereas a man defeats the Moon inside his wife by supplying him with an overabundance of semen, it is here the Moon or *kore aba* who provides his son with every kind of wild meat. This time, on the return visit, as it were, the child is already a hunter and himself a father, a man who can "shoot" his own way into the womb. The old man weeps when he holds his son because his embrace represents more than a transfer of food. Implicitly, it depicts an *exchange* of meat or semen that is deadly to the old man. Providing meat to a son who can shoot for himself forces the *kore aba* to consume the produce of his progeny and thus to break the taboo of *aθaoina* (see Chap. 6).

To finish the child and give it a name, women's myth suggests, a man has to revisit the scene of his own conception. He has to go back into the mother one more time and fall into the old man's arms, putting him to sleep: he "shoots" him retroactively, so to speak, while the old man is still in the midst of nourishing him. Seen in this light, the meat the hunter brings out of the forest to buy the head of his new child is spoils of victory over his father, a victory masterminded and carried out by the father's own invisible *kore* or ghost. The son goes back into mother and emerges with his father's head to offer in exchange for the head of his child.

In a myth of *θau*, women represent the head as wild meat that the hunter obtains by killing his father, carrying away his semen after a fatal embrace. But in myths of the first copulation and first menses, women portray the head as the direct product of woman's rage: it is the giant penis she severs in her hand, the firstborn child she cooks like a suckling pig, a part of the old man she cuts off in revenge for his trickery and intrusion. But when a child is born alive, the mother's role becomes peripheral, even in women's own myth. Indeed, the primordial couple seem to be no longer in conflict and no longer even man and wife but rather father and grandfather. Yet, even when women cede their role and seem to give nearly the whole credit to a pair or men, they still insist upon killing the mythic father.

### The Rites of rakukusa

*rakukusa* is the essential preliminary of *ꝺau*. In the past, women say, the day after men returned from the forest with the kill, bringing marsupials, eels, wild boar, cassowary, etc., the *amauraha* went out to collect ferns, parsley, watercress and other wild greens to cook with the meat.

> When the oven was opened the father said to us, "You women eat the *rakukusa!*" And we finished the *rakukusa* so that *ꝺau* could begin. The *ababana* cut the marsupials into pieces, salted them and said, "Let the one who bore the child distribute *ꝺau.*" . . . and the mother gave food to her *amauraha* saying, "I must give the first food to those who looked after my child." . . .
> Then she gave meat to *faba baha ꝺa* from the animals that had not yet been cut. She gave food to all the women and they ate and went on their way. Once the women had eaten, the child could grow.

*rakukusa* is payment to midwives and "providers of firewood" for life-giving services, for having assisted the birth, washed the newborn in the river, given it its first breast milk, impressed the "heat of life," netted a string bag as a cradle, brought food and firewood to the mother in confinement, etc. But *rakukusa* is also a head payment, and like any head payment it is an inducement not to curse the child. "If we do not give our heads to our mothers," women say, "'fuuuuuuusssss!' they will curse us and we will die!" When the midwives "eat the *rakusa*," one of the *ababana* explains, "their stomachs are contented and the child grows quickly. We feed the women to make them happy with the child so it will thrive."

As both compensation for helping to bring a child to life and inducement not to kill it, *rakukusa* dramatizes the central contradiction in a woman's role as *amau*. In caring for her brother's wife and child, the *amau* is both helpmate and suspicious overseer. She attends the birth not simply to assist the wife but mainly to protect her brother *against* his wife, to ensure that she does not "kill the child" in the throes of labor nor hand over to sorcerers her blood or placenta, residues of birth that Gimi regard as the father's own leavings. The *amau* is also a competitor waiting in the wings, a mother of first resort who gives the child its first milk, imparts the heat of life, and who will automatically take custody if the father defaults on head payments or if the child dies. The *amau*'s job description seems to stem from her role as her brother's wife *manquée* and to carry the lode of mythic sentiment, being designed to conceal—and perhaps overcompensate for —a jealous desire to replace her brother's wife and possess his child as her own. The *amau* is prone to curse the child she brings to life, in this sense, for the same reason the first woman murdered her own son: because she is the father's enraged and unlawful first wife.[3]

A head payment "cools the stomachs" of the recipients, Gimi say. And "belly heat" is the expression for both anger and sexual excitement. *rakukusa* wards off the curse of the *amauraha*, in these terms, by putting out the fire of incestuous desire. It safeguards the health of the newborn by treating the midwives in a collective sense as mythic mothers and supplying them with replacements for the child's head, thus preventing a repetition of the primordial cannibalism—a meal alluded to in the *rakukusa* by the collection of uncultivated greens. The gift is a bid to spare the child by playing out the myth with a new ending, replacing with other meat the boy woman murdered and cooked like a suckling pig. But as soon as *rakukusa* is over, it is celebrated again in a version that includes men, suggesting that giving the head to women alone fails to avert the catastrophe of the myth's end.

### *"We Finish the* rakukusa *So That* Ꝺau *Can Begin"*

At the start of *Ꝺau*, the paternal kinsmen announce that they have made sure to invite "all the mothers." "We want all the women to eat," they say, pointing to the whole marsupials they keep in reserve so they never have to refuse any woman a portion on account of "forgetting" her name. If a woman arrives uninvited and is refused a share in the feast, like the fairy at Sleeping Beauty's christening, she will curse the child. At the top of the invited list are women of the child's father's clan, especially the mother's *anaturaha*,

---

3. Margaret Mead's description of conflict between sisters-in-law on Manus applies with few modifications to the Gimi:

> All through adult life in Manus there is a struggle between a man's wife and a man's sister for his allegiance and his gifts. . . . The obscenity in which a jealous and outraged wife accuses her husband of making his sister into her co-wife has no parallel in the relationship of brothers-in-law. It is the wife who is the stranger, who is at a continual disadvantage in fighting the vested interests of the sister. So the community votes it good for these two traditional enemies to sign a continuous public truce (Mead 1968:77).

sometimes excluding the father's own mother (see rules of *aθaoina* in Chap. 6). Also present are *amamuraha* and *anatiraha* in both *kisa* and *amene* categories, thus including women married into clans of the father's mother (FZ, FFZ, and FMM), the mother's father (MM and MBW), and mother's mother (MZ, MMBW, and MFZ)—categories of kin that often overlap (see O'Hanlon and Frankland 1986:186).

The size of a *θau* depends upon the wealth and prominence of the child's father or father's father. Generally, some fifty adults congregate in the father's compound in the late morning to cook and receive portions of nine or ten marsupials and a pig. The *amauraha*, the father's sisters and mother's brother's wives, and women of the father's patrilineage bring huge bundles of wild greens, plantains, young maize, beans, taros, and sweet potatoes. Some scrape the skin off the tubers and others sit near the men who butcher the pig, mopping up blood with handfuls of parsley or greens and tying them into bundles. One woman takes the pig's intestines to a stream below the compound and empties and braids them for smoking over an open fire. Another stuffs the pig's innards and belly fat into bamboo tubes. Older women place whole, gutted tree kangaroos, cuscus, or bandicoots onto the hot rocks piled on planks above the oven pits and singe the fur before rubbing it off with their hands.

If the child is not firstborn, the father's mother may prepare and cook separately, inside an oven made of a hollowed tree trunk, one of the small marsupials, perhaps a ring-tailed possum, as food for the father and his brothers and *aturaha*, provided each of them has also sired more than one surviving child. As she cooked a marsupial for her sons and sons-in-law, one woman pointed out that these men would abstain from a similar meal at the end of *haro*:

> When the Moon kills us men do not help. We eat alone. . . . But when a child is born and a feast is made, men eat. Men are the reason [lit: *ami*/root] we bear children. We don't bring children from our mothers and fathers. And we don't get them from nowhere! Our husbands are the source. That's why we don't give our children in marriage to just anyone. We give them only to our husbands' sisters.

When women finish preparing food for the several *θau* ovens, they join scattered groups of older and more distantly related women who sit on the sidelines, grooming one another, feeding infants, rolling shredded bark across their thighs, or netting string. As the men start to load sections of pig and marsupial into the ovens, the new mother comes out of her house and hands each of them a chunk of roasted pork from an open fire. "That is our custom," an older woman explains. "No one should be hungry for meat.

Everyone's belly must be content." After distributing meat to the men, the mother takes bamboo tubes from the fire and serves handfuls of steaming, fat-drenched greens to the waiting women. "Some are her *amauraha,* some are her *anoha* or *anaturaha.* . . . " To her closest *amau,* her own brother's wife or husband's own sister, she presents a whole tube stuffed with meat. When she has finished her rounds, she goes back inside her house.

An hour or so later, the *amau* is called to open the oven. She pokes a long stick into the top layer of debris while the new mother's other *amauraha,* several *anaturaha* and her own mother, remove outer layers of the oven and sort the contents into piles, continually feeding themselves morsels of food as they work. Women unload the oven while men stand by and watch. They pass the new mother a package of bananas or beans, or a piece of taro, and she hands it to her husband's *amamu* or another woman of his mother's patriclan. As women reach the bottom layers, men replace them around the ovens and set out the meat for their elders to cut and apportion. Big Men consult one another on the distribution and direct younger men to lay out rows of banana-leaf plates. The new mother moves next to the Big Man in charge and whispers to him the names of women who washed her baby in the river, wiped the blood of birth from boulders, and brought her food and firewood during confinement, and he directs that a plate be laid down for each one. "Let's cut this pig and give it to everyone," shouts one of the senior men, "so the child will grow quickly."

During the prolonged calculations, some who wait demand to receive large portions on account of their attentions to the mother. "When Nubimi had the child, I brought her sugarcane, taro, bananas," an old man announces. "Her *amau* neglected her and brought her no firewood!" yells an old woman of the father's clan, prompting the Big Man immediately to pass her a chunk of meat. "Now that the time for *ϑau* has come, you have all arrived," she continues. "You should all give *me* some of the meat you get. It was I who took good care of Nubimi." The new mother herself may add, "Put aside part of the rib cage for my *amau* and her husband who looked after me. The baby urinated into his mouth so you must give him food." The child's father's brother, meanwhile, passes out bits of meat among a group of elders watching the distribution, men of sufficient age or social prominence to have *kore* prefixed to their names in address. The hors d'oeuvres quiet the hunger excited by the sight of food. "This way there will be enough to go around," the uncle says. "If we do not give out some meat in advance, we will find ourselves short."

The featured recipients of *ϑau* are the mother's real or close classificatory brothers. But these men have kept out of sight until now, hiding in shame like the groom at a wedding. They appear when their sister emerges from her house a second time, dressed entirely in red, like a bride, and carrying her baby inside a net bag made especially by her *amau*. Her husband's father takes the carrying strap out of her hand and presents the child to one of her brothers, together with a small bouquet of green blossoms called *hareabiri ðoni*, literally, "feces-smelling grass" (*[h]are*/feces + *abiri*/smelling + *ðoni*/grass). "Accusations of sorcery have passed between us," the father proclaims. "Let the child now born to your sister close that road." As the mother's brother takes hold of the child and the *hareabiri ðoni*, a Big Man of the father's clan who presided over the division of meat hands the first portion to the mother, and she passes it to her brother. The Big Man or his assistant then calls out the names of her other brothers (*asiraha*), brothers' wives (*amauraha*), mothers (*anoha*) and mother's brothers (*anatiraha*), some ten to fifteen men and women.

As the Big Man recites a name he passes the new mother a portion of meat, and the person named walks alone across the compound to take it from her hands while her brother stands beside her holding the child. At the end of the distribution, her brother hands the child back to her husband's father and responds formally to his remarks:

> You have called for an end of sorcery between us. We shall not show this grass to the child [i.e., teach him how to steal leavings, nor incite him to work sorcery against you]. Once we were enemies but now I give you this lovely boy-child to make an end of the theft between us.

The mother puts the baby back into the house and returns to begin the longer and less formal second phase of *ðau*, distributing smaller allotments of food to twenty or thirty "providers of firewood," women who symbolically generated the heat that filled her newborn with life by actually providing care during her confinement or by belonging to categories of kin expected to do so. She presents food to her own mothers, sisters, and *amauraha,* and to women of her husband's and husband's mother's patriclans, some of whom may already have received allotments from her during *rakukusa*. The new mother stands now beside her husband who hands her, one by one, the filled sections of banana leaves he receives from his senior paternal kinsmen. Toward the end of one *ðau* distribution, the husband suddenly struck his wife in the chest. "There are two women you have not named!" he cried when his kinsmen informed him of the omissions. "Speak their names now so I can hear them!" Startled but contained, the mother took two portions from her husband and handed them over to the two women.

In the mythic universe that governs Gimi kinship and exchange, a women's father secretly precedes her brother as the "true source" of her child: he is the man behind the Moon, the malevolent ghost who would stubbornly hold the child during labor and turn her womb to "mad ground."[4] Ensuring a safe exit out of the mother by placating the hidden spirit of her father is the metaphor for life itself. At every life-crisis, the *ababana* offer head payments to the *kore*'s living descendants to induce him to let go and allow the child—or initiate or deceased—into the world or afterworld. A head payment presents the maternal kinsmen with a substitute for the child during its critical passage out of the mother, arresting the moment when the head first appears. Interpreted in light of myth, the meat of *rakukusa* and *ϑau* condenses the whole escapade in which the child arose, recapitulating the first coitus and pulling back of the father's seed (see Chap. 7). To say that the mother's brother will curse a child if he does not eat the head means, in these terms, that his father the *kore*—the man once wed to the mother—will take back the child or refuse to let it be born. The person whose head is unpurchased falls ill or dies, in this sense, because he or she ceases to be released by the *kore* and returns to a place like a *neki maha*, a mad world where sons hunt their fathers and fathers thoughtlessly maim or uproot their offspring.

As the *kore*'s closest living relation, the mother's brother is the one who most requires consideration to ensure the child's safe exit from the mother. Yet the *ababana* insist that wives of the mother's brothers and other midwives receive the first payments; that women eat the *rakukusa* and quiet the "anger in their bellies" before *ϑau* can begin. By presenting the first payments to women, the *ababana* seek out the voracious *kore* in his first destination, offering a *rakukusa* to replace the food the *kore* hunted between woman's thighs and wrapped at the head of his enormous length. The marsupial, vine leaves, and other wild ingredients of *rakukusa* work as a medicine and offset women's curse by evoking their own myth, canceling their attachment to a hidden father as if he—or the meat of his desire—had become ensconced in women's bellies, engendering the same fury that drove their mythic counterpart to kill the firstborn.

But a woman's belly is an unsatisfactory conduit for evicting the mythic father because she is ambivalent and wants to keep the Moon. Though the old man's secret invasion is the root of her fury and would ruin her mother-

---

4. During Botukofe's difficult labor, it was the *kore* of her husband's father, not her own, who obstructed the birth by "holding the child," expressing his anger at having been slighted in distributions by his own descendants (see above, this Chap.). Feeling hungry, he "went back to the mother" to find food and delayed the birth. If his matrilateral counterpart, the *kore* of the mother's father, had entered her womb during labor, it would mean—not simply that his name had been forgotten at a feast—but rather that the mother's brideprice, or "heads" of her other children, had not been paid! In that case, the labor would not be merely prolonged. The curse of the mother's brother (or father) would surely kill the child.

ing if left unabated, it is also the source of her capacity to reproduce and nurture. According to women's myths, a woman becomes pregnant "in her sleep" without knowing whom she marries. When she awakes and realizes her husband tricked her, she cuts him off or kills his child. But she also hides the child she killed; she keeps the part of her husband she made big and severed and presents it to him afterward as cooked food.

If the role of the *ababana* is to give the head and recruit the child, to create a licit kinship by annulling the mother's marriage to the Moon, allaying her rage and disappointment, extinguishing the fire of first love, etc., then the ritual role of women, as men interpret and shape it, is to oppose their project. No matter how generous the *rakukusa*, no matter how frequent the head payments, women refuse the exchange men initiate. Men give women the head of the child at *rakukusa* and *ðau* just as a man donates *hato* again and again during conception, providing the child as a gift to his wife for her to care for. But in the sense that a woman cannot initiate exchanges nor return the head on her own, she ignores her husband and makes no response to his gift. Rather than give it back, she keeps his child "between her thighs" and turns it to blood.

By assembling the midwives for *rakukusa*, the *ababana* seem to make a show of the mothers' intransigence, demonstrating their refusal to return the head as the pretext for approaching their brothers in order to transact the child to life. In the aftermath of *rakukusa*, men have no choice but to celebrate *ðau*, extending the distribution of head payments to the mother's paternal kinsmen in a new effort to secure the child's release. Until the point in the *ðau* ritual when the mother's brother appears and receives the first portion of meat, the mother keeps the child "out of sight" inside her house, suggesting that *rakakusa* has been a failure, that men's offer of the head has failed to persuade the mother to hand over her child. Interpreted in this way, *rakukusa* is men's justification for excluding women from their ensuing transactions. "We are willing to exchange the head with the mother," men seem to say. "We give it to her again and again, in portion after portion and rite after rite—and in copulation after copulation. But she refuses to give it back. She makes common cause with the spirit of her father and turns the child to blood, leaving us no recourse but to appeal to her brother."

If the necessity of excluding women from life-giving exchanges is, indeed, men's hidden premise in *rakukusa* and *ðau*, it accords closely with women's own myth that gives nearly the whole credit for *ðau* to the child's father and grandfather (see above, this Chap.). But if there is no invariant sequence of mythic events, as I have stressed, there can be no single meaning of a head payment. The rites in which men and women cooperate to exchange the head represent a compromise, in this sense. The sexes act together, yet may *act out* separate fantasies, making a show of cooperation that masks the conflict over who is to blame for killing the child. The mythic terms in which women accept the gift of the head may have a different origin and motive than those in which men present it. Yet, if *rakukusa* precedes *ðau* for the reasons I have given—the same reasons women had to finish the second course of a cannibal meal before the distribution of pigs to *anatiraha* could begin (see Chap. 3)—then women eating the head at *rakukusa* is also tacit acknowledgment of guilt, an occasion for the sexes to resolve their argument, at least temporarily, in men's favor.

# PART THREE

Marriage and Male Initiation

# NINE

# The Myth of the Flutes and Principles of Exchange

## Principles of Exchange

If rites of birth enact the premise that men make life possible by confiscating the "head of the child" from women and circulating it among themselves, then rites of death demonstrate the antithesis, dramatizing the consequence to the child of the "head" falling back into women's hands so that men are forced to revert to exchanges with women. In one sense, a person dies because the *ababana* neglected to offer head payments on his or her behalf, or because the *anatiraha* refused to "eat" them (see Chap. 2). When a man dies in his prime, his *ababana* and *anatiraha* trade accusations of sorcery as they once exchanged valuables, as if blame for death were a kind of anti-gift, the inverse of the head payments that once kept the man alive.[1] But the result of men's accusations, made in elaborate divination rites conducted "out of women's sight," is mainly inconclusive. Gimi mortuary ritual culminates not in the naming of a sorcerer or guilty man but in the accusation, in a collective ritual sense, of the deceased's mothers (see Chaps. 3, 4, and 5).

When the *ababana* and *anatiraha* stop exchanging the head, it falls out of circulation. The moment men stop transacting a man to life, as it were, his mothers and sisters "steal" the body, forcing the *ababana* into direct negotiation with the thieves. In *ruhu, niniusina, beheθabaθa,* and *agesagena,* men

1. As in descriptions of Gimi mortuary ritual (Chaps. 3 to 5), the person, or subject, of head payments here again is presumed to be male. In part, this reflects the ethnographic finding that life-crisis rites for males are more frequent and elaborate, and more often described by both sexes, than those celebrated for females. More important, the generic maleness of the person expresses the logic of exchange and, indeed, of the whole culture. The symbolic maleness of the individual—including those who, upon marriage, "cease" or "fail" to be male—cannot be dismissed, it seems to me, as an artifact of my being a woman who was "treated like a man in the field," who relied too much on male informants or on Melanesian Pidgin, who avoided discussion with women of classically male topics (Faithorn 1976:86–87), etc., nor by the notion that women are somehow "inarticulate" at the "'meta' level of fieldwork" (Ardener 1975:1–2).

"give the head" to women mourners, presenting them with a replacement for the life they stole, disassembled, and put on as decorations. Rites of death blame women, as I have argued, by showing such transactions always to be in vain or one-sided. Men present women with head payments in rite after rite, but women offer only blood and bones in return.[2]

If the rites of birth and death demonstrate the problem with women, showing that they refuse to exchange the "head of the child," then the jointly celebrated rites of marriage and first-stage initiation for boys seem to implement a solution. If, in the terms of the mythic scenario that I propose the rites address, a woman insists on menstruating, if she refuses to *relinquish* a living child, then men will exchange her and the child as one, giving her away as a bride while the child is still inside her and unborn. Gimi explanations of marriage and head payments, idioms like "eating the head," "returning the head," etc., become fully understandable, I suggest in this chapter, in the context of unspoken messages communicated in rites of male initiation and marriage, especially in secret phases in which the flute is bestowed as a replica of the bride, her "blowing hole" already filled with meat that represents the hair-covered head of her father's child. When two men exchange sisters in marriage in mythic terms, each forces his sister to surrender to the other man the child she refuses to give him, a child sired by their father whom she would rather keep and turn to blood. In exchanging brides and confiscating their heads, in taking away woman's father/penis/child, men become autonomous, reversing the primordial situation in which woman was alone and had it all. As woman once possessed the flute and "hid the father," so men acquire the bride with the father still inside her: they invent the bride as a flute, or a giant penis, as though she had been cut off from her father in the midst of copulation, endowed with a vagina and filled with his child. Men exchange the brides as the way to empty them and convey their father-derived contents to male initiates, who are the brides' younger brothers. As the flute "made a man" of the bride, its passage to her brothers feminizes them, putting woman's pubic hair on their faces, so they become self-sufficient, capable of transacting the father's child without recourse to women (see Dundes 1976).

But men's solution is hardly satisfactory for, in arranging to bypass their daughters and sisters and transact the father's head entirely among themselves, they also reveal his presence, thus falling into agreement with women

---

2. The idea that women's inability to initiate exchange symbolizes both female sexual identity and secondary status is expressed by Rubin in terms that fit the Gimi:

> The girl never gets the phallus. It passes through her, and in its passage is transformed into a child. When she "recognizes her castration," she accedes to the place of a woman in the phallic exchange network. She can "get" the phallus—in intercourse, or as a child—but only as a gift from a man. *She never gets to give it away.*
> (Rubin 1975:195; my emphasis)

that it was really the father who ate the child's head and provoked the first menstruation. By blaming women for death and contriving to exclude them from the rites of exchange, men paradoxically expose the father and extend the argument they attempt to resolve.

## The Start of hau

*apina* or first-stage male initiation (lit: *abi*/spear + *na*/thing) is celebrated concurrently with a series of sister-exchange marriages. Marriages are held at other times, but when *apina* is planned they are saved up for the occasion (see Koch 1974a:402). Three or more pairs of sisters are exchanged in a series of elaborate double weddings. Before the weddings, while pairs of brides are still secluded inside women's houses, men begin *apina* by interning two or three groups of eight to a dozen or more boys in each of two or three men's houses. The combined celebrations last for about two weeks and are ideally held during the dry season (from May to September) in conjunction with a pig-killing festival called *hau* (see Read 1952:20; Langness 1974).[3] The whole complex of rites, also called *hau,* occurs once in five or ten years or more rarely, perhaps, before the *pax australiana.* Nowadays representatives from the entire Gimi language area and even beyond may converge on the host villages of a ridge or valley, bringing together some 1200 people. The rites are conducted on a twenty-four-hour cycle in a volatile atmosphere of sexual license and of potential conflict among groups brought into un-accustomed contact. Throughout the weeks of the festival, the loud or distant music of flutes is heard almost constantly.[4]

*hau* begins with the initial secret phase of *kuta* or marriage. Each pair of brides or *amau* is secluded inside the house of the mother of one and sub-jected to an initiation which is a lesser version of the rites of first menses

3. *hau* opens with an elaborate parade of *keruba* boards, painted wooden planks, up to three meters high, that are tied onto the backs of men and women of the host clans (see Salisbury 1959). *keruba* dance before and during the slaughter of pigs. During two *hau* in 1974–75, a total of some 160, and 100, animals were dispatched at the start of the festivals and on later occasions. *keruba* are a kind of soul-net that capture the pigs' departing *aunas.* When *hau* is over, the boards are left to rot in the new gardens of the pigs' owners so that, as they decompose, they will release the pigs' *aunas* to fertilize the ground and help restore the depleted supply of tubers and other crops.

Descriptions of *keruba* boards and other dance shields called *kafi* (see Langness 1974:197), and of other *hau* rites centered on pigs, are omitted from the following account.

4. In April 1974, David and Samantha Gillison and I attended *hau* in a village one day's walk from Ubagubi. In July, another cycle of rites was held by a village two days' walk in the opposite direction. Ubagubi celebrated its own *hau* immediately prior to our arrival in September 1973 and, upon our departure in December 1974, we heard that a nearby settlement was planning *hau* within the next several months. Gimi say that the festivals, which are planned years in ad-vance, are traditionally staged in such closely spaced sequences—like a slow chain reaction—as word spreads that one or more hamlets have begun preparations.

(*haro*). The two are kept constantly awake, deprived of food and drink and taught songs and incantations (see Chap. 6). At night, the ritual leaders make an enormous central fire to "cook" the brides, and the two clans exchange songs of anger. Mothers of the bride complain that the brideprice was paltry. Mothers of the groom protest that the feathers, pigs, cash, and lengths of cloth they gave were the very finest.[5] The bride-givers boast of their clan forest, naming rivers, species of red birds, red flowers, red cordyline, and brilliantly colored insects to refer to the treasure they are about to lose. "A parrot as vibrant as ours is not to be found on your land," they sing. "But now we are sending one to you." Between songs, women disparage one another's efforts, and the hosts demand that everyone sing loudly and with gusto so their *aunas* fill the room.

During the day, at oven sites throughout the village, pigs are singed, gutted, boned, and stuffed with greens in preparation for the weddings (*habarena*). As visitors continue to arrive, reports circulate of elopements, infidelities, and elusive pigs that may threaten the upcoming marriages.

On the second or third night of the brides' internment, young men, some of them already married, arrive in one of the women's houses to sing *aboE* or courting songs and to "tanim het" (see Langness 1969:42; Brown 1969:83; Strathern & Strathern 1968:145). The men sit cross-legged on a platform at the rear with their bare backs to the fire while women loll on the floor facing the leaping flames. Everyone shakes his or her head rhythmically, swaying in unison to songs that suggestively juxtapose varieties of wild taro (beautiful girls) and black Birds of Paradise or black cordyline (fine men). In a lull between songs, two or three decorated actors burst into the crowded hut, clear a stage around the fire, and begin a performance of *harukaru* or ritual theater (see Chaps. 3 and 6). On most nights of *hau*, small bands of men and women tour the five or six houses where *kuta*, and later *apina*, are in prog-

---

5. During the initial closed phase of *A*'s *kuta* (fig. below), *U* and *S* sat on opposite sides of the crowded hut, one among the "mothers" (*anoha*) and the other among the "providers of bridal pork" (*anaturaha*), as the two groups of women exchanged choruses of mock insults. *U* and *S* explained: "We are sisters of *P*. So his wife is our *amau*. *A* is our sister-in-law (*amau*) and our sister (*a'au ara*) both." The event of marriage—or rather the nonevent, the nonmarriage of those in the category of *preferred* spouses like *P* and *U* or *P* and *S*—transforms them, terminologically at least, into consanguines.

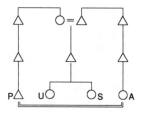

ress, repeating, on any one night, the same repertoire of *harukaru*. They waken the dozing singers with scenes of sorcerers' attacks or ribald vignettes of village life, a memorable adultery, a quarrel between co-wives, the decline of a man's sexual powers. Battles fought long ago, the arrival of the first Australian Patrol, the habits of prostitutes in Goroka or of white cockatoos at lower altitudes are recreated around the fire.

Each sex, sometimes in the guise of the other, acts out scenes on their own or the other sex's premises. (This is the only occasion during the rites when women enter men's houses. Women are rigorously excluded from the rest of *apina*, although men participate in all but the first nights of *kuta*.) During the last nights of *kuta*, women players appear at the door of a men's house to fetch their husbands' weapons or netted carrying bags or possum-fur caps for mounting feathers, using them to create the costumes in which they will return hours later. Male performers likewise borrow their wives' or paramours' attire before making dramatic entrances into women's houses. Each set of performances lasts about a half hour, after which the singing resumes.

Early on the morning of their weddings, the brides emerge from seclusion and one begins to adorn the other, dabbing her face with colored clays and tying on a headdress of red Pesquet Parrot feathers. On the sides of the headdress hang furry tassles of cuscus testicles that augment the "beard" tattooed on the bride's face (see below, this chap.). The bride's *anoha*, the senior women of her patrilineage, help her with the rest of her decorations. They tie on layers of new bark-string fore-skirts, tuck in lengths of new cotton cloth to make a bustle over her rear, and fasten scores of narrow bands of plaited yellow bamboo around her waist and upper arms. The *anoha* also decorate the *anaturaha*, women who reared the pigs used in her brideprice and "mothers" of her *amau*. They wrap the *anaturaha* in new string skirts, tie newly netted bags across their foreheads, paint their faces with clays or trade-store pigments, and smear their bodies with pig fat to make them glisten in the morning sun.

After her entourage is decorated, the bride reaches beneath the many layers of new skirts and removes her old one. She hands it to her mother who begins to wail on cue. Then her father starts to sob, often louder than her mother, and orders the procession to the groom's compound to begin. "Let my daughter's *habarena ugunu* [lit: *habare*/cut + *na*/thing (i.e., wedding) + *ugunu*/pig] now be delivered!" he cries. "Leave only the *anotu ugunu*, the head pigs, for my son inside the men's house." The decorated *anaturaha* pick up the many bundles of cooked pork that have been laid out in the center of the bride's father's compound. Across their foreheads, the women sling *hoge kopisa ugunu* (lit: *hoge*/string-skirt + *ko*/bag + *pi*/inside + *sa*/poss. + *ugunu*), netted bags stuffed with sections of pigs' back, head, and leg that have been wrapped in new string skirts. On their heads, they pile whole rib cages and charred bamboo tubes filled with pieces of meat, fat, and bananas

(*Above*) One of the *anatu*, or purchasers of the bride, carries a stick of *kabibisahara*, pig's innards that have been stuffed or braided and then roasted or smoked and hung in a row. The display shows that the animals sent with the bride are complete. "We would be ashamed," the bride's mothers explain, "if her *anatu* said, 'You eat all the insides and send us only the empty carcass.'"

(*Top right*) Wearing new string skirts, waistbands of braided yellow bamboo, and a headdress of marsupial fur and red Pesquet parrot feathers, the bride walks at the center of the wedding procession carrying the neck of a pig. She is supposed to nibble morsels of the meat en route. Men of her father's patrilineage bring up the rear carrying the headless and limbless *ano ugunu* or "big pigs."

(*Bottom right*) His upper body whitened with talc, the mother's brother of the groom escorts the bride to her new home. He holds her hand in which she carries a charred pig's heart impaled on a stick. He leads her past a display of wedding pork, including bamboo tubes tied together in pairs and filled with cooked meat, fat, and bananas. This display will be delivered with the second bride, who is the sister of the groom, when she marries the brother of the first bride in an identical ceremony to be held immediately after this one.

and tied together in pairs. The paired bamboos are called *ϑagi riϑi—abese riϑi* (lit: *ϑagi*/banana + *riϑi*/bamboo—*abese*/meat + *riϑi*). To their hips, the women fasten *kabibisahara* or "innards," sticks hung with rows of esophagus, intestines, bladder, lungs, stomach, and other organs that have been stuffed or braided and then roasted or smoked. The display of innards from neck to rectum shows that the pigs sent with the bride are complete. "We would be ashamed," women explain, "if her *anatu* said, 'You eat all the insides and send us only the empty carcass.'" In their hands, lying on banana leaves, the *anaturaha* carry flat sections of salted pork called *ϑobena* (lit: *ϑobe*/salt + *na*/thing) so that these choice parts will be the first set down in the groom's compound.[6]

The bride's kinswomen paint the *anaturaha,* anoint them with pig fat, adorn them with new clothes and cooked meat to "cool their bellies," they say, and assuage disappointment in the bride. "We don't want her *anatu* to say, 'We paid dearly for her yet she comes to us empty.' So we send *ϑobena* and the rest." Meat worn and paraded by the *anaturaha* also satisfies the honor of the *ababana,* showing that they have sent food with the bride for her to provide a sumptuous meal for the women upon whom she will depend in her early married life.

Following the *anaturaha* are the bride's *anoha* who carry other bags of cooked meat. Behind the *anoha,* at the center of the procession amidst an entourage of unmarried age-mates, come the bride and her undecorated *amau.* The one is going to her new home while the other is returning to her father's compound. Watching two brides named Gome and Pare, a man in the crowd remarks:

> Gome's *asi* [brother; lit: sibling of opposite sex] marries the *asi* [sister] of her [intended] husband. . . . One bride takes the place of the other. The two men make an exchange. Gome's *asi* takes a wife from Pare's *asi*. . . . There is no other mother who bore them. They [each pair of marrying siblings] are *kisa asi.* Each has but one mother.

Men of the bride's patrilineage bring up the rear bearing five cooked pigs, boned and gutted, which are the main wedding pork. There are two headless, limbless *ano ugunu* or "big pigs" spread on litters; and three whole

6. Among the Melpa, "brides . . . used to wear some of the bridewealth valuables. . . . It is illuminating that while between men the gesture of transference is a handing over, or a setting out of valuables for the recipients to pick up, here the woman's person is draped with them. We may take this as symbolic of the fact that women rarely act as negotiators" (M. Strathern 1972:156). I argue that Gimi women's putting on brideprice (or relics of the deceased; see Chap. 5) symbolizes their illegitimacy as donors; and that the transference of goods between men always entails the literal or symbolic *divestiture* of women, an act tantamount to the reduction of their augmented mythic status.

*natano ugunu* or "coleus leaf pigs" trussed on poles. The *ano ugunu* will be presented to senior men of the groom's lineage who may redistribute them to other clans to pay off old debts. But the *natano ugunu* are not for redistribution. They will be presented formally to the "one mother" of groom and bride in recognition of her toil:

> She worked hard. . . . When her children defecated she wiped the feces with her own hands [i.e., using *natano* leaves]. When she carried her children to her gardens, her arms ached. For this pain, the mother now must eat.[7]

Inside the groom's compound, the wedding party sets down the burden of pork in a long row on the ground. The groom's side hauls out its own prestation, identically packaged and trussed, and lays it in a parallel line opposite the bride's meat, creating an aisle that runs nearly the whole length of the compound. Amid the commotion, the grooms and their age-mates are nowhere to be seen. "The husbands are ashamed and have run away," the women say, as convention dictates. The bride stands beside her father at the far end of the aisle and, in her left hand, holds up a charred pig's heart impaled on a stick.[8] Her father wraps his hand around the hand with the heart and calls out to senior men of the groom's patrilineage who stand near his father's house at the other end of the aisle:

> Come and take her hand with the heart . . . I wanted to send her to you some time ago, but her mother opposed me. "First we must raise the pigs," she said. "Let her eat pigs and grow bigger. Then we will cut her. . . ."
> You and I are old enemies. Now let us be friends.

At the groom's end, a huddle of men ostentatiously count Australian dollars. Suddenly, from behind them, a man appears wearing a headdress of yellow cuscus fur and black cassowary plumes, his face, chest, and upper back caked with white talc. He seizes the bundle of notes and runs down the

7. The mother is enjoined from eating the pigs given in her name. She distributes the meat among her other children, co-wives and women of her husband's lineage and clan. Traditionally, she wore the pearl shells that were presented with these pigs and today keeps the small cash payments that have largely replaced the shells.

Among Jale of the Western Highlands, the agnates of a male initiate present his maternal kinsmen with a gift called "'pig-nourishing-hand-cutting-one': the pig that cuts off the nourishing hand" (Koch 1974a:404). Like the "coleus pigs" presented to a Gimi mother, the gift is designed to sever a maternal relation.

8. The Gimi word for "heart" is *rumopa*, but wedding guests refer to the heart the bride holds as *hau*, literally "liver." *hau* is also a generic term for inner organs, especially the various "livers" where thoughts and emotions originate. Glick speculates that *hau* may be the root of *[h]auna*, personal spirit or life-force (1963). Both words may be related to the name of the festival, but no Gimi made that connection to me.

aisle toward the bride and her father. Just before he reaches them he backs up, then dances forward, moving back and forth several times before he places the money, and a sprig of coffee, directly in the bride's hand. Her father takes the bundle of money and the whitened man, who is the groom's *anati,* replaces her father's grasp and leads the bride away.[9] The men who line both sides of the aisle alternate shouts of joy, drowning out the plaintive wails of the bride's maiden attendants.

As soon as the bride arrives at the groom's end of the compound she begins to decorate her *amau.* Her father picks up a bundle of *hoge kopisa ugunu* from the groom's display and loads it onto her mother's head. It is now the turn of the bride's *anoha* to be decorated with face paint, smeared with pig fat, dressed in new skirts, and loaded down with cutting pork and to lead the procession back to her father's compound. Her *anaturaha* follow, with her husband's own mother carrying the scorched heart so that her *amau,* too, can hold it when she marries. The second ceremony proceeds as a virtual repetition of the first, with the roles of givers and receivers of the bride reversed. "It is the women who change the brides," men say. In late afternoon, the mothers of one of the brides may give away another daughter, escorting her to her husband's village with pigs they received in the morning for her sister.[10]

By putting on new clothes and the sections of pork, the women who "change the brides" seem to repeat their role in mourning when they put on the man (see Chap. 5). The idea that the pigs stand for the bride's body is suggested in the explanation one woman gave for wearing the innards and other parts: "We don't want her *anatu* to say, 'We paid dearly for her yet she comes to us empty.'" During the nights of singing that precede the transfer, the bride's lineage brothers cover themselves in ashes to mourn her departure, which is the last occasion when her father will give her head to her *anati.* The manner in which her mothers send her to the groom heightens the impression that marriage—and the cessation of head payments—is a kind of death for the bride, the time when she will be "eaten" in the form of pigs.

During the days of catenated weddings, several betrothals are also ar-

9. Spectators explain the *harukaru* in which the bride changes hands. Through the gestures of his dance, the groom's *anati* says to the bride:

> We worked hard to raise the pigs and money to buy you. Now you must return the pigs and money to us. You must pick coffee that earns the money to buy pigs. . . . You must make gardens, plant sweet potato, and give us the food so we may eat.

The bride's father will give the twenty or so Australian dollars placed into her hand to her brother, the man about to marry the groom's sister.

10. During one *hau,* four of the six brides so painstakingly feted ran off on the nights of their weddings with unrelated visitors to the festival, illustrating the difficulty—and rarity—of achieving the ideal pattern.

ranged. In the evening, a delegation of five or six men, visitors from another village, arrive at the house of the man whose daughter they seek. They carry a huge pole, about fifteen meters long, covered with one- and two-dollar Australian notes (totaling some 200 dollars in 1975) and crowned with the black plumage of the Princess Stephanie Bird of Paradise. A small crowd watches while the girl's father briefly acknowledges receipt of the pole. Ideally, girls betrothed now at ages of six to twelve will be married some six to ten years later during the next *hau* cycle.

## The Seclusion of Male Initiates

As the bridal processions move back and forth between the compounds of a village, and the villages of a ridge, flutes echo inside the several men's houses where initiates have been interned. Less than a week earlier, one or two nights after the brides were sequestered, the men arrived at the women's houses to fetch their sons, boys of about eight to twelve. Seeing the men approach in early evening, women threw stones and attacked the men with sticks wrapped in stinging nettles and then ran to the men's houses to block the entrances (see Read 1965:136–37). Although the battle was a ritual, the women attacked with vigor. The men hooted war cries and hollered abuse as they pushed the boys through the women's blockade. The women fell back and regrouped in the doorway, making the men run the gamut once more. When all the boys were securely inside, the women, forbidden to cross the portal of the men's house, drifted off singly or in pairs, sobbing in the growing darkness.

The men made the boys kneel along an inside wall, each one supported by an unmarried mother's brother or matrilateral cousin who would attend him throughout his ordeal. The chaperon, a youth initiated on the previous occasion, is called *ahamo* or "one with the same name" (lit: *aha*/same + *mo*/the). The men cordon off the boys and their *ahamoha* to keep away men who recently had sex, a particular danger during *hau* when promiscuity is virtually prescribed.[11] Inside the vine cord, men who have abstained from sex stand shoulder to shoulder to block the view of initiates as four other men pull a pair of flutes or *kamiba*, literally "giant [fictitious] birds," from under a bed or out of the rafters and carry them out of the house.

The four return several hours later, two of them wearing masks and decorated as "giant insects," and two playing flutes. They crawl into the house in a line behind the wall of men, the "insects" preceding the pair of flute

---

11. I never entered a men's house. My descriptions and explanations of events that occurred there are based upon accounts of men who reconstructed the scene for me, and described related experiences, sometimes while listening to tape recordings of men's songs and speeches made during the initiations by David Gillison.

players. The standing men hoot and chant while the "birds" cry out of sight
of the initiates. As the moment of revelation approaches, the men launch
into haiku-like songs that allude to the initiates' impending birth. One song
describes marsupials "slipping out" of nests as easily and plentifully as rain
falls to earth:

> The possum-child slips out of the hole in the ground,
>> heavily, quickly as fall the rains . . .
> The possum-child slips out of the hole in the tree,
>> heavily, quickly as fall the rains . . .

As the moment draws nearer, men's songs name the red parrots and Birds of
Paradise they will "pull down" out of decorated holes in wild bamboo:

> Come down, Pesquet's parrot, come down!
>> I will pull you down [out of] the tattooed hole in the
>> wild bamboo.
> Come down, Raggiana Bird of Paradise, come down!
>> I will pull you down [out of] the tattooed hole in the
>> wild bamboo.

After about half an hour of singing, while the flute music continues out of
sight, the standing men break formation to allow the two monster-insects to
approach the initiates and crawl menacingly over their legs. Suddenly the
music stops and the flute players stand to appear before the boys. At that
moment, the *ahamoha* pull back the heads of the initiates and hold stone
axes to their throats. "If you tell your mothers, sisters, or younger brothers
that it is we men who make the *kamiba* cry," the Big Men shout, "we will cut
your throats with axes and dump you in the river!"

The *ahamoha* lay flutes in the initiates' laps while the Big Men continue
their harangue:

> Take hold of the flute! Is it heavy? Are there insects inside it?
> Do you hear their buzzing? Do they bite your hands? Put your
> ear to the hole and listen. *Nothing* is inside! It is *we men* who
> blow into the bamboo and make it cry!

The Big Men instruct the boys to close their eyes and, in silence, the
*ahamoha* place pieces of salted pork directly into their mouths. The traditional "flute food," which men say is sometimes still fed to initiates, is blood
drawn from the upper arms of Big Men and cooked with greens. Big Men
tell the initiates that the salted meat (or salty arm blood) they cannot see is
"the *kamiba*'s feces." "We give you this food to make you grow quickly," they
say. As one man afterward explained:

> If a boy eats his mother's food he will not grow. If his mother's food reaches his stomach, his whole body will sag and shrink. . . . His skin will wither, his bones will dry out, and his eyes will sink into his head. . . . Women's food is hot! Women have a heat that stops boys from growing, a heat that comes from having sex and menstruating and giving birth. . . .
>
> That's why we celebrate *apina*. We put boys into the men's house to stop them eating wherever they feel hungry, eating the foods women have touched. We give them *our* food and play the flutes to make them grow.

As older men remove the bamboo instruments from the boys' laps, they tell them:

> We don't tell our wives about the *kamiba*. We tell them it's a bird that cries. You say to yourself, "I like the woman I married but I won't tell her. . . . Even in the moment I die on her, even when I lie like a fool drooling on her chest, I won't tell her!" A woman is a delicious thing, but a grown man does not tell her what he knows.

The two flute players who crawled into the house behind the masked "insects" now stand before the initiates and face each other. They begin to play again, dancing back and forth in the central corridor of the men's house.

Later during *apina*, Big Men give the initiates more advice about how to behave with the wives they will one day supply:

> When I buy a wife and give her to you and . . . you go into her house, do not take hold of her skirt or open her legs. Tell her to do that herself. . . . A man does not put his hand on his penis. Your wife will hold your penis and put it inside her. . . . And when you ejaculate, don't die on her. . . . Get up fast! If you sleep on a woman you will grow old quickly. You'll start to cough like an old man. . . .
>
> Do not touch a woman's vagina. It is an enormous [kind of] mouth. If you touch a vagina and take food [with that hand] you will die. That is the warning of our ancestors.

### The "Vaginas" on Men's Faces

Several days after the initiates were taken into seclusion, I played recordings of the men's songs to men of other villages, visitors to the *hau*. "The men sing about women," they told me as they listened, "because women bear the children."

When men sing about a hole in the ground, or a hole in a tree, or a hole in a rock, or in wild bamboo, they sing about the hole in the flute, about woman's vagina. We get beards [*rasamunaϑa;* lit: *r/*our + *asa/*mouth + *mu/*surrounding + *aϑa/*hair, fur, or plumage] from that hole!

A new initiate mustn't play the flute or he'll get a beard while he's still a boy and stop growing. The song says, "Let the possum-child—let men—be born as fast and plentifully as rain." We celebrate *apina* so men will slip out of [women's] holes as often and effortlessly as rain falls to earth.

Adolescent initiates are called "new vaginas" on account of the hair that will soon start to appear around their mouths: rebirth during *apina* endows a boy with a "vagina" in his head in the same way as did his original emergence from his mother (see Chap. 4). But the initiates are forbidden to play the flutes, and to eat marsupials "covered in female pubic hair," until their next initiation, which is not celebrated until they have married, fathered at least two surviving children, and actually grown beards. A dozen or more years after men present "flute food" to groups of first-stage initiates in *kamiba anu ameE* [lit: *kamiba/*flute + *anu/*spirit-child + *ameE/*give], and impose stringent taboos on female foods, they celebrate *humi anu ameE,* "giving the possum-child" to a single married initiate, bestowing the right to play the flute and to consume certain marsupials "out of women's sight." The newly permitted marsupials are called *aϑahauragi* because their fur can be neatly extracted by hand (lit: *aϑa*) to expose smooth skin.

The initiate goes alone into the forest to hunt *aϑahauragi.* He brings one animal back to the men's house and gives it to a Big Man who is also his *anati.* The Big Man butchers the marsupial, giving the stomach and innards to an old man, and cooks the rest. Using his right hand, he puts a piece of the cooked meat into his mouth, immediately takes it out, and holds it under his left armpit, literally, a "crotch" (*sagana*). The initiate lowers his head under the Big Man's arm as the Big Man pronounces the initiate's flute name and places the meat directly into his mouth. "The Big Man gives him *sagana* to eat so now he can eat possums [and play the flute]."[12]

12. The male life-span is divided into nine named categories or age-grades: *anu arak* (unweaned child of either sex), *ferete arak* (*ferete/*small + *arak/*child or boy, 4–7 years), *ari arak* (uninitiated boy, 8–11 years), *maE arak* (initiated boy, 12–18 years), *aϑomebana* (non-virgin man, 18–24 years), *hakarubana* (24–40 years), *hakisabana* (40–45 years), *orarabana* (45–55 years), and *oϑesabana* (over fifty-five years).
After the celebration of *humi anu ameE,* *aϑomebana* becomes *hakarubana* for whom the re-

Marsupials categorized as *hage higi* (lit: *hage*/fat + *higi*/creature), because their fur is firmly rooted and has to be singed off before cooking, remain tabooed to all but very young and very old males. Even old men do not eat *hage higi* in women's presence because the animals sometimes sleep "with heads tucked into their crotches." Ingested in women's company, they might transmit that sleeping position to a man so that he "ate his own crotch" and fell ill. Men's taboos are based upon a pervasive association among flutes, marsupials, and female pubic hair, or *sagana,* that figures centrally in the secret that men divulge to younger men through the performances of their initiations and marriages.

### The Flute Myth

During the sleepless nights that follow the first revelation of flutes to adolescent boys, men recount the flute myth.[13] At the beginning of time, some versions say, "There were no men, only women and children." Women lived without husbands and owned the flutes. In other versions, men were merely "asleep and did not see the *kamiba,* only women did. But once Manoke [i.e., the eponymous clan founder] held the flutes, women never saw them again." The first woman kept her flute hidden under her bark-string skirts and at the head of her bed. When Manoke was a small boy, he stole his sister's flute and made her menstruate. A menstrual hut was called *kamiϑama* or "flute house" (lit: *kamiba*/flute + *nama*/house), men point out, because, "when the boy stole his sister's flute, the Moon killed her for the first time."

At the start of some versions, two sisters are initiating young girls by playing flutes inside the *kamiϑama*. The "cries" wake Manoke and he "crawls out of the men's house," making his way in darkness to the women:

> "What is that I hear crying?" the boy wondered. He left the house quietly and reached the door of the *kamiϑama,* hiding himself in tall grass. When the two women finished playing, they carried the flutes outside and set them down in the grass. They didn't see their brother hiding there. . . .
>
> The boy stole the flutes and brought them back to the men's house. He woke his age-mate, and the two of them started to play. Everyone awoke and asked, "Where did those things come from?" "The women were playing them," the boy said, "and I stole them and brought them here." . . .

---

moval of facial hair was traditionally tabooed. Only in late middle age, as an elder *orarabana* or as *oϑesabana,* did a man remove his whiskers, using a tiny bamboo cord to grasp and extract each hair.

13. Men recounted the following versions of the flute myth directly to me on other occasions.

The two sisters looked for their flutes . . . but only heard the cries. "Who took our flutes?" they wondered and followed the sounds into the men's house. They found their brother and said to him, "We made the flutes cry and it was good. Now you have brought them into your house. Keep them here with you."

The sisters told none of this to any other woman. . . . They forgot everything and died. That's why women nowadays know nothing about the flutes. When they hear them they think, "I wonder what that is? Some strange bird, perhaps, crying inside the men's house. Did a cassowary wander out of the forest? Is a giant bird hiding in the men's house?" . . . But the flute once belonged only to women. It isn't ours! We men stole it! (See R. Berndt 1962:50–51)

In other versions, the first flute was played and "seen" by only one woman who died with the secret.

That woman died and the rest never found out. Only one woman knew how to play. "I blew the flute alone," she told her brother. "But now you take it and make another so two men can play. Two age-mates can face each other and blow."

She heard the duet coming from the men's house and was pleased. "She said to her brother, 'I am a woman. But you are a man and can care for the bamboo in the men's house.' She was not angry," the myth teller added. I remarked that, in my experience, a man or woman who had been robbed became irate; and that I routinely heard men announce at feasts that they had to feed "all the women" because they were angry, as if anger were women's general condition. In response, he said that the sister only pretended to accept her loss. She took revenge "in secret," he said, without speaking of what she did:

Women have no whiskers but we men do. The reason, men say, is, "Woman's pubic hair is planted onto the mouths of men." We stole something from woman and blew into it and the hair of the vagina grew on our faces. . . .

When woman owned the flute, she used her pubic hair to close the mouth [i.e., to make a stopper for the blowing hole]. "With what shall I close this hole [lit: *asa*/mouth, opening, slit, incision]?" she wondered. Then she pulled out her pubic hair and made the plug.

Our true ancestors had no beards.[14] . . . When the boy stole

14. Only after their ancestors "held" the flutes did Gimi men grow beards. But they were much lighter in the past, men say, before white men brought razors.

his sister's flute, he didn't realize the hole was closed. He put his mouth on the plug and tried to play and afterward a beard grew. . . . Women know about this but have never seen it. They have heard the flutes but never *seen* them.

The first woman got the inspiration to make the flute—and to use her hair as a plug—by "looking down at her vagina": "The *kamiba* comes from the *kamiϑama*. . . . The first time the Moon killed woman, she was inside the *kamiϑama*. She looked down at her vagina and made the *kamiba*." Men also say, "The *kamiba* is the giant penis of the Moon," suggesting that when woman "looked down at her vagina" she saw that it was "plugged" by the Moon. She made the flute in the image of herself *at that moment,* as it were, in the midst of copulating with the Moon. Interpreted in this way, men's flute myths send a hidden message, indicating that menarche was caused not only by the boy who stole the flute, pulled out the plug of pubic hair, and blew into the hole but also by the Moon who plugged the hole in the first place. Seen in these terms, men's myth corresponds with women's own secret usages surrounding menstruation. According to women's "blood songs" and myths, a woman's blood issues not only from the "noses" of her lineage brothers but also from the giant who stole his way inside her (see Chaps. 4 and 6).

In another cycle of men's myths, as we have seen, it is again the "small boy" who opens the vagina. He climbs to the top of a huge tree, throws a stone into a lake and splashes out the fire between woman's thighs. But the boy throwing down the stone, putting out the fire, and retrieving the stone inside "a long, long net bag" around his neck, as men remark afterward, is "the same" as the Moon throwing down his penis and withdrawing into the sky. Indeed, they say that "the boy is the same as the Moon." We may recall their exegetical remarks:

> The Moon threw down his penis and had sex with the woman. . . . He put out the fire between her thighs and withdrew. . . . The Moon says, "I am the one who opens her passage." And we say to the Moon, "You are the one who enters her first and we are the ones who come after" (see Chap. 7).

Significantly, the Moon does not appear within the narrative itself. As in the flute myth, the Moon is eclipsed, making an appearance outside the main narrative in what appear to be parenthetical remarks. But the myth teller's or translator's mention of the Moon or his "giant penis" in connection with the flute plug is no mere afterthought, it seems to me, because, in implying the presence of a second, *adult* male, it directly contradicts the myths' radical insistence that the fire, or the flute, originally belonged to woman alone.

Looked at in terms of marriage and initiation ritual, this underlying antithesis of the myth's main premise becomes the hidden scenario, the secret that gives meaning to the whole complex of rites surrounding flutes. Through a succession of public and clandestine performances, as we will see, men arrange for the Moon or mythic father gradually to appear so that he is no longer outside the main action, concealed like the plug of pubic hair in a flute, disguised in a cluster of black insects, or reduced to the figure of the small boy "hiding in tall grass." According to my interpretation of the rites, the fathers of the brides and the grooms, and the Big Men and the initiates, personify the Moon and the small boy at different phases of the drama, bringing to life as separate characters, and as separate contents of woman's body, the primordial father and son. Participants in the ritual take on various mythic persona in order both to play out and to alter the mythic design.

### Flute Ritual in Marriage

Men instruct their wives to begin *kuta* several nights before the start of *apina* so that the brides, many of whom are the initiates' older sisters (as is the ideal), will emerge from seclusion and be sent off to the grooms while the initiates are still sequestered. The boys should not witness their sisters' departure, men explain, because their fathers have hidden flutes among the wedding pork to be carried in the bridal processions. The fathers of the brides disguise the flutes as containers of salt and hide them inside the brides' own net bags.

> It is the father who gives the salt. . . . He gives the "salt bamboo" to his daughter and she thinks it's just salt, but it's something else. It's her father's *nimi*. It's his bird, his *kamiba*. . . .
>
> We wrap the flutes in leaves of banana or pandanus and the bride doesn't know! We put them inside her very own net bag and she carries them to her husband thinking they are containers of salt! But her *anatu*, her husband's father, knows. "It's the *kamiba*," he says to himself and takes them out of her net bag and carries them into his men's house.[15]
>
> The father of the bride hears his flutes being played inside another house and thinks, "I've sent you my girl . . . and sent my flute with her."
>
> Hearing the new flute, women ask, "Whose *kamiba* is cry-

15. Women describe men's secret transfer to flutes in their own Bird of Paradise myth (see Chap. 6). The flutes men wrap in leaves and hide inside the bride's "very own net bag," so that she carries them unknowingly to the groom, are represented in women's myth by the (stiffened) corpse of the infant boy which the heroine *herself* "pulls out of the rafters," places in her net bag, and carries across many ridges to give to her "true husband."

ing?" And the groom replies, "My *naϑimu* [lit: *n*/my + *aϑimu*/taboo; i.e., father-in-law] sent it to me with my wife. He sent his girl and his bird here together and gave them to me. That is the new *kamiba* that cries."

Having recounted the flute myth inside the men's house to the secluded boys, men then enact the central episode in the yard outside, casting the boys' sisters in the role of the first woman. As a creature of men's myth, the first woman acts supremely alone or in concert with her sister. Personified by the bride, or a pair of brides, she becomes an unwitting go-between in men's secret performance. Her father hides his flutes inside her net bag (lit: *ko*), an overt symbol of her "womb" (lit: *hanu ko; [h]anu*/spirit child + *ko*), so that, when she arrives in her husband's compound, his father can remove them and take them into a new men's house. The men divest the bride of her phallic cargo and reveal it to a new generation of "small boys."

Deeds mythic woman performs by herself are carried out in marriage ritual by men acting through the bride. The myth states that woman invented the flute alone and made the plug by pulling out her pubic hair, implying that the flute sprang from her like hair, or like a child she produced endogenously without a man. Interpreted in light of ritual, the flute appears instead as something she got from her father, something *he* lodged at the head of her bed, under her bark-string skirts, inside her net bag, etc. In the secret terms of marriage ritual, men's myth does not proclaim the original omnipotence of women but, in accordance with women's own wish to forget, conceals a fantasied incest with the father (see Jones 1925).

Some weeks before the start of the festival, fathers of the brides of one clan request that the mothers' brothers, or a married man who is an expert, tattoo "beards" on the brides.[16] According to men's remarks, the tattoos are a kind of retaliation for the first woman's silent revenge upon the boy who stole her flute. She left him with a "new vagina"—for which men now give her a "beard."

> Men had no beards before they played flutes. . . . The boy put
> his mouth on woman's vagina, and blew, and whiskers appeared.
> That made men's stomachs hot [because] women have no
> beards. So men tattoo them.

The tattooist escorts a clan's two or three brides-to-be to a spot at the edge

---

16. If the tattooist is not himself a classificatory mother's brother, then the mother's brother attends the tattooing and is compensated separately to make sure the tattoos heal properly. As one man explained: "If the *anati* doesn't see the girl and another man cuts her, the *anati* will be angry and her face will become infected. But if the *anati* sees her and holds her [while the tattooist works] all will go well."

of the settlement amid "tall" *imperata* grass, a place like the one where the boy listened in hiding to his sisters' flutes. The young women are tattooed in turn. Each lies on her side while the expert kneels over her and covers her face from temple to chin with a *nini*-like mixture of pig fat and charcoal (see Chap. 5). Using a broken razor blade or the traditional obsidian flake, he cuts parallel lines or chevrons into the girl's blackened cheek. His wife or other female assistant pinches each of the long cuts into a ridge, a section at a time, and he makes tiny, closely spaced incisions across it, rubbing in the surrounding sooty mixture as he works. The tattooist continues this procedure until he has cross-hatched all the long cuts and rubbed blackening into the bleeding crevices. The bride turns over and he repeats the tattoos on the other side of her face.

At about the time a man commissions his daughter's tattoos, he goes into the forest to cut lengths of *kore riϑi* or "wild bamboo" to make a new set of flutes for his son-in-law. The new flutes are called *kamibabosu anu*. They are the "unborn" or "spirit-child" (lit: *kamiba*/flute + *bo*/the + *su*/poss. + *anu*/spirit-child or fetus) of his own instruments, the *he-ano*, or grandmother (lit: *he*/spirit + *ano*/mother) flutes which he stores in the rafters of his own men's house. *kamibabosu anu* have the same name and same "cry" as their *he-ano*. "The father of the bride says to the groom, 'The mother of the *kamiba* stays with me but I give you her child to cry inside your house.'"

> The father of the bride makes new flutes and sends them to his son-in-law as the child of his own. He sends his child with the child of his flute. . . . "The mother stays here," he says to the groom, "but I send away her child and give her to you."

A man identifies the new flutes with his daughter not only by referring to them as the "child" of the "mother" he still plays and possesses but also by matching their "mouths." The markings he etches around the flutes' blowing holes are the same design as the tattoos on his daughter's face (see fig. 14). As one ritual expert commented about the decorations on a wedding flute:

> When we cut [i.e., send] a girl away in marriage, whether to a distant place or nearby, we cut [i.e., decorate] the *kamiba* in the same way [indicating an imaginary instrument because I am a woman and cannot be shown an actual one]. . . . We decorate the woman and the *kamiba* together.

Some flute patterns are called *kabagena* or "insect-thing" (lit: *kaba*/insect + *ge*/? + *na*/thing) because they render the trails left by insects feeding on the underside of shedding bark or bamboo. The markings also represent the

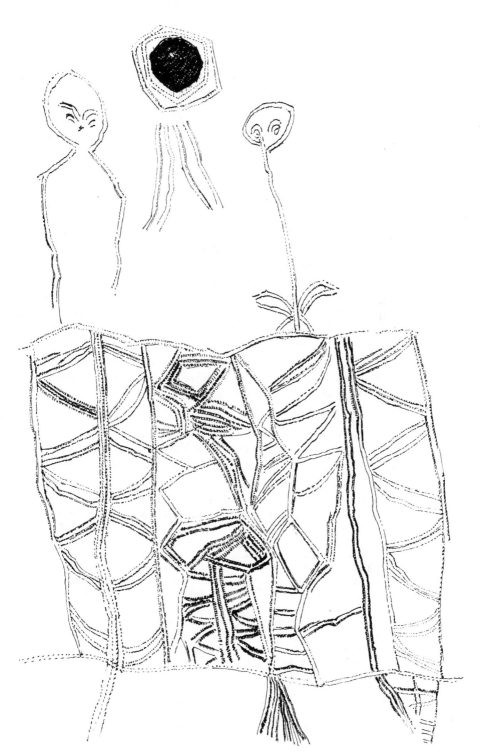

Figure 14. Incised decorations on a flute. A flattened view of the markings on a tubular flute. The black circle at the top represents the blowing hole.

mythic plug of pubic hair: a moving cluster of black insects, some men suggest, resembles a mass of woman's pubic hair. The insects' trails, which testify to their marauding appetite, also recall the relentless hunger of a newborn child whose head is covered in hair. Other flute patterns are derived from chevron-shaped folds in the casque of a New Guinea Hornbill (*Rhyticeros plicatus*). The bird's gigantic "nose" is like a penis, men remark, and serves as a mouth as well. As a ritual artifact, or pair of artifacts, the flutes display information contrary both to myth and to what Big Men announce when they reveal the instruments to initiates for the first time. The designs incised around the blowing holes show that the flutes are neither devoid of insects, nor "empty," and thus imply that the thing "hidden inside the mouth of the bamboo" is made of more than woman's pubic hair.[17]

The *kamiba* a man gives to his son-in-law consists not only of the instruments themselves, lengths of bamboo that will someday rot and have to be remade, but also of the right to play his own named "cry," a distinctive combination of sounds and contrapuntal rhythms. The gift of flute and flute "cry"—which the groom will not actually use for years (see above, this chap.)—represents the gift both of a man's daughter and of the right to "play" her his way, the right to share his unique relation with her. "A man blowing into a flute," men reveal, "is like going into a woman." And the sounds that come out are the "cries of his child":

> A man's wind is his penis. . . . We saw woman's vagina and
> made a hole in the bamboo and added marks like pubic hair.
> Blowing into the mouth [of the flute with one's hand covering
> the end] is like penetration and [releasing the hand and] letting

17. Insects etched around the mouth of the flute may symbolize not only female pubic hair but also the hair surrounding a man's anus, an association already suggested by Big Men's telling boys during *apina* that flute food, which traditionally consists of the Big Men's own blood, is "the *kamiba*'s feces" (see above, this chap.). The giant "insects" that precede the flute players into the men's house are covered in thick feces-like mud. "There is a common association between hair and feces and . . . head hair is used as a symbol for libidinous aggressive drives of all kinds" (Leach citing Berg 1967:81). Seen in these terms, the monster insects who crawl over the boys legs at the moment the flutes are revealed symbolize the flutes' fecal contents come terrifyingly to life.

The equation, hair = feces = flute plug, also proposes that men attempt to replace "women's natural procreativity." "The plugging up of the anus by the Chaga has been interpreted as being a male attempt to imitate female pregnancy" (Dundes 1976:230). A similar meaning seems to be contained in the Jale expression "to initiate a boy" whose root "may be translated with the verbs 'to build' [a house], to 'make' [a garden] or 'to defecate'" (Koch 1974a:402). Gimi men seem to equate a man's hairy orifices—anus, mouth, and fontanel—with the flute's blowing hole and with the vagina. In each case, the phallic content of the hole is both denied and alluded to in the symbolism of *surrounding* hair: insects for the anus, marsupials for the mouth, and Birds of Paradise (plumages) for the fontanel.

out the sound is like pushing the child out of the mother's vagina. That's why [demonstrating on an imaginary instrument] the blowing hole is small and the crying hole is big: one is the vagina for having sex, and the other is the vagina for bearing the child.[18]

Symbolized as flute playing, the male role in coitus is to insert and "blow out" a child. When men describe conception and parturition in literal terms, we may recall, they say that a man installs the child in a woman's belly and, after a period of sexual abstinence, "returns to the mother to finish the child" and induce the birth (see Chaps. 4 and 7). The final penetration "wakes the child" so it does not stay "asleep and die inside the mother," and the infusion of semen "closes the first mouth," sealing over the fontanel through which the fetus ate during the long months of gestation. When men discuss the symbolism of flute playing or the process of actual conception and birth, they speak of installing a child and inducing birth as the work of *one* man, of one who withdraws his wind, or penis, for a certain interval and then "returns to the mother." But in the secret exchange of flutes during *kuta,* men *perform* the male procreative role as a joint venture, as if it were achieved in the transactions between the fathers of the brides and the grooms.[19]

### The Father of the Groom Feeds the Bride Her Father's Meat

Before the father of the bride wraps his flutes in leaves and hides them inside the bride's net bag, he stuffs them with salted chunks of cooked marsupial or young pig, animals informants describe in this context as "covered with hair." Just like the mythic flute, the flutes a man sends to his son-in-law (in care of his father) are "plugged with hair" and unplayable. He sends his son with secret instructions on how to unload them:

> When the wedding pigs are killed, the father of the bride gets two good bamboos. He etches tattoos [around the sites of the blowing holes] and fills them with meat and taros and yams. He

18. "The *nama* flutes are made of a single piece of bamboo approximately two feet six inches long and four to five inches in diameter with a hole three to four inches from one end [*sic*]. When they are played, the open end near the mouthpiece is closed with a handful of mud (see n.17, this chap.). The flute is then held in the left hand with the mouthpiece against the player's lips while the palm of his right hand is used to produce the tune by alternately opening and closing the farther end. Flutes are always played in pairs, which are referred to as age-mates" (Read 1952:5). For a more technical description of these "tubular aerophones" and the sounds they make, see Moyle (1972:813) and Gourlay (1975).

19. In presuming the ideal of sister exchange, Gimi discussions of marriage—and my rendering of them—take for granted that every father of the bride is also father of a groom, so that the bride's father and the groom have a symbolic father-son tie.

doesn't tell his daughter! He tells his son and his son tells the groom:

> "When my daughter wants to eat the meat I've put into her net bag, don't let her break open the bamboos! *You yourself* take out the meat and feed it to her. Then take the flutes into the men's house. The things I filled with meat are the *kamiba* I give to you."

The father of the groom [acting for the groom] takes the meat out of the bamboos and gives it back to the bride to eat. Then he takes the bamboos into his men's house and cuts open the blowing holes. . . .

To play the flute and gain access to his bride, a man has to unplug the flute according to instruction. He, or his father acting in his stead, removes his father-in-law's meat through the end of the bamboo and "gives it back" to the bride, placing each piece directly into her mouth in the same way an *ahamo* feeds an adolescent boy who has just seen the flute for the first time, or the way a Big Man feeds marsupial meat to a married male initiate (see above, this chap.). Like a boy during *apina,* the bride closes her eyes while she eats the flute food. Then the groom's father, acting again as the groom's surrogate, opens the blowing hole by cutting out the bamboo inside the rings of "pubic hair" the bride's father incised.

The whole operation has to be kept secret from the bride. If she finds out her father's "tricks," if she realizes he disguised his flute as a container of salt, hid it inside her net bag, and sent secret instructions to the groom, or his father, via her brother, she will smash the flute and ruin men's collaboration.

> When the father stuffs the meat into the bamboo it's as if he puts a child in his daughter's belly. If she breaks open the bamboo [opens it, that is, in the way Gimi ordinarily open bamboo tubes after cooking], it would be like her killing the Moon. So her husband [or his father] has to take out the meat himself and give it back to her. It's the same as his opening her hole and removing her [child's] head. Afterward a *kisa arak,* a "true child," will be born.
>
> Then he carries the *kamiba* into the men's house and cuts out the blowing hole. . . . When he plays the flute for the first time it's as if he puts his own *hato,* his own semen, into his wife. He takes out her father's meat and feeds her himself.

The father of the bride always gives two flutes, the same informant added, because one is the *kore arak,* the firstborn child "killed by the Moon" (*kore*/ancestor, ghost or wild + *arak*/child); and the other is the *ðusa arak* (*ðusa*/cultivated or domestic), the "true child" of the husband's semen. But according to his instructions on emptying the flutes, the groom (through his father's surrogacy) has to *replace* one kind of child with the other. He has to remove the "head" of the firstborn by "[putting] his own *hato*, his own semen, into his wife." That *dis*placement of the bride's father, however, is partial: when the groom unplugs his father-in-law's flute, when he pulls out the "child" or "head" the older man installed, he gives it "back" to the bride in a single gesture, placing her father's meat directly into her mouth. The groom (or his father acting for him) transfers the "child" from one "vagina," the flute's crying hole, into another, the bride's newly tattooed mouth, filling the bride in the very act of emptying her father's flute. Once he has carried out these secret instructions, once he has emptied the flute by feeding the bride, the groom can feed her himself.[20] As author of these procedures, the father of the bride reveals his presence to the groom and offers to share with him the procreative role.

If the bride were to break open the flute and feed herself the contents, men insist, their whole project would be ruined. If her hands even touched her father's meat, she would forever "kill (or be killed by) the Moon." All her children would be *kore arak*, and she would never bear a "true child." If men allowed the bride to open the disguised flute like an ordinary cooking vessel, if they failed to prevent her from *doing the expected thing*, she would keep the fantasy of her father as her husband. By opening and emptying the flute herself, she would deprive her living husband of his role, prevent him from "removing her father's meat" through a second exit of his own making. If she stopped her husband from taking-out-and-putting-back the *kore arak* her father installed, it would remain "dead meat" and she would get no second mouth, no new vagina through which to deliver *kisa arak*. She would have only a first mouth plugged by the Moon: when she tried to eat again—to copulate with her husband—her body would shatter like a bamboo container and leak the Moon's dirty "water" (see Chap. 6). By using intermediaries and keeping their transaction secret, first and second "husbands" arrange to bypass the bride and reproduce life on their own (see n.20 above).

20. Women's Bird of Paradise myth seems to parallel and give an alternative rendering of virtually every detail of men's secret transfer of flutes (see n.15, this chap.). Here, for example, the requirement that the groom (or his father) empty the flute by removing the "head"—or dead meat—of the bride's father and then "feed it back" to the bride before he can deposit "his own semen" and make his flute "cry," etc., is paralleled in women's myth by the true husband hollowing out the tree, depositing the boy murdered by the father of the bride, and then adding his own "decorations" (lit: *autaisana*/leavings). In the *nenekaina*, tellingly, it is the bride herself who takes the dead baby out of her house, carries it to her husband, and eventually "releases all the birds" (Chap. 6).

If the fathers of bride and groom, and the bride's brother and the groom, fail to keep the secret, if they allow the bride to do what comes naturally and smash open the bamboo, their ritual performance will have failed to alter the course of her prehistory, failed to interrupt the fantasy of her first marriage. A woman who opens the flute by herself still possesses it. She remains inside the myth and can carry out her mythic vengeance against her first husband by cutting off his enormous length, murdering his child, etc. A bride who is allowed to have her way and keep the flute would defeat the men, according to the logic of men's rites. She would foil their theft and retain her mythic independence, avoiding marriage and escaping into the forest like the Torrent Lark (see Chap. 3). But according to women's myths, the bride who opens the flute would *not* automatically devour the contents. With the help of a true husband, she would release all the birds and bring the Moon's child to life (see Chap. 6).

### *"Eating the Head" after* apina

Some two or three days after the exchange of brides, and five or six days after the confinement of male initiates, *apina* concludes with the boys' dramatic emergence from the several men's houses. The night before the emergence is uncharacteristically quiet. Flutes sound only intermittantly, and there are no *harukaru*. Men enumerate the complex food taboos and other restrictions designed to ensure the delicate course of the boys' growth, protecting them both from contamination by women and female foods like marsupials, red pandanus, wild mushrooms, frogs, ground-burrowing insects, etc., and from overstimulation by hypermasculine items like the best sugarcanes and bananas, white pandanus nuts and arboreal birds (see Gillison 1980).

By early morning, men have assembled outside the men's houses to lay out the pork they will distribute after the boys' emergence. Flat, boned carcasses (representing about sixty-five pigs) are placed on banana leaves and laid out in the hot sun in two long parallel rows (see Read 1952:17). Men cut some pigs into smaller sections and quietly chant increase spells to ensure there will be plenty to eat. Their wives fan flies off the meat and shew away scavenging dogs. The initiates' mothers and fathers assemble bags of marsupial fur and plumages, stuff bamboo tubes with cooked pork and fat, and tie bundles of fat and shredded bark for making string, preparing the gifts to "buy their sons' heads" when they emerge from seclusion.

Inside the men's houses, the *ahamo* decorate themselves and their charges in red, covering their bodies with a mixture of pig fat and deep red pandanus oil and tying on stunning headdresses of red Pesquet's Parrot feathers and cuscus fur like those worn by the brides. Even after the boys are decorated, they receive "flute names" from their mothers' brothers. "The *anati* goes inside the house of his taboo [his *atu*] to deliver the child of his *kamiba*." On the eve of internment, the *anati* cut new flutes of wild bamboo and tested them in the forest where real birds could hear their first notes. Echoing the words of the brides' fathers, as men afterward explain, "the *anati* says to the boy, 'To the child of my sister, I give the name of my bird. . . . I give him the flute and say: "I give the child to you. The mother of the flute stays with me but I give you her *anu*, her spirit-child, to cry inside your house."'"

Around noon, with visitors from many villages crowded into the first compound, the boys' *anatiraha*, soot-blackened and fully dressed as warriors, burst out of the men's house. They run to the other men's houses, brandishing bows and arrows, and soon return carrying dazed, pandanus-reddened initiates on their shoulders. They disappear with the boys into the first house and, amid thundrous war cries and dances, run outside again with the whole batch of "bloodied" initiates hoisted on their backs.[21] Seeing their exhausted, disoriented sons bobbing limply above the warriors' heads, the women weep. The men run in a line around the display of pork and then reenter the men's house through the opposite door, traversing the interior central corridor before they emerge again from the original door. After eight or ten circuits of the men's house, each of which is "like the passage of a man's wind through a flute," the *anati* gently set down their charges, placing each boy beside the pile of valuables set out by his father to buy his head. The bearer is immediately handed a small package of fat and string. "The *anati* [or *ahamo*] watches out for the boy during *apina* because he wants to eat his head afterward. He wants to eat the pig he will get for showing this boy his flute and bringing him out alive!"

As soon as these head payments are made, the larger distribution of pork to other villages begins. Each village or foreign clan is called by name and, as a few representatives amble slowly through the crowd, slabs of pork or whole trussed pigs, "the most important and valuable item in the contribution" (Read 1952:19), are ostentatiously piled up for their inspection. The amount allotted depends on the number and nature of ties between host and guest. The principal recipients are traditional allies, often the same villages and clans who supply wives and initiate the youths. To the very end, the women sit beside the pigs they reared, now piled slabs of meat. Even after the piles have been carried off, the women remain, smoking idly while dogs lap up pools of fat that have collected in the leaves where the carcasses lay.

Several days after the departure of the last festival guests, Big Men escort initiates and their *ahamo* to a small hut near a stream or river. The youths are made to wash their hands repeatedly and to clean their fingernails with sticks

---

21. Initiates may be brought out of seclusion in an alternate running formation with the boys holding the hands of their *ahamo*: initiate—*ahamo*—initiate—*ahamo*, etc.

specially sharpened by the Big Men to get rid of resistant particles of "mother's food." The Big Men induce vomiting with cane in themselves, as a kind of demonstration, and then in the boys. "We vomit our mothers' milk and the sweet potato they fed us so we can grow up to take the places of our fathers," men explain, paraphrasing the motives they apply to the initiates (see Read 1952:13–15). For older boys, an almost identical rite is performed to induce bleeding from the nose that will remove "mother's [or sister's] blood" (see Chap. 6).

At *apina,* men say, a man sends his affines his son's head and "returns the *kamiba.*" The head payment the initiate's father presents to the *anati* or *ahamo* at the end of *apina* is in return for the flute he received when he married:

> When a man wants to show his son the *kamiba,* he calls for the *kamiba* of his father and of his wife's father. He shows the two flutes and kills a pig. That pig is the same as his son's head. He kills the pig so that the *auna* of the *kamiba* the *anati* shows the boy will eat the *auna* of the meat and cry. The orphaned pigs and the new initiates hear the cries of the *kamiba* and grow quickly. . . .
>
> When a man wants to show his son the *kamiba* he has to give the boy's head to his *anati.* If he doesn't, the *anati's* flute will not cry and the boy will not grow!

When a man initiates his son, some dozen or more years after he marries, he "sends back the head" he received inside his father-in-law's flute. "Returning the head" at *apina,* men say, allows the boy to "come out alive" and be born a man. The father's "gift of the head" fills the *anati's* flute: "The *auna* of the [*anati's*] flute eats the *auna* of the [father's] meat and cries." The contents of the *anati's* flute, including the "flute food" placed in the boy's mouth during *apina,* are derived in part, in this sense, from the boy's own father. The father uses the mother's brother—or his flute—as conduit to transfer his own substance into his son. And by diluting the *anati's* head, the father also tempers the *anati's* rage at losing or feeding it to the initiate, thus mitigating his desire to "take back the child." The father "finishes" his son, in this sense, by replacing the head the boy stole from his original father during

(*Top*) After nearly a week in seclusion, exhausted initiates emerge from the men's house on the shoulders of their mothers' brothers. The boys wear headdresses of marsupial fur and red Pesquet parrot feathers similar to those worn by the brides. Their bodies are covered in a bright red oil made from pandanus nuts and pig fat.

(*Bottom*) After being carried out of the men's house and paraded through the settlement, each initiate is set down by his mother's brother before a pile of cooked pork and other valuables set out by his father to "buy his head."

mythic gestation, appeasing the hunger that would otherwise make the *anati* hold him inside the flute so "the flute would not cry and the boy would not grow!"

Gimi men and women equate the impetus for exchange with the life-and-death power maternal kinsmen wield over their sisters' children. The debt of the *ababana* is virtually perpetual because the anger of the *anatiraha* is unabated, fixed, collective. A man "returns his son's head" at *apina* and on other occasions, Gimi say again and again, to ward off the "curse" of the *anati*. Interpreted in terms of the secret usages surrounding flutes, these routine statements imply that, unless the *anati* is appeased, he will succeed retroactively to his father's mythic role, taking the initiate's mother as his wife and withdrawing the boy, holding him in the grips of an incestuous myth so he cannot grow and become a man. The recurrent image of the *anati*'s plugged and silent flute evokes his complete wedding to the mother and "holding" of the initiate, as the *kore* "holds the unborn" during a difficult labor, symbolizing the inertia of so much rage and desire. To open the flute, the boy's father inserts a new head: he feeds the *anati,* or his flute, and appeases him so he will let go of the boy. The father's head payment at the end of *apina* forestalls the *anati*'s curse and keeps the boy in good health, in these terms, by repeating the first extraction of his head from the marriage flute, reinstating the divorce of the mythic parents and again rescuing their child.

### The Final Stage of Male Initiation

Before a man celebrates *apina* for his eldest son, he undergoes the final, ultrasecret stage of his own initiation.[22] His father-in-law and other senior male affines escort him to a clearing in the forest where they hastily construct a *kamiϑama,* a "menstrual hut" or "flute house," of palm fronds and banana leaves. Inside the hut, an elder makes a tourniquet of peeled banana stems and lets blood from the initiate's arm, shooting a vein inside his elbow with a miniature bow and obsidian-tipped arrow. The blood spurts onto a bed of edible greens that the men have set out on a banana leaf. When the greens are well splattered with blood, one of the elders folds the leaf and hangs it in a sling over a slow-burning fire. The men go out of the hut, leaving the initiate alone while his blood simmers, and decorate their heads and bodies with leafy bamboo vines. They return in a happy procession, two of them blowing the "mother of the flutes," a bigger, deeper-sounding instrument made from the base section of a variety of large bamboo and played only on this occasion (see Salisbury 1965:60).

---

22. This initiation rite was described to me by David Gillison who was shown it by men who hoped that divulging their own secrets would persuade him to be more revealing about the true source of cargo (see Chap. 7).

After some fanfare, the men lay these most sacred flutes in the initiate's lap and threaten to kill him if he reveals the secret they are about to reveal to him. Then they wrap the mother flutes in leaves, load them into net bags, and sit down to eat the greens cooked in the initiate's blood. One of the elders places some of the food directly into the initiate's mouth, exactly as an *ahamo* feeds an adolescent initiate the *"kamiba's* feces," a piece of salted pork or of a Big Man's cooked arm blood; or as the groom places his father-in-law's "flute food" into the bride's mouth; or as a menstruating woman eats without ever letting her hands touch the food (see above, this chap.; and Chap. 6). As the men finish their meal, they become ebullient and make their way back to the compounds laughing and singing.

The secret name of the mother flute is *kuma*, a kind of lizard that lays its eggs inside wild bamboo and, as men point out, eats the *sese* insects that also nest there and feed off the bamboo's moist inner walls. Consuming a meal of his own blood inside a "menstrual hut" or "flute house," the initiate ingests yet another kind of "flute food," another rendition of the edible "plug" in his mother's vagina. Like the lowly *sese*, he is interned inside his house or "mother" and eats her *from within*. The initiate/fetus "eats the head" of the father's penis and is then himself devoured by the father, as it were, when his elders consume his arm blood. Considered as intrauterine drama, the men's communal meal carries out the Moon's reabsorption of the firstborn and inverts the symbolism of the wedding flutes. As the initiators once bestowed their daughter in the shape of their penis, as a son, with a "beard," etc., they now take back the groom as their menstruating bride, eating his blood as symbol of her maidenhead and the head of her firstborn child.

If my analysis is correct, it raises the question of why men enact a fantasy of intrauterine cannibalism, autocannibalism, and homosexuality as the ultimate achievement of manhood. Why do men celebrate the sterility of the marriage they collaborated to create after its success is already established?

Men conduct the marriage transaction, I have argued, as if the father of the bride were making a series of *visual* revelations to the groom; as if, through his gift of flutes, in the way he decorates and fills them and instructs the groom to empty them, etc., he were trying to correct a false impression created by the flute myth. As the sender of flutes, the bride's father assumes the role of the Moon or "first husband," revealing himself as the myth's missing person: he shows the groom, as if he were the boy who tried to play the flute, at first, without removing the plug, that the plug consists of something more than his sister's pubic hair. The purpose of marriage, in this sense, is to make the groom aware of the real contents of woman's body and to transform his mythic identity; to convert him from a thief and recidivist in incest, a small boy hiding in tall grass, etc., to a second husband capable of participating in an exchange with the first. The difficulty of the transition is indicated by the fact that the groom is nowhere to be seen at his own wedding and hardly participates in the transactions that bring him a wife.

A man cannot present *ba ϑa ϑa* nor make a head payment until he understands what they are. And he cannot simply be told what they are because the real contents of the flute—what really happens inside his mother's body—is unspeakable. Over the course of his various initiations, his matrilateral kinsmen and, later, his affines *show*—and *feed*—him the secret through the rites surrounding the sacred flutes. The blueprint for marriage and exchange lies, in this sense, in men's ritual visualizations of fantasies of prenatal life (see Chap. 7). In the final stage of male initiation, the flute plug or head of the unborn child appears in a kind of ultimate version. To understand the meaning of the *kuma* rite, and to decipher the marriage rules, we have to review what men have already divulged about the flute plug during *apina* and *kuta*.

## Unspoken Lessons of Male Initiation and Marriage

There is great emphasis, throughout both male initiation and marriage, upon the flutes' contents and understanding the true nature of the mythic plug. Men recreate the plug in various forms: as salted pork or arm blood fed to first-stage initiates, as decorations around the flute's blowing hole, as tattoos around the bride's mouth, and as the original head payment—the "hair covered" meat stuffed into the marriage flutes and later "returned" at the end of *apina*. In the sense that *apina* and *kuta* are masterminded by an absent father, or pair of fathers, or by men who act mainly behind the scenes, the many recreations of the plug are like attempts by the mythic father to show the son, and later the groom who bears the son's "same name," that the mother's vagina is not empty, nor stuffed with pubic hair as he is first told, but rather filled with "the head of a child" placed there by the father himself.

One of the ways a man "puts a child in his daughter's belly" is by having her face tattooed: the bride's "beard" shows that her father fed her, or filled her mouth, in the same way he plugged her flute. The father sends instructions to the groom to unplug the flute by feeding the bride in a certain way, taking food from the end of the flute and placing it directly into the bride's mouth—while her eyes are closed. The father's instructions on mouth-to-mouth feeding recall the prenatal scene, when the father nourishes his child before its eyes are opened by sending food from the head of his penis directly into the child's hair-surrounded "first mouth" (see Chap. 7). When a man gives his daughter and his flute to a son-in-law, in these terms, he transfers the in utero history of their relation, sending off his penis while it still feeds her, while it still fills her "first mouth" and gives shape to her whole body (see Fenichel 1954). He creates the flute in the image of their prenatal marriage: his penis is enormous—as big as her whole body—because she is still in the womb. She is still combined with him, locked in his "hot embrace," still being fed through the head.

By having his daughter tattooed, a man at once gives her his child and turns her into a son—a child with a "beard." Because the bride is not a boy, however, the marriage to her father is sterile: his child gets stuck in the birth canal, turns to blood and closes her playing hole (see n.17, this chap.). To unplug her, and stop the hemorrhage, he finds a boy like his son, one with the "same name," and teaches him how to play her, how to "waken," "finish," and "blow out" the child he installed. Interpreted in this way, marriage replaces a sterile "homosexual" union between a man and his daughter with a fertile one between the man and his daughter's husband, who stands in the mythic relation of his own son.

The dramatic steps men take during *kuta* to hide the flute from the bride and to prevent her angry outburst thus seem to conceal a deeper threat to their enterprise based upon men's own wishes. Men's failure to stop the bride from having her way symbolizes their inability to reproduce the flute plug in *removable* form—to pull it out of one "vagina" and put it back inside another—thus splitting their territory, separating first and second husbands, distinguishing the orifices, and identities, of father and husband so they are no longer one and the same; so the "small boy" is no longer "the same as the Moon" (see above, this chap.). If the bride smashes the flute, in this sense, it means her father and husband remained stuck together inside her, locked in head-to-head combat over which one inhabits and possesses her. The more hidden meaning of the bride's "menstruating forever" may be that her father and husband would remain in a deadly marriage of their own, fused like the primordial father and son.

The myths and rites associated with men's sacred bamboo flutes suggest that men's ritual life, and indeed the whole structure of Gimi exchange, are based upon attempts to resolve the symbolic incest and homosexuality implicit in fatherhood, to undo the phallic interchange that unites a man with his children, making *both* sons and daughters his clone-like offshoots. The method of siring a child and the object of exchange are alike to recapitulate the fantasy of ejaculation in such a way that a man is *not alone* inside his wife and thus need not reingest his own substance, need not "eat the head" of his own child. By sending the bride in duplicate, pairing her not just with another bride but also, secretly, with a pair of flutes, and endowing her thereby with *two* "vaginas," Gimi elders arrange to divide the moment of auto-devouring and autoexchange, so to undo the incestuous fusion of father and child.

In order to "finish the child"—both on the eve of actual delivery and at the climax of ritual—men "return the head" to the father and thus reverse the fantasy of reabsorbing ejaculate or pulling back the child's head. When the bride arrives, the groom, or his father acting in his stead, removes her father's meat from the end of the flute and feeds it to her, taking the head out of one "vagina," the flute's crying hole, and immediately "putting it back" inside another, the bride's tattooed mouth. By this gesture, he returns the father's head, performing the reabsorption of semen during coitus as the *simulation* of return. The method of dislodging the bride's father, of supplanting the initial filler of her flute and acquiring her child, is for a man who is not the son, but who has his "same name," to *seem* to return the father's head by inserting it into a mouth that looks like the father's mouth, because it is bearded, but is really a duplicate, merely a recreation of the one he still possesses. The enterprise is risky and has to be carried out in secret—and usually through the surrogacy of the grooms' fathers—because simulating perfect identity between the groom and the bride's brother, and between the mouths of the bride and her father, evokes a corresponding identity between act and myth, thus tending to reinforce the fantasy rather than overturn it.

After the flutes have been exchanged and reciprocally unplugged by extracting the meat, the grooms' fathers play a duet that empties them again, repeating through their music the whole dramatic sequence of substituting their "heads." An unplayed instrument is not merely silent, according to myth, it is plugged with woman's pubic hair, filled by a hidden father, etc. When the player inhales before blowing into his instrument, he repeats the boy's first attempt to play. He pulls back his wind and, in the mythic manner, eats his father's head. When he releases his breath to fill the hollow chamber, he sends back the head and pushes out "cries" from a second hole, reviving his father in his child. With the next inhalation and during rests, in the soundless gaps that give each named tune its distinctive cadence and rhythm, the flute player replugs the blowing hole and "kills the child," silencing the cries he just blew into the world. But the whole performance is a simulation: the flautist does not reabsorb his own father's head—nor kill his own child—because (unlike primordial woman) he does not play alone. The wind he revokes by inhaling, the "child" or "cries" he withdraws into his mouth, resemble those he released in his last breath but come from the mouth of another man, a man with the "same name."[23] The child inside his flute cries the same tune but has a different father.

When initiated affines play the music of coitus together, they make the mythic conception of the firstborn reversible, undoable, and without cata-

---

23. A pair of flute players, called "age-mates" like the flutes, have normally exchanged sisters or daughters.

strophic end. By reproducing the first time in the flutes' sounds and contra-puntal rhythms, they split the moment of climax, divide the going in and coming out into parts for two men to play. In terms of the myth that flute playing echoes, the unspoken motive for the exchange of head payments is to get possession of the other man's child and keep it out of woman, to en-liven her dead contents so they fly away and never reenter her same hole. Begetting a child in the ritual sense is always an act of rescue, a project of "finishing" what another man began and left behind unawares. Each man brings to life what the other lost the first time he ventured into a woman. Yet retrieving another man's child is also a voyage of return: the only method of "finishing the child," men say, is to "go back into the mother" and release it from the Moon's "hot embrace." When a man returns to his wife to induce the birth, he encounters a man like his father and makes him a final offer of his penis or wind. To bring out the child, or make a flute cry, a man also has to save his own life by placating the old man's jealous rage and homosexual desire.

In the way men concoct the ritual plug, in the way they decorate flutes and brides, they reveal that a wife has a man hidden in her mouth, a penis amid her pubic hair, and that he, too, devours the child. Every time they feed an initiate flute food, they perform the motive for this paternal cannibalism. When an *ahamo* feeds his adolescent charge the *"kamiba's* feces," the salty arm blood of Big Men, during *apina;* when the groom pulls salted "hair-covered" meat out of his father-in-law's flute and puts it back in the bride's mouth during *kuta;* when a married man takes a bite of marsupial meat from a Big Man's armpit during *humi anu ameE;* when, several years later, he eats his own cooked arm blood during *kuma;* and when a female initiate eats food between tongs during *haro;* each one "eats the head" of the primordial father and incites him to devour the child in revenge. Placing pieces of salted meat, or salty blood, or food that might be tainted with blood, directly into the mouths of brides and initiates enacts the *first* intrauterine transfer of food, the first passing back-and-forth of nourishment from head to head or urethra to fontanel (see Chap. 7). The feeding of initiates in rite after rite opens the myth to show the father's role in creating the flute, in depositing the hairy head of his child and closing the vagina to other men.

Viewed in this light, the flute myth conceals the real reason the boy got a beard when he stole his sister's flute. Having heard the haunting music, he hid in the tall grass outside her door and tried to enter. He approached her vagina but, from his vantage point amid her pubic hair, could not see his father's penis. He was blind to the plug because it represented his own un-born self being fed through the head and combined with his father. His lips not only touched his sister's hair, they "ate the head" her hair concealed. His sister, too, ingested their father's head before she was born, acquired his identity and incited his rage. But at marriage, she loses the head and it passes to her brother. When a woman marries, her brother steals the flute and gives it to her husband: a man with her brother's same name plays her father's song, blows out his child and so ends the pregnancy that began before she was born, while she still incarnated the head of her father's penis and automatically devoured his infusions. The marriage rite ends the bride's congenital pregnancy and begins another by repeating the original feeding—the original transfer of the head or penis—through a new hole. By removing the flute food and then feeding it "back" to the bride, as men emphasize he must do, the groom (or his father) creates a second "vagina for bearing the child" (see above, this chap.). This latter-day feeding of the bride is also the first instance of a head payment; it represents the first attempt to placate the violated mythic father, to return the head the child stole from him and thus to forestall his retaliatory curse.

The rite sends a crucial piece of information to the groom. It shows him that the head of the child comes to him inside his bride and has to be returned *inside another bride,* sent back inside the same package in which it arrived. It thus explains why he cannot participate in his own marriage: he cannot send back the head because he has yet no daughter in whom to conceal it. To enter into marriage exchanges, according to the rules, he has to learn how to "finish the child" by delaying his return to the mother— pausing not merely for breath or the duration of a pregnancy—but for generations, providing a final head payment to placate the father by concealing it inside his daughter. This information governing the choice of a spouse for his son is fed to him gradually, over the course of his own initiations, through successive revelations of the flutes' contents. As an adolescent and young married man, he "eats the head of the child" in consecutive forms, coming to an understanding of its true nature with his own mouth. By eating the various flute foods his elders supply, he acquires a "head" from the father and is able to fill a flute of his own.

The final revelation to a married male initiate, the idea his elders make him "eat" before he can exchange the heads of his own children or find them spouses, is the consequence of *no* exchange, which is the consummation, in fantasy, of men's incest and homosexuality. When men intern the initiate in a "menstrual hut" and consume his arm blood, in my interpretation, they enact the myth of men's primordial relation, devouring him in the way the Moon withdrew his own fallen seed from a lake of menstrual blood, or as the *kuma* lizard feeds on *sese* insects inside her own nest. The *kuma* rite of blood eating plays out for the initiate what happened inside the first woman during the prehistoric coital era. In the darkness of the *kamiϑama,* his elders dramatize the mythic fusion of men's heads or penes, showing him how father and son combine inside the mother to keep her body filled and closed, so she cannot be exchanged. The unspoken message of a man's final initiation is that his marriage may fail, not just because his wife wants to stay married to a fantasy of her father, but also because the father is a greedy old man who tries to keep all his children as boy-brides and "eat their heads" forever.

In exchanging and playing flutes, and in feeding the contents to brides and initiates, Gimi men enact unspoken secrets of procreation as the premises of exchange. The transfer of brides, brideprice, and head payments undo the myth of the first time, rescue the child, avoid the calamity myth predicts, etc. But the exchanges also perserve the secret union of fathers and sons by seeming *not* to alter the myth. Though the rites are a sham—because the groom is not a son, nor is the father resident within the bride, nor is it possible to enact a myth—their efficacy depends upon the success of such illusions. When the groom, or his father, opens the bride's father's flute and pulls out the meat that represents the "head of his child," he alters the myth by making the father appear at the mouth of the flute. But the groom achieves this, and disidentifies himself from his mythic persona, by assuming that of another boy with the "same name." He separates his head from the head of his own father by unplugging another man's flute. Through the marriage transaction, father and son end their mythic homosexual attachment by giving it a new ritualized form, pulling themselves out of the same woman by duplicating her vagina, creating a second hole and second instrument as perfect replicas of the first.

### Ransoming the Space of a Lifetime

Interpreted in terms of myth and of secret rites involving flutes, the rules by which Gimi link transfers of head payments and brideprice are like a strategy of delay, a means to purchase the space of a lifetime by ransoming the child from prenatal attachments. The whole sequence of ritual payments seems designed to induce the *anatiraha,* as ritual counterparts of a hidden mythic father, to vacate the mother and release her child into the hands of living men. Like the capricious *kore,* maternal kinsmen have the power to curse their sisters' children, revoking the lives they unintentionally gave away. The *anati* is forever liable to reassert his mythic marriage to the mother and refuse a substitute for her child's head. But *anatiraha* are not merely "cursers" and child eaters. Like the *kore bana* or Moon or giant penis whose prerogatives they inherit, they also represent the original father and ultimate source of life. In order for a man to stay alive and produce descendants, he has both to sever maternal attachments and to retain them, a contradictory aim he achieves by trading-off his daughter's life against his own.

Exchanges of the head negotiate lifetimes of different durations for men and for women. When a girl marries, her *ababana* cease making head payments to her *anati* on her behalf and, unlike a boy, she herself does not continue to make the payments after marriage. But a man continues to give his head to his *anati* and, later in life, he gives his head to his *anati*'s son when he gives the son his daughter as a wife for *his* son, concealing it in the flute he sends with the bride (fig. 15). Rather than continue to ransom his daughter and keep her as a full member of his patrilineage, a man sends her back to his maternal kinsmen as a wife, as replacement for his FM and the repository of his own head. The rules of marriage and exchange allow him to refinance his own life, as it were, by sacrificing his daughter, using her body as the vehicle to convey his head a second time to his mother's brother's lineage, represented a generation later by his mother's brother's son. Marriages coincide with the first stage of male initiation, in this sense, not only to arrange the secret transfer of flutes from the brides to their younger brothers but also to enable the brides' fathers to purchase a second lease on life at their daughters' expense (fig. 16).

### Breaking Apart the Myth: Exchanges as Acts of Cancellation

When exchanges of brides, flutes, and head payments are interpreted in light of the secret rites that precede or accompany them, the objects seem to give material form to the unspoken content of men's myth and to condense the whole era in which woman presided by keeping secret her marriage to the Moon. The first woman plugged her flute to hide the Moon's child. When that child—a "small boy"—dared to remove the plug and leave her "house," she killed him and began to menstruate. Men transact flutes out of women's sight, in this sense, so they can "bring the boy out alive!" In marriage and first-stage male initiation, men reconstruct the myth of woman's body and exchange its hidden content as a way to defeat the first woman and avoid the death of her child.

The "feces" *ahamo* extract from the *kamiba* and feed to adolescent initiates, the meat the groom pulls out of the wedding flutes and feeds to the bride, the blood a married man's senior male affines let from inside his elbow, cook, and "feed back" to him, and even the food the *haro* initiate grasps between sticks (see above, this chap.; and Chap. 6), are all prototypes of a head payment. Each represents the flute plug as a removable—and therefore live—phallic object. When men transfer this payment or "plug" from one mouth to another, removing it from the mouth of a flute and placing it into the mouth of bride or initiate at the climax of a rite, they perform a secret version of marriage, opening mythic woman and liberating her contents,

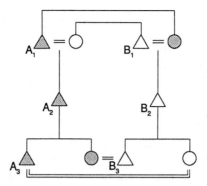

Figure 15. The "head" of a male is purchased twice, giving him a second lease on life at his daughter's expense. $A_1$ sends the "head" of $A_2$ to $B_1$ at *ϑau* and *apina*, etc. $A_2$ sends his own "head" to $B_1$ and $B_2$ inside the flute he gives with his daughter in marriage to $B_3$. All these arrangements are reciprocal in the sense that sister exchange is the ideal.

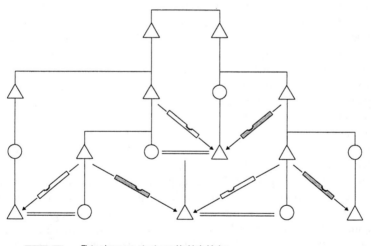

Flute a boy sees at *apina* and holds in his lap

Flute a man receives at *kuta* with his wife

Figure 16. Marriage and the movement of flutes.

breaking apart fatal combinations that in her—and in the flute myth—remain unseen.

If men's transfer of brides and head payments cancels the unity of myth and brings males into a world outside their mothers, it also shifts the blame for death onto the liberators. Once men reconstruct the myth in ritual objects—once they reveal the phallic nature of the plug—they name the father (see Mitchell citing Lacan 1974b:393–95). In men's myth, woman creates and plugs the flute alone. But in the marriage rite, the flute is shaped and filled by the father of the bride. To make it cry, to remove the child the father installed and bring it to life, the groom or his lineage have to provide ransom in the form of head payments. The payments declare the father's guilt in the sense that their purpose lies in arresting his secret marriage to the bride, enabling the donors to replace him or his son in the act of installing or stealing her flute. To refuse or return a head payment, in these terms, is to assert the underlying premise of the myth rather than its surface evasion, as if the bride's father were to refuse to renounce her as a wife, refuse to give up his right, and the right of his son, to take back—and, in that sense, devour—the child he put inside her. When informants insist that head payments are not returnable, or that the return of the head would automatically "curse the child," according to this interpretation, they mean that reciprocity would cancel the cancellation of the mother's brother's rights and establish the unstated mythic reality in which he assumes the role of cannibal father.

Interpreting Gimi exchanges as acts of cancellation, as creating new ties by undoing others that exist as unspoken fantasies, displacing maternal attachments by revealing the hidden father, etc., does not account for their being staged as dramatic rites of give-and-take. If returning a child's head payment is tantamount to condemning it, as Gimi repeatedly say, why do they also state that the head payments they receive are engendered by the ones they gave and, therefore, subject to the same taboos? Why do Gimi celebrate marriages one after another in identical rites with objects identically decorated, packaged, and presented so that they appear to be getting back exactly and at once what they gave away?

Exchanges are designed, as I have suggested, to overthrow a mythic past. Ritual converts myth to visual reality, introducing artifacts that in various ways reproduce mythic items and relations so that—through the act of exchange—the myth is reordered, its catastrophic end revised and averted. As demonstrated dramatically in the rites of cure for infants (see Chap. 8), reordering the myth is achieved in the context of one's own past: it means replacing the components of *one's own* myth for those of another who ideally bears the "same name." The technology of negation requires that a duplicate myth already exist; that every first time have an antecedent in the way the first Gimi man had a father who didn't know how to "finish" him. In order to replace, rather than merely repeat, one's own fantasied relations, someone else has to do the same thing at the same time. Exchanges retaliate against one's own myth and kill the father, in this sense, by going back inside an identical but other myth to "finish the child": "I fend off my father—and finish myself—by offering him a convincing substitute for me, a head that looks like mine, that often has my same name, but is actually yours." Head payments simultaneously contradict and reinforce mythic reality because they are "not me" yet "the same as me;" they are both removable substitutes for mythic items and their equivalents.

The "head" moves in the same two directions as coitus itself: transfers of head payments mutually extract the plugs from two sets of flutes. Each first gift, each removal from the flute's "vagina," each rescue of the firstborn from a primal scene, is a replacement inside another. The going out and the coming back are parts of the same movement, like emptying the father's flute and feeding the bride, or blowing out his "child" and putting back his song. When lineages or clans exchange sisters in serial marriages and carry identically prepared gifts of pork back and forth between compounds or hamlets, what each side immediately reciprocates, it seems to me, is not simply wives or pigs but the cancellation of its own mythic past: the equivalence of the displayed objects manifests the identity not only of the objects themselves but also of the invisible relations the public exchange is designed to postpone. The true identity of brides and head payments is not with each other, in this view, but with flutes and flute plugs or menstrual blood, sacred objects each sex keeps out of sight of the other—not because they are unknown—but because each represents a myth of body content or design at odds with the myth of the other sex.

### The Gimi Meaning of Secrecy

What is the meaning of secrecy in Gimi ritual? For men, the secret of the flutes lies in the true nature of the plug. During his initiations, a man learns "with his mouth" that the plug is a phallus and that the first woman was not alone nor without a husband. But such male secrets are entirely in keeping with the secrets of women, paralleling the revelation to the bride that her menstrual blood originates not in herself but in the "noses" of lineage brothers and as the consequence of her first marriage to the Moon. The secret of each sex is something that originated with the other—as a flute or as menstrual blood—something that it steals from the other sex and has to hide. Like menstrual blood, flutes are lethal the moment they are *seen* by the other sex. And like menstrual blood, flutes are a magical source of productive power. In the same way that a woman's capacity to bear children and "give talk" to crops and pigs derives from secretly retaining vestiges of her blood, so does men's success in hunting and warfare, their capacity to stage rituals and ensure the yields of gardens and pig herds, depend upon hiding the flutes in the rafters of their houses. Each sex acquires the power to create wealth and reproduce life by hiding what it stole from the other.

But the fact that both sexes are thieves does not mean that each inherently possesses, in a reciprocal way, what the other lacks. On the contrary, it shows that both want the same thing; that flutes and menstrual blood are but variants of each other, alternate versions of the "head" or penis of the mythic father. Women and men acquire the father's head in the same way: both steal or "eat" it in utero. And both want to keep it *hidden,* to keep the penis "still inside," still in the midst of copulation, and, therefore, enormous and fully potent. Each sex conceals the traffic in the stolen object because, to expose the father's head, to let menstrual blood or sacred flutes be seen by the other sex, would remind the primordial father of what he lost and unleash his fury.

Only men can come to terms with the mythic father. A woman gets his penis *first:* he feeds her while her brother is still a "small boy"—still "the same" as the father. But she refuses to give back her father's nourishing gift and delivers his child as menstrual blood. So the father—while remaining inside her and out of sight—arranges for his son or "head" to escape: the theft of the flute is a *collaboration* between the absent father and unborn son that launches the son in exchange and brings him to life. Whereas women try to keep the stolen child entirely hidden, men make a duplicate set to give away. The father of the bride matches the flutes and daughter he sends away, the part of himself he "cuts off" at *habarena* or marriage (lit: *habare*/to cut + *na*/thing), with the mother instruments he hides in the rafters of his men's house. He is thus able to return to the mythic father, that is, to the father of the groom, what looks like the original "head of the child." But the exchange between fathers leaves their daughters altered and bereft: they acquire a "second vagina" and are robbed of the firstborn.

Gimi ritual secrets refer to the hoarding not of information but of reproductive power as if it were an indivisible object like a child or a flute. The capacity to bring life to people and goods is wholly possessed by one sex *at the expense of the other* in different eras, in the mythic past or ritual present, before the birth of the child or afterward. Ownership of flutes is eternally moot because, like "birds," they have a life of their own and tend to fly into the hands of the other sex (see Gillison 1983a:49). The flutes' volatility symbolizes the sexes' conflicting desires for phallic identity. This conflict, I have argued, both governs the rules of exchange and performance of public rites, yet remains outside informants' discussions. Men and women go to great lengths both to enact the equivalence of publicly exchanged objects and to hide their association with other, phallic objects, like flutes and menstrual blood, which they do *not* exchange. The separate, secret rites men and women perform before and during the communal celebrations are parts of a ritualized war that keep their conflicting desires out of the public domain.

The rites of *apina* recapitulate the flute myth in order to rescue the initiate from its end, which is the onset of menstruation and death of the firstborn. Being born a second time inside the men's house innoculates the boy against the mythic father and enables him some day, after an appropriate delay, to "return to mother," to reenter the father's territory and come out alive—and with a wife and child of his own. The Big Men forbidding him to play the flute at *apina* is like the promise of another when he marries. The flute the *ahamo* lays in the initiate's lap is a gift-in-earnest of a bride. It is "the phallus . . . affirmed in the boy, who [will some day have] it to give away" (Rubin 1975:195).

# PART FOUR

## The World of Sorcery

# TEN

## "Only Men Understand Sorcery"

Sorcery was once part of war, but "since the government arrived and banned warfare," men lament, "we have all become little boys working sorcery!" Whenever a man or woman becomes ill, sorcery is reckoned as the cause. Only men practice sorcery and only men are targets, but women and children may be attacked as a means to strike their husbands and fathers. At the start of fieldwork, women confiscated the meat I offered to their children during feasts because pigs reared in other villages, and even vegetables cooked in the same ovens, were like a poison to young children: men who owned the pigs might be working sorcery against their fathers or be in cahoots with sorcerers. "In the days when we fought with bows and arrows and our enemy sent us food, we never fed it to our children because they would have died," men told me. "Big Men ate the enemy's pig inside the men's house and hunted marsupials for the children."

When Samantha and other girls ran ahead on a path or wandered to the edge of a garden, women called them back in case sorcerers lurked nearby. The first time Samantha went swimming, the mother of one of her friends climbed onto a boulder in the middle of the river. She took her husband's old shirt out of her net bag and began to tear it to shreds, placing each shred in a small fire at her feet. "Now my husband will not get sick," she explained. "Men can take this kind of thing and work sorcery with it." When the fire was out, the girls doused the ashes, further destroying the link between the man and his shirt and spoiling its use to a sorcerer. When Samantha and I chewed sugarcane in the midday heat of a garden, the women instructed us to swallow every drop of juice and to keep the husks until we came upon moving water or returned home, making sure nothing that had been inside our mouths fell unneutralized to the ground.

Listed and explained in terms of sorcery, the daily routines of Gimi life portray a people living in fear. Yet rarely did anyone appear anxious, ruminative, or sullen, a demeanor Gimi describe disparagingly as "pulling one's nose." When a dispute arose during the course of the day, it was saved for the evening newshour, a period just before dusk when men and women throughout the village climbed to the high points of their compounds and exchanged yodeled salvos to arrange for a formal grievance or *kot* the next day (see Chap. 2 n.12). During the early months of fieldwork, while I still communicated mainly in Melanesian Pidgin, I could not connect the suspicions increasingly confided to me with the way I perceived people's moods and the general atmosphere of village life. The usual easy conversation around earth ovens or along the narrow paths that connect compounds and gardens at first made me think of precautions against sorcery as akin to looking both ways before crossing the street or following other routine safety rules.

## To Talk in the Sun

"Sorcerers attack in the sun not the rain," men say, referring not only to the middle of the day but also to the drier time of year when men hunt and stage large-scale rituals, affording opportunities for close contact and the theft of leavings. But people usually fall ill in the wet season, succumbing to the effects of "thefts" made during the dry season. About once a week during the period from October to June, someone's illness requires a meeting of local enemy clans and, if the illness is grave, of enemy clans from other villages.[1] The meeting is called *fobirikaina* or "sun talk" (lit: *fo*/sun + *biri*/happen, occur, be, etc. + *kaina*/talk) because it is convened around noon, when the sun is highest overhead.

At the start of *fobirikaina*, a crowd of men gathers in the compound of the sick man.[2] Many seek out the shade of peripheral bamboo and banana plants to distance themselves from the "hot talk" of Big Men who huddle in the bare, sun-drenched center of the compound. "Only we Big Men, only men with names, sit in the sun til our heads ache," Tahamaoga announces. Only

---

1. Much of the following description of sorcery accusations and administration of cures applies to the period before the opening of Ubagubi Rural Health Center in 1981. Since that date treatment has been provided in the village for malaria, pneumonia, abortion, malnutrition, tropical ulcers and abscesses, pleurisy, bronchitis, asthma, dysentery, diarrhea, arthritis, osteomylitis, gastroenteritis, measles, injury, pelvic inflammation, worm infestation, meningitis, impetago, scabies, dental decay, anxiety, venereal disease, hepatitis, and childhood diseases like whooping cough and mumps.

2. On the rare occasions when a sorcerer attacks a woman directly, he usually acts on behalf of her husband to punish her infidelity; or as the "hired gun" of her husband's enemy, to penalize her husband. When a woman falls victim to sorcery, her illness or death is counted primarily as a loss to her lover or husband, and it is upon *his* history and relations that the search for the sorcerer and a cure are based.

As far as I know, full scale *fobirikaina* are not held for women.

During a sorcery meeting or *fobirikaina,* literally, "sun talk," held in the victim's compound, traditional enemies station themselves outside the fence to answer charges and make counter-charges

Big Men can take the heat of confrontation and bring to light the names of those in their own ranks who traffic in other men's leavings. When a man and his brother both fell ill after leaving their natal clan and taking up residence with Patomena clan in another part of the village, suspicion fell upon Patomena's traditional enemies. Though they lived in another village, several of them had lately begun to visit a sister's son who lived near the stricken brothers. While sleeping in their nephew's men's house, it was rumored, Patomena's enemies revealed their nefarious intentions to Q, an unmarried man of low status who slept in the same men's house and was a sister's son of their sister's son. Patomena charged that their enemies paid Q to show them Patomena's houses and gardens and to steal the brothers' leavings; and that Q had actually taken feces and broken off strings from their wives' skirts in order to get hold of semen absorbed in the fibers. Only a Big Man has the authority to challenge such accusations by demanding, "Who among you has *seen* this? Tell us *who* it is!" In the midst of *fobirikaina,* a Big Man of *Q*'s clan shouts, "Who has seen *Q* escorting foreigners through the village? I see the men of my clan and I tell you they have not worked sorcery against you!"

Women and children sit at the opposite end of the compound out of ear-shot. "Women think only about rearing pigs and planting food," men told me when I asked why women were excluded from *fobirikaina.* "Women cannot hear talk. Only men can do that!" Before pacification, men say they had to keep women away because those born in enemy villages might "run home" to tell fathers and brothers the details of their husbands' suspicions and war plans, giving the impression, contrary to their first explanation, that they feared women understood men's words too well. "Men ate the sorcery pig, the *rubese ugunu* [lit: *rubese*/sorcery + *ugunu*/pig; i.e., the payment to steal leavings] inside the men's house so that women and children wouldn't see them. Only women who knew how to keep their mouths shut [mainly postmenopausal women] were given some of the meat." Nowadays, especially in the early years of a difficult marriage, a man may accuse his wife of taking payment from her father's allies and attempting to steal his own or his father's leavings. But, in general, sorcery is the one misuse of intimacy for which men are mainly to blame.

Surrounding the stricken man's house is a crude fence of bamboo stakes, called *rotana,* to keep out women and children. When I asked about the fence, the men told me, "Remember, a woman has a vagina where the Moon kills her and where her husband, too, pays regular visits. . . . If she were to step over the sick man, or over his food or weapons or net bag or anything that belonged to him, his wounds would fester and his fever rise. He would get hotter and hotter until he died." In emphasizing the physical threat of a woman's presence and the danger inherent in her sex, men seem to translate fears about her actual relations with other men, her loyalties to kinsmen, into a mythic capacity to harbor a hostile "husband" in her genitals.

### The Nature of Suspicion and Accusation

The purpose of *fobirikaina* is to "name names"; to identify publicly the man who cast the fatal spell and force him to undo it. "Name the man who passed our leavings to you!" a Big Man shouts before the gathering of men. "Name the man who passed your leavings to us!" "Give us the name of the man you saw accepting the *rubese ugunu* or lurking alone [i.e., waiting to receive it]." But the very nature of sorcery makes such sightings nearly impossible. An attack or theft of body leavings is carried out by one man, moving silently and unseen; or by conspirators whose movements leave no trace and whose faces the victim is made magically to forget. Even men who actually witness a sorcery payment being made, or about to be made, do not understand at the time what they are watching and take no notice. "I thought the meeting, comment, question, etc., had no other meaning," men protest afterward. "I had no thought of sorcery because sorcery was at work!"

Sorcery has an overwhelming power to lull suspicion so that, even when accusations are made, they are likely to be false. The one named as sorcerer is apt to be the sorcerer's target. "Here is how accusations are made," one man explained:

> One man wants to work sorcery on another. Say, I want to work sorcery on M. So I accuse you, who are M's close ally, his brother or age-mate: "You've taken my leavings and are working on them!" Knowing yourself to be innocent, you think I must be working sorcery on you so you stay far away from me. By falsely accusing you I remove M's best protector and put him off guard. M thinks *you* are my target and is careless with his leavings. Without you around I get close to him and take what he leaves behind and work sorcery on it and kill him! That's how accusations work. . . .
>
> When you eat you mustn't throw away the leavings. You must hold onto them and put them in your bag. You mustn't think, "Ah, they are accusing him. *He* is the one they are after," and become careless. Because if you are careless with your leavings, and forget where you lose them, a sorcerer will take them. His accusations are a trick!

Sorcerers act invisibly, yet to accuse a man of sorcery one has to see him. To "see" a sorcerer, therefore, to recognize the real meaning of his acts and gestures, one has to understand his motive, to know his relation to the victim, to know why he considers himself his victim's victim. When a man falls ill, his kinsmen create a public list of men whom they believe have reason to believe that they were harmed by him—or by his close associate. During *fobirikaina*, the sick man's kinsmen air family history, reciting offenses he or close male agnates have committed or are suspected of having committed. His brother may have enticed another man's wife to run away and marry him; his father's brother may long ago have committed a murder; the wife of his brother's son may recently have died in childbirth, etc., moving the survivors or relations to seek revenge. The stricken man's father or brother is often first to address the crowd, portraying him as a dutiful son or age-mate who, having innocently attracted a new wife, or properly avenged a death, is now the victim of misguided retaliation.

The longer an illness endures, the more life threatening it becomes, the older and more prominent the victim, the more frequently are *fobirikaina* convened in the case of a single illness; the more painstaking and public is the review of the victim's past, the more of his kinsmen, ancestors, and enemies the search encompasses; until, near or after the death of a Big Man, the review of an individual life seems to recall the history of an entire region. But that history is a shifting battleground where Big Men's recollections collide. As preamble to a public accusation, a Big Man of the victim's clan situates his illness or death at the end of a long list of killings and counterkillings that began decades ago. His speech testifies to his clansman's innocence by altering the causes and consequences of each death in the series, recasting descendants of the survivors of an ancient war as no longer victims of a rout but sorcerers filled with unprovoked fury. He shifts the logic in an entire pattern of vendettas, arguing that, by its position in the sequence, *this* attack cannot be justified as retribution.

To name the current sorcerer during *fobirikaina,* Big Men have to renegotiate a part of history. But they cannot dwell too much on the past. "If we talk about our old enemies," one orator yells, "the ones we ignore will kill you or me and leave the other of us in bitter regret. Let's stop our false talk so that no more men die and leave us holding our livers." . . . "We trade accusations while our enemies look on and laugh. Instead of recalling old resentments we should be naming names!" Yet the past is always alive in the present, shaping the disputes of *fobirikaina.*

### Sorcery and War

According to Gimi accounts of their history, internecine wars were deadlier than wars between settlements and created in the few survivors bitter and persistent foes whose descendants still use sorcery to take revenge. Two men of clan E remembered that their paternal grandfather, the Big Man K, had suspected his elder-brother clan of sorcery and instigated their massacre. "E was a big clan. There were two men's houses and one men's house worked sorcery against the other." . . .

> It was a time like now. There were many deaths and much talk of sorcery. "Where are the sorcerers coming from?" we asked ourselves. . . . then K's younger brother became sick. . . . B, a medicine man from the village of Gotuha, offered to cure him: "Go into the forest," B said, "and bring me marsupials and I will make a medicine for your brother." But it was a trick.
>
> B made a poison. He pretended to eat it and gave it to K's brother. "There is something inside my stomach!" K's brother cried and began to shake violently. It was the kind of poison that rots your insides while you swallow it. . . . Afterward he drank a soup his wife had made and then he emptied his bowels and died.

Suspecting his "elder brothers" of sorcery, the Big Man *K* summoned his allies and mounted an ambush:

> "Now I have found out *who* is killing us!" *K* said to himself, realizing that *B* was sent by his elder brother clan. "We will finish them off!" he vowed. . . . *K* killed pigs and sent them secretly through the forest to his allies [in other compounds of the village and in a neighboring village, issuing the standard invitation to make war]. When his allies had eaten the meat, they tightened their bows, mounted cassowary plumes on their shields and came in the night. . . .
>
> We [i.e., men of *K*'s clan and their allies] assembled before dawn and laid in wait outside the men's house. Twenty men waited in silence outside each door. . . . When a man came out to urinate we shot him, and he didn't get up to fall a second time. We entered through the opened door, and the men inside saw their brothers and were not alarmed. . . .
>
> Five men waited outside each woman's house. . . . The women and children came outside to relieve themselves for they, too, were without fear. But their *auna* had already left them [i.e., they were as good as dead]. We shot them all. Dawn came, then morning, and still we were shooting! If a man ran out [of a woman's house], twenty men ran him down and shot him.
>
> The men inside the men's house made a wall of their shields and shouted to the others, "We're going out. Get behind us!" But as they were about to break out of the house we set fire to it and . . . shot them in disarray. . . . One man—or two men—got away and went to Gotuha. But they were not inside the men's house nor in a woman's house. One had spent the night in a menstrual hut [i.e., in an assignation]. His name was *R*. He took his spear and his wife and ran to the river. . . .
>
> The woman was carrying her infant daughter. "The child is weighing us down. We will be killed in our tracks!" *R* said. "They did not cut off your penis nor close my vagina," said his wife. "I can still bear another." They said these things to each other and killed their child with a rock. They smashed the head and ribs and left it inside the net bag and ran away like rats to Gotuha.

Comparing the escaping couple to rats inspires a digression on how a cornered mother rat kills her firstborn. A rat burrow has two doors, one at each end like a men's house, the men explain. To trap a rat, one man digs up the main tunnel entry and, upon reaching the inner chamber, calls out to his comrade who is waiting at the rear "hiding road." The rat hears the men at both doors and is frantic to escape, but she hesitates, thinking of her children:

> "How can I leave them?" she says to herself. . . . She picks up one child in her mouth and enters the hiding road. She hears her other child crying. "I hear my other one but I see only you," she says to the child in her mouth. "You are a lovely child and I will eat you first." The mother eats her firstborn along the escape route. . . . "You cannot forage for yourself nor move as fast as me," she realizes . . . so she eats her child before she runs away. And then we kill her.

The tale of the mother rat leads to the subject of eating firstborn children:

> A firstborn child is a powerful thing. When a firstborn died no one ate it because eating a firstborn made one get old quickly and die. . . . But women sometimes ate a Big Man [even when he was firstborn]. . . . Women could eat a firstborn child. . . . A woman could eat her own child but a man, never! A woman and her brother could eat her child but never the father! (See above, Chap. 3)

Like a mother rat who devours her firstborn and better-loved child to save it from an external foe, a clan who massacres a brother clan uses intimacy to become a deadlier enemy within. When the raiders entered the men's house, "the men inside saw their brothers and were not alarmed." Like mother love, the relation between brothers, or men who are close allies, may be prone to a cannibal-like treachery, a desire wholly to destroy the one who is nearest and "unseeing" like a trusting child. The two members of the younger-brother clan that instigated the massacre say that their grandfathers tried to annihilate the elder-brother clan. "We didn't want a child of theirs to grow up and work sorcery against us!"

> "We shot them *all!*" our fathers told us. "We threw their bodies into swamps and ate their pigs. We ate the pigs but not our enemies because, if we had, our bodies would have turned yellow." . . .
> Talk of sorcery led to killing in the old days, and if we keep talking about sorcery now we will end up fighting again!

### The Inside Man

Like cannibalism and fratricidal war, sorcery is based upon the misuse of intimacy. If men want to ensorcel someone who lives far away, they hire an "inside man," someone who lives in his village, to act as their local agent by stealing leavings or arranging an ambush. The man named as local sorcerer is likely to be out for revenge on his own account because of the death of a son or brother. If the accused insider were innocent, he is reprimanded during *fobirikaina*, he would have warned the victim's clansmen so they could have staked out his garden and intercepted the foreigners in the act of delivering the *rubese ugunu*, the local sorcerer's fee of pork and, nowadays, money. Often, the inside man is accused of taking the initiative by carrying the leavings of those he suspects to their traditional enemies in another village. "Sapiau! You! Sitting over there!" Tahamaoga shouts at the start of his oration. "Your hands reach into distant places—into Vami and Gotuha. . . ." Sapiau protests: "Now that your brother is dead, men of Gotuha say I am the killer. They accuse *me* of stealing his leavings and carrying them to Gotuha. But I didn't deliver anything there."

The inside man may also be accused of "pulling" the foreign sorcerers into the village. "The man from here who wants to work sorcery—that one man—," another man explains, "pulls our enemies. We say to him, 'You hold our enemies by their ankles.'"

> When a man dies, his clan think men of his own village have killed him. . . . They butcher a pig in secret so that none of their enemies, nor any woman, sees them. They take out the liver and the innards and eat them together with the head and some meat. Then they wrap up the backside and the limbs and slabs of the carcass and carry them to our enemies in another village [as payment] to work sorcery against us!

The men who deliver the *rubese ugunu* share a meal with the recipients to ratify their plan and return home. But the "one man" who is the instigator stays behind to lead the two or three foreign sorcerers back to the outskirts of his village, or he arranges to meet them there when they arrive:

> There is one man who brings them here. . . . He goes into hiding and builds a *rubesenama* or "sorcery house" (lit: *rubese/* sorcery + *nama*/house) along their route in the forest. . . . He prepares food for them and gives them a secret place to sleep, and in the morning he shows them the man he wants to kill.

The mercenaries lie in wait with the inside man, but it is he who enters the victim's garden or follows him into the forest. "He alone shoots him with a poisoned dart or . . . slips a wire around his neck so he cannot cry out." The foreign accomplices hold the victim immobilized as the sorcerer "pierces his heart" by inserting poisoned slivers of bamboo into his armpit. Then they feed the victim a bespelled tuber of sweet potato to make him lose all memory of the attack and let him go. They return to their forest hideaway, one man carrying the actual perpetrator on his shoulders to prevent his feet from touching the ground or getting wet. The cold ground or water would "cool" his body and deactivate the sorcery he just performed.

> There is something hot inside a man who has worked sorcery, and if it goes cold his victim will not die. A man who performs a spell doesn't eat sweet potato nor greens, nor any food full of water, until his victim dies. He smokes tobacco and sleeps all day and does not leave his house. Sorcery is hot, and a sorcerer must keep the heat inside his body. When his victim falls, then he can eat and go outside again. . . .
> The sorcerers sleep together for five or six days, drinking no water or sugarcane, touching no food any woman has touched.
> . . . When their victim dies, . . . his *auna* flies into the forest and tears apart their *rubesenama.* Then the sleeping men awake and realize, "Yes. Our man is dead. Now we can eat sweet potato and drink water and return to our houses." (See Lindenbaum 1979:61)

After the attack, while the sorcerers retire to the *rubesenama,* the ensorcelled man returns home and falls mortally ill. His wife asks him where he has been and he tells her that he went into the forest to collect vines for tying a fence, or that he spent the afternoon in his garden planting sugarcane, having utterly forgotten the ambush on the road. But men of his lineage suspect the true cause of his condition and concoct an antidote containing a ground-burrowing insect, crushed earth worms, pig fat, banana skin, and the leaves of certain trees. They rub the mixture under his armpits and around his collarbone to make the tiny entry sites of the sorcerer's bamboo slivers become visible and "open up." His brothers "look inside him" and, seeing that sorcerers have attacked him, feed him another antidote to make him remember the incident and name the men.

Once the stricken man remembers what happened to him "on the road," his comrades run to the houses of the men he names and make everyone inside "hold ginger root":

> "The men who worked sorcery on me came from *that* place!" he says when his head opens up. We get ginger root and *run* with it. We run through the night and the pouring rain until we arrive at the houses he names. We go inside and make everyone—even children and young men—hold the ginger under his arm. . . . We don't sleep! We run back to our brother and give him the ginger before dawn. He eats it and breaks into a sweat, and his face falls [i.e., his expression changes]. And so we *see* who has done it.

He falls fast asleep and his sweat dries. When he wakes up he says, "Go back to that place and bring me more ginger."

The first ginger is a diagnostic: if the sick man eats it and becomes "hot"—if he breaks into a sweat, trembles, urinates, passes wind, or passes out—the man who worked sorcery against him, or a member of his clan, has held the ginger in his armpit. To recover, he has to ingest a second dose held by the same man or his near relation. The second time he will "get hot" and fall asleep again, but he will wake up "cold" and cured. Ginger transmits the "heat" between men but is itself "cold," men say, because it is planted beside compounds and is not "wild" (lit: *kore*).

### Who Is the Internal Enemy?

Who is the "one man" who unobtrusively picks up the crumbs of tobacco that fall from another man's pipe or the sweet potato skins he carelessly discards on the ground, and then ensorcels them, or passes them to the man's enemies in another village? In over three-quarters of the thirty or so sorcery disputes I recorded in which individuals were named, the accused were co-resident *abogofa* or affines (see Knauft 1987). Indeed, a man's *kisa abogo*, his real FZS or MBS, or *kisa atu*, his wife's own brother, is often the first man accused of killing him and is, in any case, expected to react guiltily when he falls seriously ill or dies. A man's *abogo* or *atu* is the first to offer comfort or express remorse, to attend him in his death agonies, and to grieve when he dies by covering himself in mud or slashing his ear. The *abogo* is also first to exonerate himself by supplying an exhaustive account of his recent whereabouts.

To prove his innocence, the accused may invite his accuser's wife to make a garden on his land, giving her the chance to retaliate by stealing his leavings and passing them to her husband. More often, the accused yields to pressure to send his own wife and child, or a brother's wife and child—who is the classificatory sister and sister's son of his accuser—to live in his accuser's compound.

> That is our custom. Whoever worked sorcery against us, say, Dabisa clan, we ask them to send us one of their wives who is a woman of our clan, our sister, and her child. And Dabisa sends them and we give the child ginger to take back to his fathers. His fathers hold it in their armpits and the child returns and gives it to his *anati* to eat. If his *anati* does not recover, he says to the child, "Your father did not work sorcery against me. Take the ginger to another place."

If the accused lineage had actually worked sorcery against the sick man, men hasten to point out, the woman and child they send would be the last to know. "I would not *see* it!" insisted one man, referring to the time he was sent with his aged mother to live in the compound of a dying cousin:

> With me around, my fathers closed their mouths and talked in secret. "There is his child," they would say. "The moment his *anati* falls ill he will go to him and make him cold."
>
> Later on, when my *nanati* took sick and I was in his house and I gave him a smoke or something to eat, he would break into a sweat; or he would get up to urinate and collapse. When he recovered a little he would say to me, "Your lineage, your fathers and brothers, are working sorcery against me. Go back to them and bring me ginger they have held."

The accused lineage "throws mother and child into the mouths" of their accusers. They send their son to sleep beside his ailing *anati* so he will be on hand in a crisis to hold the ginger or to run with it back to them. The offer of such care is, of course, a challenge that it prove ineffective and demonstrate the innocence of those who supply it. In the idiom of Gimi kinship, a man's "taboo" or brother-in-law is his enemy while the son of his "taboo" is like his own child. This contradiction is constantly played upon in accusations of sorcery.

> "Here is your *amaga*," say the accused. "My brother bore him. We have to look into his eyes so how could we work sorcery against you? You are his *anati* so how could we poison you? If you die, my brother's son will cover himself in mud and ashes. He will slash his ear and cry. How could we face him? . . . Your sister bore my brother's son. You bore him. We could not push him into our stomachs! No! Nor could we kill your son. Because we bore him . . . because he is our own child."

An affine is an enemy by definition, Gimi men say, but the affines who live in one's midst "don't speak clearly. They don't say, 'I am your taboo and you are mine.' No. They trick us. They oil our skins with flattery." Men of affinal clans who become too friendly are likely to be accused of sorcery; and then to protest their innocence by claiming either to be the *anumona*, the "children" (lit: *anu*/spirit-child + *mo*/the + *na*/thing) of their accusers, incapable of betraying their *he-ano* or "spirit mothers." Or they claim to be *an-oha* and *anatiraha*, "mothers" and "mother's brothers," devoted to protecting "our own children." During *fobirikaina*, one man accused a classificatory sister's son and member of an affinal clan: "I am not your enemy but you carried my leavings to Vami and I found out! I think it's *you*—not my old Vamian war enemies—who want me dead!" The accused protested, "I am your *anu*." "But you lie," the accuser retorted. "You hide things from me who is your *anati*."

When one brother-clan, usually the elder or *a'au*, accuses the other of sorcery, they may threaten to unleash the protective fury of their *anumona*: "'You want to kill our mothers,' our children will say to themselves. 'Well, you are not many!' They will look at their mothers and feel sorry for us and say, 'Shoot us too! Kill one of our mothers and we'll kill two of you!'" But the *anumona* themselves may demur and claim neutrality: "We, your children, hear our mothers accuse one another, but we shall not interfere. We shall not support one against the other." The "mothers" then accuse their "children" of having kept silent while their "brothers" were plotting to kill them; or of having instigated the sorcery by whispering false accusations to the other brother—or "mother." "You alone divide us!" they shout to men of the affinal clan during *fobirikaina*. "You blow cool on our brothers while they give us the heat and we die. You tell us lies. It is you who are hitting the head of our ground [i.e., dividing the ground between us, turning our brothers into enemies]."

If someone in the "hot" center of the compound accuses a man by name, the accused picks up a stone, stands and throws the stone against a rock on the ground, declaring, "I did not see [the one you accuse me of killing]. . . . Do not accuse me! He [the dead man] was the blood of my heart. He was my own child." Or he says, "I am your mother and did not kill you [i.e., your father, brother, wife, etc.]." The oath taker then retrieves the stone, casts it over the compound fence, and spits forcefully onto the ground. If a man gives false witness, his stomach will swell grotesquely, testifying to his guilt. The men sitting near him spit at the same time because hearing a lie can have the same effect as telling one. "Anyone who hears the false words [of an oath] and swallows his saliva will get sick. His stomach will fill with fluid and swell until he dies." But false accusations are lethal mainly because, as orators repeatedly declare, they lead to attacks on the innocent and allow sorcerers to continue their work unhampered.

## The Nature of Sorcerers and Their Techniques

### *The Sorcerer as Bad Mother*

Sitting on the sidelines, listening to men publicly accuse one another of being deceitful "mothers" and treacherous "children," of seeming too friendly and getting too close, "oiling the skin with flattery" in order to steal a man's leavings, etc., I notice the women and children around me. Women nurse and coddle their infants. When a child cries, the mother rocks it rhythmically in her arms, singing, kissing, squeezing, patting, rubbing, bouncing, biting, and whispering sweet nonsense to soothe it. Even when an infant is placid, the mother, father's sister or mother may offer her breast or masturbate it. Women steadily groom their infants and dispose of wastes with meticulous care. A woman uses her fingers to wipe mucous from her baby's nose or pus from its ear, rubbing the discharge into her thigh until it is absorbed and disappears. If her child has sores or a rash, she gently lifts off the scabs with a soft twig or cassowary-bone needle and collects the pus and flakes of dried blood in a leaf. She folds the leaf into a tiny package and tucks it into her net bag, disposing of it later in a river or fast stream.

Children defecate freely in their mothers' laps, and the mothers collect the feces in coleus leaves, wrapping the leaves tightly, tying them with bark string, and placing the packet inside their bags. If some feces fall to the ground, the mother mixes them into the soft earth with her heel. All these measures protect her child—and her husband if the child is unweaned— from falling under a sorcerer's spell. During rites of marriage, we may recall, men celebrate the mother's role as feces remover par excellence, presenting the mother of the bride with meat called *natano ugunu* (lit: *natano*/coleus leaves + *ugunu*/pig) to compensate "her labor in removing feces and carrying her child about." The definitive act of motherhood, in Gimi terms, is also the originating crime of sorcery: it is the *unseen* or unperceived removal of body leavings; the experience—as adults may imagine it in a child—of losing a part of oneself without feeling or realizing it. In motherhood, as in sorcery, two people are utterly close, yet only one is truly aware or able to see the other; only one collects and disposes of the other's wastes while the other is oblivious and without suspicion. As those who nurture and give care, mothers are also the original "thieves" of body leavings.[3]

3. I am grateful to Robert Paul for the following insightful commentary on my interpretation of the Gimi Oedipus complex and underemphasis of the mother.

> . . . so much does the interpretation rest upon a "positive" Oedipal reading, and on the primacy in the Gimi conceptual system of the father, or of the father in the mother or in her womb, that I begin to notice the absence of the mother—Oedipal or pre-Oedipal both. . . . Given the kind of child rearing and nurture, in particular, which Gimi male children receive, one would have to expect a good deal of concern about mother in the pre-Oedipal dyad. And of course the Oedipal triad . . . is not only about father.
>
> When one reminds oneself that the ideology claims that reproduction is only possible thanks to males and their compromise formations enacted in exchange, and that women are only destructive, one begins to get a sense that of course this whole ideology is itself defensive against very deep anxieties and fears arising out of envy of mother, and of simultaneous fear of separation and also of reabsorption in symbiotic union.
>
> I would propose the following hypothetical dynamic to account for the observed Gimi data and the collusion of both men and women in sustaining it: I would begin . . . by placing Oedipal anxieties of men at the core: growing up involves the threat of castration, while turning back threatens either or both loss of or reabsorption by the mother. The usual defense for men is a regression to the anal phase, in which issues of homosexuality, gifts, sadism, dominance and subordination, and

### *A Sorcerer Is a Lonely Man*

When asked to describe a sorcerer in the abstract, men do not compare him to a mother. "A sorcerer is a man alone who hides what he does," they say. He is a recluse who sleeps most of the day and goes on the prowl at night to steal food from other people's gardens and to open graves and eat morsels of the dead. He is always on the look-out for discarded shreds of sweet potato skins, husks of corn or sugarcane, pandanus seeds, bits of tobacco, anything carelessly abandoned by others. "An old man or a widower or a young man may be a sorcerer but not a man with a wife," men explain, "because a woman is completely cold. A woman's body is filled with water and ruins his spell."

While ordinary men have wives whose company they avoid, a sorcerer is a man without a wife who seeks out the wives of other men. He follows the wife of a prospective victim to her garden. "A sorcerer makes his way noiselessly," one woman said. "While I am gathering sweet potato or weeding he approaches me and—ever so gently—breaks strings off my skirts and carries them away and kills my husband" by ensorcelling the semen absorbed in the bark string. In the past, a sorcerer trailed a woman to her menstrual hut and still comes to watch her give birth and hold the child in her arms because "he has no child of his own." A woman is the repository of her husband, the ground that soaks up his "fallen" self. She carries him about with her as semen absorbed in her skirts, as a fetus embedded in her womb, as a child lying in her arms, as menstrual blood "dying" between her thighs. By following the wife, the sorcerer gets close to his victim while the victim himself is in absentia or unaware of the sorcerer's presence.

A sorcerer's most potent spells are those that induce his victim to copulate with his wife while he watches them from behind a tree or a hidden corner of

---

magical omnipotence or anal narcissism are salient. Men retreat from the positive Oedipus complex to the "negative" one, with the father as the loved object, defensively, to avoid the dangers of rivalry with and castration by father. But the men's negative Oedipus complex exactly parallels the women's "positive" one, since in both, the father is loved, and the desire is to exclude the mother. Men and women, then, each have reasons for wanting to eliminate mother from reproduction and even go so far as to blame the danger of women on men—the father in the mother, the Moon, the sorcerer, etc. I have the impression that Gillison . . . has to some degree colluded with both Gimi men and women in their effort to erect an ideology which serves to defend against anxiety aroused by the Oedipal mother, who, after all, is there in the primary myths, as the bad mother behind the sorcerer, as the first woman with the flute, etc. Putting father in her womb denies her "castration," which soothes the anxiety of the men, retaining the fantasy of the phallic woman; while the women like the idea of having father's penis/baby in their wombs for their own, less conflictual, Oedipal fantasy reasons.

their garden. Afterward he retrieves the semen that "falls out of the vagina" onto the ground. "The man ensorcelled with his own semen doesn't get sick he dies so fast! He goes to sleep feeling ill and dies before he awakes." The voyeurism, anger, and symbolic homosexuality implicit in acts of sorcery are often associated with adultery. Some men attribute desire for a woman to resentment of her husband and to having witnessed the conjugal act. As Rabofo reported:

> One night I was awake and about while everyone was asleep. I was standing near a door and heard two voices. . . . I put my ear to the wall and listened. The woman was saying to her husband, "Stop! Go away!" Then they lay down and started making love. The man held his wife and said, "You have sex with other men and I know about it!" "With *whom?*" the wife demanded. "You look Rabofo in the eye. You are always staring at him."
>
> "I don't know what you're talking about!" the wife said. "You're lying! . . . You have sex with Rabofo!" he insisted. I heard him speak my name though I had nothing to do with that woman. "You can't have sex with me!" she said. "I don't want to be with you while you speak of another man." But he said, "First I'll put my penis inside you and then we'll talk." The woman took off her skirt and the man entered her. . . .
>
> I was listening outside the door and I thought, "You accuse me falsely so I *will* have sex with your wife!" . . . My belly was hot!

### Techniques of Sorcery

Having gotten hold of his victim's "fallen" substance by sleeping with his wife or by some other ruse, the sorcerer wraps it tightly in leaves or stuffs it into a narrow bamboo tube and looks for ways to make the packet disintegrate. He tries to locate a corpse, especially of a woman who just died in childbirth, intending to insert the leavings packet in her vagina or in her abdomen by making a slit below the navel. If he cannot find a woman, he may use the body of a man, implanting the leavings in the "hairy" anus or armpit (see Chap. 9 n.17). As the corpse rots, men explain, its fluids invade the packet so it "gets hot" and decomposes, causing a corresponding rise in temperature, decline, and disintegration in the victim.

When someone dies and a man, or several men, of an enemy clan become sick at about the same time, the enemy may come forward and accuse the bereaved clan of attempting revenge by implanting their leavings in the corpse. If the deceased is a woman who died in childbirth, the enemy clan may summon their allies and arrive in an armed delegation, demanding to open the grave and inspect the corpse in the light of day. They would not come by stealth at night, they say, because they would encounter the deceased's affines or paternal kinsmen who lie in wait for the sorcerer. He is likely to come at night and try to stand near the grave, hoping to attract his victim's *auna* into the ginger root he clutches in his hand. The ginger absorbs the *auna* as it escapes the corpse, and, once it is "filled," the sorcerer returns home alone and eats it as a kind of preemptive strike, devouring his victim's *auna* before it can attack him. Plaintiffs who approached a grave to retrieve their leavings in darkness thus might be mistaken for the sorcerer.

When a grave is opened, the corpse is handled by a woman. When the deceased is male, the handler is likely to be a classificatory daughter married into the plaintiff's lineage. She lifts the body so the men standing around her can see that no leavings packet has been placed beneath the buttocks. Often, however, the deceased's kinsmen refuse to allow such direct access to the corpse. Instead, they may invite their accusers to dig a narrow shaft into the grave and pour in water drawn from a fast-moving stream that would "cool the sorcery" and arrest decomposition of the leavings. But they may only allow a search of the ground above the grave: when a sorcerer inserts a leavings package in a corpse, he is supposed to wrap it in vine strings and tie the ends of the strings to tiny sticks on the surface, enabling him in the weeks ahead to monitor any disturbance that would undo his work.

Often a sorcerer has no access to a corpse. He may substitute a decaying wild banana stem, cutting a hole or "vagina" near the base and inserting the leavings. He seals the hole and waits for the banana to turn "completely yellow." The banana's fluids seep into the package, having the same effect as would those of a corpse. Instead of a wild banana, the sorcerer may use a *neki maha*, depositing his victim's leavings in the marshy area around a river outlet or in the peripheral algae or "yellow water" of a stagnant pool (see Chap. 8). If he cannot find a decaying banana nor enter a *neki maha*, he may hang the packet from the ceiling of a tree hollow, preferably a marsupial's abandoned nest, and build a fire on the ground. As the heat slowly rises over the course of days or weeks, it "enters" the leavings and precipitates a corresponding meltdown in the man from whom they were stolen. "When a young man dies, we say, 'the sorcerer killed him by cooking his *autaisana*.'"

The various niches where a sorcerer sequesters his victim's leavings—the vagina, abdomen, armpit, or anus of a corpse, the base of a decaying banana stem, the "mad ground" of a *neki maha*, the smoldering hollow of a tree—all give access, actually or in substitute form, to the rotting interior of a woman's body; all represent a disintegrating vagina in more or less overt ways. The sorcerer locating or manufacturing such a niche and inserting his victim's leavings "heats" not only the leavings and, correspondingly, the victim but also the sorcerer himself. The sorcerer "gets hot" from performing his spell, from hiding another man's leavings inside a rotting or burning hole, suggesting that the hole exists not only in the corpse or banana, etc., but also inside himself. "There is something hot inside a man who has worked sorcery, and if it goes cold his victim will not die." To keep the "heat" the sorcerer has to avoid even the remotest contact with women, abstaining from water and juicy foods because they are "wet" like women and shunning other men because they live and copulate with women and "take the food of their hands." Sequestering the leaving's packet initiates a quiescent, smoldering copulation inside the sorcerer's own belly which he makes every effort to prolong, and let "sleep undisturbed," through abstinence, inactivity, and complete avoidance of living women.

Men compare the heat sustained in a sorcerer's belly to the fire inside the men's house where, in the past, warriors heated their weapons after a battle. By placing arrows near the fire and keeping them constantly hot, men could cause the wounds the arrows had inflicted to fester and become infected as if they were still lodged in the enemies (see Codrington 1891:310). The fire in a men's house had the same long-distance power to inflame a wound as the heat of sexual intercourse. When a newly married woman cuts her leg and the cut becomes ulcerated, she refuses to have sex with her husband because the heat of their sex is infecting her leg. Similarly, a man with a sore takes no food from his wife, and avoids anything she has grown, because her touch would convey the heat of their union to his sore and cause it to ulcerate. Like the warrior who kept his arrows hot next to the fire, the sorcerer who keeps the heat of his spell in his stomach stays connected to his victim by reproducing the invisible aftereffect of coitus, evoking its power to keep in close touch those who have been sexually intimate.

We have already seen that Gimi implicitly compare a sorcerer's crime with the definitive aspects of a mother's care, and that men link fratricidal war with the cannibalism of a mother rat. Categorically, at least, the sorcerer himself is likely to be a mother's brother or male "mother." But his rites give him maternal identity in a further, mythic sense by endowing him with a filled and impenetrable "vagina" and making him unapproachably "hot" like the first woman. According to men's myth of Primordial Fire, the vagina of the first woman was on fire and burned to ashes the penis of any man who tried to enter. One night, a small boy led the woman up a mountain and made her lie down beside a lake. The Moon threw his penis out of the sky, splashed into the still water, and put out woman's fire: her insides "went cold," and she began to menstruate (see Chap. 7). If we look at a sorcerer's work in terms of the myth of first coitus, it seems to condense the whole episode. Hiding his victim's leavings in a smoldering or rotting vagina is like the Moon throwing his penis into the blaze between woman's thighs and leaving in his wake a pool of cold blood. The sorcerer ignites his own fire, as it were, when he sequesters his victim's leavings. He ventures inside the vagina like the Moon and then gets hot like the woman on the ground. And like the Moon in men's myth, he stays out of sight. A sorcerer's identity is rarely revealed despite men's extraordinary efforts to name him, as we see in Chapter II. The sorcerer's ultimate anonymity, like the Moon's disappearance from the main narrative of men's myths, leaves the whole blame for sorcery and death "between woman's thighs." By evoking myths of first coitus, the sorcerer's rites show again that, at the level of final cause, Gimi attribute death to the onset of motherhood and murder of the firstborn.

# ELEVEN

# The Rites of Cure

## Cures during *fobirikaina*

The purpose of "naming names" during *fobirikaina* is to undo the sorcerer's work. If the victim's kinsmen find out the sorcerer's identity and the location of his secret niche, they can stop the disintegration of leavings by removing the packet or by pouring in water drawn from a swift river or waterfall. Through greater knowledge of the past, powerful memories, and gifts of oratory, Big Men possess a privileged means of deciding who is guilty. But to know who attacked the victim one has to *see* the attack through a kind of reviewing that words alone cannot provide. Words are invisible and, therefore, inherently duplicitous. Big Men can look into history and identify the sorcerer's clan by placing his victim's life, and the lives of his close allies, within the complex regional configuration of enmity and alliance. But public airing of recent conflicts and renegotiation of past events merely cast nets of suspicion, providing the outline of incidents that may have caused a man's demise. The proof—and the cure—lie in catching the sorcerer in flagrante delicto, a necessity that requires his repeating his original attack. To "name names" Big Men need the visual confirmation of the rites that follow their initial orations.

When the sick man does not recover after the first *fobirikaina*, suspects may be made to undergo private tests of guilt, providing Big Men with the kind of evidence they need to make further accusations or issue denials. "I don't name a man for no reason!" a Big Man shouts during a second or third round of *fobirikaina*, insisting that an oracle using red pandanus has already verified his accusation. The suspect, or men of his lineage, were made to prepare red pandanus fruit "with their own hands" and to feed it to the stricken man's wife and firstborn child, or to wives and children of his brothers or fathers, and then to eat it themselves together with their own wives and children. During the next several days, men "watched the bodies" of the victim's

317

children, especially his firstborn, to see if they "turned yellow" or became covered in sores, indicating that they had "eaten with their father's enemy." "A child who eats with his father's enemy will not endure. His belly will swell and his hair will grow long and thin and death will overtake him."

The pandanus oracle "names" the sorcerer by forcing him, in effect, to repeat his crime before witnesses. The red pandanus is a substitute for the victim's *autaisana;* it represents both his wife's menstrual blood and his own "fallen" semen, the stuff the Moon killed and the sorcerer stole. By feeding the sick man's wife and firstborn child pandanus he himself concocted, the performer of the oracle again sequesters stolen leavings inside a hidden mouth or vagina. If the child becomes sick or "turns yellow," he or she reacts in the same way as the rotting banana stem or corpse into whose "mouth" the sorcerer inserted the father's leavings. The child's illness thus mimics the response of a fetus when its head is "fed" or "touched" by the father's penis (see Chap. 7), and thereby indicates that the red pandanus he or she ingested was indeed "the same" as the father's stolen *autaisana;* that it was prepared and inserted by the hands of the actual thief or his close relation.

Performance of an oracle can catch the sorcerer red-handed. But even when it incriminates the inside man and his brothers, it is only the start of a cure because it cannot implicate the men who were "pulled by their ankles," collaborators who also worked sorcery and whose bodily presence is required to undo it. The *ababana,* therefore, call new meetings, demanding that anyone they suspect, as well as representatives of clans or villages linked to the suspects, reassemble in their compound and make a kind of global direct contact with the victim.

After the first round of speeches, the father, brothers, or sons of the stricken man move him into the doorway of his house. Other men of his lineage slaughter a pig in the middle of the compound and carry it to the small fenced taro garden beside the men's house, which is used only to feed adolescents after initiation or unmarried or celibate men. There they gut the pig and singe off the hair over an open fire. Big Men divide the carcass into sections, reserving the liver, kidney, heart, or tongue, an emptied section of small intestine, and bits of meat from the breast bone, for the two or three medicine men who are also crouched inside the enclosure. The medicine men are members of a local or foreign enemy clan that has been implicated by the ginger or pandanus oracle, or by marsupial oracles (see Chap. 4), or named by a Big Man of the victim's clan or by the victim himself.

The medicine men cut up the innards, spread them on a large leaf, and then stuff their mouths with chunks of salt, ginger root, and the dried leaves and barks of wild trees they brought from their own territory. They chew these ingredients and spit them out in unison, sending fast streams of thick liquid onto the raw pork. "Spit is the same as sweat," the men say. "It heats the *rakukusa*." The inclusion of spit and imported leaves and barks ensures that the sick man will eat "something of his enemy, something of his enemy's forest." But the wild ingredients and spittle alone are too "hot" for the patient to swallow. The medicine men "cool" the *rakakusa* to edible perfection by also chewing ginger or leaves of *Zebrina* species and salt, cultivated or manufactured foods that are "cold." Then they fold the medicine inside the large leaf, insert it into a bamboo tube, and place the bamboo on an open fire inside the garden enclosure. The men lay the fat-coated stick they used to push the packet into the tube on top of nearby cordyline shrubs or insert it in the fence: "We don't want the *kore* to come in the night and eat the *auna* in the fat. If the *kore* eat with the sick man he will die. If the *kore* eat his medicine they will carry him away with them."

The pig used to make the *rakukusa*, especially the blood and fat, are permeated with the sick man's *auna* which acts like a magnet for his ancestral *kore*. By butchering the pig and preparing the medicine inside the taro garden or *rotana,* men protect it from the ravenous ghosts of paternal relations and from other sorcerers who would steal the pig's blood or bones and use them to work new sorcery. The enclosure also protects the *rakukusa* from contact with women. At any time during the process of preparation and consumption, as men cut up the medicine, lay it on a leaf, chew it, spit it out, wrap it in leaves, insert it in a bamboo tube and afterward remove it, unwrap it, apportion and eat it, morsels may fall from men's hands and mouths onto the ground. If a woman or child or man who recently had sexual relations—presumably, any man in the main part of the compound—were to step over a morsel, the medicine would "go cold" and lose its efficacy. "If a woman stepped over a drop of pig's blood she would defeat the medicine," men explain. "She would ruin it. The medicine would go cold and the sick man would not recover." Men take pains to keep the medicine "hot" by averting what seem to be parallel dangers—preventing *kore* from devouring it, sorcerers from stealing it, and a woman (or anyone who recently has been inside her, like a child or sexually active man) from stepping over it, literally, "passing it between the thighs." The various precautions taken during the preparation of the cure thus recall the site of the attack.

Most women sit out of earshot during *fobirikauna,* but, in cases of dire illness, there are usually a few women in the main part of the compound. The patient's wife may be crouched inconspicuously outside the fence around the taro garden removing feces to prepare the pig's bowel for braiding and cooking in the main oven. If the man is prominent, the wife of one of his sons may sit beside him near the center of the clearing stroking his upper body and fanning him with a fig branch to provide relief from the sun. To deflect the tiny invisible arrows that sorcerers sometimes launch at midday, a man of his lineage drapes *hu ϑu* vines over his shoulders or plants a *huϑu* branch into the ground behind him. Amid the leaves above his head, he ties pieces of cooked pig's lung because the lungs are filled with *ano* or fluid, "a female thing that cools the sorcery inside him." In the section "On the Meaning of Hot and Cold" (see below, this chap.), I discuss apparent inconsistencies in the effects of "hot" and "cold" that emanate from women and female objects.

While the *rakukusa* still cooks on the open fire, one of the medicine men leaves the enclosure and approaches the patient. He whispers into his ear, then holds pieces of the pig's singed and salted liver above his head. "Pull men's *auna*s from every quarter!" he invokes the sun. "You who have worked sorcery over there . . . over there . . . over there . . . ," he says, turning in a circle and pausing in each direction, "*your* food is Nomoa [the patient] about to eat." The rite is "the same as holding ginger," men afterward explain. "Men of Hagibu, Vami, Heroana, Mane, Kuasa, Gusereve, whoever among them worked sorcery against Nomoa will not walk here! So we call out to the sun and the *auna* of the sorcerer—wherever he is—enters the liver. Nomoa eats the liver and it makes him cold and ends his sickness." The medicine man may also untie the piece of pig's lung from the branch above the patient's head and feed it to him, too, as another way of having him "eat men's *auna*s." Then he and the other medicine men and several of the victim's close paternal kinsmen—but not his own father, father's brothers or sons—eat pieces of the singed liver. They pass other pieces to a group of his male affines and sometimes to his wives, young children, unmarried daughters, and son's wives who have stationed themselves outside the enclosure. "Only men eat the medicine," men respond to my query. "If a woman ate it, it would go cold. But the liver, skin, and small bowel [among other soft parts] of a pig are cold, and women and children can eat them."

During the cooking of *rakukusa,* men of the victim's lineage and clan load sections of pork tied with greens into a steaming earth oven in the main part of the compound while their wives fill peripheral ovens with vegetables. When the *rakukusa* is cooked, men remove several planks of the garden fence or *rotana* to create a "new opening" through which the patient enters. The medicine men empty the contents of the bamboo onto banana leaves. One of them picks up a piece of cooked meat and, facing in the direction of the village of the sick man's main traditional enemies—likely his own village—repeats the invocation to the sun and hands the meat to the patient. Then he sits down again to eat his own medicine, sharing it with senior men of the victim's clan who also enter the enclosure, and with others who remain outside the fence. If the sick man's mother is old and widowed, she may follow him into the enclosed space "because she has no husband," neither man nor Moon.

The victim's *ababana,* the hosts of *fobirikaina,* meanwhile distribute sugarcane to the assembly and provide water in wide bamboo poles for men who no longer have teeth to strip and chew the hard cane. "Let everyone drink this sugar," the Big Men exhort:

> Young men, old men, Big Men, and boys! Don't one of you sit aside or stay inside your house and let yourself be passed by. We must all come together and drink. The one among you who hides is the one we will shoot with our talk [i.e., accuse]. Everyone must drink this sugar because our father [brother, son, etc.] is sick . . . because sorcerers are trying to kill him in his prime.

The Big Men repeat these exhortations later when they unload the main oven and cut, salt, and distribute the cooked pork. "We don't want this man to die. We killed a pig to feed our enemies. . . . to cool the man among us who worked sorcery against him." "Let us drink sugar and eat pig together in one place and end it!" The *ababana* feed "watery" foods to a congregation of their enemies and allies on the premise that the sorcerer is likely to be among them. Having been unable to discover the sorcerer's niche and remove their kinsman's leaving, or to "cool" it in situ by pouring in the "wild" water of their ancestors, they attempt now to break the sorcerer's hold by pouring water into *him*. A man who has worked sorcery and denies it by eating or drinking during *fobirikaina* "will later fall ill so that everyone *sees* who is guilty."

Absence from *fobirikaina* is an indication of guilt. "When a man dies, we watch who comes to see him. If one man, or the sons of one man, do not come, that is the man who killed him." The deceased's patrikin publicly condemn those who have not paid their respects:

> We buried Rakati and sat in our houses but you did not come. You did not come to see us. . . . Rakati's mother did not die. Nothing happened to his father. They are still there! Why didn't you go to them so they could look into your eyes . . . ? Because you stayed inside your houses we think it is you who worked sorcery on him.

Yet dutifully attending funerals and *fobirikaina* is no guarantee against being accused, as Rakati's *kisa abogo* bitterly complained: "I went to his compound wailing and covered in mourning clays and *you saw me!* My own clan told me if I stayed inside my house I would be accused. I did not speak to you then [i.e., accuse someone else to protect myself]." Only the patrilineage of the sick or dead man ought to initiate accusations. During *fobirikaina*, it is the duty of the *ababana* to move unobtrusively through the crowd to overhear other men's whispered conversations and to ask oblique questions that will give clues to the sorcerer's identity.

Before the main distribution of meat, especially when the patient is thought to be gravely ill, one of the invited enemy Big Men stands at the front of the assembly and holds out a piece of cooked pig fat. About a dozen men, all of one clan, file past his outstretched arm, each one touching the fat and returning to his place in the shade. When one clan is through, the Big Man places the touched fat on a leaf and picks up another piece, holding it out for the men of another clan. He repeats the procedure until he has collected pieces of fat touched by representatives of every enemy clan or village in attendance. Then the *ababana* carry the stricken man out of his house, covering his upper body in a shroud. Or else they support him in his doorway so that only his lower body is outside the house, and they begin a test like the one performed on a corpse (see Chap. 4). His enemies file past him, each man bending down to rub a piece of the touched fat over his shin or to smear it across his toes.

His father, brothers, or sons squat on either side of him, watching intently to see if, during the moments a piece of fat touches his leg, he breaks into a sweat, trembles, coughs, spits up phlegm, urinates, defecates, releases intestinal gas, or loses consciousness. His succumbing, even fleetingly or barely perceptibly, to any of these symptoms reveals that the man who ensorcelled him, or one of his clansmen, is touching him again at that very moment, making him "get hot and die" by repeating the original contact. The sorcerer's touch provokes a little death that replaces the real one his spells will otherwise cause. As the suspects bend down, one after another, to rub fat on Harato's leg, a Big Man of his clan names other men of the village who have recently been cured by this technique:

> When they stole *S*'s *autaisana* we killed a pig and everyone gathered to eat it. The men who came to eat the meat rubbed fat on his leg and he recovered. When they took *B*'s *autaisana* we did the same thing and *B* got better. So now we kill this pig to feed our enemies!

When several men of one clan are gravely ill or have died and all believe they are targets, *fobirikaina* is a larger and more formal affair. Its purpose may not be to find a specific culprit or cure but to prevent further attacks by "closing the road of sorcery." The victims' clan summons their most distant enemies, representatives of clans they suspect of providing *bisuari*, a lethal bark, or performing sorcery as paid accomplices of inside enemies. The *ababana* provide these men with whole cooked pigs or large sections, often redistributing meat they just received in other villages as marriage or death payments. The *ababana* also kill pigs from their own herds and butcher them by removing the skeleton and cutting the flayed, headless outer body into slabs. They create sections of "bones," "skin," and "meat," including

During a sorcery meeting, one of the invited enemy Big Men holds out a piece of cooked pig fat for the men of his clan to touch one by one. Afterward, this piece of fat, and others that have been touched in a similar way by members of other clans, will be rubbed on the sick man's foot or shin to see if contact with any piece causes him to break into a sweat, tremble, cough, pass out, etc., thus identifying the sorcerer's clan.

innards, but present only the slabs of "skin" and bamboo containers stuffed with "meat" to the foreign visitors.

The hosts display the cooked pork in the hot sun, including meat which may have been carried from other villages and begun to smell strongly of rot. They stack the pieces in piles, setting six or seven piles in a row to represent as many pigs, and carry the prestations across the open compound, setting down each one in front of a representative of a distant clan. "Pork cannot be given in secret," men remark as they watch the meat being presented. "Pork given in secret is payment for sorcery. Men and women must *see* the meat we give."

During the transfer, the donating Big Man announces:

> If a man of this village buys poison from you or brings you our
> *autaisana,* you must tell us *who* it is. . . . Do not come here to
> work sorcery against us. When a man from our village tries to
> pull you here, run to tell us! And we will banish that man.

The meat he presents now is a gift. "Don't think about repayment," he says.
"I give you this freely." His announcement is generally the cue for the visitors to produce some potent piece of sorcery material, such as a body orna-
ment or piece of cuscus fur which supposedly fell from the Big Man's own
headdress while he danced during a recent *hau* or initiation. They claim to
have received it, together with a fee in cash and cooked pork, from one of his
local enemies. If such "fallen objects" are ensorcelled in distant places, men
explain, there is no chance to reach the sorcerers in time to make them touch
ginger or hold pig fat.

The host clan also makes a presentation to the inside man and his cronies,
to men they suspect of having recently pulled outsiders "by their ankles" or
conveyed *autaisana* into their hands—mainly, their *anatiraha* and *abogofa.*
To these local instigators and prime movers of the plot, the hosts give some
pigs' "skins" but mostly "bones," skulls with jaw bones attached, sections of
"arms" and "legs," rib cages, backbones, etc., because "the bones must be
eaten here." They present these parts to the wives and children of the local
suspects, many of whom are their own classificatory sisters, daughters, and
grandchildren. They call each woman or child by name and, one by one,
they step into the main arena and come forward to accept allotments of
meat.[1] The women and children carry the meat back to their compounds
and turn it over to the men on whose behalf they received it.[2]

1. Nearly all gifts of food are presented publicly to women, even outside the context of life-
crisis rites. Even routine head payments are made to the wife of the *anati.* In distributions of
pork at a Melpa wedding, there is a sense in which "women are thought of as the primary recipients of pig meat" (M. Strathern 1972:111). As among the Melpa, a Gimi woman's inclusion in a
distribution of meat acknowledges her status (see ibid., 96). But in acknowledging a woman's
status, I argue, the gift also highlights the status of women in general as those who invariably
receive and are, therefore, in an inferior position.

2. The convention of presenting "skin" and "meat" to enemies from other villages but retaining the "bones" parallels, in the context of home consumption, a distinction between the sexes.
"We give meat and blood to the women," men say, "but we eat the bones." Despite the public
appearance, in which women step forward to receive large sections of pork, men take back from
women and keep for themselves the largest and choicest share on the bones.

Gimi food taboos give the same deceptive appearance. A general consumption ethic equates
abstinence or moderation in eating with masculine virtue and strength and indiscriminate in-
dulgence with female lassitude. While males in their prime are traditionally surrounded by
stringent taboos to separate them from women and female foods, women are treated as un-
regulable (but see rules of *aϑaoina,* Chap. 6). Since many antifemale taboos are designed to

Between 4 and 5 o'clock in the afternoon, when the main distribution of pigs is ending and most women and children have left, a Big Man of the host clan addresses the crowd of men:

> When men talk of sorcery, I stay inside my house. I don't go to my garden. I don't enter the forest. Look how my fingernails have grown long from idleness! . . . If you come upon a woman asleep in her garden, let her alone. Don't steal her skirt strings. Don't think of working sorcery against her man.

A Big Man from a distant village, the recipient of many "skins," responds:

> When a man from your village, or a neighbor, brings us leavings from one of your clansmen, I will say to him, "The man you want to kill is my comrade." And I will bring [those leavings] here to you and close the road of sorcery between us.

Then the host turns to a Big Man of a local enemy clan:

> A poison has come to us from far away. If I stay here with you, if my clansmen continue to live in this place, I am afraid the foreign sorcerers will kill us.

But his local enemy reassures him and pleads that he stay:

> Let your clan and mine not part! We used to go easily into each other's houses. . . . Now the talk of sorcery keeps us apart. We are afraid you will accuse us of drawing you into false friendship.
>
> If you find out that one of us has brought back poison, name the man and I will say to him, "Throw it away!" We are not dogs. We are not pigs. . . . We cannot live alone among the trees. We are men and have to live among men.

Months after a distribution of pork to foreign sorcerers, when a member of a local enemy clan becomes sick, the enemy clan may then accuse the hosts, in retrospect, of treachery, citing their presentation of pork on this occasion as having "opened the road of sorcery, not closed it. . . . You killed pigs and sent them to men of a distant place so they would eat them and

---

guarantee the purity and strength of warriors, they have no doubt declined since pacification. Nevertheless, my impression in 1973–75 (unsupported by quantitative data) is that men receive more food of higher quality than do women. Commensal taboos which prevent a man from eating banana, sweet potato, taro, or other foods that have been partially consumed, stepped over, or even touched by a woman or child, usually result in his being given the entire item at the start.

return here to kill one man!" The clan that gave the pigs points out, "We did not kill a wild pig and give it to them. When they kill pigs they will summon us, and we will go there and bring back the meat they give us." Pigs that are not wild, not "thrown" in one's path by ancestors but reared by the living and invested with their *auna,* have to be returned in kind. In sorcery transactions, as men repeatedly say, there is never a return gift. The payment for sorcery is never "cooled" because the repayment is theft. The return of the *rubese ugunu,* the sorcerer's fee, is the theft of his victim's leavings, a crime that fills the sorcerer with heat. When the victim's clan summon their enemies to feed them sugarcane and pork to "cool their stomachs," they attempt to spoil the sorcerers' conspiracy by making public reparations for the meat that was shared in secret to seal their pact.

## The Theory of Sorcery and Essence of Cure

"Everything about sorcery is hidden," men say. It is "the talk a man hides in his stomach, the words that make his stomach hot." Sorcerers work alone or in silent conspiracy and move without being seen. By the time a sorcerer's work is discovered, it is over and done. By the time a man falls ill, his *autaisana* are stolen and disintegrating; his enemies have been "pulled by their ankles" and paid off and their ambush magically erased from memory. Sorcery is known only through its consequences so that, though it is utterly concealed and invisible, its reality is manifest and never open to doubt (see Levy-Bruhl 1923; Evans-Pritchard 1976 [1936]). The intrinsically real ex post facto character of sorcery is represented by the very nature of leavings. They are the residues of a meal or copulation, tangible remains of something that is done, consumed, expended, and no longer open to view. The aim of curing is to expose what has already happened and disappeared. To stop a man from dying, the sorcery has to be made publicly visible and undone; the sorcerer has to be named; the thing he stole pulled out of its niche and restored to the victim; the act he committed in secret repeated before an assembly of men.

In theory, a sorcerer is extravagantly antisocial and conspicuous. He is a recluse, voyeur, "spoiler of the dead," and thief, and often a man possessed by the rampaging *kore* of his dead relations. When Rabofa's sister died in his arms, he said, her *kore* "went inside" his liver and stomach and drove him to set fire to his own house. "I was like a drunk man. I didn't have a thought for my belongings. . . . I just burned down my house!" After a Big Man died, two of his sons ate the fruit of a red pandanus growing near his grave. For weeks afterward, the two yelled in the night and roamed the village, stealing firewood, pointing arrows in people's faces and terrifying children: by eating the fruit, they had ingested their father's *kore* and become *neki*. The sorcerer may be flamboyant or reclusive but in either case tends to resemble his victim. A man who has just performed a spell behaves like the Big Man who fears sorcery, stays inside his house, lets his fingernails grow long from idleness, avoids social gatherings, etc. Indeed, in particular cases, a sorcerer is impossible to identify from outward behavior. Despite repeated cries to "Name the man!" men say, the true sorcerer is rarely revealed. Those publicly accused during *fobirikaina* tend to be either men "without names," men too inconsequential to be believably guilty, or men with "great names," Big Men above suspicion. When a man gets sick, a Big Man of his clan may privately seek out a Big Man of the clan he suspects and convince him to call a meeting of his own clan and flush out the culprit. "'Go to the river and get rid of it!' the suspected Big Man instructs his own clansman."

More often, Big Men related to a suspected—or even publicly named—sorcerer go to great lengths to protect him because they view him not as a sorcerer but as an ordinary man possessed by the enraged *kore* of a father, brother, son, wife, etc., using the only means available, since pacification, to carry out his duty.

> On his deathbed, *H* told his three sons, "When I am dead, get hold of my age-mate's feces and work sorcery on them so that he can die, too." His sons were afraid the sorcerer would eat ginger and they would never know who killed their father. One of them worked quickly. He got the feces and put them inside the base of a wild banana, inside a hole he made with his knife. He covered the hole so that no one would ever find it. But he told the Big Men what he had done.

Cures administered during *fobirikaina* compel the sorcerer to renew contact with his victim yet allow him to remain unidentified. When medicine men spit into their medicine, or hold a piece of singed pig's liver to the sun to imbue it with enemy-*auna,* or feed the stricken man pieces of ginger held under enemy armpits, or rub pieces of held pig fat on his shin, etc., they provide the victim of sorcery with generic leavings, leavings of men related to the sorcerer as members of his own clan or lineage. The essence of cure is not "naming the man," in this sense, but having him return to the scene anonymously or vicariously, in the person of an interchangeable clansman, and repeat his crime in public, in a way that forces him to donate spit, sweat, or *auna* and thus to put back the leavings he stole. The sorcerer's return gift restores the sick man to wholeness, "coldness," and health because it recasts the original theft and misuse of intimacy as part of a collective exchange of male substance.

Chapter Eleven

## On the Meaning of Hot and Cold

The sorcerer's rite, his stealing a man's leavings and secreting the leavings packet in an orifice of a female corpse, or a female orifice of a male corpse, or a "vagina" in the stem of a rotting banana stem, etc., is a symbolic sexual act that "heats" his own body. Yet the remotest contact with an actual woman, or with anything she has touched, or with anything faintly resembling her sexual anatomy puts out his fire and destroys his lethal hold over his victim. "Women are cold and ruin sorcery," men say. They are as cold as the forest floor and as "filled with water" as frogs and other creatures that dwell in icy streams. Yet men also say that a woman exudes a volatile heat that infects the food she handles, inflames her husband's sores, raises his fever, stunts her son's growth, and fatally "fills the nose" of any ordinary man who dares to watch her give birth to a child. A woman is "hot" from having sex and giving birth, yet she "cools" a sorcerer and wrecks the medicines made to remedy his work. By stepping over any ingredient or implement used to prepare a cure, she turns it "cold" and destroys its healing effect.

According to women's myths, woman was not always a creature of cold rivers and the ground. In one nonesoteric tale, the first woman is represented as a cassowary. The cassowary once lived in trees and could fly like other birds. She was "hot" and soared toward the sun.

> At first the cassowary did not live on the ground. She lived in trees and knew how to fly. But she ate unripe fruit [lit: tree-offspring]. She plucked fruit when it first appeared—while it was still in flower—and ate it all up. The parrot and the Hornbill watched the cassowary and asked her, "Why do you do that? The fruit isn't ripe or ready but you eat it anyway."
>
> "I'll eat the unripe fruit and leave you two the fruit that ripens," the cassowary replied. "No," the other birds said, "Let's let *all* the fruit ripen." But the cassowary didn't listen and kept eating new fruit. The parrot and the Hornbill decided to play a trick on her.
>
> The branch where the parrot slept was on the left, and the branch where the Hornbill slept was on the right. The cassowary slept in the middle. While she was gone, the parrot and the Hornbill made a deep hole in her branch and stuffed it with moss to hide what they had done. . . .
>
> At darkness the cassowary alighted on her branch. Pprrrh! the branch crashed to the ground. "What have you done?!" she cried. "You ate the fruit before it was ripe so you shall stay upon the ground," the other birds said. "We will eat the fruit when it ripens. The fruit we do not eat, the fruit we let rot and fall to the

ground, that shall be yours." The cassowary was once a bird like other birds.

Woman was "hot" and able to fly, according to women's myth, while she possessed her own branch. Men say that a woman is contagiously hot when she has sex or menstruates or gives birth to a child, while she is copulating with her husband or the Moon or while a child is "passing between her thighs." To portray the first woman as a cassowary who once knew how to fly, and had a branch of her own, is thus to compare her to a woman who, in a transient way, possessed a penis—during coitus or birth, fleeting eras when she was combined with a man. But according to this myth (a just-so story which, unlike the other *nenekaina*, gives no excuse for the heroine's fall) she misused her perch by eating unripe "tree-offspring" and was banished. The other birds kept their perches and gained exclusive access to the food supply—men kept their masculinity, in other words—by engineering the cassowary's downfall, cutting off her branch and forcing her to eat what was already fallen and dead. The two birds severed the cassowary's perch by making a deep hole and filling it with tree moss, the material women use as tampons. They cut off her giant penis and filled her vagina with menstrual blood, which men and women describe as "cold," "rotten," "stinking," "smelling of death," "dead," etc., and as the blood of a father or brother.

Like the small boy unplugging woman's flute or extinguishing her fire, like the giant penis eating his way inside the sleeping woman, the birds forcing the cassowary off her branch opens her hole: while she sat in the tree and was heated by the sun her hole was nonexistent or impenetrable. She was like a virgin whose opening is closed or so small, men say, "no man can fit his penis inside it." While woman was a virgin-cassowary, she possessed the Sun's giant penis: she was closed and could fly like a man. But she began to eat unripe fruit, literally, "children of the tree-branch." During her marriage to the Sun, she devoured the "head" he hid inside her. She ate the unready fruit of his loins and was banished to cold ground.

### Sun, Moon and Sorcerer

The Moon is the Sun's younger brother. According to my interpretation of men's myth of Primordial Fire (see Chap. 7), it is the Moon, or his stand-in the giant tree, who himself devours unready offspring. In men's myth, a small boy who is "the same as the Moon" leads the woman to a mountain lake, climbs an enormous tree, throws a stone into the lake, splashes out the fire "between her thighs," and retrieves the stone inside the long net bag around his neck. I have suggested that the boy and his deeds present an image of semen, or a humunculus, rising through the penis, ejaculated from the head or urethra, "killed" in the fall and reabsorbed. In order to extinguish woman's fire—to end her prior marriage to the Sun—the Moon sacrifices his firstborn but does not abandon him. He pulls the stone-cold boy back into the head or "first mouth" from which he spit him out.

During translations of their own myths, some men remarked to me that the Moon is a *rubese bana* or sorcerer. If we examine a sorcerer's work in terms of the Moon's mythic feats, then his efforts to steal his victim's leavings—by becoming the wife's lover, getting hold of semen encrusted on her string skirts, retrieving her menstrual or parturitory blood or pieces of her child's corpse, etc.—are like attempts to take leavings from a woman whose fire is out, whose vagina is cold and dead, as the boy retrieved the stone from the still lake. In the second phase of his work, when he deposits the leavings inside a corpse or rotting banana stem or *neki maha* or smoldering tree hollow—a sequestering that "heats" his own body—the sorcerer seems to incorporate what fell to the ground in the way the Moon's giant penis pulled back the lifeless stone. The link between sorcerer and Moon further implies that the cause of death is an enforced return to the head of the giant penis, a reentry into the "first mouth" while it is still wide open, still "spitting," still in the midst of putting out woman's fire.

The sorcerer transfers his victim's leavings from one vagina and puts them back inside another that exists both outside him, in a corpse or banana or *neki maha,* etc., and in his own "head." His work initiates a hidden coitus that decomposes his victim. By remaining inactive and reclusive, sleeping all day inside the *rubesenama,* abstaining from food and drink, smoking tobacco, shunning women, etc., he arrests the coitus in his belly, prevents it from reaching climax and ending too soon, before the victim is fully reabsorbed and disintegrated. A sorcerer is able to kill his victim invisibly and at a distance by making himself as *still* as the sleeping first man or the huge tree, motionless figures in the myths of both sexes that, until the myths' endings, copulate at a great distance and retrieve their "heads" without awakening or leaving the house—without ejaculating, reducing in size, or going cold. Having sex with a woman, eating food from her hands, touching the cold ground, getting wet, drinking water or sugarcane or eating juicy foods, getting up and moving about, etc., "cool" the sorcerer because they hasten or resemble the *end* of coitus, forcing him to withdraw from the only place where he can unite absolutely with his victim.

Like the Moon or tall tree, a sorcerer is an aloof but monumental phallus who conceals a stilled primal scene. That hyperphallic condition paradoxically turns him into a kind of bad mother. The sorcerer's fallen-and-buried leavings resemble not only the Moon's fallen-and-pulled-back head but also the cassowary's unripe and devoured fruit. In the context of women's myth, the sorcerer's retrieval of fallen seed is like the cassowary's eating unripe "children of the tree-branch." The sorcerer appears to be an ordinary man in the way a cassowary seems to be an ordinary, if oversized, bird. But a sorcerer, like a cassowary, has a secret "filled" vagina: his penis is wound up inside him like a coil of rope inside a net bag. The coitus is endless—stilled, solidified, and put away inside him so he cannot move or have sex like other men. A sorcerer has no wife and cannot "fly." He is like the first woman who is on fire, or possesses her own branch, or owns her own flute: his hole is invisible and *always filled*. By carrying out his spells and assuming mythic proportion, the sorcerer becomes not simply a bisexual figure but the embodiment of a ceaseless and silent congress. He "heats" his body into the mythic circumstance in which his victim arose, assuming the omnipotence of the primordial couple, of a mother whose whole body has the shape of a penis. His solitary posture, like that of the Moon or cassowary-woman or flute owner, is a paradox of complete union, incarnating the fantasy of a combination that disappears in fusion.

### Heat and Stillness: The Fantasy of Perfect Union

The sorcerer keeps the "heat" inside him by an attitude of stillness and reclusion. Like the Moon or tall tree or first man asleep in his house, he remains stationary or out of sight, yet his reach is vast and penetrating. Like the Moon's rays or first man's penis or the *auna* of a dreamer, a sorcerer is able to invade the most intimate spaces. His ubiquity and power, capacity to move silently and unseen, to steal leavings nearly by the force of his presence, etc., are combined with immobility and a tendency to "sleep inside the house" while other men are active and abroad. Indeed, sorcerers operate inside the settlement with the same license and capriciousness—and the same invisibility and stillness—with which certain ancestral *kore* dwell in the clan forest. Rather than move with peripatetic ease toward a distant sleeping woman, the eponymous founder of Remofi clan never left his mountain cave and kept all the women imprisoned with him. He was a terrifying giant who stole leavings from his victims without moving. According to a man of Remofi clan:

> The Man who was the ancestor of all us Remofi, the man called Remofi, was no ordinary-sized man! He was enormous, as big as the cave where he lived at Bikobikafi at the headwaters above the River Kaho. Go there and see yourself how big it is! . . . His name was Remofi, and he had many, many wives. He married a thousand women and never went anywhere. His body was too heavy for him to do anything but sit. He defecated inside his house, and his wives carried his feces outside. That's what they say.

Everyone wanted to see Remofi. And everyone who looked at him died! They pissed and shat on the spot! Remofi was *huge*. To summon his wives and children he didn't even open his mouth. "Mmmmmmm," he let out, "mmmmmmmm," from the pit of his stomach, and the ground shook. The whole earth shook. That's what I've heard.

This Remofi bore Titabuda and Titabuda bore Baiabese and Baiabese bore my father's father [whom the storyteller doesn't name because he has his same name]. Look, there aren't so many men between me and the very first man, between me and Remofi. . . . The cordyline they planted when he died is still growing. And my father says his bones—his enormous bones—are still there in the cave.

Once Guduha went into this cave and picked up a skull. He rolled tobacco and blew smoke through the eye socket, and afterward he went mad. He poured water into the skull through the hole and drank from it.[3] He became filled with *kore* and walked around in a mad state and we pitied him.

Remofi cannot speak nor move and requires a thousand women to remove his feces. Like a newborn, he is a demanding creature whom everyone wants to see. But he is no ordinary babe, as anyone who gets close to him discovers. Those who enter his cave irresistibly deposit leavings, lose their heads, and "die." Entry into Remofi's cave has the same effect upon his admirers as has a sorcerer inserting leavings into a "vagina." Like one of Remofi's visitors, the victim of sorcery returns involuntarily to the prehistoric site where he was conceived. If we look at Gimi sorcery as a set of performances, real and fantasied, whose cryptic dogma is myth, then the sorcerer seems to embody a malevolent ancestor who is at once enormous, like the Sun or Moon, and childlike; as the first man was both a "giant" and "unfinished" or fetal-like. The sorcerer draws his victim into the mad cave of conception by going there himself. He remains still, undisturbed and hidden inside his house, a posture that conjures between himself and his victim the unsurpassably close relation—the "hot embrace"—of father and child the first time they met head-to-head in the vast expanse of the womb. The sorcerer tries to sustain that critical moment by retaining his body "heat."

Women associate coldness directly with ejaculation. In secret love magic they teach a bride on the eve of her departure, they tell her she can excite her

---

3. Many of the skulls found in caves outside the village are broken open at the back, suggesting that the brains may have been extracted for eating. But no Gimi made that association to me.

husband by telling him his *ano* or "water" makes her "feel cold and shiver." "When you want your husband to get an erection, sing this song to him":

> Your *ano* flows down inside me
> And I shiver and shake. I feel cold,
> Cold as the River Furubitabana.
> When your water flows down in me,
> I feel cold and I shiver.

The second verse is the "husband's reply":

> I let my boil burst and my water flows down inside you.
> I shiver and shake. I feel cold.
> I let my boil burst inside you and
> I shudder cold as the wind.

A woman "feels cold," in song and in myth, when her fire is put out; when a man—or a boy in a treetop or a pair of birds—has extinguished her incendiary first love. During the bride's initiation or *haro,* men of the groom's lineage enact the role of fire extinguisher by filling a bamboo tube with water drawn from a clan river and spraying it on the bride and later "forcing" her to drink it. The river water, referred to in the ritual as *kore abe* or "ancestor urine," a euphemism for ancestral semen, "cools the bride" so that she is safe for the groom to enter (Gillison 1980, 1987). The groom relights the bride's fire and then extinguishes it again by discharging his own "heat"—"bursting his boil" in women's contemptuous phrase—and becoming as "cold" as the vagina he cools. "Heat" originates in sexual union but is dissipated by its fulfillment in climax and ejaculation.

If we interpret "heat" as coitus and "cold" as ejaculation, detumescence, and withdrawal, then the ritual condition of being "hot" or "cold" varies, not with sexual identity but with the sexual moment and relation (see Mead 1970:248–49, n.28). A man becomes "hot" or "hotter" when sexually united with a woman even in the remotest ways, by her stepping over him or sharing his food; or by his taking leavings from her "vagina"—from her string skirts, menstrual hut, birthing site, etc. A woman is "hot" when joined with a man in ways that may be similarly removed or metaphoric; when she is married to the Sun or "killed by the Moon" or when a child is born. Like the cassowary who lost her perch, a woman becomes cold, "as cold as the forest floor," "wet," inundated, etc., afterward, as the site where a child exited or semen "fell," where heat was lost and desire died. In certain circumstances, like sorcery, her body becomes the transmitter of what culminated there, as if she could impose the result of one man's act upon the next man who penetrates her or upon the next "hot" object that "passes between her thighs."

She is "cold" and "filled with water" and makes things cold because, once she has married or come of age, she herself has been made cold by a man or by the Moon. A woman is a put-out fire that puts out fire. Men treat the end of their own desire as if it were a female trait, as if a man's loss of sexual "heat" and potency were a component of woman's own nature, a condition she may transmit to other men by contagion.

### Heat and Homosexual Connection

When men say that a woman is "cold," they also seem to mean that her sex, or men's desire for it, destroys the symbolically homosexual "heat" between men. In a ritual vignette men perform late at night inside the men's house during the seclusion of first-stage initiates, they dramatize the female role of "cooling" the friendship between unmarried age-mates, a bond conventionally expressed by young warriors' braiding each other's hair. Three young men play the parts of two age-mates and a girl. The boys' long hair is represented by vines hanging in rows from bands tied around their heads.

> The "age-mates" sit by the fire and take turns weaving bright yellow strings of bamboo through long plaits in each other's "hair." The "girl" arrives and, seeing them together, sings:

> Beautiful Redhead! You make braids and your head pains!
> Go up to the headwaters, lovely yellow bamboo, and
> > Cool yourself there.
> Stand in the shade of the *kiba* tree and let me gaze at you.

Discussing the play with me afterward, one of the "age-mates" paraphrased the girl's song:

> "You don't need braids in your hair. How beautiful your head is without them! You are as lovely as the yellow bamboo threaded through your hair. Why sit here, in an unshaded place, while he makes your head pain? Go to the headwaters where the yellow bamboo grows, go to the place where you belong, and let the flowing water cool you. Go into the high forest, to the shade of the *kiba* tree, and I will make you cold. Look at my body and you will cool off."
> A woman is a cold thing.

To a man in the midst of man's work—sorcery, warfare, ritual—an actual, living woman is always "cold" because contact with her forces him to discharge the sexual "heat" that, by connecting him symbolically or *invisibly* with another man, enables him to use his power in the world. That empowering, seamless connection between men is modeled upon the very sameness of father and child at the moment of conception, the head-to-head exchange that generates all new life and originates inside the mother (see Chap. 7). The man-to-man bond that a real woman would destroy occurs paradoxically inside a mythic or ritually devised woman. The sorcerer or warrior connects himself to his victim by penetrating a woman-not-a-woman, becoming potent or "hot" inside the vagina of a corpse or banana stem or wound of an enemy, a hole that is actually or metaphorically dead, putrid, swamp-like, filled with blood, infected, etc., like the vagina of a menstruating woman or *kore badaha*. These dead female orifices are also teeming with life because, in the process of decomposing their contents, they produce new amalgamations, new head-to-head connections between men.

By performing secret rites, a sorcerer enters and incorporates this hidden female territory so that, by controlling his own body state, he manipulates his victim and other objects and events in the external world. Sorcerer and victim move independently about the settlement, yet they are invisibly united, a circumstance attested by their both being "hot." By stealing and sequestering his victim's hair or feces, by retrieving arrows whose tips are covered with enemy blood and placing them next to a fire, by pulling back the stone-inside-his-neck-bag, recoiling his giant penis with the "dead meat" wrapped at the head, etc., the sorcerer, warrior, Moon, or first man consummates a *long-distance* relation with another man, a relation that is sustainable only as long as it is secret and invisible, still and undisturbed; only as long as the mother inside whom it transpires is a corpse, a house, a cave, or a myth. Contact with an actual woman and arousal to the point of climax, experienced even in the remotest sense, by eating "watery foods" or leaving the house, etc., debilitates the sorcerer or warrior or first man because it forces him to withdraw from the mother's terrain and thus to fall out of touch with the other man who stands, by implication, for the mythic father-child.

### Rites of Cure: Cooling the Sorcerer Releases the Victim

When a sorcerer is forced to repeat in the Sun what he did alone by the Moon's rays, "inside a hole," etc., he undoes his dark deed, aborts its consequences, and provides a cure. He is forced to activate, and thus bring to a climactic end, the tie he has kept "hot," festering, internalized, dormant. The rites of *fobirikaina* try the suspect by making him *actually touch* the ailing man or corpse, making him do at close quarters what the sorcerer is able to sustain only by keeping a great distance. The pubic rites try the suspect by making him grasp the victim's toe or foot, rub his shin with cooked pig fat, feed him "burning hot" raw ginger that has been held under enemies' "hairy" armpits, or medicine laced with their spittle, or pig's liver "shot" by the sun with their *auna*. The toe, foot, or lower leg substitutes for the victim's penis (see Chap. 4); and the soft white fat, "hot" ginger, spittle, or sweat, etc., reproduce seminal discharge or the aftermath of coitus. If the suspect is, indeed, the sorcerer or a member of his clan, his feeding "semen" to the victim or holding his "penis" will make him "get hot and die": his whole body will ejaculate and show the sorcerer recommitting his crime, inducing climax, stealing substance, etc. The victim's involuntary release of "heat"—a corpse letting go of urine, feces, or intestinal gas; a sick man breaking into a sweat, trembling, or passing out—catches the sorcerer red-handed.

The demonstration produces a cure, or prevents the sorcerer from claiming another member of the deceased's clan, because, to provoke a release of "heat" in his victim, the sorcerer has to release his own heat and thus put back what he stole. To make a sick man "hot," a suspect has to donate the sweat of his hand or underarm or some other leaving. Suspected sorcerers who live in other villages add leaves of their clan forest and spit into the medicine they prepare so the sick man will ingest "something of his enemy." "If the sick man eats something of the man who worked sorcery against him, his illness will end," men say. "The sorcery would go cold and could not hold him." If the medicine men are indeed the culprits, their concoction will "heat" the victim and fill him with "water" so that he sweats, passes urine, or loses consciousness and then "goes cold" and recovers. When a man ingests a substitute for semen of the man who ensorcelled him, according to my interpretation, he climaxes and lapses into a postcoital sleep, a temporary loss of *auna*, or *petite mort*, from which he recovers.

Even when he does not recover, his paternal kinsmen still insist that his enemies line up and hold his foot so that he can "name" the killer and thus prevent more casualties in their ranks. Even a dead man can testify. His body can still respond to the sorcerer's touch, feel the heat, and let go. When the sorcerer prepares the medicine, holds the ginger, or touches the dead man's food, he puts back the *auna* he stole, converting his theft, and his invisible hold upon the victim and his clan, into a public exchange of substance. The exchange simultaneously opens and "cools" the bodies of both men: it unplugs the sorcerer's hole, so to speak, dissipates the heat of disintegration, and allows his victim's *auna* to escape.

### Creating a Second Exit

Before every cure or diagnostic proceeding, the victim's agnates perform a brief rite that alters the original mythic site of encounter with the sorcerer. Before suspects line up to rub pig fat on the sick man's shin, his comrades pull him, or just his leg or lower body, out his doorway or out a specially made opening in the *rotana,* the bamboo fence built around his house when he fell ill and went into seclusion. If he is well enough to walk into the taro garden where his medicine is being prepared, his kinsmen uproot stakes in the fence so that, after he has eaten, he can leave through a newly made exit. Soon after a man dies, his kinsmen tear a hole in the wall opposite the doorway of his wife's or mother's house where he was carried in his final hours so that, before suspects line up to hold his foot, his kinsmen can pull the lower half of his corpse out the torn opening (see Chap. 4).

Even in lesser rites, curers take pains to construct a second exit. When a child or adult is gravely ill, the father or other close agnates go into the clan forest to draw water from a fast-moving river, an overt symbol of ancestral "semen," and seal it inside a bamboo tube by tying a leaf over the open end. Before the father drips the water over the head of his dying child, before other clansmen pour the water over a leavings packet retrieved from a sorcerer's "rotting" niche and placed above the victim's head, before they pour the water into a grave shaft where they suspect their enemy have buried leavings, etc., they cut a slit in the side of the bamboo container so "the water does not leave the bamboo through the hole it entered." In each case, the victim's saving reconnection with the demonic *kore* or sorcerer is made to occur after the father or other kinsmen pull him, or the *kore,* "out a new door," removing one or the other through an opening other than the one through which he entered—or was symbolically inserted—through the theft and sequestering of leavings.

The bamboo tube containing river water invested with ancestral *kore,* the woman's house where a man dies, the fence surrounding the house where a man lies sick, these represent woman's body in the generic sense. "Woman is man's house," according to one current expression; and, in ritual, any bamboo container may be associated with the flute and, therefore, with the first woman. If the bamboo, or woman's house, or fence is a woman, a ritual embodiment of the mythic mother, then the father who makes a slit on the side of the tube before he drips water over his dying baby, the *ababana* who tear a hole in the house wall or remove planks from the fence, create a new exit like a "crying hole" in a flute, a second "vagina for bearing the child" (see Chap. 9). Looked at in these terms, cures for sorcery all begin by removing the victim from the scene of the crime, getting him out of the "vagina" where the sorcerer ensconsed him, or his leavings, like a plug in the mythic flute.

In the context of curing ritual, the open end of a bamboo container, the door of a house, the gate in a fence—any regular or *original entrance*—stands for the sorcerer's first and only hole, for the "vagina" in a corpse or rotting banana or in his own hot belly. In terms of men's myths, the sorcerer's first entrance lies at the head of his giant penis and represents his urethra *during* the first copulation: it symbolizes the moment when he was still inside the first woman and could automatically retrieve what he lost, "pull back" the child who stole life from him. The sorcerer's work is a symbolic taking-back of life, an enforced return to the source, equivalent to the Moon retrieving his own ejaculate or "fallen head." In that sense, the cure—pulling the leavings packet out of the sorcerer's secret niche, or pulling the victim or his lower body or limb out a new hole in a house or fence—is like rescuing the small boy from the treetop or unplugging the flute; it is like engineering a live birth through a new opening, a second birth to replace the mythic demise of the firstborn. The specially made second exit in a bamboo tube, fence, or house arrests the victim's decline, in these terms, in the same way as does the exchange of substance between sorcerer and victim: like the men's reciprocal losses of "heat" in spit, sweat, urine, feces, wind, etc., the new openings release the sticken man from the "head" of the mythic father or mother's brother and usher him into a world outside the mother. It is no coincidence that sorcerer and victim are typically related as affines and that their exchange recapitulates the secret exchange and mutual unplugging of flutes at marriage. I return to this interpretation in the Conclusion.

The rite of making a second exit in the sorcerer, or in some other ritual embodiment of the mother, symbolizes birth, or rebirth, as a hard-won interruption in the intrauterine cycle of death. The sorcerer's original sequestering of leavings—inside a corpse (especially of a woman who just died in childbirth), a heated marsupial nest, a *neki maha* crammed with frogs, snakes, and other fetal-like creatures who incarnate the *kore* of those who were stillborn or died as children—appears, in this analogy, as the installation of a child in the womb. The sorcerer remaining inactive while the leavings disintegrate is like a deconstruction of the main part of pregnancy when the father abstains from sex so the child can sleep and enlarge undisturbed. In the last days of pregnancy, men say, a man copulates with his wife "once more" to wake the child. "The semen makes the child tremble and fills it with strength." When the victim's kinsmen attempt to rescue him by finding the sorcerer's niche, pulling out the leavings to stop their disintegration; when they hold the leavings packet over his head and pour on water to "cool" and deactivate the sorcerer's spell; when they dig a shaft into a grave and pour in water from a running stream, etc., they create a ritual representation of the final ejaculation or "return to mother" as the means to "finish the child," induce birth, and open a new hole.

The Gimi universe contains two kinds of water, the swamp or *neki maha* and the rushing mountain torrent or waterfall, the one still "like a sorcerer," the other a swift-moving cure. The two types of water refer to opposite but sequential kinds of power or productivity: the first is "sleeping," silent, concealed, low-down, dark, Moon-lit, filled, coalesced, retained, stagnant, "hot," and corresponding to coitus and gestation; the second is "awakened," "crying," exposed, high-up, light, Sun-drenched, emptied, separated, "cold," and corresponding to ejaculation and birth. In dirges and songs of male initiation, men express the idea that a river, the vital effluent of ancestors, produces life by discarding its contents extravagantly along the banks, throwing up rich detritus and soil as it moves swiftly on its course. Men sing of giant trees in the same way, attributing their great height to the upward movement of male life-force, the surging of ancestral *kore* through the massive trunk toward the sun until it bursts forth like an ejaculation at the crown, sending out fruits and birds of every kind.

Men use the image of birds that come to feed in upper branches and then, startled by a hawk or hunter, fly away en masse, as a symbol of male initiates emerging from seclusion in the men's house. Like birds feeding in treetops, the initiates take nourishment from the "heads" of Big Men so they can be born in an explosive discharge at the end of *apina*, riding out the door of the men's house on their *ahamo*'s shoulders. "The *oromo* [*Paradisaea raggiana* or Count Raggi's Bird of Paradise] is like a man," men say, because it seeks the company of other males. "Men could be like the *oromo*. The boys we bear are as beautiful as new birds, but we get too close to them and kill them with sorcery. Young *oromo* learn to fly because [their fathers] do not touch their bodies nor steal their leavings!"

In initiation songs, men represent the birth of their sons into manhood with images of sudden induced flight, hectic dispersal from a massive source like a river or giant tree. Men model ritual birth upon actual birth as the deliberate achievement of the father, as a dramatic separation from the head of a mythic giant, or grandfather, which the father provokes and assists. The flying arrow that puts feeding birds to flight creates an image of a man "shooting" at a tree and inducing ejaculation on a monumental scale. Male creativity—and the cure for sorcery—seem to lie in the disturbance or interruption of an entropaic gestation like the growth inside still water or a tree before it fruits, a profuse but silent fertility that kills and consumes its own unless actively ended and revealed. A man has to "wake the child" and bring it out a new hole so it does not "stay asleep and die inside the mother."

### The Fatality of Mother Love

The sorcerer is identified not simply with the Moon or *kore* or giant penis but with what he accomplished, with his disappearing inside the first woman, extinguishing her fire and ending her marriage to the Sun—or to some eternally prior father figure. In this analogy to myth, the sorcerer's rites reduce his victim to the status of the firstborn whom the Moon devours, or withdraws into his "head," in the midst of coitus with the first woman: the deadly "heat" or secretly homosexual contact between sorcerer and victim can be sustained only inside some facsimile of the mother or vagina. The sorcerer's identity is with neither the Moon nor the first woman, in this sense, but with their union, as if he embodied an arrested version of the myth's main event. The sorcerer's relation to his victim replicates the relation between the copulating primordial pair and the child they never stop creating-and-devouring, burning to ashes, reducing to menstrual blood, turning to stone or a plug of pubic hair. The notion that the sorcerer's secret niches exist inside him, and that his stealing and sequestering leavings are tantamount to pulling them out of one vagina and putting them back inside another, suggests that his rites turn his own body into a flute he unplugs and replugs, as if he himself were the first woman/giant penis heated indistinguishably into one.

The sorcerer, or seamlessly bound first pair, always has the mother's shape, and appears to be alone, because the father disappears inside her. In images of the first flute, cassowary and python, the myths of men and women seem to ascribe death, or the first menstruation, to mother love, as if the mother were a solitary phallic creature who willfully "ate unripe fruit" or sent her offspring into a conflagration. But in other, more esoteric myths, women reveal that the first woman's aloneness—and foul deed—are the consequence of her first marriage. In tale after tale, the heroine marries her father unknowingly and, when she realizes what she has done, kills her child in a frenzy of guilt and revenge. Then she "gives back" the child, offering it as a meal to her unsuspecting father-husband (see Chap. 3). She transforms the child her husband gave her into the blood she keeps "between her thighs." In men's myths, the same notion of immediate transformation of semen into blood, of the oneness of departure and return, the inseverability of life and death are symbolized by the Moon "pulling back the stone." The concept of death-in-return to the mother seems to represent a convergence of women's and men's fantasies: by "going back into the first hole" the deceased both reunites with the hidden father and consummates the mother's wish for the return of her first love. In death, it might be said, a man realizes his mother's wish to take him back and to keep her father as an invisible and indivisible part of herself.

If a sorcerer, indeed, appropriates the power of a mother to reabsorb her child and to overcome the separations in existence, might it be true, after all, that Gimi men secretly believe women possess a creativity superior to their own? That they really see the first woman as supreme as their own myth insists? Do men actually rate the sleeping/concealed/coalesced/gestative mode of production higher than the awakened/exposed/emptied/ejaculative mode? And are the women who seem to agree with men's low assessment of their sex, the ritual leaders who berate brides and female initiates, merely demoralized by the lengths to which men go to deny their secret envy (Bettelheim 1954; Mead 1970; Lidz and Lidz 1977)?

Women and men agree that "women dream first" and can "see the *kore*," the patrilineal ghost who initiates conception and, when angered, inhibits birth. But only men insist that women, on account of witnessing birth and seeing the *kore*, have the power to see what men do in hiding, and even to know what they secretly feel. Women's power to dream often gives them the initiative in marriage, men say. BoðaEha attributed his first interest in his wife, Revakione, to her dreaming of him and causing him to dream of her the same night. According to BoðaEha, Revakione dreamed that she saw him while she was with her mother in the garden. "I held her vagina and said, 'I want to marry you.' And Revakione replied, 'I will marry you.'" That same night, BoðaEha remembered:

> I saw Revakione in a dream. I took my bow and arrows and my ax and went to my garden. Revakione was going to her garden, too, but she saw me and followed me instead. I turned around and asked her, "Where are you going?" "I want to follow you," she said. And I asked, "Are you mine that you wish to follow me?" "I am yours," she said. We walked together to my garden. I threw a lighted firestick at her, but it didn't fall to the ground. It stuck to the upper part of her arm and burned her. I got some water and poured it on her to put out the fire.
>
> I saw all this at night in my dream. The next day on the road . . . I met Revakione carrying red pandanus and said to her teasingly, "*nabogo!* Let me buy some of your pandanus!" I spotted the sore on her arm. "What hit you, *nabogo?*" I asked her. And she replied, "You burned me last night." That's how she revealed herself to me. "You burned me last night with a firestick. I saw you in my dream. I think of you all the time and want to marry you," she said.
>
> She went to her father and said, "I want to marry BoðaEha." Her father came to my house and asked me, "Did you really want to buy red pandanus or were you tricking her?" . . . Then her father told his brothers, "You can take payment from BoðaEha. My daughter likes him only." And my father gave them payment.
>
> That is how we two met in our dreams and were married.

Because women "dream first," some men say, they have the initiative in matters of love and in becoming pregnant: the *kore* visits the woman first, showing her the sex of the child, and then returns the same night to "trick" her husband. But in granting women this kind of priority, men seem to deny the earlier arrival, and superior power, of a father in the literal and figurative sense, underrating both the social role of men who arrange their childrens' marriages and the spiritual input of ancestral *kore* who deposit the fetus and control its emergence into the world (see Jones 1925; Spiro 1968). Women may "dream first," but they dream—and become pregnant—only *after* the *kore* enters them. A woman's father allies himself with the *kore* or Moon in order magically to control her fertility. Considered in this light, men's tributes to women's initiative and insight, and their myths about the female origin of the world, are a means to conceal the mythic Father by treating him as attribute and hidden power of the Mother. Men deny the Father's role by assigning it to an angry ancestor or sorcerer or life-destroying Moon, to a man who—by dying or becoming invisible or impossibly distant—is able to penetrate the Mother first and *seem always to be part of her,* as intrinsic to her as pubic hair or menstrual blood or the plug in her flute.

If this is men's vision of the Mother, I have argued, it fits women's own view. According to my interpretation of women's secret rites and myths, women conceive of their bodies as fused or coalesced with an invisible and ambivalent male element. They portray themselves as inhabited by the Moon or their brother's "noses," as pursued by sorcerers and secret lovers; and they equate this illicit male presence with both the creativity and deadliness of menstrual blood, with both their talent for nurturance and tendency to pollute whatever they touch. Women view motherhood, in these terms, as the exposure and cutting off of their mythic selves, as the gradual loss of secret male contents acquired—or stolen—during prenatal congress with the Father.

Sorcery beliefs and the rites of *fobirikaina* suggest that men regard the Mother, or the Womb, as an intractable holder of power; as an inert vessel—like a flute or house—that can be filled with music, lit, heated, made to exude secrets, etc., only when a man inserts his wind or sends back his penis and encounters his predecessor. When men credit women with a unique capacity to "see the *kore*" and treat them as mythic originators, in this sense, they treat as woman's invention the thing her body *conceals,* denying that another man somehow, invisibly and unaccountably, arrived in her beforehand. Men and women claim to communicate through their dreams in a way that parallels the kind of intercourse I hypothesize between their separate myths—by agreeing to omit or underrate the presence of the Father. In dreams and myths, both sexes disguise the incestuous origin of life by treating it not as an event but as *attributes* added to the Mother or hidden inside her body. The sexes' ensuing mythic argument, and Gimi society itself, seem to be founded upon this augmented version of woman. The rules of marriage, rites of exchange, and cures for sorcery are all designed in this sense to deconstruct woman's body and to repossess her misappropriated assets.

# CONCLUSION

# TWELVE

# Myth as Ultimate Reality

Gimi men claim that the continuity of society, and their own authority, rest upon the secret of bamboo flutes. I have treated the underlying or unconscious content of the flute myth—extrapolated not only from men's exegeses but also from a tacit dialogue between men's and women's versions—as comprising *the* organizational premise of Gimi ritual and exchange. From that perspective, the fundamental problem of social relations is one of dissociation. The deepest structure of kinship and marriage, the core relational pattern, stems in Gimi terms not only from the drive to reciprocate but also from the need to sever fantasied connections, to open woman's body, annul her first marriage, and resurrect the firstborn child as the symbol of individual life. The operative symbolism of exchange reflects not only the requirement for integration or sociality but, more prominently, the wish to avoid it. For the Gimi, I have argued that reciprocity is the most immediate form not simply of "integrating the opposition between the self and others" as Lévi-Strauss says (Lévi-Strauss 1969:84) but also of creating that opposition as if it did not, or need not, exist.

The equivalence of objects is less the precondition for exchange than its ritually concocted result; less the intrinsic character of an item than a resolution to the dilemma of having to give up parts of the mythic self and yet keep it intact—of men having to renounce their sisters when they would rather "marry their sister, commit incest, and have no need of any other woman in order to reproduce life" (Godelier 1986:158). Gimi principles of equivalence and rules of marriage allow both men and women to achieve the desired impossibility, to get back or keep the persons and things they must give up, to lose a sister or brother yet acquire a "sister" or "brother," to reinstate myths of their past at the same moment as they exchange them away. The exchange is conducted in terms that tend to deny its existence, giving the illusion that the separations it creates, the expulsion, disengagement, or opposition of relations it achieves, have not really occurred and need not exist. The sym-

345

bolism of exchange treats opposition, or the escape from myth, as if *it* were the fantasy, as if "the joys eternally denied to social man, of a world in which one might *keep to oneself*" (Lévi-Strauss 1969:497; original emphasis) were not lost but attained as the very essence of the social contract.

Gimi exchanges dissociate or "break apart" mythic elements through the divestiture and accusation of women. The decoration of women mourners with remains of the deceased, the loading of flutes into brides' net bags, and the embellishment of women who accompany the brides with every kind of wedding pork allow men to carry out exchanges as if they were rescuing something—or someone—who appears to be part of the mother but was in fact stolen from the father. The content of Gimi mortuary ritual, the year-long series of rites in which women have to give back, in exchange for head payments, mourning raiments made from the deceased's clothes and net bags, blackening and clays used to adhere his spirit to the face and body, etc., suggests that women having eaten a man "in secret"—as a matter of fact or fantasy—has the meaning of making him *seem* part of them, of creating an illusion of female power through misappropriation and misuse of the male. At marriage, women transport the bride with cooked pork, symbolizing her death as an object of exchange. She is reduced to her mother's cargo in the marriage transaction, and, as such, carries the same phallic lode as a man's corpse in mortuary ritual. This interpretation of the public exchanges at death and at marriage is in keeping with the content of women's own eso-teric rites in the sense that they, too, contain an image of woman's body as coalesced with, or housing, a dead male element.

The combined scenarios of men's and women's myths and secret rites sug-gest that life arises in, and is sooner or later reclaimed by, a *hidden* mythic father. The father is personified in ritual by the mother's *ababana* or paternal kinsmen in the sense that they enact his mythic rage and resentment and accept compensation for his mythic losses. In public discourse, in the term "to menstruate," *hibo fa* (lit: *hik*/Moon + *mo*/the + *fa*/hit, strike, implant or kill), and in the equation of the firstborn child with "Moon's blood," the primordial father is symbolized by the Moon. The Moon is like Chronos. He devours his every child, turning his head into the site of perpetual car-nage, a metaphor for uninterrupted incest, for the horror of one generation swallowing the next before it is born so that time and kinship are lost. The Moon commits his crimes in darkness, in the hidden precincts of Woman's Body, because he is ensconsed there in eternal copulation. The Moon never goes outside, never sees the light of day, so that Woman seems to be alone. *She* appears to be the cannibal and to own the flute on account of her seam-less union with the Moon. But she merely "holds the *kamiba*": men take it away and leave the whole blame in her hands.

*The War between the Sexes: The Theft and Countertheft of Flutes*

Taken together, various Gimi theories of procreation indicate that the sexes are created alike in the image of the mythic father. But the male remains the father's clone-like offshoot while the female is altered at marriage to "house" a new man. When a woman marries, according to women's myths, she herself cuts off the giant father. But in men's myth, and according to the logic of men's secret rites, woman's brother steals her flute and opens a "second vagina" so she can accommodate a new husband—one who is not like the Moon and who has her brother's "same name." If marriage and first menses represent woman's loss of her birthright, whether by theft or her own renunciation, then the "theft" of a man's corpse—considered not as an illicit act nor entirely "women's idea," as men insist, but as a culturally orchestrated show of protest—symbolizes woman's attempt to refill the hole her marriage created and take back her father's flute.

In the era before Australian control, the dead were installed on roofed-in platforms, exposed to the elements and supposedly left to rot in peace. But there were occasions, as Gimi men and women recall, when a man's mothers and sisters, in a frenzy of grief, returned secretly to his garden, pulled him off the platform and ate him. Even when carried out entirely as ritual fiction, women's theft of a corpse may be interpreted as a kind of retaliation for the theft of woman's flute in the mythic past. Interpreted in these terms, the series of mortuary rites in which men buy back the *auna* of the deceased from women mourners are tantamount to men repossessing the sacred object they originally stole from women at marriage (Gillison 1983a).

After a death, paternal kinsmen apportion sections of cooked pork in a way that supposedly recapitulates the consumption of a corpse, as if pigs were merely the second course of a cannibal meal women undertook as part of a conspiracy against men. Men insist they were utterly unaware of women's plot and looked on afterward in horror, adding that women preferred to eat men and leave female corpses at the disposal of sorcerers. By providing the deceased's "mothers" with other meat to replace the "head" they have already eaten, the paternal kinsmen open women's bodies and create safe exit for the dead man's spirit. The head payment is paradoxically a reclamation of the male in the same way that a man emptying the bride's flute, and feeding her "back" her father's meat, reclaims the flute and puts it back into circulation among men. But the *manner* in which a woman is "fed back the head" in the series of rites that end her mourning, and during her marriage, maligns her, I have argued, because it denies her capacity to return men's gift *in living form* and thus gives men the pretext to appropriate her child before it is even born.

Head payments deliver the deceased into a forest afterworld. They arrange his rebirth and escape from women by attributing death to women's illegitimate hunger, compensating women's loss as if it were spoils of a willful and capricious theft. A woman in mourning is treated like a bride, as if she had "plugged her hole" in secret to consummate an illicit marriage, compelling her present husband (or men of his lineage) to offer her another "head" as replacement. As soon as the *ababana* or husbands finish handing out head payments to women mourners, they distribute parts of the same animals to the women's fathers and brothers, compensating them, too, for the release of the dead man's spirit. If the offer of head payments condemns mourning women, then, in corollary fashion, it implicates their paternal kinsmen in the same matrimonial crime and, paradoxically, mitigates women's blame. The gift acknowledges the hidden presence of a mythic father, an enraged and ravenous Moon, suggesting that neither bride nor cannibal acts alone. But the acknowledgment is kept as a secret among men, and women are left publicly alone with their guilt. Head payments ransom the life of an individual by buying out the father's original interest, but they do so in a way that keeps him out of sight and still hidden inside the mother. By returning to the mother to finish the child, that is, by continuing to exchange the head after marriage, men are able to come to terms with the mythic father and, unlike women, to mitigate their guilt.

### The Flute as Core Symbol

In the past, Gimi say, men forbade women to see the flutes on pain of death. In the late 1950s and early 1960s, the cult began to fade after missionaries carried flutes out of the men's houses, showed them to women and children, and burned them. But before the start of my first fieldwork in late 1973 there was a revival of traditional practices, and men in many Unavi villages were rebuilding the men's houses to initiate their adolescent sons and telling them that the flute's haunting, syncopated cries were made by a newborn *kamiba*, an imaginary cassowary-like bird whose mother comes out of the forest on rare occasions to give birth inside the men's house. During first-stage initiation, men tell the boys that "the *kamiba* is a woman" and that "nothing is inside! It is we men who blow into the bamboo and make it cry!" Years later, men reveal that a player's wind is his "penis" and that the "cries" he blows out of the flute are his "child."

Based upon analyses of myths and rites surrounding the sacred flutes, I have suggested that the *kamiba* is more than an icon of woman's body. Playing it condenses the whole prenatal era, summarizing the process by which a man installs his child, leaves it to sleep during gestation and then goes back to finish it and induce birth. The flute arrests and objectifies much of what transpires in the womb, crystallizing in a ritual artifact the intrauterine events that determine human relations and anatomy. The father deposits and nourishes the child during many acts of intercourse so that the child's whole body is like an enlarged mirror-image of the penis. The fontanel is called the "first mouth," men say, because the mythic first man, a prototype of a fetus, had no mouth and took in food through a gaping hole at the top of his head. The "open," throbbing, hair-surrounded fontanel through which the unborn ingests nourishment seems to correspond to—and to reflect—the orgasmic urethra. From this perspective, the fontanel memorializes the first period of intrauterine life when the giant penis fed the child through the head. But in direct remarks, men compare the fontanel not to a urethra but to a vagina, pointing out that it is the first part of the child to touch and enter the birth canal. Discussing the symbolism of objects and qualities, Gimi men readily refer to a woman's sex but rarely make direct associations with the male.

Men imply a relationship between the urethra and vagina in the sense that they say the head of the penis is inundated with menstrual blood and other vaginal fluids postcoitus, which is why men warn each other against falling asleep after orgasm. The fact that men envision menstrual blood as flooding the penis during sex suggests that they see the father as not only nourishing the child in utero but also as exchanging substance with it; and the fact that blood always shows in the birth canal before the head of a living child suggests that that very first head-to-head transaction was a disaster: the father killed the firstborn by withdrawing him into the "vagina" at the top of his "head." This first murderous father was not the child's eventual "true father" but the Moon, the ancestral *kore,* the giant penis who invaded his mother's house while she slept unaware. *This* father arrived inside the mother during her own conception, when she herself was a blind fetus and ate her father's head. Even after she is born and married to another man, he is reluctant to leave her body, and she is ambivalent, often giving him safe refuge in the crevices where she hides her menstrual blood.

As ritual artifact, I have argued, the flute arrests such complicated scenarios of intrauterine life, combining relations among generations, parricide and filicide, copulation and death, gestation and birth, etc., as if they were simultaneous and the same (Gillison 1989). The "unnoticed" plug of pubic hair symbolizes the Moon's lurking habitation of woman's body; and the blood that "first appears" when the boy pulls out the plug reveals the Moon's expulsion and his retaliation in the killing of the firstborn. The flute a man manufactures when his daughter marries presents her body in the shape of his penis, or the giant penis of the Moon, symbolizing their perfect but lethal marriage. By mythologizing his daughter, shaping her to fit his ancient desire, he transforms her into a gorgeous instrument, an object to entice another man who has the same name as his son. When a man gives his daughter in marriage, literally, *habarena,* a "cutting," he stops making head payments on her behalf and "cuts her off." He sends her away *in the midst* of their mythic union, while his "head" is still inside her, making her both irresistible—filling her mouth with siren cries that summon the boy—and accessible through a new opening. Interpreted as ritual enactment of the Moon killing the first woman, the father's various constructions of the bride, his having her face tattooed with a beard, etching matching "pubic hair" on the flute and stuffing it with hair-covered meat, etc., represent his giving her away by amputating part of himself, creating a second vagina in her to match the one in his own "head," sacrificing the "hole" of his desire to another man.

### The Exchange of Flutes: Deconstructing the Mother

The iconography of the flute shows that a bride, or mythic mother, conceals the father. Men construct the bride as the secret vessel of her father, converting his rage and desire into her own attributes—her pubic hair, "beard," menstrual blood, and even the shape of her body. Men make the father disappear, as it were, so they can placate him and come to terms in the absence of his debilitating anger, offering him a new "head" to replace the one he sacrifices inside his daughter. Personified in the two fathers of the brides, the mythic father orchestrates the whole operation from behind the scenes, contriving his own absence as a liberating ruse (Bidou 1989). The brides' fathers fill the flutes with "hairy" meat and make them unplayable, as the mythic flute was plugged with pubic hair, and then exchange them in secret. As their daughters depart for the grooms' compounds, the men hide the instruments inside their net bags so that, upon arrival, each may empty the other's flutes and cut open blowing holes inside rings of "pubic hair" the other man incised. The exchange effectively unplugs the flutes—and the brides—by removing the "heads" the fathers installed.

After flutes are exchanged, they have two "vaginas," a blowing hole where the player inserts his wind or "penis" and a sounding hole where the "cries of his child" emerge. Like a flute, a woman's body after marriage is divided into two zones, a silent lower "vagina" where her husband goes in and an upper body where she cradles his child and produces a flow of milk, soothing words and tender songs (see Devereux 1972:218). Like the prepartum and postpartum taboos that keep a man away from his pregnant and lactating wife, the opening of a second hole in the flute symbolizes the segregation of woman's sexual and reproductive functions so that she is wife or mother but never both at the same time nor in the same hole. "It is as if two aspects of the human being—sexuality, on the one hand, and the production and growing of children, on the other—had been split off one from the other" (Mead 1970:260).

The exchange of flutes deconstructs the mother, in this sense, assigning her reproductive functions to a "second vagina" in order to avoid the mythic collision between her father and husband/child. In the flute myth, a small boy goes to his sister's house and steals her flute. But when he puts his lips to the blowing hole, he finds that the hole is plugged and no sounds come out. When he removes the plug and blows into the empty chamber, the myth says, "the Moon kills woman for the first time." According to the myth's latent symbolism, the boy enters the mother while she still copulates with the Moon or mythic father, and his head gets stuck in her hole. When he pulls out his head, her hole fills with blood—the blood of the firstborn, blood of his own murdered self. Entering his mother/sister costs the small boy his life: he displaces the Moon but the Moon pulls him back like a stone. In men's myth, the marriage of brother and sister ends in the mutual destruction of father and child.

But in marriage ritual the flutes are exchanged and opened in a new way: the creation of a second vagina saves the brother, and converts him into a husband, by averting the unseen collision with his father. In the paradoxical manner of ritual transactions, the means of avoiding calamity is to appear to repeat it, to perform a "mock calamity" that defeats the real one (Frazer 1963 [1922]). When a pair of (fully initiated) brothers-in-law play the flutes, each replays the mythic encounter with his father in a way that avoids the mythic outcome. Each reverses his own death in utero by redoing, in place of his "same-named" partner, the first head-to-head exchange. Each player sends in his wind, offering his "head" to the hidden father. In the rhythmic pauses when the music stops, the father devours him, retaliating for the son having put his lips on the plug and eaten the father's head. But the son—or flute player—does not really die because the head he inserts is merely a replica of his own, donated by his brother-in-law. With the next breath, the next gift of his head, the player escapes the father and comes back to life in sounds that "fly" out the other end of his flute. The mythic son resurrects himself and excretes his father in the child he pushes out of the flute's higher second hole.

When brothers-in-law play the flutes together, each recapitulates the *other's* first marriage and death. But the "dead heads" they leave inside the woman—recreated during *hau* in the *kamiba* "feces" fed to initiates, in the "killed" meat stuffed into the flutes and fed to the brides, etc.—will not die as did their mythic counterpart. The back-and-forth movement of flutes between men, and of a man's wind inside the flute chamber, rescues the firstborn child by switching the Moon's cast-off parts so that he *remains divided:* the Moon cannot simply reabsorb his fallen issue and reduce it to blood because the head returned to him—the one blown into the mouth of the flute during *apina, kuta,* and other rites—is not the same as the one he lost. It looks like his own but comes from another man.

Ritual overturns the mythic result through the use of facsimiles contrived by absent fathers. In the marriage rite, the groom is no longer the brother. But because he receives the brother's "same name" he can play his part in the exchange that cancels the mythic theft. Understanding how to create and deploy ritual facsimiles is the essence of male knowledge; it is the information men reveal to their sons and sisters' sons without words, through demonstrations performed during a whole series of initiations. When Big Men reveal the flutes to adolescent initiates, they tell them that "nothing is inside!" But then they make the boys close their eyes and instruct the *ahamo* to feed them the *"kamiba's* feces," chunks of salted pork or salty blood drawn from the Big Men's arms. Having insisted the flutes were empty, the leaders of the rites convey a contradictory message by feeding the initiates the flutes' contents in the form of their own blood or "feces." Years later, when the boys marry, their elders revise this information about the flute's contents, showing them that the flutes are filled—not with the father's feces—but with the hairy head of his child.

Men's secret rites imply that the bride is an eternally bad mother. If left to have her way, she would never let go of the father. Men place plugged flutes on her back as the icon of her guilt and immorality, of her harboring the father, reducing the firstborn to "blood between her thighs," etc. If, as Lévi-Strauss has argued, "the emergence of symbolic thought . . . required that women, like words, should be things that were exchanged" (Lévi-Strauss 1969:496), among the Gimi it is because such exchanges allow men to use women's wish for the father as cover for their own. In sister exchange, and in the simultaneous "secret" transfer of flutes as phallic symbols of the brides, Gimi men disguise the fulfillment of incestuous and homosexual wishes, treating the conjugal relation as a relation to their wives' fathers and brothers as stand-ins for their own. By manufacturing flute-woman as primary object of exchange, men treat the forbidden encounter with the father as if it could occur *only* in mythic prehistory, before birth, in the darkness of woman's body: they obscure the father's role in an unnoticed plug of hair and blame the mother for their ills.

### The Gift as Accusation: Head Payments That Blame the Mother

The Gimi notion of death can be defined, in one sense, as the moment head payments cease to persuade the primordial pair to remain apart; the moment the Moon disappears again inside the mother and she swallows the child. From the perspective of myth, head payments are perpetually owed alimony and ransom, inducements offered to the Moon and his wife to divorce and to liberate the child they engendered as hostage. Head payments propel the individual through life, and into afterlife, by continuing in rite after rite to undo the fatal entanglement in which every child is conceived and tends always to become reabsorbed. Each undoing is temporary because the anger and remorse of the primordial father always come back to life. The man who gives away "the head of his child" with his daughter loses a vital part of himself. Though he agrees to part with it when she marries, he feels robbed every time she bears a child and tries to reclaim his gift by cursing the child. At every crisis in a person's life, at every moment of achievement or vulnerability, the *ababana* publicly "return the head" the mother's father bestowed inside her, exposing the content of his flute so that it becomes separate from him and he cannot take it back.

Rites of exchange tend to be repeated and lifelong because they advance the process of disengagement by constructing relational distinctions *on the model of their dissolution*. The exchange of flutes and head payments create an affinal alliance, but the form of the payments reproduces the incestuous first marriage so that the exchange also repeats the union it is designed to interrupt or override. Through the act of exchange, men enter woman's mythic prehistory in order to cancel her ancient attachments and avert a fatal collision inside her body. But to avoid that collision they represent its *occurrence* in a condensed, material form: the flute and the gift of the "child's head" recreate woman's first marriage to the Moon as movable, and removable, objects. The exchange of flutes simultaneously undoes *two* first marriages: each recipient extracts the plug in the other's flute; each evicts the Moon on behalf of the other.

The symbolism of this expulsion, the terms in which exchanges—and flute playing itself—mutually cancel incestuous first marriages, is to reorganize woman's anatomy, to construct a second vagina as perfect replica of the first, so that the gift seems to be a "return of the head," a reentry into the Moon's same hole. Although the head payment exposes the Moon's presence inside the first woman, and thus acknowledges his role in instigating the deadly first union, the effect of its transfer, and of exchanges in general, as I argue, is to blame the mother. It is she who tries to keep the "head" when men return it to the father by depositing it in her look-alike mouth, inside her net bag, etc. It is *her body* that has to be opened and emptied because she is intractable and would keep his child unborn. The Moon, personified by the bride's father and brother and by men in general, is merely reluctant and can be persuaded with gifts to quit her body. Indeed, he is in cahoots with her husband from the start, helping him to steal and empty the flute.

## Marriage and Head Payments as Ultimate Rites of Cure

Gimi men design flutes—and, by analogy, their whole society—not to valorize female fertility but to cure the fatal consequences of men's own desires. Interpreted in terms of the flute myth, as men themselves advise, Gimi life-crisis rites are men's repeated attempts to solve their own mythic attachments as if they stemmed from a correctable fault in woman's anatomy. Tattooing a beard on the bride, cutting out the playing holes in wedding flutes, making a "new opening" on the side of a bamboo water container or in a fence or house wall, etc., may each be regarded as provisioning the first woman with a second vagina to be used *solely as exit,* a place where the spirit of the newborn or sick or deceased can come out of mother without encountering her enraged and ravenous "first husband" on the way in. The ritual emptying of a bride, flute, fenced enclosure, house, etc., reorganizes the mother so that father and child are not forced to "travel the same road"; so that a man does not have to "blow" into the hole where his wife menstruates. The rites create an escape route so that the doomed first child—represented by the initiate, groom, sorcery victim, or deceased—can flee the primordial father and come back to life.

The myth of a plugged flute, or bad mother, is embodied not only in actual flutes and in women themselves but also in bamboo water containers, houses, fences, and the bodies of sorcerers. The sorcerer's method of attack is to steal his victim's leavings and place them inside a corpse or rotting banana stem or *neki maha,* a secret, disintegrating niche that corresponds to a vagina hidden in the sorcerer himself. Acts of sorcery internalize the whole myth of first coitus and place the sorcerer in a condition like that of a bride, as if the Moon had disappeared inside him, taken refuge in a stilled copulation, and were blocking his exit. The method of cure is to "cool" the sorcerer, remove the leavings from his niche, make a new hole in a bamboo tube, etc., as if these measures could open the sorcerer, as if his body, or the one where he sequestered the leavings, were a flute that could be unplugged, equipped with a "crying hole" and made to let go of the child.

Rites of sorcery arrange a deadly reunion between men who have met before inside the mother: sorcerer and victim are often related, at least categorically, as mother's brother and sister's son, a relation that carries the mythic significance of father and unborn child. If acts of sorcery realize the fatal potential of men's homosexual and incestuous wishes, then rites of marriage and exchange offer the cure. At the climax of *ðau,* the feast that celebrates the birth and naming of a child and the first gift of the head, the father's father, or men of his lineage, hand the child to the mother's brother. Holding the newborn and a bouquet of "feces-smelling grass," a symbol of past sorcery thefts, the father's father says to the mother's brothers: "Accusations of sorcery have passed between us. Let the child now born to your sister close that road!"

In virtually explicit terms, men characterize marriage and the birth of children as the means to end thefts of one another's leavings or "feces." If sorcery is the disastrous result of father and son coming back together inside the mother, then marriage is a rematch with a different outcome: rather than reenter his father's "head" and die in the womb, the son—revived in the groom who takes his name—"blows out" the father and emerges reborn in his child. Marriages stage the mythic father-son encounter in a way that reverses the outcome of sorcery. Through the transfer of flutes, a pair of "brothers" pull out the sorcerer's or Moon's plug, transforming feces into child, theft into exchange, a lethal head-to-head encounter into fertile "homosexual" alliance.

The transformation is never complete, never accomplished once and for all, because the mythic father is eternally angry. To keep their children alive and flutes empty, his sons have to keep extracting the plug, exchanging head payments at every crisis, continuing to defuse the mythic parents and restore their dead issue. According to the ritual design—and at the father's own behest—men absent him from their transaction and thereby deny his guilt: they conceal the father's presence in the flute plug or child's head. But the subterfuge puts men in a bind. By hiding the father inside the mother, treating her pubic hair or menstrual blood as expressions of his relation with the child, they also empower the mother. To disentangle their own affairs and find a cure for sorcery, men have to overthrow the mother: they have to open her body and expose the father joined head-to-head with the child. But they do it as a secret among themselves. The oneness, passionate attachment, and fatal conflict between father and son remain hidden inside the flutes, objects that men hide from their wives and that the women, for reasons of their own, consent publicly not to know.

# APPENDIX

# Kinship Terminology

The following list gives formal referents of Gimi kinship terms. The list is divided into four parts:

I   Terms for agnates and affines used by a male ego.
II  Terms for affines used by a male ego to refer to his own wife, agnates' spouses, and their relations.
III Terms for agnates and affines used by a female ego.
IV  Terms for affines used by a female ego to refer to her own husband, agnates' spouses, and their relations.

Outside the nuclear or extended family, two people are likely to be related in a number of ways, creating a range of choice in actual usage (see Glick 1967). The marriages of oneself and one's children are the main events that determine the route, or series of intermediate ties and kinship terms, a person uses to trace his or her connection to another. To take the simplest example, a woman calls her FBSD *naramo,* "my daughter," unless (or until) she marries the woman's own son, in which case the younger woman becomes *nanatu,* "my daughter-in-law." Reciprocally, a man calls his FBSD *namabu,* "my son," unless (or until) he marries the man's own daughter, in which case the younger man becomes *na ϑimu,* "my son-in-law."

Distinctions of generation may be invoked to mark significant disparity in age within a generation.

Terms are used in both address and reference except where *A* indicates a term used only in address.

Terms extended in the classificatory sense are prefixed, in reference, by *amene,* which informants say means literally "other-than-*kisa*" (lit: *kisa*/true or real).

*n* means "my."

## I    Terms for agnates and affines used by a male ego

| | | | |
|---|---|---|---|
| + 2 | | *kore naba* | FF, MF, any male agnate or affine in the second (or higher) ascending generation |
| | | *he-nano* | FM, MM, any female agnate or affine in the second (or higher) ascending generation |
| + 1 | | *naba* | F, FB, any male agnate of own father's generation, MZH |
| | A | *natu* | true F (lit: *n*/my + *atu*/taboo) |
| | | *nano* | M, FBW, MZ, any female affine of own mother's generation |
| | | *nanati* | MB, MBS (if considerably older than ego), any male affine of own mother's generation |
| | A | *naba* | true MB, true FZH |
| | A | *kisa nano* | true MB (lit: *kisa*/true + *n*/my + *ano*/mother) |
| | | *namamu* | FZ, any female agnate of own father's generation; W of any *nanati*, any *amau* of own M |
| | A | *nano* | true FZ, true MBW |
| | | *natu* | FZH, H of M's *amau* other than *nanati* |
| o | | *nasi* | Z, FBD, any female agnate of ego's generation |
| | | *na'au ara* | elder B, son of F's elder B; W of *na'au ara* (who may be addressed as *nano*) |
| | | *nara* | younger B, son of F's younger B; W of *nara* (who is not *nanatu*; see below) |
| | | *nabogo* | MBS, FZS, MBD, FZD, any male or female affine of ego's generation; W of *nabogo* |
| | A | *nasi* | true MBD, FZD, MZD |
| | A | *nara* | sons of M's true younger B and F's true younger Z |
| | A | *na'au ara* | sons of M's true elder B and F's true elder Z |

|  | *nanogai* | MZS, MZSW (lit: *n*/my +<br>*ano*/mother + *gai*/?) |
|---|---|---|
| − 1 | *namabu* | S, BS, FBSS; any S of *nara* or<br>*na'au ara* |
|  | *naramo* | D, BD, FBSD; any D of *nara* or<br>*na'au ara* |
|  | *namaga*<br>(reciprocal *nanati*) | ZS, ZD; any S or D of *nasi* |
| A | *namabu* | true ZS; any S of *kisa nasi, kisa*<br>*nabogo,* or *kisa nanogai* (unless<br>married to own D) |
| A | *naramo* | true ZD; any D of *kisa nasi, kisa*<br>*nabogo,* or *kisa nanogai* (unless<br>married to own S) |
| − 2 | *naga rau/nama ϑi* | child of *naramo, namabu, namaga,*<br>and *naga rau* |

## II Terms for affines used by a male ego to refer to his own wife, agnates' spouses, and their relations

| + 1 & 2 | *na ϑimu* | WFF, WFM, WMF, WMM<br>WM, WF, WFB, WFBW, WFZ,<br>WFZH, WMZ, WMZH,<br>WMB, WMBW, etc., i.e., all<br>those who (ideally) shared in<br>the brideprice given for ego's<br>wife (but see rules of *a ϑaoina* in<br>Chap. 6) |
|---|---|---|
| o | *nanaro* | W |
|  | *na'au ara/nano* | W of elder brother |
|  | *nara/nanatu* | W of younger brother |
|  | *natu* | W's elder sister |
|  | *natu/naramo* | W's younger sister |
|  | *naune* | W's sister's husband (lit: "my<br>rival")[1] |

1. *naune* means "my rival" or "my enemy," men explain, in the sense that the husband of a sister of a man's wife married a woman whom the man himself might have married, yet he is not of the man's own lineage or clan. He is "some other man who married my wife's sister" (see R. Berndt 1954:33). If two men call each other *naune*, their sons may call each other *nanogai* (see above). *naune* is like *nanati*, Gimi men also say, because, like a mother's brother, *naune* may perform the nose-bleeding operation (see Chap. 6).

| | | | |
|---|---|---|---|
| | | *natu/naϑimu* | ZH, WB, WZH, WFBD, WFBDH, WFBS, WFBSW, etc., i.e., H of any *nasi* and child of any sr. *naϑimu* and his/her spouse (other than *nasi*) |
| | | *nanatu* | BW, i.e., any lineage or clan wife of own generation to whose brideprice ego contributed |
| − 1 | | *naϑimu* | DH |
| | A | *namabu* | WBS, WZS; S of *natu* other than *naϑimu* |
| | | *nanatu* | SW; any lineage or clan wife in first descending generation to whose brideprice ego contributed |
| | A | *naramo* | WBD, WZD; D of *natu* other than *nanatu* |
| − 2 | | *naϑimu* | DDH; H of *namaϑi* or *naga rau* |
| | | *nanatu* | SSW, WBSW, WZSW, etc., W of *namaϑi* or *naga rau* |

**III**  **Terms for agnates and affines used by a female ego (terms for agnates and affines in the first and second ascending generations are the same as those used by a male ego)**

| | | | |
|---|---|---|---|
| 0 | | *nasi* | B, FBS, any male agnate of ego's generation |
| | | *na'au ara* | elder Z, daughter of F's elder B |
| | | *nara* | younger Z, daughter of F's younger B |
| | | *nabogo* | MBS, FZS, MBD, FZD, any male or female affine of ego's generation |
| | A | *nasi* | true MBS, FZS, MZS |
| | A | *nara* | daughters of M's true younger B and F's true younger Z |
| | A | *na'au ara* | daughters of F's true elder Z and M's true elder B |
| − 1 | | *namabu* | S, ZS, FBDS; any S of *nara* or *na'au ara* |
| | | *naramo* | D, ZD, FBDD; any D of *nara* or *na'au ara* |

360

|  |  | *nama ϑi* <br> (reciprocal <br> *namamu/he-nano*) | BS, BD; any S or D of *nasi* |
|---|---|---|---|
|  | A | *namabu* | true BS; any S of true *nasi* or true <br> *nabogo* (unless married to own D) |
|  | A | *namaro* | true BD; any D of true *nasi* or true <br> *nabogo* (unless married to own S) |
| − 2 |  | *naga rau* or *nama ϑi* | child of *naramo, namabu, nama ϑi,* <br> and *naga rau* |

## IV Terms for affines used by a female ego to refer to her own husband, agnates' spouses, and their relations

| + 1 & 2 |  | *nanatu* | HFF, HFM, HMF, HMM <br> HF, HM, HFB, HFBW, HFZ, <br> HFZH, HMZ, HMZH, HMB, <br> HMBW, etc., i.e., all those who <br> (ideally) contributed to ego's <br> brideprice |
|---|---|---|---|
| o |  | *naba ϑo* | H |
|  |  | *nanaro* | co-W |
|  |  | *namau* | BW, HZ, i.e., W of any *nasi* or any <br> *asi* of own H |
|  |  | *natu* | ZH, i.e., H of *nara* |
|  |  | *natu* or *na ϑimu* | ZH, i.e., H of *na'au ara*; or H of <br> *namau* who is not *nasi* |
|  |  | *namahu/nara* | H's younger brother |
|  |  | *nanatu* | HBW, i.e., lineage or clan wives of <br> own generation to whose <br> brideprice ego contributed pigs |
| − 1 |  | *na ϑimu* | DH |
|  |  | *namabu* | HBS, HZS (other than *na ϑimu*) |
|  |  | *nanatu* | SW; any woman in first <br> descending generation to whose <br> brideprice ego contributed pigs |
|  |  | *naramo* | HBD, HZD (other than *nanatu*) |
| − 2 |  | *na ϑimu* | DDH; H of *nama ϑi* or *naga rau* |
|  |  | *nanatu* | SSW, HBSW, HZSW, etc., i.e., W <br> of *nama ϑi* or *naga rau* |

# GLOSSARY OF GIMI TERMS

Morphophonemic Note: The morphophonemic changes in Gimi are caused either by the glottal stop (*k* or *g*) or by vowel harmony. There are no consonant clusters, and the only final consonant is the glottal. When *k* or *g* is contiguous with another consonant (at either word or morpheme boundary), the following changes occur:

> *k* or *g* + *m* becomes *b*
> *k* or *g* + *n* becomes *ϑ*
> k or *g* + *r* becomes *t*

Before all other consonants *k* or *g* is deleted. The exception to the rule is the *n* in *na*/thing which never changes (McBride and McBride 1973). An apostrophe indicates that *k* or *g* is usually glottalized or silent. At other times, glottalization is optional; that is, it varies with the speaker's dialect.

| | |
|---|---|
| *ababanu* | Patrilineage or patriclan (lit: *aba*/father + *bana*/man) |
| *abiare* | Light-colored clays and muds used to cover the body and "hold the (deceased's) *auna* on the skin" in mourning |
| *abogo* | Cross-cousin; *abogoraha* ( pl.) |
| *abogofa* | Affinal clan |
| *aϑaoina* | Set of taboos that restrict consumption of the produce of "one's own hands" (see Chaps. 2 and 6) |
| *aϑarena* | Contamination of (women's) hands (lit: *aϑa*/hand + *re*/noun ending + *na*/thing) |
| *aϑuso* | Body matter that consists of marrow, nasal mucous, gray matter, etc., and that flows as *hato* (semen) into the penis during copulation |
| [*h*]*agesagena* | Fat-soaked things (lit: *hake*/pig-belly fat + *sa*/poss. + *ge*/? + *na*/thing); mourning raiments (armbands, |

kneebands, skirts, turbans, etc.) made from torn pieces of the deceased's clothing and net bags, smeared with pig fat to "hold the *auna*," and worn by women

Ritual celebrated by deceased's *ababana* to end the year-long mourning period and to "buy back the *auna*" by providing women with cooked meat in exchange for their removing the *agesagena*, burning them and consigning the ashes to a clan-owned river

*ahamo*  One with the same name (lit: *aha*/same + *mo*/the); *ahamoha* (pl.)

*ahamoina*  The practice of same-naming or two persons with the same name (lit: *ahamo* +*i*/? + *na*/thing), e.g., sisters-in-law (*amauraha*), brothers-in-law (*aturaha*), or an initiate and his/her chaperon

*a'au ara*  Elder sibling of same sex

*amabu*  Son; *amabuha* (pl.)

*amaga*  Sister's child (for a male ego); *amagaraha* (pl.)

*amamu*  Father's sister/mother's brother's wife/mother's *amau*; *amamuraha* (pl.)

*amau*  Husband's sister/brother's wife (for a female ego); *amauraha*, *imiuraha* (pls.)

*amene*  Other-than-*kisa*, i.e., a classificatory or "not true" relation

*anati*  Mother's brother; *anatiraha* (pl.)

*[n]anatu*  "Woman [my] pigs made a wife"—"woman/man whose pigs made [me] a wife," e.g., for female ego, son's wife, husband's brother's wife, etc., and husband's mother, father, and paternal kin generally; for male ego, son's/brother's wife; *anaturaha* (pl.) (see Appendix)

*ano*  Mother; *anoha* (pl.)

*ano*  Water, i.e., any body fluid other than blood (esp. urine, semen, sweat, forehead oils, and other oils of the skin, death liquors, etc.)

*anotu*  Head or head payment; see *arabosu anotu*

*[h]anu*  Fetus or spirit-child; invisible aspect of the child

*[h]anu'o*  Womb (lit: *[h]anu*/fetus + *ko*/bag)

*anumona*  Spirit children (lit: *anu*/spirit-child + *mo*/the + *na*/thing), i.e., clan of sisters' sons

*apina*  First-stage male initiation (lit: *abi*/spear + *na*/thing)

| | |
|---|---|
| *ara* | Younger sibling of same sex; and, for a male ego, younger brother's wife; *araha* (pl.) |
| *arabosu anotu* | Head payment called "the head of the child" (lit: *arak*/child + *mo*/the + *su*/poss. + *anotu*/head) |
| *arak* | Infant or child; visible aspect of the child (in contrast to *anu*, above) |
| *ara'e a'au'e* | Brother clans (lit: *ara*/younger brother + *a'au*/elder brother) |
| *aramo* | Daughter; *aramofa* (pl.) |
| *ari'aϑa* | Hair, fur, or plumage |
| *asa* | Mouth, opening, slit, cut, incision, wound, etc. |
| *asi* | Sibling of opposite sex or man/woman of my generation whom I may not marry, including, for a male ego, MBD, FZD, and MZD; *asiraha* (pl.) (see Appendix) |
| *atu* | Affine (lit: *atu*/taboo), e.g., for a male ego, wife's brother; *aturaha* (pl.) |
| [*h*]*auna* | Life-force (lit: *au*/body or skin, i.e., visible body surface + *na*/thing); invisible animating aspect of a person, ghost (*kore*), animal, or plant manifested in breath, voice, pulse, heart beat, etc., and in the capacity for growth, and present in all *autaisana* |
| *autaisana* | Body exuviae (urine, feces, sweat, tears, hair, blood, etc.) and discarded scraps of food or tobacco |
| | Body decorations (headdress plumages, string skirts, marsupial fur pieces, necklaces, armbands, etc.) (lit: *au*/body or skin + *tai*/dir. + *sa*/poss. + *na*/thing) |
| *baϑaϑa* | Brideprice (lit: *baϑa*/woman) |
| *baϑaha* | Woman |
| *bana* | Man |
| *beheϑa* | Fern |
| *beheϑabaϑa* | Death ritual (lit: *beheϑa*/fern + *ϑabaϑa*/spine); in which the deceased's *ababana* "buy back the *auna*" by providing mourning women with cooked meat in exchange for their burning the dried central spines of ferns that were cooked in the ovens of *ruhu* and *niniusina* to symbolize the uncultivated greens once eaten with human flesh |
| *be'a 'aϑa* | Age-mate |
| *biϑokaina* | Men's myths; stories of the men's house (lit: *biϑo*/? + *kaina*/speech or talk) |
| *faba baϑaha* | Women who are nonkin or of no category of relation |

|  |  |
|---|---|
|  | (lit: *faba*/nothing + *baðaha*/woman) but who are nevertheless included in distributions at feasts |
| *fiða* | Second crop of sweet potato planted without fallow some twelve to eighteen months after a first crop; (see *aðaoina* in Chap. 6) |
| *fobirikaina* | Sorcery meeting (convened around noon) or "sun talk" (lit: *fo*/sun + *biri*/happen, occur, be, etc. + *kaina*/speech or talk) |
| *forita'ara asa* | Fontanel (lit: *forita'ara*/first, top, frontal, or vanguard + *asa*/mouth) |
| *habarena* | Wedding (lit: *habare*/cut[ting] + *na*/thing) |
| *haðana* | Poison that men say a woman makes from the combined sexual fluids of her lover and herself and secretly feeds to her husband |
| *haro* | Rites of female initiation (lit: *haro*/thatch) at whose climax men climb onto the roof of the woman's house and thrust a huge sugarcane pole through a hole in the thatch |
| *harukaru* | Ritual theater |
| *hato* | Semen |
| *hau* | Ritual festival including pig kills and joint celebrations of marriage and first-stage male initiation |
| *he-ano* | Grandmother or spirit mother (lit: *he*/spirit [irregular form of *kore*] + *ano*/mother) |
| *hibo fa* | To menstruate (lit: *hik*/moon + *mo*/the + *fa*/hit, strike, shoot, implant, kill) |
| *hibosubak* | Moon's songs (lit: *hik*/moon + *mo*/the + *su*/poss. + *bak*/song) sung to end menstrual periods; see *korabak* |
| *huðikaina* | Curse (lit: *huði*/curse + *kaina*/speech or talk) |
| *kagora asa* | Vagina (lit: *kagora*/vagina + *asa*/mouth) |
| *kamiba* | Flute (lit: *kamiba*/giant [fictitious] bird) |
| *kamiðama* | Menstrual hut (lit: *kamiba*/flute + *nama*/house) |
| *kareta* | Grayish-white beads of Job's tears strung into necklaces and worn by women in mourning |
| *keterama* | Menstrual hut (lit: *kete*/shame + *nama*/house) |
| *ki'3* | Guilt, remorse |
| *kiri* | Python |
| *kisa* | True, real or own (relationship), esp. as opposed to *amene*, meaning not-*kisa* or classificatory |
| *korabak* | Blood songs (lit: *kora*/blood + *bak*/song) sung by women to end their menstrual periods |

| | |
|---|---|
| *kore* | Ghost; an honorific title like "sir" or "madam" prefixed to names of persons of advanced age or elevated status |
| | Wild, spirit, ancestral |
| *kore abe* | Ghost urine, a euphemism for ancestral semen, i.e., the fast-moving water of rivers and waterfalls |
| *kore baϑaha* | Wild or spirit woman (lit: *kore* + *baϑaha*/woman); heroine of *nenekaina* (women's myths) and villain of *biϑokaina* (men's myths); term of insult used by one woman to another |
| *kore bana* | Wild or spirit man; villain of *nenekaina* |
| *kore riϑi* | Wild bamboo (lit: *kore*/wild or spirit + *riϑi*/bamboo); spirit bamboo used to capture deceased's *auna* and locate murderer in hours immediately following death |
| *kuma* | Lizard that lays its eggs inside wild bamboo; secret name for "the mother of the flutes" |
| *kuta* | Rites of marriage |
| *nasobakaina* | "Food talk" or garden magic (lit: *nasoba*/food + *kaina*/speech or talk) |
| *neki maha* | Marsh, swamp, gully, stagnant pool, river outlet, graveyard (lit: *neki*/mad, deranged, intoxicated, etc. + *maha*/ground) ritually associated with female interior |
| *nenekaina* | Women's myths (lit: *nene*/allegory or gist + *kaina*/speech) |
| *nimi* | Bird, flute |
| *nini* | Mixture of carbon, powdered ash, and *ϑarI* with which women blacken their faces in mourning |
| *niniusina* | Death ritual (lit: *nini* + *usi*/wooden bowl + *na*/thing); in which deceased's *ababana* "buy back the *auna*" by providing mourning women with cooked meat and fat (carried in an *usi*) in exchange for their removing the *nini* from their faces |
| *rakukusa* | Medicine |
| | Ritual held prior to *ϑau* that marks emergence of mother and child from monthlong postpartum confinement |
| *rotana* | Fence of bamboo stakes erected around the house of a sick man to keep out women and children |
| *rubesebana* | Sorcerer (lit: *rubese*/sorcery + *bana*/man) |
| *rubesenama* | Bush shelter where sorcerers wait for their spell to take effect (lit: *rubese*/sorcery + *nama*/house) |

| | |
|---|---|
| *rubese ugunu* | Clandestine payment made to sorcerer (lit: *rubese*/sorcery + *ugunu*/pig) |
| *ruhu* | Rites of death |
| *sagana* | Crotch (also referring to underarm) |
| *ϑarI* | Mixture of pig fat and red pandanus oil used to coat the body on ritual occasions and in the concoction of *nini* |
| *ϑau* | Rites of birth |

# BIBLIOGRAPHY

Allen, Michael R. *Male Cults and Secret Initiations in Melanesia*. Melbourne: Melbourne University Press, 1967.

Alpers, Michael, and D. Carleton Gajdusek. "Changing Patterns of Kuru: Epidemiological Changes in the Period of Increasing Contact of the Fore People with Western Civilization." *American Journal of Tropical Medicine* 14 (1965): 852–79.

Ardener, Edwin. "Belief and the Problem of Women." In *Perceiving Women*. Edited by Shirley Ardener. New York: John Wiley and Sons, 1975.

Bakan, David. *The Duality of Human Existence: Isolation and Communion in Western Man*. Boston: Beacon Press, 1966.

Bamberger, Joan. "The Myth of Matriarchy: Why Men Rule in Primitive Society." In *Women, Culture and Society*. Edited by M. Z. Rosaldo and Louise Lamphere. Stanford: Stanford University Press, 1974.

Bardwick, Judith M. *Psychology of Women*. New York: Harper and Row, 1971.

Barnes, J. A. "African Models in the New Guinea Highlands." *Man* 62 (1962): 5–9.

———. "Genetrix: Genitor :: Nature: Culture?" In *The Character of Kinship*. Edited by J. R. Goody. Cambridge: Cambridge University Press, 1973.

Barth, Fredrik. *Ritual and Knowledge among the Baktaman of New Guinea*. New Haven: Yale University Press, 1975.

Bateson, Gregory. *Naven: A Survey of the Problems Suggested by a Composite Picture of a Culture of a New Guinea Tribe Drawn from Three Points of View*. Stanford: Stanford University Press, 1958 [1936].

Berndt, C. H. "Women's Changing Ceremonies in Northern Australia." *L'Homme* 1 (1950).

———. *Myth in Conflict: A Study of Myth in the Eastern Central Highlands of New Guinea*. Ph.D. diss., London School of Economics, University of London, 1955.

———. "The Ascription of Meaning in a Ceremonial Context, in the Eastern Highlands of New Guinea." In *Anthropology in the South Seas*. Edited by J. D. Freeman and W. R. Geddes. New Plymouth, New Zealand: Avery Press, 1959.

———. "Women and the 'Secret Life.'" In *Aboriginal Man in Australia: Essays in Honour of Emeritus Professor A. P. Elkin*. Edited by R. M. Berndt and C. H. Berndt. Sydney: Angus and Robertson, 1965.

Berndt, R. M. "Contemporary Significance of Pre-Historic Stone Objects in the Eastern Highlands of New Guinea." *Anthropos* 49 (1954): 553–87.

———. "Kamano, Jate, Usurufa and Fo:re Kinship of the Eastern Highlands of New Guinea: A Preliminary Account." *Oceania* 25 (1954–55): 23–53, 156–87.

———. *Excess and Restraint: Social Control among a New Guinea Mountain People.* Chicago: University of Chicago Press, 1962.

———. "Warfare in the New Guinea Highlands." *American Anthropologist* 66, pt. 2 (1964): 183–203.

———. "The Kamano, Usurufa, Jate and Fore of the Eastern Highlands." In *Gods, Ghosts and Men in Melanesia.* Edited by Peter Lawrence and M. J. Meggitt. Melbourne: Oxford University Press, 1965.

Bettelheim, Bruno. *Symbolic Wounds: Puberty Rites and the Envious Male.* Glencoe, Ill.: Free Press, 1954.

Bidou, Patrice. "Quand le père est absent: Essai a partir d'une mythologie Amazonienne." In *Le père. Metaphore paternelle et fonctions du père: L'interdit, la filiation, la transmission.* Paris: Denoël, 1989.

Bloch, Maurice. "Symbols, Song, Dance and Features of Articulation: Or Is Religion an Extreme Form of Traditional Authority?" *Archives Européenes de Sociology* 15 (1974): 55–81.

———. "The Past and the Present in the Present." *Man,* n.s. 12 (1977): 278–92.

———. "Almost Eating the Ancestors." *Man,* n.s. 20 (1985): 631–46.

Bloch, Maurice, and Jonathan Parry. "Introduction." In *Death and the Regeneration of Life.* Edited by M. Bloch and J. Parry. Cambridge: Cambridge University Press, 1982.

Bowden, Ross. "Kwoma Death Payments and Alliance Theory." *Ethnology* 27 (1988): 271–90.

———. "Historical Ethnography or Conjectural History? A Critical Analysis of *Sepik River Societies.*" *Oceania* 61 (1991): 218–35.

Boyd, David J. "The Production and Management of Pigs: Husbandry Option and Demographic Pattern in Eastern Highlands Herds." *Oceania* 55 (1984): 27–49.

Brown, Paula. "Chimbu Death Payments." *Journal of the Royal Anthropological Institute* 91 (1961): 77–96.

———. "Enemies and Affines." *Ethnology* 3 (1964): 335–56.

———. "The Chimbu Political System." *Anthropological Forum* 2 (1967): 36–52.

———. "Marriage in Chimbu." In *Pigs, Pearlshells and Women.* Edited by R. M. Glasse and M. J. Meggitt. Englewood Cliffs, N.J.: Prentice-Hall, 1969.

Brown, Paula, and H. C. Brookfield. "Chimbu Land and Society." *Oceania* 30 (1959–60): 1–75.

Brown, Paula, and Georgeda Buchbinder, eds. *Man and Woman in the New Guinea Highlands.* Special Publication no. 8. Washington, D.C.: American Anthropological Association, 1976.

Brown, Paula, and Donald Tuzin, eds. *The Ethnography of Cannibalism.* Washington, D.C.: Society for Psychological Anthropology, 1983.

Buchbinder, Georgeda, and Roy A. Rappaport. "Fertility and Death among the Maring." In *Man and Woman in the New Guinea Highlands.* Edited by Paula

Brown and Georgeda Buchbinder. Special Publication no. 8. Washington, D.C.: American Anthropological Association, 1976.

Bulmer, R. N. H. "Political Aspects of the Moka Ceremonial Exchange System among the Kyaka People of the Western Highlands of New Guinea." *Oceania* 31 (1960): 211–38.

Burridge, K. O. L. *Mambu: A Study of Melanesian Cargo Movements and Their Social and Ideological Background.* New York: Harper and Row, 1960.

Chodorow, Nancy. "Family Structure and Feminine Personality." In *Woman, Culture and Society.* Edited by M. Z. Rosaldo and Louise Lamphere. Stanford: Stanford University Press, 1974.

Chowning, Ann. "The Recognition and Treatment of Abnormal Mental States in Several New Guinea Societies." In *Psychology in Papua New Guinea.* Edited by M. A. Hutton, R. E. Hicks, and C. J. S. Brammal. Port Moresby: Australian Psychological Society (Papua New Guinea Branch) and Society for Papua New Guinea Psychological Research and Publications, 1973.

Clark, William. *Place and People: An Ecology of a New Guinean Community.* Canberra: Australian National University Press, 1971.

Codrington, R. H. *The Melanesians.* Oxford: Clarendon Press, 1891.

Cook, Edwin A., and Denise O'Brien, eds. *Blood and Semen: Kinship Systems of Highland New Guinea.* Ann Arbor: University of Michigan Press, 1980.

Delaney, Carol. "The Meaning of Paternity and the Virgin Birth Debate." *Man,* n.s. 21 (1986): 494–513.

Delany, Janice, Mary Jane Lupton, and Emily Toth. *The Curse: A Cultural History of Menstruation.* Rev. ed. Urbana: University of Illinois Press, 1988.

Descola, Philippe, and Jean-Luc Lory. "Les guerriers de l'invisible: Sociologie comparative de l'aggression chamanique en Papouasie Nouvelle-Guinée (Baruya) et en Haute Amazonie (Achuar). *L'Ethnographie. Voyages Chamanique Deux,* nos. 87–88 (1982): 85–111.

Devereux, George. "Considérations ethnopsychanalytiques sur la notion de la par enté." *L'Homme* 5 (1965): 224–47.

———. *Ethnopsychoanalysis.* Berkeley: University of California Press, 1972.

Dundes, Alan. "A Psychoanalytic Study of the Bullroarer." *Man,* n.s. 2 (1976): 220–38.

———. "Projection in Folklore: A Plea for Psychoanalytic Semiotics." In *Interpreting Folklore.* Bloomington: Indiana University Press, 1980.

Durkheim, Emile. *The Elementary Forms of the Religious Life.* Translated by J. W. Swain. London: George Allen and Unwin, 1954 [1912].

Durkheim, Emile, and Marcel Mauss. *Primitive Classification.* Translated by Rodney Needham. Chicago: University of Chicago Press, 1963 [1903].

*Encyclopaedia of Papua New Guinea.* Melbourne: Melbourne University Press, 1972.

Ernst, Thomas M. "Aspects of Meaning of Exchanges and Exchange Items among the Onabasalu of the Great Papuan Plateau." *Mankind* 11 (1978): 187–97.

Evans-Pritchard, E. E. *Theories of Primitive Religion.* Oxford: Clarendon Press, 1965.

———. *Witchcraft, Oracles and Magic among the Azande.* Abridged with Introduction by Eva Gillies. Oxford: Clarendon Press, 1976 [1936].

Eyde, D. B. "Sexuality and Garden Ritual in the Trobriands and Tikopia: Tudava Meets the Atua I Kafika." *Mankind* 14 (1983): 66–74.

Faithorn, Elizabeth. "Women as Persons. Aspects of Female Life and Male-Female Relations among the Kafe." In *Man and Woman in the New Guinea Highlands.* Edited by Paula Brown and Georgeda Buchbinder. Special Publication no. 8. Washington, D.C.: American Anthropological Association, 1976.

Feil, D. K. "Women and Men in the Enga *tee.*" *American Ethnologist* 5 (1978): 263–79.

Fenichel, Otto. "The Dread of Being Eaten." In *The Collected Papers of Otto Fenichel.* 1st ser. New York: W. W. Norton, 1953.

———. "The Symbolic Equation: Girl = Phallus." In *The Collected Papers of Otto Fenichel.* 2d ser. New York: W. W. Norton, 1954.

Ferenczi, Sandor. "Gulliver Phantasies." *International Journal of Psycho-Analysis* 9 (1928): 283–300.

Finch, John. "Structure and Meaning in Papua New Guinea Highland Mythology." *Oceania* 55 (1985): 197–213.

Forge, Anthony. "The Golden Fleece." *Man,* n.s. 7 (1972): 527–40.

Fortune, R. F. "The Rules of Relationship Behaviour in One Variety of Primitive Warfare. *Man* 47 (1947): 108–10.

———. "New Guinea Warfare: Correction of a Mistake Previously Published." *Man* 60 (1960): 108.

———. *Sorcerers of Dobu.* London: Routledge and Kegan Paul, 1963 [1932].

Fox, Robin. *Kinship and Marriage: An Anthropological Perspective.* Harmondsworth, Middlesex: Penguin Books, 1967.

Frazer, Sir James George. *The Golden Bough: A Study in Magic and Religion.* Abridged ed. New York: Macmillan, 1963 [1922].

Freud, Sigmund. *The Interpretation of Dreams.* Translated by James Strachey [1958]. Pelican Freud Library vol. 4. Harmondsworth, Middlesex: Pelican Books, 1976 [1900].

———. *Totem and Taboo.* Translated by James Strachey [1950]. London: Routledge and Kegan Paul, 1960 [1913].

———. *Introductory Lectures on Psychoanalysis.* Translated by James Strachey [1963]. Pelican Freud Library vol. 1. Harmondsworth, Middlesex: Pelican Books, 1973.

———. *Three Case Histories: The "Wolf" Man, the "Rat" Man, and the Psychotic Doctor Schreber.* Introduction by Philip Rieff. New York: Collier Books, 1963.

———. "Contributions to the Psychology of Love: The Taboo on Virginity" Pp. 217–35 in *Collected Papers,* vol. 4. Translated by Joan Riviere. London: Hogarth Press, 1956a [1918].

———. *Delusion and Dream and Other Essays.* Introduction by Philip Rieff. Boston: Beacon Press, 1956b.

———. "Fetishism." *International Journal of Psycho-Analysis* 9 (1928): 161–66.

———. "Some Psychical Consequences of the Anatomical Distinction between the Sexes (1925)." In *Women and Analysis: Dialogues on Psychoanalytic Views of Femininity.* Edited by Jean Strouse. New York: Grossman, 1974.

———. "Female Sexuality (1931)." In *Women and Analysis: Dialogues on Psychoanalytic Views of Femininity.* Edited by Jean Strouse. New York: Grossman, 1974.

————. "Femininity (1933)." In *Women and Analysis: Dialogues on Psychoanalytic Views of Femininity.* Edited by Jean Strouse. New York: Grossman, 1974.

Gajdusek, D. Carlton. "Physiological and Psychological Characteristics of Stone Age Man." *Engineering and Science* 33 (1970): 26–62.

————. "Kuru in the New Guinea Highlands." In *Tropical Neurology.* Edited by John D. Spillane. New York: Oxford University Press, 1973.

Gajdusek, D. Carlton, and Michael Alpers. "Genetic Studies in Relation to Kuru. I. Cultural, Historical, and Demographic Background." *American Journal of Human Genetics* 24 (1972): S1–S38.

Gardener, Don S. "Performativity in Ritual: The Mianmin Case." *Man,* n.s. 18 (1983): 346–60.

Gell, Alfred. *Metamorphosis of the Cassowaries: Umeda Society, Language and Ritual.* London: Athlone Press, 1975.

————. "Reflections on a Cut Finger: Taboo in the Umeda Conception of the Self." In *Fantasy and Symbol.* Edited by R. H. Hook. London and New York: Academic Press, 1979.

Gillison, Gillian. "Fertility Rites and Sorcery in a New Guinea Village." *National Geographic Magazine* (July 1977).

————. "Images of Nature in Gimi Thought." In *Nature, Culture and Gender.* Edited by Carol MacCormack and Marilyn Strathern. Cambridge: Cambridge University Press, 1980.

————. "Cannibalism among Women in the Eastern Highlands of Papua New Guinea." In *The Ethnography of Cannibalism.* Edited by Paula Brown and Donald Tuzin. Washington, D.C.: Society for Psychological Anthropology, 1983a.

————. "Living Theater in New Guinea's Highlands." *National Geographic Magazine* (August 1983b).

————. "Incest and the Atom of Kinship: The Role of the Mother's Brother in a New Guinea Highlands Society." *Ethos* 15 (1987): 166–202.

————. "L'horreur de l'inceste et le père caché: Mythe et saignées rituelles chez les Gimi de Nouvelle-Guinée." In *Le père: Metaphore paternelle et fonctions du père: L'interdit, la filiation, la transmission.* Paris: Denoël, 1989.

————. "The Flute Myth and the Law of Equivalence: Origins of a Principle of Exchange." In *Big and Great Men: Personifications of Power in Melanesia.* Edited by Maurice Godelier and Marilyn Strathern. Cambridge and Paris: Cambridge University Press, and Editions de la Maison des Sciences de l'Homme, 1991.

Glasse, R. M. "Cannibalism in the Kuru Region of New Guinea." *Transactions of the New York Academy of Science* 29, ser. 2 (1967): 748–54.

————. "Marriage in South Fore." In *Pigs, Pearlshells and Women: Marriage in the New Guinea Highlands.* Edited by R. M. Glasse and M. J. Meggitt. Englewood Cliffs, N.J.: Prentice-Hall, 1969.

————. "Some Recent Observations on Kuru." *Oceania* 40 (1970): 210–13.

————. "Le masque de la volupté: Symbolisme et antagonisme sexuels sur les Hauts Plateaux de Nouvelle-Guinée." *L'Homme* 14 (1974): 79–86.

Glasse, R. M., and Shirley Lindenbaum. "Fore Age Mates." *Oceania* 39 (1969a): 165–173.

———. "South Fore Politics." *Anthropological Forum* 2 (1969b): 308–326.

———. "Kuru at Wanitabe." In *Essays on Kuru*. Edited by R. W. Hornabrook. Faringdon: E. W. Classey Ltd., 1976.

Glasse, R. M., and M. J. Meggitt, eds. *Pigs, Pearlshells and Women*. Englewood Cliffs, N.J.: Prentice-Hall, 1969.

Glick, Leonard B. *Foundations of a Primitive Medical System: The Gimi of the New Guinea Highlands*. Ph.D. diss., Graduate School of Arts and Sciences, University of Pennsylvania, 1963.

———. "Categories and Relations in Gimi Natural Science." *American Anthropologist* 66, pt. 2 (1964): 273–80.

———. "The Role of Choice in Gimi Kinship." *Southwestern Journal of Anthropology* 23 (1967): 371–82.

———. "Musical Instruments in Ritual." In *Encyclopaedia of Papua New Guinea*. Melbourne: Melbourne University Press, 1972.

Gluckman, Max. *Custom and Conflict in Africa*. Oxford: Basil Blackwell, 1963.

Godelier, Maurice. "Le visible et l'invisible chez les Baruya de Nouvelle-Guinée." In *Langues et techniques: Nature et société*. Edited by S. Thomas and L. Bernot. Paris: Klincksieck, 1972.

———. "La sexe comme fondement ultime de l'ordre social et cosmique chez les Baruya de Nouvelle-Guinée." In *Sexualité et pouvoir*. Edited by A. Verdiglione. Paris: Payot, 1976.

———. *La production des grands hommes: Pouvoir et domination masculine chez les Baruya de Nouvelle-Guinée*. Paris: Fayard, 1982 (see 1986).

———. *The Making of Great Men: Male Domination and Power among the Baruya*. Translated by Rupert Swyer. Cambridge and Paris: Cambridge University Press and Editions de la Maison des Sciences de l'Homme, 1986.

Godelier, Maurice, and Marilyn Strathern, eds. *Big Men and Great Men: Personifications of Power in Melanesia*. Cambridge and Paris: Cambridge University Press and Editions de la Maison des Sciences de l'Homme, 1991.

Goody, Jack. "The Mother's Brother and the Sister's Son in West Africa." *Journal of the Royal Anthropological Institute* 89 (1959): 23–34.

Gough, E. Kathleen. "Female Initiation Rites on the Malabar Coast." *Journal of the Royal Anthropological Institute* 85 (1955): 45–80.

Gourlay, K. A. *Sound-Producing Instruments in Traditional Society: A Study of Esoteric Instruments and Their Role in Male-Female Relations*. New Guinea Research Bulletin no. 60. Port Moresby and Canberra: Australian National University Press, 1975.

Graves, Robert. *The Greek Myths: 1* and *The Greek Myths: 2*. Harmondsworth: Penguin, 1955.

Green, André. "Atome de parenté et relations oedipiennes." In *L'identité: Séminaire dirigé par Claude Lévi-Strauss*. Paris: Quadrige/Presses Universitaires de France, 1977.

Greenfield, H., and J. Clark. "Energy Compensations Related to Child Bearing in Young Lufa Women." Goroka: Papua New Guinea Institute of Medical Research, 1974.

Greenstadt, William M. Review of *The Origin of the Gods: A Psychoanalytic Study of Greek Theogonic Myth,* by Richard S. Caldwell (Oxford University Press, 1989). *International Journal of Psycho-Analysis.* In press.

Hayano, David M. "Marriage Alliance and Warfare: A View from the New Guinea Highlands." *American Ethnologist* 1 (1974): 281–93.

Hays, Terry E., and Patricia H. Hays. "Opposition and Complementarity of the Sexes in Ndumba Initiation." In *Rituals of Manhood.* Edited by Gilbert H. Herdt. Berkeley: University of California Press, 1982.

Herdt, Gilbert H. *Guardians of the Flutes.* New York: McGraw-Hill, 1981.

—, ed. *Rituals of Manhood: Male Initiation in Papua New Guinea.* Berkeley: University of California Press, 1982a.

—. "Sambia Nosebleeding Rites and Male Proximity to Women." *Ethos* 10 (1982b): 189–231.

—, ed. *Ritualized Homosexuality in Melanesia.* Berkeley: University of California Press, 1984.

Herdt, Gilbert H., and F. J. P. Poole. "'Sexual Antagonism': The Intellectual History of a Concept in New Guinea Anthropology." *Social Analysis,* special issue 12 (1982): 3–93.

Hertz, Robert. *Death and the Right Hand.* Translated by Rodney and Claudia Needham. Glencoe, Ill.: Free Press, 1960 [1907, 1909].

Hiatt, L. R. "Secret Pseudo-Procreation Rites among the Australian Aborigines." In *Anthropology in Oceania.* Edited by L. R. Hiatt and C. Jayawardena. Sydney: Angus and Robertson, 1971.

Hogbin, Ian H. *The Island of Menstruating Men: Religion in Wogeo, New Guinea.* Scranton: Chandler Publishing Co., 1970.

Hugh-Jones, Christine. *From the Milk River: Spatial and Temporal Processes in Northwest Amazonia.* Cambridge: Cambridge University Press, 1979.

Hugh-Jones, Stephen. *The Palm and the Pleiades: Initiation and Cosmology in Northwest Amazonia.* Cambridge: Cambridge University Press, 1979.

Jones, Ernest. "Mother-Right and the Sexual Ignorance of Savages." *International Journal of Psycho-Analysis* 6 (1925): 109–30.

—. *The Life and Work of Sidmund Freud* (1953–57). Edited and abridged by Lionel Trilling and Steven Marcus. New York: Basic Books, 1961.

Kaberry, P. M. *Aboriginal Women.* London: Routledge, 1939.

Keesing, Roger M. "Introduction." In *Rituals of Manhood.* Edited by Gilbert H. Herdt. Berkeley: University of California Press, 1982.

—. "Kwaio Women Speak: The Micropolitics of Autobiography in a Solomon Island Society." *American Anthropologist* 87 (1985): 27–39.

—. "Ta'a geni: Women's Perspectives in Kwaio Society." In *Dealing with Inequality.* Edited by Marilyn Strathern. Cambridge: Cambridge University Press, 1987.

Kelly, Raymond C. "Witchcraft and Sexual Relations: An Exploration in the Social and Semantic Implications of the Structure of Belief." In *Man and Woman in the New Guinea Highlands.* Edited by Paula Brown and Georgeda Buchbinder. Special Publication no. 8. Washington, D.C.: American Anthropological Association, 1976.

————. *Etoro Social Structure: A Study in Social Contradiction*. Ann Arbor: University of Michigan Press, 1977.

Kirk, G. S. *Myth: Its Meaning and Functions in Ancient and Other Cultures*. Cambridge: Cambridge University Press, 1971.

Klein, Melanie. "Early Stages of the Oedipus Conflict." *International Journal of Psycho-Analysis* 9 (1928): 167–80.

Knauft, Bruce. *Good Company and Violence*. Berkeley: University of California Press, 1987.

Koch, Klaus-Freidrich. "Sociogenic and Psychogenic Models in Anthropology: The Functions of Jale Initiation." *Man*, n.s. 9 (1974a): 397–422.

————. *War and Peace in Jalemo: The Management of Conflicts in Highland New Guinea*. Cambridge, Mass.: Harvard University Press, 1974b.

La Fontaine, J. S. "Ritualization of Women's Life Crises in Bugisu. In *The Interpretation of Ritual*. Edited by J. S. La Fontaine. London: Tavistock Publications, 1972.

————. "Descent in New Guinea: An Africanist View." In *The Character of Kinship*. Edited by Jack Goody. Cambridge: Cambridge University Press, 1975.

Langness, L. L. "Some Problems in the Conceptualization of Highlands Social Structure." *American Anthropologist* 66, pt. 2 (1964): 162–82.

————. "Sexual Antagonism in the New Guinea Highlands: A Bena Bena Example.: *Oceania* 37 (1967): 161–77.

————. "Marriage in Bena Bena." In *Pigs, Pearlshells and Women*. Edited by R. M. Glasse and M. J. Meggitt. Englewood Cliffs, N.J.: Prentice-Hall, 1969.

————. "Ritual, Power and Male Dominance in the New Guinea Highlands." *Ethos* 2 (1974): 189–212.

Lawrence, Peter. *road belong cargo*. Manchester: Manchester University Press, 1964.

Lawrence, Peter, and M. J. Meggitt, eds. *Gods, Ghosts and Men in Melanesia*. Melbourne: Melbourne University Press, 1965.

Leach, E. R. *Political Systems of Highland Burma*. Boston: Beacon Press, 1954.

————. *Rethinking Anthropology*. London: Athlone Press, 1961.

————. "Virgin Birth." *Proceedings of the Royal Anthropological Institute for 1965* (1966): 39–50.

————. "Magical Hair." In *Myth and Cosmos*. Edited by John Middleton. Garden City, N.Y.: Natural History Press, 1967.

————. *Claude Lévi-Strauss*. New York: Viking Press, 1970.

Leenhardt, Maurice. *Do Kamo: Person and Myth in the Melanesian World*. Translated by B. M. Gulati. Chicago: University of Chicago Press, 1979 [1947].

Lepervanche, Marie de. "Descent, Residence and Leadership in the New Guinea Highlands." *Oceania* 38 (1967–68): 134–58, 163–89.

LeRoy, John. "Burning Our Trees: Metaphors in Kewa Songs." In *The Yearbook of Symbolic Anthropology* 1. Edited by Erik Schwimmer. London: Charles Hurst, 1978.

————. *Fabricated World: An Interpretation of Kewa Tales*. Vancouver: University of British Columbia Press, 1985a.

————, ed. *Kewa Tales*. Vancouver: University of British Columbia Press, 1985b.

Lévi-Strauss, Claude. *Totemism*. Translated by Rodney Needham. Boston: Beacon Press, 1963 [1962].

————. *The Savage Mind*. Chicago: University of Chicago Press, 1966 [1962].

———. *Structural Anthropology*. Translated by Claire Jacobson and Brooke Grundfest Schoepf. Garden City, N.Y.: Anchor Books, 1967.

———. *The Elementary Structures of Kinship*. Translated by J. H. Bell, J. R. von Sturmer, and R. Needham. Boston: Beacon Press, 1969 [1949].

———. *The Raw and the Cooked: Introduction to a Science of Mythology 1*. Translated by John and Doreen Weightman. New York: Harper Torchbooks, 1970 [1964].

———. *From Honey to Ashes: Introduction to a Science of Mythology 2*. Translated by John and Doreen Weightman. New York: Harper Torchbooks, 1974 [1966].

———. *Tristes Tropiques*. Translated by John and Doreen Weightman. New York: Washington Square Press, 1977 [1955].

———. *The Origin of Table Manners: Introduction to a Science of Mythology 3*. Translated by John and Doreen Weightman. New York: Harper and Row, 1978 [1968].

———. *Myth and Meaning*. The 1977 Massey Lectures. New York: Schocken Books, 1979.

———. *Paroles données*. Paris: Plon, 1984.

Lévy-Bruhl, Lucien. *Primitive Mentality*. Translated by Lilian A. Clare. London: Geo. Allen and Unwin, 1923 [1922].

———. *The Notebooks on Primitive Mentality*. Translated by Peter Riviere. New York: Harper Torchbooks 1978 [1949].

———. *Primitive Mythology: The Mythic World of the Australian and Papuan Natives*. Translated by Brian Elliott. St. Lucia: University of Queensland Press, 1983 [1935].

Lewin, Bertram D. "The Body as Phallus." *Psychoanalytic Quarterly* 2 (1933): 24–47.

———. "Anal Eroticism and the Mechanism of Undoing." In *Selected Writings of B. D. Lewin*. New York: Psychoanalytic Quarterly, 1973.

Lewis, Gilbert. *Day of Shining Red: An Essay on Understanding Ritual*. Cambridge: Cambridge University Press, 1980.

Lidz, Ruth W., and Theodore Lidz. "Male Menstruation: A Ritual Alternative to the Oedipal Transition." *International Journal of Psychoanalysis* 58 (1977): 17–31.

Lincoln, Bruce. *Emerging from the Chrysalis: Studies in Rituals of Women's Initiation*. Cambridge, Mass.: Harvard University Press, 1981.

Lindenbaum (Glasse), Shirley. "The Social Effects of Kuru." *Papua and New Guinea Medical Journal* 7 (1964): 36–47.

———. *Kuru Sorcery*. Palo Alto, Calif.: Mayfield, 1979.

———. "Cannibalism: Symbolic Production and Consumption." In *The Ethnography of Cannibalism*. Edited by Paula Brown and Donald Tuzin. Washington, D.C.: Society for Psychological Anthropology, 1983.

LiPuma, Edward. "Sexual Asymmetry and Social Reproduction among the Maring of Papua New Guinea." *Ethnos* 44 (1979): 34–57.

Lory, Jean-Luc. "Quelques aspects du chamanisme Baruya (Eastern Highlands Province, Papouasie, Nouvelle-Guinée)." *Cahiers OSTROM Série Sciences Humaines* 18 (1982): 543–59.

Lowman-Vayda, Cherry. "Maring Big Men." *Anthropological Forum* 2 (1968): 199–243.

McArthur, N. "The Age Incidence of Kuru." *Annals of Human Genetics* 27 (1964): 341–52.

McBride, Sam, and Nancy McBride. *Grammar Essentials for Gimi, Eastern Highlands*. Kainantu: Summer Institute of Linguistics, 1973.

MacCormack, Carol, and Marilyn Strathern, eds. *Nature, Culture and Gender*. Cambridge: Cambridge University Press, 1980.

Malinowski, Bronislaw. *Argonauts of the Western Pacific*. London: George Routledge, 1922.

———. *Sex and Repression in Savage Society*. London: Kegan Paul, 1927.

———. *The Sexual Life of Savages in North-Western Melanesia*. London: George Routledge, 1929.

———. "Myth in Primitive Psychology." In *Magic, Science and Religion and Other Essays*. New York: Doubleday, 1954 [1926].

———. *Coral Gardens and Their Magic, Volume I. Soil-Tilling and Agricultural Rites in the Trobriand Islands*. Introduction by Edmund R. Leach. *Volume II: The Language of Magic and Gardening*. Introduction by Jack Berry. Bloomington: Indiana University Press, 1965 [1935].

Marshall, Mac. ed. *Siblingship in Oceania: Studies in the Meaning of Kin Relations*. ASAO Monograph no. 8. Ann Arbor: University of Michigan Press, 1983.

Mathieu, Nicole-Claude. "Biological Paternity, Social Maternity." Translated by D. Leonard. *Feminist Issues* 4 (1984 [1977]): 63–71.

Mauss, Marcel. *The Gift: Forms and Functions of Exchange in Archaic Societies*. Translated by Ian Cunnison. New York: W. W. Norton, 1967 [1925].

Mead, Margaret. *Growing Up in New Guinea: A Comparative Study of Primitive Religion*. New York: Dell Publishing Co., 1968 [1928].

———. "The Marsalai Cult among the Arapesh, with Special Reference to the Rainbow Serpent Beliefs of the Australian Aborigines." *Oceania* 4 (1933): 37–53.

———. *Sex and Temperament in Three Primitive Societies*. New York: William Morrow, 1935.

———. *Male and Female: A Study of the Sexes in a Changing World*. New York: William Morrow, 1949.

———. *The Mountain Arapesh, Volume II: Arts and Supernaturalism*. Garden City, N.Y.: Natural History Press, 1970.

Meggitt, M. J. "Male-Female Relationships in the Highlands of New Guinea." *American Anthropologist* 66, pt. 2 (1964): 204–24.

———. *Blood Is Their Argument: Warfare among the Mae Enga of the New Guinea Highlands*. Palo Alto, Calif.: Mayfield Publishing Co., 1977.

Mihalic, F. *The Jacaranda Dictionary and Grammar of Melanesian Pidgin*. Port Moresby: Jacaranda Press, 1971.

Mitchell, Juliet. "On Freud and the Distinction between the Sexes." In *Women and Analysis: Dialogues on Psychoanalytic Views of Femininity*. Edited by Jean Strouse. New York: Grossman Publishers, 1974a.

———. *Psychoanalysis and Feminism*. New York: Random House, 1974b.

Montagu, M. F. Ashley. *Coming into Being among the Australian Aborigines*. London: Routledge & Kegan Paul, 1974 [1937]. Cited in Delaney 1986.

Moyle, Alice. "Music." In *The Encyclopedia of Papua New Guinea*, 2:809–17. Melbourne: Melbourne University Press, 1972.

Newman, Philip L. "Religious Belief and Ritual in a New Guinea Society." *American Anthropologist* 66, pt. 2 (1964): 257–72.

———. *Knowing the Gururumba.* New York: Holt, Rinehart and Winston, 1965.

Newman, Philip L., and David J. Boyd. "The Making of Men: Ritual and Meaning in Awa Male Initiation." In *Rituals of Manhood.* Edited by Gilbert H. Herdt. Berkeley: University of California Press, 1982.

Newton, Douglas. *Crocodile and Cassowary: Religious Art of the Upper Sepik River, New Guinea.* New York: Museum of Primitive Art, 1971.

———. "Untitled: An analysis of Kwoma Compositional Principles and Kwoma Ideology, New Guinea." New York: Museum of Primitive Art, n.d.

Nilles, J. "The Kuman People of the Chimbu Region, Central New Guinea." *Oceania* 21 (1950–51): 25–65.

Obeyesekere, Gananath. *Medusa's Hair: An Essay on Personal Symbols and Religious Experience.* Chicago: University of Chicago Press, 1981.

———. *The Work of Culture: Symbolic Transformation in Psychoanalysis and Anthropology.* Chicago: University of Chicago Press, 1990.

O'Hanlon, Michael. "Handsome Is as Handsome Does: Display and Betrayal in the Wahgi." *Oceania* 53 (1983): 317–33.

O'Hanlon, Michael, and Linda Frankland. "With a Skull in the Netbag: Prescriptive Marriage and Matrilineal Relations in the New Guinea Highlands." *Oceania* 56 (1986): 181–98.

Oliver, Douglas L. *A Solomon Islands Society: Kinship and Leadership among the Sinuai at Bougainville.* Cambridge, Mass.: Harvard University Press, 1955.

Ortner, Sherry B. "Is Female to Male as Nature Is to Culture?" In *Woman, Culture and Society.* Edited by M. Z. Rosaldo and Louise Lamphere. Stanford: Stanford University Press, 1974.

Ovid. *The Metamorphoses.* Translated by Horace Gregory. New York: Viking Press, 1958 [A.D. 8].

Paul, Robert A. "Did the Primal Crime Take Place?" *Ethos* 4 (1976): 311–52.

———. "Symbolic Interpretations in Psychoanalysis and Anthropology." *Ethos* 8 (1980): 286–94.

———. *The Tibetan Symbolic World.* Chicago: University of Chicago Press, 1982.

Poole, F. J. P. "Transforming 'Natural' Woman: Female Ritual Leaders and Gender Ideology among Bimin-Kuskusmin." In *Sexual Meanings.* Edited by Sherry B. Ortner and Harriet Whitehead. Cambridge: Cambridge University Press, 1981.

Radcliffe-Brown, A. R. "The Mother's Brother in South Africa." In *Structure and Function in Primitive Society.* New York: Free Press, 1965.

Rank, Otto. *The Myth of the Birth of the Hero.* New York: Alfred A. Knopf, 1964 [1914].

Rappaport, Roy A. *Pigs for the Ancestors: Ritual in the Ecology of a New Guinea People.* New Haven: Yale University Press, 1968.

———. "Marriage among the Maring." In *Pigs, Pearlshells and Women.* Edited by R. M. Glasse and M. J. Meggitt. Englewood Cliffs, N.J.: Prentice-Hall, 1969.

Read, Kenneth E. "Nama Cult of the Central Highlands, New Guinea." *Oceania* 23 (1952): 1–25.

———. "Cultures of the Central Highlands, New Guinea." *Southwestern Journal of Anthropology* 10 (1954): 1–43.

———. "Morality and the Concept of the Person among the Gahuku-Gama." *Oceania* 25 (1955): 233–82.

———. "Leadership and Consensus in a New Guinea Society." *American Anthropologist* 61 (1959): 425–36.

———. *The High Valley.* New York: Scribner's, 1965.

Reay, Marie. "A High Pig Culture in the New Guinea Highlands." *Canberra Anthropology* 7 (1984): 71–77.

Reik, T. *Ritual: Four Psychoanalytic Studies.* New York: Grove Press, 1962 [1946].

Reiter, Rayna Rapp, ed. *Toward an Anthropology of Women.* New York: Monthly Review Press, 1975.

Richards, A. I. *Chisungu: A Girls' Initiation Ceremony among the Bemba of Northern Rhodesia.* London: Faber and Faber, 1956.

Rigby, Peter. "The Structural Context of Girls' Puberty Rites." *Man,* n.s. 5 (1970): 434–44.

Róheim, Geza. "Dying Gods and Puberty Ceremonies." *Journal of the Royal Anthropological Institute* 59 (1929): 181–97.

———. "Women and Their Life in Central Australia." *Journal of the Royal Anthropological Institute* 63 (1933): 207–65.

———. *The Eternal Ones of the Dream: A Psychoanalytic Interpretation of Australian Myth and Ritual.* New York: International Universities Press, 1945.

———. *Psychoanalysis and Anthropology.* New York: International Universities Press, 1950.

———. "The Origin and Function of Magic." In *Magic and Schizophrenia.* Bloomington: Indiana University Press, 1970 [1955].

Rosaldo, M. Z., and Louise Lamphere, eds. *Woman, Culture and Society.* Stanford: Stanford University Press, 1974.

Ross, John Alan. "The Puberty Ceremony of the Chimbu Girl in the Eastern Highlands of New Guinea. *Anthropos* 60 (1965): 423–32.

Rubin, Gayle. "The Traffic in Women: Notes on the 'Political Economy' of Sex." In *Toward an Anthropology of Women.* Edited by Rayna Reiter. New York: Monthly Review Press, 1975.

Sagan, Eli. *Cannibalism: Human Aggression and Cultural Form.* New York: Harper and Row, 1974.

Sahlins, Marshall. "Poor Man, Rich Man, Big Man, Chief: Political Types in Melanesia and Polynesia." *Comparative Studies in Society and History* 5 (1963): 285–303.

———. *Stone Age Economics.* Chicago and New York: Aldine, Atherton, 1972.

———. "Raw Women, Cooked Men, and Other 'Great Things' of the Fiji Islands." In *The Ethnography of Cannibalism.* Edited by Paula Brown and Donald Tuzin. Washington, D.C.: Society for Psychological Anthropology, 1983.

Salisbury, Richard F. "Unilineal Descent Groups in the New Guinea Highlands." *Man* 56 (1956): 2–7.

———. "Correspondence." *Man* 66, 67 (1959): 50–51.

———. "Despotism and Australian Administration in the New Guinea Highlands." *American Anthropologist* 66, pt. 2 (1964): 225–39.

———. "The Siane of the Eastern Highlands." In *Gods, Ghosts and Men in Melanesia*. Edited by P. Lawrence and M. J. Meggitt. Melbourne: Oxford University Press, 1965.

Sandler, Joseph. "The Body as Phallus: A Patient's Fear of Erection." *International Journal of Psycho-Analysis* 40 (1959): 191–98.

Schiefflin, Edward L. *The Sorrow of the Lonely and the Burning of the Dancers*. New York: St. Martin's Press, 1976.

Schlossman, Howard H. "The Role of Swine in Myth and Religion." *American Imago* 40 (1983): 35–49.

Schneider, David M. "The Distinctive Features of Matrilineal Descent Groups." Introduction to *Matrilineal Kinship*. Edited by D. M. Schneider and E. Kathleen Gough. Berkeley: University of California Press, 1961.

Schwimmer, Erik G. *Exchange in the Social Structure of the Orokaiva*. London: Christopher Hurst, 1973.

———. "Male Couples in New Guinea." In *Ritualized Homosexuality in Melanesia*. Edited by Gilbert H. Herdt. Berkeley: University of California Press, 1984.

Segal, Hanna. "Notes on Symbol Formation." *International Journal of Psycho-Analysis* 38 (1957): 391–97.

———. *Introduction to the Work of Melanie Klein*. London: Hogarth Press, 1973.

Seligman, C. G. *The Melanesians of British New Guinea*. Cambridge: Cambridge University Press, 1910.

Sexton, Lorraine D. "'Wok Meri': A Women's Savings and Exchange System in Highland Papua New Guinea." *Oceania* 52 (1982): 167–98.

———. "Pigs, Pearlshells, and 'Women's Work': Collective Response to Change in Highland Papua New Guinea." In *Rethinking Women's Roles*. Edited by Denise O'Brien and Sharol Tiffany. Berkeley: University of California Press, 1984.

Sillitoe, Paul. "Man-Eating Women: Fears of Sexual Pollution in the Papua-New Guinea Highlands." *Journal of the Polynesian Society* 1 (1979): 77–97.

Skultans, Vieda. "The Symbolic Significance of Menstruation and the Menopause." *Man*, n.s. 5 (1970): 639–51.

Slater, Philip E. *The Glory of Hera: Greek Mythology and the Greek Family*. Boston: Beacon Press, 1968.

Sörum, Arve. "Growth and Decay: Bedamini Notions of Sexuality." In *Ritualized Homosexuality in Melanesia*. Edited by Gilbert H. Herdt. Berkeley: University of California Press, 1984.

Spiro, Melford. "Virgin Birth, Parthenogensis, and Physiological Paternity: An Essay on Cultural Interpretation." *Man*, n.s. 3 (1968): 242–61.

———. *Oedipus in the Trobriands*. Chicago: University of Chicago Press, 1982.

Steadman, Lyle. "Cannibal Witches in the Hewa." *Oceania* 46 (1975): 114–21.

Stephen, Michelle, ed. *Sorcerer and Witch in Melanesia*. New Brunswick: Rutgers University Press, 1987.

Strathern, Andrew J. "Descent and Alliance in the New Guinea Highlands: Some Problems of Comparison." *Proceedings of the Royal Anthropological Institute for 1968* (1969): 37–52.

———. "The Female and Male Spirit Cults in Mount Hagen." *Man,* n.s. 5 (1970a): 571–85.

———. "Male Initiation in New Guinea Highlands Societies." *Ethnology* 9 (1970b): 373–79.

———. *The Rope of Moka: Big Men and Ceremonial Exchange in Mount Hagen.* Cambridge: Cambridge University Press, 1971.

———. *One Father, One Blood: Descent and Group Structure among the Melpa People.* Canberra: Australian National University Press, 1972.

———. "Kinship, Descent and Locality. Some New Guinea Examples." In *The Character of Kinship.* Edited by Jack Goody. Cambridge: Cambridge University Press, 1975a.

———. "Why Is Shame on the Skin?" *Ethnology* 14 (1975b): 347–56.

———. "Men's House, Women's House: The Efficacy of Opposition, Reversal, and Pairing in the Melpa Amb Kor Cult." *Journal of the Polynesian Society* 88 (1979): 37–51.

———. "Death as Exchange: Two Melanesian Cases." In *Mortality and Immortality: The Archaeology and Anthropology of Death.* Edited by S. C. Humphries and H. King. London: Academic Press, 1981.

———, ed. *Inequality in New Guinea Highlands Societies.* Cambridge: Cambridge University Press, 1982a.

———. "Witchcraft, Greed, Cannibalism and Death: Some Related Themes from the New Guinea Highlands." In *Death and the Regeneration of Life.* Edited by Maurice Bloch and Jonathan Parry. Cambridge: Cambridge University Press, 1982b.

Strathern, Andrew J., and Marilyn Strathern. "Marsupials and Magic: A Study of Spell Symbolism among the Mbowamb." In *Dialectic in Practical Religion.* Edited by E. R. Leach. Cambridge Papers in Social Anthropology 5. Cambridge University Press, 1968.

———. *Self Decoration in Mount Hagen.* London: Gerald Duckworth, 1971.

Strathern, Marilyn. *Women in Between: Female Roles in a Male World, Mount Hagen, New Guinea.* London: Seminar Press, 1972.

———. "The Achievement of Sex: Paradoxes in Hagen Gender-Thinking." In *The Yearbook of Symbolic Anthropology Volume I.* Edited by Erik Schwimmer. London: Charles Hurst, 1978.

———. "The Self in Self Decoration." *Oceania* 49 (1979): 241–57.

———. "No Nature, No Culture: The Hagen Case." In *Nature, Culture and Gender.* Edited by Carol MacCormack and Marilyn Strathern. Cambridge: Cambridge University Press, 1980.

———. "Culture in a Net Bag: The Manufacture of a Subdiscipline in Anthropology." *Man* 16 (1981a): 665–88.

———. "Self-Interest and the Social Good: Some Implications of Hagen Gender Imagery." In *Sexual Meanings.* Edited by Sherry Ortner and Harriet Whitehead. Cambridge: Cambridge University Press, 1981b.

———, ed. *Dealing with Inequality: Analysing Gender Relations in Melanesia and Beyond.* Cambridge: Cambridge University Press, 1987a.

———. "Producing Difference: Connections and Disconnections in Two New Guinea Highlands Kinship Systems." In *Gender and Kinship: Toward a Unified Analysis.* Edited by Jane F. Collier and Sylvia J. Yanagisako. Stanford: Stanford University Press, 1987b.

———. *The Gender of the Gift.* Berkeley: University of California Press, 1988.

Turner, Victor W. *The Forest of Symbols: Aspects of Ndembu Ritual.* Ithaca: Cornell University Press, 1967.

Tuzin, Donald F. "Yam Symbolism in the Sepik: An Interpretative Account." *Southwestern Journal of Anthropology* 28 (1972): 230–54.

———. "Sex and Meat-Eating in Ilahita: A Symbolic Study." *Canberra Anthropology* 1 (1978): 82–93.

———. "Ritual Violence among the Ilahita Arapesh: The Dynamics of Moral and Religious Uncertainty." In *Rituals of Manhood.* Edited by Gilbert H. Herdt. Berkeley: University of California Press, 1982.

———. "Miraculous Voices: The Auditory Experience of Numinous Objects." *Current Anthropology* 25 (1984): 579–96.

Van Baal, J. *Reciprocity and the Position of Women.* Amsterdam: van Gorcum, 1975.

Van Gennep, Arnold. *The Rites of Passage.* Translated by Monika B. Vizedom and Gabrielle L. Caffee. Chicago: University of Chicago Press, 1960 [1908].

Waddell, Eric. *The Mound Builders: Agricultural Practices, Environment and Society in the Central Highlands of New Guinea.* Seattle: University of Washington Press, 1972.

Wagner, Roy. *The Curse of Souw: Principles of Daribi Clan Definition and Alliances in New Guinea.* Chicago: University of Chicago Press, 1967.

———. "Misreading the Metaphor: 'Cross-Cousin' Relationships in the New Guinea Highlands." Unpublished ms., 1972.

———. "Analogic Kinship: A Daribi Example." *American Ethnologist* 4 (1977): 623–42.

———. *Lethal Speech: Daribi Myth and Symbolic Obviation.* Ithaca: Cornell University Press, 1978.

Watson, James B., ed. *New Guinea: The Central Highlands.* Special Publication. *American Anthropologist* 66, pt. 2 (1964).

———. "Tairora: The Politics of Despotism in a Small Society." *Anthropological Forum* 2 (1967): 53–104.

———. "Society as Organized Flow: The Tairora Case." *Southwestern Journal of Anthropology* 26 (1970): 107–24.

Wedgewood, Camilla H. "Girls' Puberty Rites in Manam Island, New Guinea." *Oceania* 4 (1933): 132–55.

Whitemen, J. "Girls' Puberty Ceremonies amongst the Chimbu." *Anthropos* 60 (1965): 410–22.

Whiting, Beatrice. "Sex Identity Conflict and Physical Violence: A Comparative Study." *American Anthropologist* 67 (1965): 123–40.

Williams, F. E. *Orokaiva Society.* Oxford: Oxford University Press, 1930.

———. *Bull-Roarers in the Papuan Gulf.* Territory of Papua, Anthrop. Rep. 17. Port Moresby: Walter Alfred Bock, 1936.

———. *Papuans of the Trans-Fly.* Oxford: Oxford University Press, 1969 [1936].

Worsley, Peter. *The Trumpet Shall Sound: A Study of "Cargo" Cults in Melanesia.* New York: Shocken Books, 1968.

Wurm, S. A. "New Guinea Languages." *Current Anthropology* 2 (1961): 114–16.

———. "The Languages of the Eastern, Western and Southern Highlands, Territory of Papua and New Guinea." In *A Linguistic Survey of the South-Western Pacific.* Edited by A. Capell. Noumea: South Pacific Commission, 1962.

———. "Australian New Guinea Highlands Languages and the Distribution of Their Typological Features." *American Anthropologist* 66, pt. 2 (1964): 77–97.

Yanagisako, Sylvia J., and Jane F. Collier. "Toward a Unified Analysis of Gender and Kinship." In *Gender and Kinship: Toward A Unified Analysis.* Edited by Jane F. Collier and Sylvia J. Yanagisako. Stanford: Stanford University Press, 1987.

Young, Michael W. "'Our Name Is Women: We Are Bought with Limesticks and Limepots': An Analysis of the Autobiographical Narrative of a Kalauna Woman." *Man,* n.s. 18 (1983): 478–501.

———. "The Tusk, the Flute and the Serpent: Disguise and Revelation in Goodenough Mythology." In *Dealing with Inequality.* Edited by Marilyn Strathern. Cambridge: Cambridge University Press, 1987.

# INDEX

Index

Sorcery, 126; and animals and plants, 224–
26; and childbirth, 48, 244; and female
conduits, 130, 131, 135, 147, 209; and
invisibility of, 118, 300–301, 314, 317,
326, 331; and menstruation, 187, 219;
and payment for, 305, 324, 326; as per-
verse mothering, 309–10, 313, 314, 336–
40; principles of, 30, 219, 231, 297, 327,
330–31, 332, 334–35, 339–42, 354–
55; and regional history, 302, 317; as
revenge, 125, 225, 301, 327; techniques
of, 305–6, 312–15; compared to myth,
314–15, 330, 331–32, 335, 339–40; and
warfare, 297, 302–4. *See also autaisana*
(leavings); Big Men; Cures; Hot/cold;
Male homosexuality; Mother's brother;
Pigs
Sorcery accusations: and affines, 307–9, 321,
338; as "anti-gift," 251; and falseness of,
302, 309; and nature of, 300–302; as
trigger for war, 30, 302–3
Sorcery meetings (*fobirikaina*), 298–302,
305, 309, 317–26; and exclusion of
women, 300, 309–10; for women,
298n2; as rites of cure, 335
Spirit. *See kore*
Strathern, Andrew, 33
Strathern, Marilyn, xvi, xvii, 175n8, 176,
324n1
Subsistence, 36–43
Sugarcane: as male crop, 40; and menstruation, 178; in myth, 161
Sun, as male symbol, 233; in women's
myth, 328–29; and sorcery, 298, 320,
339. *See also* Hot/cold
Sweet potato, 38, 41; and *fiða* (second
cropping), 42, 194, 195; and magic, 167,
168, 169, 170–71; and mythic origin of,
199, 200, 201. *See also* Garden magic;
Gardens

Taboos. *See* Food taboos; Menstruation,
practices surrounding
Taro, 27, 39, 40, 169; and blood magic, 181,
184–85; in flutes, 273; and garden

magic, 167, 168, 169, 171; endangered by
sex, 192
Tattooing, of brides, 269–70; of flutes, 273.
*See also* Beard
Theater. *See* Ritual theater
*ðau* (rite of birth), 236–40, 241–47; rationale for, 243–47; in ritual theater, 98;
in women's myth, 236–40
Timing, of rituals, 253n4, 268
Trade, 38n10
Tricks: in cannibalism, 84, 102n10; in
dreams, 208, 341; in marriage ritual,
274; in myth, as symbol of incest, 92–
95, 97, 114, 161, 163, 197, 213; in seduc-
tion, 94, 95, 189

Ubagubi, 25, 26–29; atmosphere of daily
life, 297, 298; and *hau*, 253n4; in the
past, 28

Van Gennep, Arnold, 18
Visual knowledge: and flutes, 281–87, 290, 352

Wagner, Roy, 23, 24, 56, 57
Warfare, 29–36, 314; internecine, 302–4;
and refugees, 31, 32, 34; in ritual theater, 72–75; preferred to sorcery, 117, 297
Weddings. *See* Marriage ritual
Widows: and death ritual, 127, 128, 135, 136;
in myth, 89–91, 148, 159–66; and promiscuity, 210; and rules of inheritance,
88n9, 144
Woman's nature, 210, 211, 219, 220–21,
324n2; and anger, 266; and coldness,
234, 311, 319, 328, 333–34; in myth, 340
Women's self image, 342, 346
Women's myths. *See nenekaina*
Womb: in myth, 213, 220, 238–39; in ritual,
111–12, 115; as sterile vessel, 210, 218; symbolized by net bag, 269. *See also kore
ridi; neki maha;* Procreation theories

Yams, 169; in flutes, 273; and garden magic,
168, 169; endangered by sex, 192; in
myth, 161; and symbolism of, 160n4